The Fishermen of Eastbourne

TED HIDE

S.B. Publications

By the same author:
The Pleasure Boatmen of Eastbourne

Front Cover: *Fisherman John Hide on board (at tiller) his fishing Lugger 3NN*
'Four Sisters' on Eastbourne beach C.1880, with sons
John, Edward, and Dennis on board.

Title Page: *Eastbourne Fishermen's and Boatmen's Arch.*
Visit of Prince and Princess of Wales, 31st August 1883.

Back Cover: *Fishermen of Eastbourne C.1870.*
The Hide family. Left to right. Father - George Snr. son - Samuel Beckett,
grandson - John, son - George Merrick Jnr. son - John, seated on the family capstan.
Background is now the site of 'Fusciardi's' Ice Cream Parlour, Marine Parade.

First published in 2009

ISBN 978 185770 352 8

Designed and Typeset by EH Graphics (01273) 515527

Contents

The Fishermen of Eastbourne

This book materialised from family research and developed into a record of the fishing community from early days up to the later 2nd World War and Post War years. I do give examples of the Hide family and other families way of life and involvement in the fishing industry of Eastbourne and of tragic and heroic incidents that took place onshore and at sea.

Also a little about local smuggling and shipwrecks on our shore and of the characters that have enriched Eastbourne's maritime heritage.

Some facts about the beginning of our lifeboat history in Eastbourne and of the skill and bravery that our fishermen displayed in saving of lives serving as crews of the lifeboat.

To the hard life that fishing has always brought, must be added that of the fishermen's wives, married and widowed. Of the worry when their men folk were at sea - a hazardous occupation with a high death rate. Apart from the worry, imagine the ever-pervading smell of fish and the labour intensive job of keeping a home going. Fishing clothes heavy with salt and fish waste, raising a family and all that went with their lot as fisher folk. Hard labour indeed for women over many years, coupled with the anxiety of the wives, mothers and sweethearts of our lifeboat crews when at sea during violent weather, having assisted in the launch and the wait for their safe return.

As with the book 'The Pleasure Boatmen of Eastbourne' the following is a record especially for those present day Eastbourne families whose ancestors were part of the fishing community that occupied the beach at Eastbourne from early times. Throughout this chronological record of events where possible, dates, names of fishermen and boats are given. As to names, the same Christian names were given through generations of seafaring families and it has been difficult to differentiate between father, son, cousins etc. Some surnames to recall are: Swain, Knight, Simpson, Hurd, Paul, Penfold, Prodger, Breach, Adams, Erridge, Allchorn, Tutt, Tyrell, Huggett, Mockett, Sayers, Wood, Matthews, Boniface, Hide, Novis, Elms, Hardy, Hunt, Godden, Reed, Chester, Waymark, Crick, Mitchell, Carter, Andrews and many more, names still to be found among the inhabitants of Eastbourne to this day, although not to any knowledge amongst those that fish out of Eastbourne today.

Eastbourne's local newspapers have been a valuable source of research and a great deal of information has been gleaned from them starting c.1862 and prior to that from the East Sussex and Brighton publications. As to information from Eastbourne Council, unfortunately important Council documents, plans and records relating to the Foreshore and Fishing Stations have not come to light during research. Hopefully they are not lost forever.

I am grateful to the following for the help and support given to me: - Brian Allchorn, Pearl Tyler (nee Prodger), the late Fred 'Mucky' Erridge, the late Jack Hurd, the late Frank Smith, The Langford sisters - Thelma and Pam, Mike Strong,

Ken and Jim Simpson, Gary Brookshaw and the sponsorship of Cornfield Law, Lionel Jones, David Simkin, the late Olive Wilkins (nee Simpson), the late Phil Webb, Rowland Pragnell, Chris Erridge, Sue Huggett, Mavis Clack, Michael Partridge, Judy Grimes, Alan Hayes, Andrew Chester, Tony Allchorn, Jane Lade, John Mockett, the late Mike Longley, Chris and Judy Allchorn, Michael Watson, Lawrence Stevens, Betty Harris (nee Hide), Dennis 'Bonny' Boniface, Dr. Clifford Gillam, Eastbourne Fishermen's and Boatmen's Protection Society, "The Fishermen's Club", and many others.

Also many thanks to Liz Howe for the design and typography of this book and to my son Richard who has again assisted with the collation and editing of my work.

Sea Houses. East-Bourne. 1850.

Introduction

The principal source of the supply of fish for England was for many centuries the English Channel. Along our southern shores the harbours and ports had their boats suited to their particular conditions and in Eastbourne's case, launching off and hauling up the beach for which the boats were purpose built. In early times fish was a main source of food especially for local Eastbourne inhabitants, evidence of countless fish bones have been found in local Saxon site excavations.

The method of catching fish from early days inshore was by line and hook, seine and kettle net systems. Deep-sea fishing would see drift nets and long line (line and hook) used. Then by the 1820's an additional method, trawling, was introduced. The first trawl, it is said, was used in the North Sea and soon caught on around Britain's coast.

Of resolute stock, Sussex fishermen were quoted thus by F. E. Sawyer 'Sussex Fish & Fisheries' 1882 - *'The Sussex fishermen are a mixed race, partly Spanish, partly Norman French, partly Teutonic (Saxon) in origin, warring with one another'* and of course the French who poached their fishing grounds. The fishermen of Eastbourne added to their income by smuggling contraband during the 17th, 18th and 19th centuries and on occasions, acts of piracy when they attacked, boarded and stole cargo from passing merchant ships.

In 1565 Eastbourne had 140 households with 700 inhabitants and in 1621, about the same. In 1676 inhabitants remained at 700 and similarly in 1724. So, a pretty static population with some living and fishing from the shingle 'Stade' that would later become the Sea Houses. In all probability fisher folk cottages were there before the known 'Sea Houses' with living conditions somewhat primitive in their shingle/flint built cottages.

The original shingle 'Stade' Fishing Station at Eastbourne (where the Marine and Royal Parades now stand) did not have a water link with the interior of Sussex, so fish caught in those early times were taken by wagon to Lewes and London and for local needs to the fish markets at Hastings and Brighton. Eastbourne boats would also land fish at these towns and they in turn landed fish at Eastbourne. With the coming of the railway to Eastbourne in 1849 locally caught fish were freighted to the London market at Billingsgate for many years.

Between 1700 and 1800 Eastbourne, being very agricultural, shipped out wheat and wool by boat from the 'Stade' receiving coal and other commodities in return. Chalk from the quarry at Holywell was shipped out to Hastings, Rye and Hythe to be made into lime. For local use lime was produced in fired kilns on site. Today at low tide can still be seen the channel cut through the rock reef off Holywell for the chalk boats to get to the beach. Fishing, in a small way took place from Holywell up to the 1890's.

The winter months of the 19th century saw boats from the east coast of England fish the herring round into the Channel and in the summer months follow the mackerel down. Our Eastbourne Luggers would join the fishing fleets of Hastings,

Brighton, and Newhaven in the northern voyages up to the North Sea for the herring. Then, in later years, wait for the herring to arrive off Eastbourne. As with the herring so with mackerel, northern voyages taking place during the months of May, June and July and in later years, when the mackerel arrived off Eastbourne the boats followed them down to the west country and off Ireland selling their catches at ports of call. Consequently our fishermen were away from their families for long periods.

Eastbourne fishermen also fished locally for sprats that came round in December, January and February. Off Eastbourne and down to Rye Bay for plaice, sole, skate, whiting, dogfish (huss) and many other fish in addition of course to lobsters, crabs, scallops (pronunciation 'scollops') whelks, prawns and cod. Locally caught fish was smoked, bloatered and kippered on the 'Stade' in wooden huts called 'Dees' specially built for this purpose. During the 1950's-60's, sprats were still being smoked and today smoked local fish is still produced in a small way.

As previously stated, fish was a staple food of the local inhabitants and fishing community, in particular 'salt herring' with vast quantities being salted down in barrels. Stories come through local fishing families of how their ancestors used to be utterly fed up with having nothing to eat but 'salt herring' when times were hard.

Operating during those years was the lugsail rigged un-decked boats called 'punts' about 15 - 20 feet in length and used for inshore fishing. The half open decked Lugger some 27 feet long was called a 'Shinaman' and the larger fully decked lugsail rigged boat a 'Lugger' used for going deep sea.

1879 saw the enactment of The Eastbourne Improvement Act and the fishermen forced to move from their ancient site by the Sea Houses to make way for the building of a sea wall and Royal Parade. The Fishing Station then moved to its present site east of the Great Redoubt in the years 1882 - 84.

The Eastbourne fishing fleet never reached the size of the Hastings fleet, although in the late 1880's there was a large fleet of Luggers operating out of Eastbourne from the new Fishing Station. Built locally the big Eastbourne 'Luggers' with their brown tanned lugsails were known as 'Bourners', decked with accommodation space for a crew of 4 to 7 men including a boy. Tonnages were various 7 - 30 tons according to length. Some 20 - 40 feet in length, they had finer lines and were faster than their Hastings counterparts. It was these Luggers that would have sailed up to the North Sea and down the English Channel through to Ireland.

It has been said that Luggers were used as Pleasure boats. This was not the case, they were too heavy and the Lugger sail rig would have been difficult to manage with passengers on board. The large custom-built pleasure yacht with her sleek lines and cutter type sails and dandy rig was ideal. At Eastbourne John Mockett's 'Skylark' and Ben Bates 'Britannia' were prime examples. The smaller 'Lugger' sail rigged punt fishing boat was widely used as the Eastbourne Boatmen pleasure craft until the motorised boat came into being.

It was some task to haul the Lugger up the shingle beach, but this the fishermen did with the aid of capstans using horses, donkeys and manpower. At times injury and death occurred during this operation. It was a thriving time for fishing at Eastbourne in the 1880's and into the 1890's. A Mr Leybourne-Popham who went into partnership with local boat builder George Gausden had a large Lugger fleet built and fished out of Eastbourne during this period. For commercial and personal reasons Popham moved his boats westward in the 1890's and the volume of fishing at Eastbourne was never quite the same.

Locally, with the development of Eastbourne as a resort and the building of hotels and boarding houses, the fishing community took to pleasure boating during the summer months whilst the fishing side saw a steady demand for lobsters, crabs, scallops, whelks, shrimps and excellent fresh fish. The beach was a busy place when fishing boats landed their catches which were sold by auction on the beach directly as they were landed off the boats. It wasn't until 1899 that Eastbourne had its own purpose built fish market. (This market closed down in 1970). Fish hawkers with their barrows and particular 'cries' plied their wares through the streets of Old Town, the poorer East End and the upper class area of Meads.

C.1912 saw the gradual introduction of the motorised fishing boat making life somewhat 'easier' for the fisherman. For a time fishing flourished locally but Eastbourne's fishing fleet did diminish over the years due to poor prices and import by rail of cheaper fish from the markets at Grimsby and Lowestoft. Although providers of essential food, fishermen never received the subsidies afforded to the farming community. So with this decline went the fishing families of Eastbourne, a special community, all gone.

With the building of the Sovereign Harbour/Marina, it could be that one day the Fishing Station will disappear, another part of Eastbourne's heritage gone forever.

Chapter One

Early Days at Eastbourne - Fishing and Smuggling

An early mention of fishermen in East - Bourne from the Parish records show in 1296 names recorded as Tutt, Erridge, Reed, Bodle and Bartholomew. 1605 the drowning of fishermen John Howell, John Body and James Cobby is recorded and in 1756 records show John Breach and Thomas Dennis who were also drowned.

An interesting entry in a publication 'Epitaphs and Monumental Inscriptions' 1806, reads as follows: - Epitaph to Thomas Lock - A fisherman of East-Bourne who was too fond of a liquor called moonshine.

> Ye men of East-Bourne and the neighbouring shore,
> Bewail your loss! Tom Lock - he is no more!
> Where will you find a man of equal parts?
> Vers'd in the Boatman's and the Kitchen arts?
> Equally skilful, if at land or sea
> And to behold a perfect prodigy.
> His neck distended to uncommon size,
> His croaking voice and then his swollen eyes
> Were sure emblems of the life he led,
> You'll not much wonder that he now lies dead.
> 'Twas Moonshine brought him to this fatal end,
> Not one dark night did e'er poor Tom befriend;
> In vain for him did e'er poor Sol display,
> 'Twas moonshine, either night or day.

'Moonshine' was the popular name for smuggled spirits, which had been run in the 'darks' (moonless nights).

Eastbourne Parish records show fisherman Thomas Lock married Anne Ladd by licence, September 26th 1743.

1758.

The following gives some insight into life at the Sea Houses, where the original Fishing Station or 'Stade' was situated: -

Samuel and Susan Beckett lived at the Sea Houses. Samuel being the landlord of the Angel Inn. From the diarist Thomas Turner, the Georgian village shopkeeper of East Hoathly, Sussex, there is a fascinating account of Samuel and the Beckett family.

Turner writes: -

27th September 1758, 'In the morn my brother and self set out for Eastbourne

where we arrived about 7.30. We breakfasted at Sam Beckett's where we also dined on a shoulder of lamb roasted with onion sauce and potatoes'.

10th July 1759, 'My wife paid Sam Beckett 16d in full for 4lbs of lobster received by him today'

30th October 1759, 'Mr Beckett made my wife a fine present of some fine whiting and a flounder'

17th June 1760, 'Mr Sam Beckett made my wife a present of 3 fine mackerel'

30th June 1764, (Saturday) 'After breakfast John French and I set out for Eastbourne. The reason for my journey was this: Mrs French's wagon with her son and servant was yesterday a-bringing a cord of wood to my house, and just at that instant of time as they were before my door, came by Sam Beckett's post-chaise and 4 horses in their road from Uckfield to Eastbourne (their home); and in driving a great pace and together with a sufficient degree of carelessness and audacity, they, in their passing the fore-horse in the team, in order to get into the road again before the other horses, drove against him and (I presume by accident) drove the shaft of the chaise into the rectum of the horse about 9 inches, and then pierced through the gut into the body, of which wound the horse died in about 7 hours.

Now as I see the accident, Mr French desired I would go with him to talk to Mr Beckett about it... we see Mr Beckett, who behaved extremely civil and agreeable; Mr French and he agreed to leave it to Mr Fagg (J.P) and Mr Porter (the Rector of East Hoathly) to appoint what he should pay for the damage etc. sustained. Mr Beckett keeping a public house, we dined there on some pork and beans and a beef pudding. We came home very safe and sober about 7.30. Mr Beckett made me a present of a few mackerel. I bought of him 6 pieces of clear lawn, to be delivered to East Hoathly for £12'.

5th Sept 1764 'In the forenoon accompanied Mr French and Mr Porter to Hailsham to settle the affair between Mr Beckett and Mr French relating to Mr Beckett's post

Fishing at the Sea Houses 1813.

chariot killing Mr French's horse the 29th June last, of which accident I was the spectator and therefore went as a witness; but however our journey was to no purpose, for the affair could not be settled, both parties being rather obstinate, and I am afraid Master Beckett's clan are hardly good principled and honest'.

1762.

Small boats and wrecked goods were occasionally sold or auctioned at the Angel. The Sussex Weekly Advertiser 11th October 1762 carried an advertisement for the sale of two fishing boats by 'Inch of Candle'.

The advert read as follows: -

'On Tuesday 19th October, Instant, at Samuel Beckett's, at the Angel, at the Seaside, at Two o clock in the Afternoon, Two Sprit - sail boats now lying upon Eastbourne Stade; one called the 'Belle Isle', 19 feet in length, 8 feet 3 inches in breadth. Having Two Trawls, with Trawls heads and Drags, with all Utensils there belonging; the other called the 'Sea Horse', 19 feet 8 inches in length, 10 feet 9 inches in breadth, in good repair with all Utensils there belonging. Also Sixty Shares of Mackerel nets, the nets belonging to the Two Boats; to be sold together or separate. To be viewed to the day of sale, at Samuel Beckett's aforesaid'.

(In the 18th century, bidding at auctions was allowed during the burning of an inch of candle. The bid that was made as the candle went out was the bid accepted).

Sam Beckett's death was reported in the Sussex Weekly Advertiser on the 2nd July 1770. *'Last Friday se'night died at Eastbourne Mr Beckett who kept one of the Sea Houses there. His death was occasioned by a mortification in his foot, which caused his leg to be cut off. The operation was performed on Wednesday and he died on Friday. He was followed to his grave by his widow and fifteen children all by the same woman'.*

Susannah Beckett carried on as landlady of the Angel Inn and from a visit by William Hickey, a well-to-do man about town and an attorney in the services of the East India Company, we learn something of what in all probability is about the Angel Inn and Mrs. Beckett.

In August 1776, Hickey along with 3 male friends had been sailing a cutter in the English Channel en-route to Brighton when they met strong winds and high seas off Beachy Head. This combined with a severe case of seasickness and they had to drop anchor off Eastbourne. The whole party were ferried ashore through tremendous surf by local fishermen.

'Eastbourne then was only an insignificant fishing town consisting of 8 or 10 scattered houses'. They were unaware that the nucleus of the place lay inland (Bourne, around the Parish Church). *'The fishermen conducted us to the only public house in the village, a miserable looking dwelling from the outside as ever I beheld, where to its appearance we expected neither victuals, drink or any sort of comfortable refreshments'.*

They were, in due course to be pleasantly surprised however. The landlady soon had a blazing fire going in the very clean room that was put at their disposal. She had no butcher's meat, but could provide fish and poultry. *'Being told we should be content with whatever she could produce, she promised to do her best and in*

Sea Houses 1838.

half an hour we sat down to a beautiful white tablecloth. She brought in as fine a dish of fish as ever was seen at Billingsgate with excellent lobster and oyster sauces. This was followed by a pair of tender, well dressed chickens and we finished an ample repast with good old Cheshire cheese'. They washed their meal down with ale, thinking nothing better would be available. A casual enquiry revealed the landlady did have wine that she thought might not be good enough for gentlemen of quality. Nevertheless, a bottle was called for and having sampled it one of the gentlemen declared it to be as high-flavoured a claret as any in his own cellar. The consequence was a liberal potation, with two bottles being drunk each. Another surprise awaited them for upon calling for the bill, the landlady made a demand of eighteen pence (1/6d) each amounting to six shillings (6/-) *'Six shillings, my good lady,'* said one of the gentleman, *'is indeed a most moderate demand, but you must tell us what we are to pay for drink as well as eating'.*

'Oh, dear gentlemen' she replied, *' I can make no charge for that. You are most heartily welcome to the wine and I'm glad you were able to drink it. The case is, my poor boys now and then run over to Guernsey on little matters of business and generally bring home with them a few dozen bottles of wine which I seldom find occasion to use, and as it costs me nothing you are heartily welcome, and much good may you do with it'.*

By a few more questions Hickey and his friends ascertained that her 'poor boys' were more or less professed smugglers. With considerable difficulty Hickey and friends prevailed upon her to accept a guinea for *'as excellent a repast as ever four hungry fellows sat down to'* (Memoirs of William Hickey by Peter Quennell).

1772.

Fisherman William Hide married Sarah a daughter of Samuel and Susannah Beckett and raised a family of 8 children in a house situated at the Sea Houses. At that time Eastbourne was still made up of three hamlets - Meads, Sea Houses, Southbourne

Fisherman William Hide (1750-1823), copy of pencil drawing.

and the village of Bourne (Old Town) having a total population of 1,668. The military took up a presence in Eastbourne due to war with France and it was between 1800-1810 that the Martello Towers were built along the south east coast through to Seaford. These coastal defences were copied from a Tower of the sort at Martella Bay in Corsica, which offered stiff resistance to a British Force that attacked it in 1794. Some Towers still remain to this day and can be seen locally along Pevensey Bay, at Seaford and of course our own Wish Tower.

In 1803, when Napoleon was threatening to invade England, an Act of Parliament was passed authorizing a general mobilisation of all males between 17 and 55 years. The list for the Southern Division, Pevensey Rape, Sussex, contains names of Eastbourne fishermen and seamen. The list can be viewed towards the end of this book.

As already mentioned there was much military presence in Eastbourne during this period of time and up to 1815 (Battle of Waterloo) England was generally at war with the old enemy, France. The residents of Eastbourne would have been well aware of this fact having a front line view of skirmishes at sea in the Channel off Eastbourne from the late 1700's. Fishing was a hazardous occupation in more ways than one.

The following reports give an insight to incidents off Eastbourne, the details coming from the Compton Place Accounts & Correspondence Volume 117.

Letters from Robert Gibbs to a Mr Capper:

22 Oct. 1778.

'The day I drew up her Ladyship's letter I was with Mr Acton holding a Court Baron for the Manor of Eastbourne. News was brought into the room that two Privateers were engaged; We who were on low ground could see little of it but others on the heights saw the Frenchman taken and the two prizes retaken and all sent to Dover'.

11 Nov. 1778.

'Last Thursday the 5th, the finest Fleet I have ever seen passed by to the West. I was at Hollywell and counted ninety-three, all large ships with three masts within two miles of shore, and from her Grace's dressing room, the wood being cut they made a fine appearance through the trees and from all the windows on that front of Bourne Place'. (Compton Place)

Sea Houses viewed from Bourne Place, 1785.

27 Nov. 1778.

'I have just overheard that a large ship from America is ashore at Burlen-Gap (Birling Gap) and seven passengers have lost their lives, we have had a great deal of wet and blowing weather'. (The ship was the "Golden Fleece" having sailed from New York)

1 Nov. 1779.

'A fine Fleet went to the west, 11 Oct. The Press gang has not taken a man belonging to this Parish and but very few others'.

(Press Gang. This tale was told by fisherman Fred Erridge, 'Eastbourne afforded a good supply of sailors for the Royal Navy over the years, the terror of the village folk as soon as a man-o'war boat was seen making for the shore was something he remembers being told as a boy. A trick used to elude the Press gangs tells the story of an able-bodied fisherman dressed up in his grandmother's clothes, sitting before a fire, with knitting needles in hands'.)

A further tale is told by the Reverend Budgen, that when Spencer Compton (Lord Wilmington) was at Bourne Place in the late 1700's, the residents of Eastbourne made applications to him for protection against the 'Press Gangs'. A John Tutt, owner of a coasting sloop of 50 tons was granted protection, but he failed to name on the back of the protection order two of his crew and they were 'pressed' at Eastbourne. To Lord Wilmington another request for protection was made by the master of the 'Mackerill Cock' of 3 tons, for himself and his two men for the fishing trade.

A report on Impress Gangs regarding Fishermen November 1805;

'Impress immunity withdrawn from fishermen not having more then 5 children. Also withdrawn from fishermen employed in fishing boats under 10 tons'. (A shortage of seamen after Battle of Trafalgar October 1805?)

From Brewer's Dictionary of Phrase & Fable:

The term 'The Andrew' meaning the 'Royal Navy' derives from those years when one Andrew Miller acquired such a reputation as a Press Gang operator about the Portsmouth area that it came to be said that his victims had been snatched into 'The Andrew'.

Back to the Compton Place Accounts.

6 Dec. 1779.

'*We have had exceedingly bad weather here. All the Marshes between here (Bourne Place) and Langney is one continued sheet of water*'.

10 Jan. 1780.

'*Last Tuesday a fine Fleet passed by here from Lisbon and last Saturday a small French privateer drove a sloop on shore loaded with barley for Lewes. The barley is now unloading near the Wish (Wish Tower) and the French was obliged to go off without her*'.

The Mr Gibbs who wrote these communications must have been employed in some capacity at Bourne Place. It is known that he was an Officer of the Levels (Willingdon & Bourne Levels) from 1782 - 1784.

The accounts also show a Benjamin Dutton's claim for work done at the Bourne Stade (the fishing beach that is now part of the Marine/Royal Parade) dated Feb - June 1783:

'*Work at the groins at Bourne Stade includes mending Broadbourne groin, groin by Mrs Beckett's house and repairing Rattle groins - £18. 12s. 0d*'.

Now back to the war,

7 Feb. 1780.

'*In the morning a French frigate came close in here and cut off two Brig's from the land that they were endeavouring to run ashore and as we returned from Church we had the mortification to see them captured and on their way to France*'.

1 May. 1780.

'*Sunday the 23rd a French 20 gun ship was taken off Beachy Head*'.

21 April. 1781.

'*A Fleet of 140 odd sail has been passing by here. They are unwilling to return to Dover and the west wind has kept them off here ever since*'.

This is the last of Mr Gibbs' letters.

An interesting place of research is Brighton Fishermen's Museum situated beneath the promenade in one of the 'Arches'. Many Sussex maritime records are held there and it is well worth a visit for the visual display alone.

Brighton Fishing Museum, reference 10304.

April 1789.

'*One night last week a ship from Cadiz bound for Amsterdam laden with cochineal and dollars, was run down by an Indiaman off Eastbourne. The crew immediately* took to their boats and had only time to save their clothes and a few chests of dollars, before their ship went to the bottom. They afterwards put into Eastbourne'.

The following War reports are from the Sussex Weekly Advertiser, Lewes.

14 Nov. 1796.

'Last Tuesday about 4 o'clock in the morning a Frenchman of genteel appearance who had just landed from an open boat at East - Bourne, was taken into custody by the piquet guard of the nightly patrol. On examination the next day, he said he came from Dunkirk where a great number of troops were in readiness to embark on some grand expedition. Some letters were found about him and intercepted; but we have been unable to learn their contents. We understand he is still in custody'.

'Several sail of shipping were at the same time observed at a distance off East - Bourne and as they could not answer the signals hoisted in consequence by the Telegraph (from Beachy Head), it is supposed they belonged to the enemy, whereof information was conveyed by means of signal posts along the coast to Portsmouth'.

26 Dec. 1796.

'Last Tuesday se' n-night about 9 in the evening, a Ramsgate sloop with 3 men onboard was driven onshore under Beachy Head by a French schooner, the Commander of which afterwards had the audacity to land some of his men for the purpose of setting the sloop on fire which they soon affected by the help of a barrel of pitch tar which was on board the sloop. The crew having to escape the enemy, concealed themselves behind some rocks hard by, witnessed the transaction and after the French had returned on board, they made the best of their way to East - Bourne and communicated the circumstances, but too late to save the sloop, which was totally consumed'.

As previously stated it was a dangerous occupation being a fisherman along the south coast during the late 18th Century. In fact there is a report of Eastbourne fishermen being taken by the French in 1798, 'amongst other fishermen seven or eight belonging to East- Bourne were with their boat seized by the French and taken prisoners to Calais; after 4 months detention they were, through a friend's influence exchanged for French prisoners'.

The war with France checked the fishing industry and the great loss sustained by the conflict was felt for many years. No large boats were again sent out till 1824.

Smuggling was prevalent among the local fishermen of Eastbourne and the surrounding area towards the end of the 18th Century. The Sussex Weekly Advertiser reported the following smuggling activity: -

7 Nov. 1796.

'Last Tuesday night Captain Haddock of the "Stag" Revenue cutter, belonging to Rye, took off Pevensey a smuggling boat laden with 600 tubs of contraband spirits and a quantity of tobacco, which he afterwards landed and lodged in His Majesty's warehouse at East-Bourne. The boat could have out sailed the revenue cutter had there been enough wind to escape'.

The recollection of an old Eastbourner in 1885 tells an interesting tale of how the Coast Blockade men (forerunners of the Coastguard) were duped in Eastbourne c.1815. The tale goes:

'Information was passed to the Captain of the Coast blockade that after nightfall on Christmas Eve a large quantity of contraband spirits would be landed by Beachy Head.

Eastbourne in those days was nearly all fields with just the Round House and a few fishermen's cottages on the shoreline. A gang of smugglers duly landed at the Head with a quantity of tubs and were arrested by the Blockade men, marched off to the Watch House and imprisoned. But to the chagrin of the Blockade men whilst they had been at Beachy Head another gang of smugglers had landed at Langney Point and taken tubs of spirits ashore quite undetected and 'spirited' the contraband away up country.

To explain, on the protest of innocence the gang arrested at Beachy Head requested their tubs of 'spirits' be tested. They were and found to contain just seawater. On releasing them the Blockade Captain vowed never to commit all his men on an anti smuggling operation again'.

Another reminiscence of an Eastbourner John Vine in March 1895 tells of 'Free Trading' as smuggling was also known, by Eastbourne fishermen in 1818 when *'James Vine, Hide, Allchorn, Bentley, Weston and other were drowned by the upsetting of their smuggling eight oared galley'.*

A further incident reported in the Sussex Weekly Advertiser 1818 tells of *'an English smuggling Lugger, upset on going into Boulogne harbour, when all hands on board, seven in number perished. Two of them belonged to Eastbourne'.*

Further tales of local smuggling tell that fisherman Samuel Hide, the eldest son of William and Sarah was convicted for smuggling in 1822. He was sentenced to 5 years penal servitude on H.M. Ships of war and sent to Portsmouth but was released after a month and restored to his family at Eastbourne. (It may have been because he was 50 years old). The local report said, *'the bells at Eastbourne were a ringing on the joy of the occasion, and the day concluded with a supper at the Anchor tap-room, to which about 60 jolly fellows sat down and were superlatively happy'* Not like his youngest brother James 'Navarino' Hide, fisherman and smuggler. He was convicted in 1824 and sentenced to 5 years on H.M. Ships. He got his nickname by serving at the Battle of Navarino in October 1827, when a combined British, French and Russian fleet defeated the Turkish fleet. He married Susan Allchorn a member of the Eastbourne seafaring family and lived for many years at No.37 Marine Parade, a cottage in the twitten between Seaside and Marine Parade, still there to this day.

Navarino's nephew Richard Hide (b.1817) relates in his reminiscences in the year 1888 reported in the Eastbourne Gazette, of how fisherman Samuel Knight was arrested and jailed for smuggling and of his uncle 'Navarino' and the crew of a smuggler boat being caught in the Channel by a man 'o' war and being sent to servitude in the Royal Navy.

Arthur Beckett the Sussex historian wrote an article on 'Navarino' and the Hide family in the Sussex County Magazine. No.10. Volume 11, October 1928. In the article he remembers 'Navarino' as *a 'short bow legged man, who wore a tan coloured blouse and very baggy trousers, well patched and a sou'-wester. He would*

James 'Navarino' Hide (1798-1883).

often sit on Marine Parade and if a gen'l'man took a seat beside him he would spin the yarn of his naval days and on finishing would exclaim 'Choke a rat sir' Choke a rat' being 'Navarino's way of asking for the price of a tot of rum or pint of beer. If successful 'Navarino' immediately made his way to the Anchor Tap, a favourite resort of the longshoremen of the day'.

Another brother John was also involved in a smuggling incident of the 1820's, reported in the book 'Contraband County' by Mark Bullen. An excellent book on local smuggling.

'A six quart tub of spirits found floating in the sea at Eastbourne by John Hide, a local fisherman. Whilst in the act of making off with his find he had the misfortune to run into two Blockade men who bade him stop and surrender the cask. Panicking somewhat, he dropped it, whereupon the staves broke and the contents were lost. He was taken into custody for being in possession of smuggled goods, found guilty and sentenced to five years naval service. The reporter of this incident was aghast at the fate of the poor fisherman and said some distinction should be made between a man going to the seaside for the express purpose of assisting to run goods and another who accidentally picks up a cask of spirits from the sea, and endeavours to secure it as a legal prize' A petition was sent to London pleading the man's good character and innocence of any criminal intent. John Hide was released.

It was in January 1833 that a fatal affray with smugglers took place at Eastbourne at 2 o'clock in the morning, on the beach (now Grand Parade) a little west of the Sea Houses. The report in The Times stated

'A boat landed and was delivering her cargo when the coastguard arrived on the spot. They were well outnumbered, the smugglers numbering 400. The coastguard to start with were only

Marine Parade C.1870.

three, one whose name was Pett was shot dead when he fired his pistol as a signal for assistance. After considerable firing on both sides the smugglers were put to flight leaving 3 coastguard men injured. It was not known whether any smugglers were injured. Only four tubs of spirit and the boat was taken. The body of Pett was taken to the Wish Tower, where he was declared dead by Doctor Sinnock. The reports from the pistols in the dead of night excited great alarm among the inhabitants'.

Eastbourne fisherman George French was sentenced to 6 months hard labour at the 'House of Correction' Lewes, on a smuggling offence. His wife Ann petitioned for his release stating that he had 9 children to support and another baby due. *'Humbly prayed that the Lords of the Treasury please take her case into consideration'.*

French was the son of widow French; formerly proprietor of machines for sea bathing and 43 local residents signed the petition.

The local Collector and Controller of Taxes had the last word. *'The petitioner's husband was committed for having been found on board a boat with stones slung and adapted for the sinking of small casks. We are also informed that he is a reputed smuggler. It appears to us on consideration that Mrs French's petition's chief, if not only object is to screen the parish from the support of the family while French is in confinement'.* French was not released.

From a report of September 1878 the following was discovered:

'Whilst digging foundations for the Mutual Improvement Society Hall (lately the Tivoli Cinema and Constitutional Club) on what was part of Field House field, some 12 inches under the surface was discovered a brick arch, beneath which was a cavern 16 feet in diameter. The use of the cavern was not certain but in all probability a hiding place or storage for the smugglers that infested that part of the Sussex coast many years ago'.

Smuggling contraband still continues and has over the years progressed to 'people' smuggling and illegal drugs with £ millions involved. As to local modern day smugglers one Eastbourne ex-fisherman and fish wholesaler Barry Domsalla trading as Linella Fisheries, well known on the beach in the 1980-1990's, having taken over Jack Prodger's Net shop, was arrested off the west coast of Scotland aboard a vessel carrying a large quantity of illegal drugs valued at £20m. In March 1999 he along with others was charged with drug smuggling, found guilty and sentenced to 10 years imprisonment. Another smuggler Michael Harris of Pevensey Bay also involved got 6 years.

As to 'people' smuggling it was in May 2004 using inflatable speedboats, Chinese illegal immigrants were smuggled across the Channel and landed at Newhaven by Marcus Wakelin of Eastbourne and Allan Gallop from Peacehaven. On being arrested both appeared at Court where it was disclosed that Wakelin had received £9,000 and Gallop £20,000 for ferrying the illegal immigrants into England. Gallop was jailed for 4 years and Wakelin 3 years.

Returning finally to the subject of Eastbourne and the war with France, a scare went up in the middle of the night in April 1796 that must have caused concern to the residents.

4 April 1796.

'*Between 1 and 2 o'clock on Thursday morning last, the inhabitants of East-Bourne were greatly alarmed by the Highland drummers beating to arms and the consequent parading of that Regiment; but more specially when they learnt the occasion of the bustle and they found that such dreadful preparation was necessary for the repulse of the French who were then landing in Pevensey Bay. The Highlanders turned out with the utmost alacrity, marched in solemn silence with great resolution to the seaside, but had no opportunity in displaying their bravery for the alarm had been given in error, by some people of a big coal brig, who had mistaken one of our ships that was in the Bay and pretty near on shore, for the purpose of impressing men, for one belonging to the enemy*'.

Some 142 years later a similar occurrence is alleged to have happened at Pevensey Bay during the 2nd World War. An Eastbourne Gazette magazine article reports '*Germans landed on the night of 4th February 1942 and were repulsed by a unit of the 5th Canadian Infantry Brigade*'. A local man George Humphrey working for the Eastbourne Gazette did research into the incident and from evidence gathered, the probability of a landing was by a small group of German commandos.

From early days fishing took place at the Sea Houses 'Stade'. 'Stade' is a word signifying a place on shore where vessels may run ashore for the discharge of cargo etc. This was the traditional Fishing Station for the fisher folk of Eastbourne with an ease of landing, naturally protected by Beachy Head from the prevailing southwest winds. A known haven for shipping during inclement weather, especially during the days of sail.

Holywell, Meads, was also another fishing quarter but never to the same extent as the 'Stade'. It is said that the original fishing hamlet of Holywell disappeared into

Holywell C.1880. Originally a chalk quarry. A gap in the shoreline rocks can be seen where chalk boats came ashore.

the sea many years ago. This theory can be borne out by the fact that the sea has encroached inland without doubt. The name Holywell pronunciation is as with two 'L's i.e. Holly-well is the local pronunciation and you hear non-Eastbourners pronounce it quite wrongly as Holy-well. Fanny Harriet Hide, nee Coppard, was born in Holywell House, Meads in 1839 and her son fisherman Edward Hide was born there in 1875. They and their forebears the Hart family who built Holywell House, gave their pronunciation as HOLLY-WELL.

The Samuel Cant map of Eastbourne 1739 shows Holywell being spelt as Hollywell and an 1852 survey of the coast and inshore waters again shows the spelling Hollywell - spelt as it sounded. The Figg Map schedule of 1816 shows No.890 Holly Well Furlong. The problem with the pronouncing of Holywell probably started with John Royer's book of 1787, when he wrote of the spring in Holly-well having healing powers and it may well be he spelt it as Holy-well to give emphasis to his tale. Then in 1861, Eastbourne was advertised as being a resort with special qualities for invalids, the spring again was said to have healing powers, but analysis proved this not to be true. The name could derive from *'a well, close to a Holly tree'* another is *'hollow well'* or *'well in the hollow'*. More likely *'hollow well'* thus pronounced *'HOLLYWELL'*. Examples of 'Holly' pronunciation instead of 'Holy' are, Holyhead, Holyrood Palace and Holywell in Wales to name but three.

Fishermen of Holywell C.1880.

The 'Stade' Fishing Station was situated between Sea Houses, Marine Parade, and to where the Great Redoubt stands (also known as Grand Redoubt, now for some strange reason called Redoubt Fortress. The Figg map dated 1818 calls it Broad Bourne Tower). The 'Stade' was part of the Crumbles or Waste, as it was also known. The Waste was a vast shingle area that spread from near the site of the Pier past Langney Point down through to Pevensey Bay with an area inland to the roads known as Seaside, St.Anthony's Avenue and the Coast Road to the hamlet of Wallsend (now Pevensey Bay). This shingle waste was said to be in possession of the Lord of the Manor of Eastbourne. When the Manor of Eastbourne was sold in 1555, farmlands and other properties were shared between three purchasers. The shingle Waste remained undivided. This could indicate that the Waste never had been part of the Manor, as going back in time all the Waste would not have been there but gradually increased over the years with the movement of seabed shingle and tides. (Dungeness is a good present day example for a build up of shingle)

Ownership of most arable land was in the hands of the Manor owners, but the shingle was regarded as waste. Manor tenants and others would freely use the boulders and shingle for building purposes. No tithes were ever levied on the shingle/waste.

It was in 1850 that the waste 'Crumbles' was divided up between the then two principal Lords of the Manor of Eastbourne, the Cavendish (later Dukes of Devonshire) and Gilbert families. Fisherman George Hide whose cottage was on the shingle waste at the original Fishing Station said *'he never paid a rent or tithe, nor had a landlord'*. An old Eastbourne fisherman Tom Reed (born early 1900's, died aged 93 years), wrote in his reminiscences *'In those days, the fisher folk of Eastbourne built their own cottages and paid rent to no one, but eventually the Duke of Devonshire ordered them to pay 1/- per week rent'* That tale has persisted through generations of the fisher folk of Eastbourne.

In the early years of the 18th century the joint Lords of the Manor took it upon themselves to erect capstans on the 'Stade' and made a charge for all vessels landing and off loading cargo with the exception of boats belonging to local fishermen. This assumption over the Waste/Crumbles by erecting capstans was in their own interests and obviously keeping the natives happy by not forcing a charge on them. The Lords of the Manor were the only people who could afford the cost. They also placed groynes and maintained them.

Whilst they appeared to be benevolent to the local fishermen they were only looking after their own interests and received income from the commerce generated by vessels using the 'Stade'. They were in essence, speculators. The Waste/Crumbles speculation paid dividends for the 11th Duke of Devonshire. Look at the £millions made from the development of the Crumbles for the Sovereign Harbour. But he had to overcome the 'Beast of Bolsover' socialist Denis Skinner MP, for Bolsover, an ex-miner and champion of the working classes and a near neighbour of the Duke at Chatsworth. The Duke's first application for an Act of Parliament for the development of the Crumbles as a Harbour failed due mainly to the actions of Denis. At that time in the 1970's a Labour government was in power but with a change of government the Duke's application was soon passed. The Eastbourne Harbour Act 1980 came into being and today we have the Sovereign Harbour. But is it really a Harbour or just an excuse for a huge treeless, grass free housing estate/cum Marina?

Back to the 'Stade' and the capstans. The following is an extract from the 'Compton Place Accounts correspondence' 1728-1818.

May 11th 1732.

An account as what every Master of a Vessel or Boat that shall be loaded or unloaded at Eastbourne Stade, is to pay for an acknowledgement to the Lords of

the Manors of Eastbourne for the use of the capstans set up there, as those that do not make use of them.

	If they use Capstan	If not
Every vessel of 44 tunn & upwards	£1. 5s. 0d.	£0. 5s. 0d
Every vessel not exceeding 40 tunns and above 30 tunns	£0. 10s. 0d	£0 3s. 0d
Every large decked fishing boat not belonging to the Stade	£0. 5s. 0d	No payment
Every small fishing boat not belonging to the Stade	£0. 1s. 0d	No payment
Every boat laden with chalk	£0. 6s. 0d	£0. 1s. 0d

'Every fishing boat that belongs to the place is not to pay any acknowledgement for the use of the capstans'.

The Stade was used by various vessels namely, fishing boats from Hastings, Newhaven, Brighton and Littlehampton, merchant vessels from home and abroad, coal ships from the North, chalk boats and boats that loaded wheat to ship out of Eastbourne, remembering that it was an agriculture area at that time. A document showing income and expenditure for the years 1732-1734 showed Income - £13.8s.0d. Expenditure - £9.9s.3d.

In 1802, Mr Nicholas Gilbert and Mr Inigo Thomas had ideas for the partitioning and development of the Waste/Crumbles. They were two of the three Lords of the Manor of Eastbourne, the biggest landowner being Lord George Cavendish. They did try and influence Lord George into joining their scheme, but he declined. Later in 1830, Mr Inigo Thomas of Ratton, Lord of the sub manor of Eastbourne Parker sold his interest in this to the other two Lords at that time, Lord George Cavendish and Mr Gilbert (in the right of his wife, Mary Ann Gilbert) giving them equal shares in the Manor of Eastbourne.

When Lord George Cavendish died and was succeeded in 1835 by his grandson William Cavendish, as 2nd Earl Burlington, later 7th Duke of Devonshire and Mary Ann Gilbert was succeeded by her son John Gilbert in 1845, the two inheritors both had ideas for the development of their properties and agreed on the advantage of dividing the Waste/Crumbles between themselves. A Mr Driver was called on to make a survey and to recommend a fair division. A plan and schedule was the final outcome and was approved in 1850 by the Enclosure Commissioners.

The Crumbles award plan and schedule 1850, shows the Net houses and premises occupied by local fishermen at the original Fishing Station. Net houses on Steddles (Steddles being support posts on which there were mushroom shaped attachments to stop the rats etc gaining access to the Net houses). and Dees are also mentioned. Dees were where fish was dried and smoked. Interestingly we see that fisherman James Brown was living in an old boat on the beach. The Eastbourne Census 1851 also shows where some of the fishermen named in the 1850 plan and schedule were residing.

1850 ENC. COMM.

No on plan	Description of Premise	Lessee 1845	Term of Lease	Annual Reserved Rent	Lessee 1850
60	Cottage in 2 Tenements, Front court, yard at rear, cont's Washhouse & 2 garden, cont's. sheds	Commissioners of Her Majesty's Customs	Yearly Tenant	—	—
61	A Net House	—	Yearly Tenant	—	John Wymark
62	A Net House	—	ditto	—	Henry Knight
63	A Net House	—	ditto	—	Thomas Swaine
64	A Net House	— Turner	ditto	—	Samuel Alchorne
65	A Net House	Rich's Harmer, Edw'd Alchorn, Fred Dyer	ditto	—	William Heathfield
66	A Net House	Hide & Allchorn	ditto	—	William Knight
67	A Net House	— Dyer	ditto	—	W. Dyer
68	A Net House	Wm Heathfield	ditto	—	
69	A Net House	James Hide	ditto	—	
70	A Net House	John Hide	ditto	—	
71	A Net House (An old Boat)	—	ditto	—	
72	A Net House (on Scaddles)	— Simpson	ditto	—	John Simpson
73	A Portion of the Beach partly enclosed	—	ditto	—	Not in award
74	A Net House	Mrs Ogle	ditto	—	
75	An old boat (converted into a dwelling)	William Heathfield	ditto	—	
76	A Net House (on Steddles)	James Brown	At Will from Michas 1805	1.10.0	Not in award
77	A Net House (on Steddles)	— Wymark	Yearly tenant	—	
78	The Towel House and Waiting room for Bathers	Sam'l Allchorn	Yearly tenant	—	
79	Tea Houses & Ground enclosed by post and rails	Richard Reed	At Will (yearly tenant)	5.0	William Dumbrill
		Major Willard	At William Michas 1815 (yearly tenant)	1.1.0	Not in award

Schedule of 1850 plan showing fishermen's Net shops and allied premises.

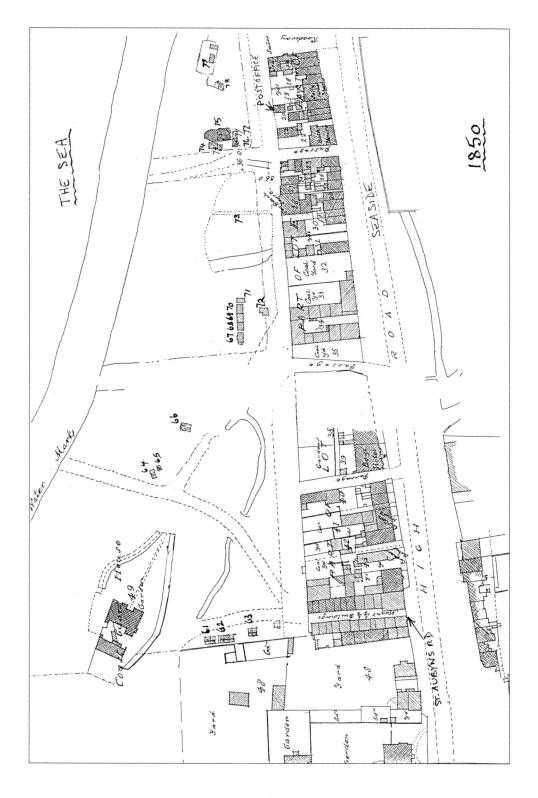

The example copies of the above give a picture of how the Fishing Station, beach and associated properties were situated along what are now Marine and Royal Parades.

The fishermen of Eastbourne in 1809 were protected by HMS 'Iris' a frigate on station to engage any French privateer, that dare approach.

'The period 1803-1815 saw prosperity in Eastbourne due to a large military presence, but with 1815 seeing the end of the war with France, troops would have been thrown onto the labour market. A period of depression and unemployment ensued in Eastbourne and the Cavalry Barracks in Old Town were later turned into the Workhouse'. An excerpt from 'The Methodist' by D Dunn Wilson.

This wasn't the first Workhouse in Eastbourne. The first report of a Workhouse was in 1737, sited at Pillory Barn, Old Town. The Barn still stands today and can be seen in Bradford Street. The next site from 1754 was at Broadbourne on the Waste/Crumbles near to where the Leaf Hall stands in Seaside, then to a site in Grove Road and finally to the Cavalry Barracks in 1826. This site became St. Mary's Hospital until a few years ago when it and the remaining Barrack building was demolished to make way for a housing estate named Letheren Place.

In an attempt to provide funds for helping the poor of Eastbourne, the inmates of the Workhouse were taught to weave and spin. Poor parents of *'girls not under the age of 9 years and boys no less than 8 years old'* were instructed to send their children to join the workforce. If they refused their poor relief was reduced or stopped.

In 1826 the Vestry minutes for January 23rd show a William Riddle allowed a sack of barley to fatten his hog, but had to send his girl Rosette to work at the Workhouse.

March 1826 shows that fisherman James Hutchings applied for £2 towards his house rent, but this was not allowed because he had been fighting and appeared before the Vestry with a black eye. He was allowed one weeks flour when he went off fishing.

On July 30th 1827 fisherman Henry Huggett applied for a loan of £9 to purchase fishing nets for catching mackerel. This was granted on condition that he paid the money back by Old Michaelmas Day 1828.

January 1827 saw the authorisation of new Stocks to be erected at Meads by the Constables. D Dunn-Wilson went on to say *'In this period there was no industrial development and the fishing was said to be poor'.* The population of Eastbourne in 1821 was 2,607.

Work and income could be had from time to time through unfortunate circumstances such as shipwrecks that happened on the coast of Sussex, salvage and salvage pay was a welcome income to the fishermen of Eastbourne. An example can be found in George Sims' Notes and Protest Notes of William Balcombe-Langridge held in East Sussex Records Office, Lewes, reference MP916. They show that on 11th March 1825, *'the brigantine 'Antonia Ulrica' went aground at Beachy Head en-route Rio Janeiro to Antwerp. Cargo salved consisted of: 1,630 bags coffee, 20 cases of sugar, 3,900 oxen and cow horns and 11 casks tapioca. Special salvage was paid to James Hide, Samuel Allchorn, John Hide, James Knight, Samuel Knight, Cosavir Knight, William Knight, Thomas Mitchell, Edward Allchorn, William Heathfield, John Hurd, William Coppard, George Cox, Thomas Weston, John Simpson, Richard Benner, Samuel Coppard, William Dyer, Benjamin Haslett, James Smith, Richard Welch, George Dyer and James Evans'.* Some of the above named were crewmembers of Eastbourne's first lifeboat. A list from the notes show they were paid for working a long tide 5/- each and a cost of £1.17.6d allowance for bread, cheese and beer. James Knight and 14 other fishermen were paid a total of £3.10.0d for their exertions in taking an anchor out to the stranded boat to prevent it drifting.

A Shipwreck and Eastbourne's first lifeboat service 1833.

The first Eastbourne lifeboat was named 'Samaritan' having been built by the local boat builders John and William Simpson. The 'Samaritan' was 25 ft long, had a beam of 8 ft 6ins and was pulled by 10 oars. John Fuller, M.P. of Rose Hill, near Brightling, Sussex, financed the lifeboat. He was known as 'Mad Jack' and is interred in the pyramid type mausoleum, which can be seen in Brightling churchyard to this day.

After the 'Thames' an East-Indiaman of some 1,500 tons was wrecked at Pevensey Bay, Eastbourne in 1822, it is said he had the 'Samaritan' built and given for the use of the people of Eastbourne. After the wrecking of the 'Thames' several rescues at sea were made by the locally stationed Coastguard but no mention of the lifeboat.

A report from the Sussex Advertiser, 25th February 1833 about the shipwrecked 'Isabella' quoted *'How truly gratifying it be to the feelings of Mr Fuller of Rose Hill, to learn he has been the cause of saving a whole ship's crew from a watery grave, on having humanely given, for the use of this part of the coast, a Lifeboat'.*

It was on 21st February 1833 that Eastbourne fishermen being members of the lifeboat crew were involved in rescuing 29 persons off the sailing ship 'Isabella' wrecked at Eastbourne. The following are accounts of the rescue: -

Brighton Guardian. 27th Feb 1833. Shipwreck. - 'On Wednesday last, this part of the coast was visited by a tremendous storm of wind and rain, which continued during the whole day. Between 6 and 7 am, the ship 'Isabella', 340 tons burthen, from the Port of London, James Wildgooss, master and outward bound for Madeira and Demerara was seen off the Boulder Bank, near the Wish (Wish Tower) Eastbourne, in evident distress. A tremendous sea drove her on the Boulder Bank, where she lost her rudder and consequently the crew having lost all command of the helm. The Eastbourne lifeboat was launched through tremendous surf and on reaching the 'Isabella' two of its crew boarded her but were ordered off by Captain Wildgooss and Mr Adam Hamilton in charge of the lifeboat was ordered to stand by. The 'Isabella' in an hour or so after, floated off the Boulder Bank, where she sprung a leak and again ran aground on the sands near Walls End, Pevensey. Here she lay at low water mark, exposed to all the fury of the waves, which broke over her with tremendous force, blowing out her decks and washing away casks, planks, etc. It was not till this happened that the Captain could be persuaded to leave her. It gives us pleasure to state that the crew and passengers, (29 persons) were all safely landed a little to the east of Walls End (Pevensey Bay) in the lifeboat belonging to

John Fuller Esq. of Rose Hill. Among the passengers were a Mr & Mrs Le Maitre with their three children, who were going to settle in Demerara, Le Maitre having obtained a situation under the Government, (Mrs Le Maitre is the second daughter of Mr William Woodhams of Lullington, near Alfriston, Sussex and first cousin of Mrs J.Padgen, of Meads, Eastbourne). Great credit is due to those who managed the lifeboat, which brought the shipwrecked crew on shore in the midst of tremendous surf. The sea has done great mischief to the vessel; but we are happy to state that a great part of the cargo has been safely landed. It consists of 200 quarters of wheat in bags; 80 chaldrons of coals; between 60 and 80 thousand bricks, a quantity of lime in casks and a variety of general articles for colonial consumption. Messrs Stone & Filder of Eastbourne together with Mr Beville of the Customs and Messrs Boykett Breeds of Hastings, the agents for Lloyds, have been indefatigable in their endeavours to secure the stores; but our correspondent states there are 'Plunderers in overwhelming numbers' ' The lifeboat which is always kept ready by Mr Adam Hamilton, Principal Officer of the Customs, was on this occasion commanded by that gentleman himself and the following brave little crew worked at the oars and exerted themselves to the utmost:- Samuel Knight, William Knight, Thomas Knight, & Samuel Knight Jnr, John, James and George Hide, John Simpson, William Simpson, George Simpson, Edward & Samuel Allchorn, George Cox, James Hutchings and Thomas Mitchell, all fishermen belonging to Eastbourne'.

A query about the rescue stated by other sources is that 'the first part of the rescue took place at the Boulder Bank when 11 persons were taken ashore'. Not so, when the lifeboat made alongside the 'Isabella' Coxswain Adam Hamilton was ordered by Captain Wildgooss to 'stand by'. This he did and when the 'Isabella' was driven aground at Walls End (Pevensey Bay) the 11 passengers were then taken off and a return trip by the 'Samaritan' took off the Captain and crew.

Other sources also state the first Eastbourne lifeboat appeared to have no name. It clearly states in the Eastbourne Gazette published October 1862 *'The 'Samaritan' was sea tested in a strong S.W.wind with heavy seas running by officers of the Lifeboat Institute. Under canvas she mounted the heavy seas with great buoyancy and fully maintained her character as a good sea boat'.*

The Eastbourne Gazette 9th December 1863 reports, when the lifeboat 'Mary Stirling' took over service from the old original lifeboat, it names the old lifeboat as 'Samaritan'.

Quote - *'The old boat the 'Samaritan' has saved about 50 lives. She was built at the expense of John Fuller, of Rose Hill, who handed the right of the gift over to his nephew, A E Fuller, this gentleman, as we are further informed eventually gave the boat to the inhabitants of Eastbourne'.*

It is also stated the 'Samaritan', which is about 8 feet shorter than the 'Mary Stirling' (new boat), had been given to the town and not to the Lifeboat Institute.

The Eastbourne Gazette, 1888 in an article 'Reminiscences of Eastbourne' by Mr John Vine (an old inhabitant, born 1811), he writes *'The first lifeboat, we had a lifeboat and although it lacked the improvements of modern boats, it was much more staunch than many of the lifeboats of today. She was called the 'Samaritan' and given to the town by Jack Fuller as he was popularly called, of Rose Hill. She*

Eastbourne lifeboat 'Mary Stirling' replaced the original lifeboat 'Samaritan' in 1863. Coxswain Joseph 'Joker' Huggett is standing extreme aft in boat.

was built from timber grown on his estate and proved a most sea worthy boat, doing some exceedingly good work in her time'.

From information through an old Eastbourne boatman/fisherman Reuben 'Old Screw' Wood (Sept.1905) he said quote, *'The 'Samaritan' was sold out of service in 1860's and turned into a river boat, the river, in this case being the Thames'.*

The first regular Coxswain of the 'Samaritan' was Samuel Knight and for the 1842 'Watts' and 1845 'Twee Cornelissen' rescues was in command and continued until 1853 when Joseph 'Joker' Huggett took over as Coxswain and Huggett was in command when the lifeboat 'Mary Stirling' replaced the 'Samaritan' in 1863. The 'Mary Stirling' built by Messrs Forrest of Limehouse was brought to Eastbourne by train. Christened by Lady Fanny Howard of Compton Place, the daughter of the Duke of Devonshire the 'Mary Stirling' was launched off the beach.

Certainly the inhabitants of Eastbourne and Sussex come in for great criticism over the 'Isabella' incident. From the account of Captain J. Wildgooss, after all on board had landed safely with only the clothes they stood up in.

'By this time many hundreds of the country people had collected on the beach; and when the tide ebbed from the wreck a most disgraceful scene of plundering ensued. That in a civilized country like England and within 70 miles of the metropolis such enormities could be committed - that bands of men, many of them armed, should come down to a wreck, setting all law and authority at defiance, to plunder and carry away everything they could lay their hands on, is a disgrace to the nation and human nature. Such conduct might be expected from the natives of the coasts of Africa or New Zealand, but that it could take place on the coast of Sussex is really dreadful. I express my thanks to Captain Wills and the officers and men of the Coast

Guard under him, particularly Lieutenants Hewett and Jackson, on whose station the ship went ashore, for their valuable assistance; and but for whose great vigilance and unremitting exertions in protecting the property, everything would have been carried off by the overwhelming numbers of lawless ruffians who came down, even from distant parts of the country, for that purpose'.

A passenger Mr P.L. Le Maitre wrote in the 'Times' 21st March 1833;

'Spirited anathema against the disgraceful and anti-social outrages practised by the wretches, who, after our lives had been saved, with reckless cruelty spread themselves far and wide along the coast for the plunder of every remnant of property the dreadful violence of the elements had spared. Such enormities and their general impunity are alike disgraceful and call, indeed, most loudly for the active interference of the proper authorities. I have so severely and extensively suffered by the monstrous practice and on the next ensuing morning after the wreck I personally secured, amid a crowd of wreckers, one of these ruthless villains and assisted by the Coast Guard, safely lodged him in the Tower commanded by the active and excellent Lieutenant Hewett, from which custody he was fully committed for trial at Lewes extra Assizes'.

Mr Le Maitre went on to express his thanks to Adam Hamilton and the lifeboat crew, the local physician and surgeon and the generous Eastbourne coachman who had all refused to make a charge for their services. So some Eastbourners restored faith in mankind. Mr Le Maitre's experience of the wrecking of the 'Isabella' and criticism of her captain is contained in a correspondence of letters in the 'Times' March 1833 - well worth reading.

Over the years rich pickings were had from wrecks along the coast of Sussex especially around Beachy Head. From legal and illegal salvaging, good money could be made by the seafaring community. The 'Antonia Ulrica' 1825 was a prime example.

1940 saw the bombing and beaching of the SS. Barnhill east of Langney Point. Thousands of tins of food and other contents were washed ashore, gathered and taken by the inhabitants of Eastbourne. Plunderers?

The assistance to the 'Isabella' was the first recorded service of the Eastbourne lifeboat 'Samaritan'. For this service the Lifeboat Institution awarded £20 to 'Samaritan's' crew and sent thanks to Adam Hamilton Principal Officer of Customs for the efficient state in which the lifeboat was kept. It is also recorded in 1827 that Mr Hamilton applied for a chain to haul up the lifeboat clear of the breakers - the cost £27. In 1837 the lifeboat was kept in a boathouse built for that purpose, alongside the Coastguard Watch House 100 yards from high water mark.

John 'Mad Jack' Fuller had bronze medals specially struck to commemorate the rescue. These were presented to each member of the crew. On one side, the portrait of John Fuller with the words *'John Fuller, Esq., Rose Hill, Sussex'*, on the other *'Presented to (name) for his conduct in saving the lives of twenty-nine shipwrecked persons, 1833'*. John Fuller died later in 1833 bequeathing the lifeboat to his 1st cousin Augustus Eliot Fuller, M.P. for East Sussex and he subsequently gifted the 'Samaritan' to the town of Eastbourne in the 1850's.

The early 1800's saw the education of working class children of Eastbourne take

John Fuller medal. 'Isabella' rescue, 1833.

place in a building attached to the bell tower of St Mary's Church under Reverend Brodie. In 1856 his daughter Julia provided a school (Brodie Hall) at the east end of town, erecting a flint-faced building situated in the grounds of Christ Church, Seaside. Church services were held in the School until completion of the Church in 1859. Christ Church became known as the 'Fishermen's Church'. The school was built to accommodate 100 children but records show, in 1888 attendance stood at 175, many of them being children of the fishing community.

Back to Fishing.

Brighton Fishing Museum, reference 13554 14th December 1835.

'Off Eastbourne early Wednesday morning, a French chasse maree from Bordeaux bound to Calais laden with wine, ran into our homestead and hoisted a signal of distress. The fishermen ever alert on these occasions immediately manned a boat and put off to her assistance, where they learned that during the night the Captain in a fit of insanity, threw himself overboard and was drowned and those on board had totally lost their calculation. The vessel was escorted to Newhaven to procure a pilot to take charge of and conduct her to her destination port'. Salvage fees for the Eastbourne fishermen.

Brighton Fishing Museum, reference 13579. August 1836.

'A female Sun Fish taken off Beachy Head last week, was exhibited on the beach by two Eastbourne fishermen, who had captured this curious inhabitant of the deep. It measured about 6 feet in length and 7 feet transversely from the extremity of the dorsal to that of the anal fin. Its weight was estimated at between 600lbs and 700lbs. It was announced in a handbill as a one eyed sea devil. These fishes, called moles or sunfishes have jaws without teeth and the tail is so short and high that the fish looks like a portion had been cut off, giving it a most singular truncated appearance. The skin is very hard and divided into small angular compartments and a thick gelatinous substance is spread under the skin. The species is not uncommon in European seas, but is rarely seen near our shores'.

On March 25th 1837, there was published in 'The Penny Magazine' an article on mackerel fishing. Here are some details from it.

'The name for the mackerel is derived from the Latin 'macula' the spotted or streaked fish, hence the term 'mackerel- sky' applied to the well known cloud formation. The weight of the mackerel is generally less than two lbs, but one individual sold in London weighed 5 lbs and a quarter. The ordinary lengths being 14 - 16 inches but some make 20 inches. The fishing season commences on the Sussex coast early February, some fish are taken in January but the numbers taken

Original print of Mackerel boats off Beachy Head, 1837.

are small and when sold in London sell for 1/- to 2/- each. To fish mackerel, fishermen have to go out a considerable distance at sea to catch, as mackerel do not approach the coast until May - June, which were the busiest months. In June they spawn. (This is when they come in really close to the shore). They move North to South and vice versa. There being three modes of fishing, - Drift net, with Luggers, Sean (seine) nets, close inshore with small boats Punts and by line - lines with baited hooks from Luggers and Punts'.

Sussex Fishermen's Superstitions from the book 'The Fisheries of the World. 1883. By F Whymper'

'With herrings the Hastings and Eastbourne fishermen believed that ' the herrings come to see the bonfires on Guy Fawkes Day'. As a fact they were generally first caught on the Sussex coast on that or the following day. Sussex fishermen have a superstition regarding a large herring of a blood red colour (called the 'King Herring'), which acts as a pilot to the school or shoal of herrings. If caught in a herring net, it is at once thrown overboard, as keeping it would bring bad luck and moreover cause the shoal to be lost for want of a pilot. When dead this fish resembles other herrings but it is said that when alive the blood red colour could be seen even on a dark night and when the fish is in the sea'.

A Sussex saying is: 'In June Mackerel are in tune'.

Every night during the mackerel and herring fishing seasons, as the nets are cast, the fishermen repeat as each (buoyant) barrel (one attached to every ten nets) leaves the side: -

'Watch, barrel! Watch! Mackerel (or herring) for to catch.
White may they be, as a blossom on the tree,
God send thousands, one, two, and three,
Some by the head, some by the tail,
God send mackerel and never fail'.

At the last net the Master says, 'Seas all', were he to make the mistake of saying 'Last net' the popular belief is that he would never see his nets again.

A Brighton proverb is 'Plaice are in season when wheat is in blossom'.

Six good things in Sussex are 'A Chichester lobster, a Selsey cockle, and Arundel mullet, a Pulborough eel, an Amberley trout and a Rye herring'.

From a report of November 1884, an Eastbourne superstition was; if any crewmember had killed a cat, this brought bad luck on the whole boat and catches would be down.

Another interesting local custom was, when codfish were caught they were dispatched with the human process of hammering the noses of the cod with a staff, this being to make them 'die lissome'

Beware in Yorkshire! 'At Flamborough if a women enters a cottage while the men are preparing their lines, she has to immediately fall to her knees and repeat the Lord's Prayer before she is allowed to leave'.

Drift net fishing was the most common method of this period, drift nets being some 20 feet in depth, by 120 feet long. Several of these nets joined together stretched at times to some ³/₄ to 1¹/₂ mile in length. The nets were usually shot in the evening and hauled at dawn. The amount of catch fluctuated from season to season.

The boats, Luggers, were generally 30 feet in the keel, built of Oak or Ash and copper fastened. They had great depth of waist and were broad of beam. Sussex boats were noted for their durability and considered as fast and as safe a boat on any coast in the United Kingdom.

All fishing boats were required to be licensed by an Act of Parliament and the Commissioners of Customs were authorized to grant or refuse licences and to prescribe within what distance of the English coast they should be employed. These impediments often occurred through the reports of the local Officers of the Revenue, who suspected certain fishermen of smuggling. Whether justly or not they could stop fishermen from pursuing their lawful occupation. The fishing limit would be not to proceed further than 3 - 4 leagues (1 League = approx. 3 miles) from the coast to fish. Valuable fishing grounds were abandoned to the French, Belgian and Dutch on the opposite coast and they freely fished all that was restricted to the English fishermen. The licences were not granted unless securities were given and this was the subject of many complaints.

This licensing system was relaxed in 1832 and the fishing limit extended to within one league of the French, Belgian and Dutch coast, but securities were still required. What these were is not known and a secret report (smuggling) upon suspicion only of the local Officer of Customs made it difficult to obtain a licence. As is obvious the object of these regulations was to protect the Revenue against smuggling but it did not secure this effect, as the French, Belgian and Dutch boats could not be brought into this operation. The result of all this was for the smugglers to bring in new ways by which to baffle the Officers of the Revenue.

So in 1837 when this report was published it was desired that this particular licensing system be also abolished so that our fishermen should be able to proceed wherever there was a catch of fish to be caught, care being taken not to infringe on the rights of the French, Belgian and Dutch coasts.

The penalties for smuggling would still be in full force against the Custom-house laws and those engaged in lawful pursuit of fishing would no longer be annoyed by the regulations and call for securities.

The Mackerel season April- June 1837 was poor. This is borne out by a letter written 9th October 1837 by John Hide's accountant, Mr James Lay of Eastbourne to the executor of the estate of a James Breach. Hide owed £12.4s.7d.to the estate. The letter reads:

Sir,

Mr John Hide has handed me your letter respecting the debt due to the estate of James Breach - from personal knowledge I have of him I can state no man is more willing to pay than he is, but the disastrous mackerel season has thrown him, & landed other fishermen in a situation that they cannot pay - if you put your tenant in execution it would be his ruin, but leave him alone until the herring season is over which is just commencing and you will be sure to have your money. To make the poor man easy will you oblige me with an answer, which will oblige, your servant?
Jas Lay.
Eastbourne Oct 9th 1837

Mr James Lay is listed in the Eastbourne 1841 census as an accountant aged 74 living with his wife Elizabeth in the Old Town area.

So the disastrous mackerel season had put John Hide and perhaps other fishermen into debt. A good herring season was hoped for and indeed it was. He and the other fishermen would no doubt have paid off their debts. The Sussex Express for that year tells us the poor mackerel season was compensated for by a good herring season October - November.

A report reads '*On Tuesday evening a Worthing herring boat with 3 men and 30,000 herring on board, bound for Brighton, struck a rock off Beachy Head and immediately sunk. Fortunately an Eastbourne fishing boat was at hand and rescued the unfortunate men from their truly perilous situation, in the absence of which they must have found a watery grave. Our herring season has commenced very prosperously, one boat having caught 60,000 and another 50,000 in a night. We are very glad to hear these good tidings and trust it will in some measure compensate for the failure of the late mackerel season and partially alleviate the distress so universally felt by its unproductiveness*'.

The next issue of the Sussex Express reports '*The Eastbourne fishermen have been unusually successful today, having brought on shore 17 lasts, that is 170,000 herrings, which they are retailing at 2s and 1s 6d per hundred of 128*'. As the season continued it was stated that more herring had been brought ashore by the Eastbourne fishermen than was ever known by the oldest man or woman living in the parish.

A poor fishing season would reflect on many of the townsfolk who depended on the fishing industry for a living, so much so that it could be the workhouse for some. (A local publication states *'fishing was always a minority line in Eastbourne'*.) Against this opinion it should be pointed out that, fish was for centuries a staple food of those that lived beside the sea, especially the peasant working classes. Local archaeological digs have produced vast quantities of fish bones giving evidence of a main diet. Failure of the fish to arrive caused great hardship. The fishing industry in Eastbourne brought a living and gave sustenance to many a person and family and the arrival of the fish was met with great joy.

Times were hard in Eastbourne on the employment front. February 1837 saw a number of able bodied labourers parading the streets singing songs of inducement to buy the matches they were selling, having been thrown out of work and being without other means of support. The annual March Fair in South Street passed off very quietly and the complaint of the dullness of the Fair was evidence of the extreme destitution of the lower classes.

Brighton Fishing Museum, reference 13642 3rd May 1838

'At Eastbourne about ten of our boats, with some others, landed about 3,000 mackerel here on Monday. They were immediately packed and sent off to the London market'. So a turn up for the Eastbourne fishermen and it would be interesting to know how transportation took place. (No railway existed at Eastbourne until 1849). Possibly by horse and cart to the nearest Station in Sussex.

A fisherman of this period John Hide (1786 -1860) an elder brother of 'Navarino' Hide was married to Ann having three children, George b.1814, Ann b.1816 and Mariah, b.1819. John and his family lived near to the Stade by the Sea Houses. He was well to the fore in the fishing community and for many years from 1819 was the designated 'Letter Receiver' (Post Office) for Sea Houses. In 1839 he became Chairman of the Eastbourne Fishermen's Compensation Fund Society. A first meeting of Owners & Masters of Fishing Vessels and fishermen of Eastbourne was held on 1st March 1839 at the Kings Arms Public House, Seaside (this was the original Kings Arms demolished c.1890 which stood between Hanover Road and Redoubt Road, now occupied by a terrace once named Jubilee Terrace, opposite to where the present Kings Arms stands today). The Compensation fund was at the suggestion of Mr & Mrs Henry Ogle, benevolent friends of the fishermen, who resided close to the 'Stade' in a house called Sea Beach House. Later occupied by the Streatfield family. (Known today as Sea Beach House Hotel, Marine Parade).

John Hide (1786-1860). Fisherman and Letter Receiver.

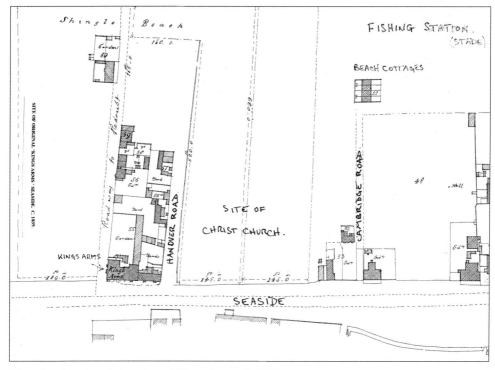

Plan showing site of the original Kings Arms, C.1839.

The idea was for a Society or Association to be instituted and be entitled '*The Eastbourne Fishermen's Compensation Fund Society*'. The Society book makes interesting reading and is partly produced here. The Society was formed as the fishermen had had two lean years of fishing (except a good herring season in 1837) and much damage to nets and gear. But the first half-year report held at the Kings Arms on 9th August 1839 shows no demands on funds although fishing voyages had been unproductive.

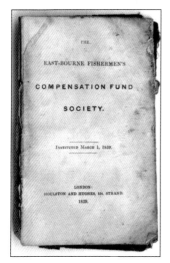
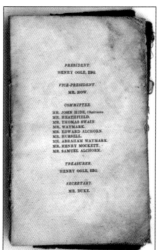

Copies of original Compensation Fund Society book, 1839.

A report of October 1839 shows *'catches poor and Eastbourne fishermen look likely to apply for relief in the Workhouse this winter'*. As previously stated a lot of inhabitants relied on the fishing trade for a living. Fishermen at that time numbered some 100.

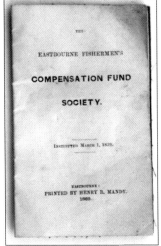 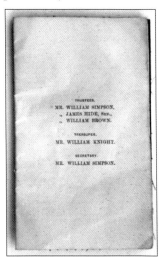

In 1869 this original 'Compensation Fund' was reconstituted and the original book of rules (1839) adopted, published and printed by a local man, Henry R. Mandy. Trustees of the Fund were fishermen, William 'Old Laddie' Simpson, James 'Navarino' Hide and William Brown, Treasurer William Knight and Secretary William 'Old Laddie' Simpson. This

Copies of original Compensation Fund Society book, 1869.

Compensation Fund ran until 1903 when at a meeting in the Beach Hotel it was disbanded and the monies, some £250, were given to Charity.

C.1840 'A bit of Postal History'.

The 'Post Office' at the Sea Houses in those days (1840-50's) was a receiving house for mail and had been so from 1819 and probably before. John Heatherly's 1819 *'Guide to East Bourn'* mentions the receiving house for letters at the Sea Houses - the Main Post Office in 1819 being at East-Bourne village below the Parish Church. Between 1840 - 50 the Main Post Office moved to Southbourne (Town Hall area).

The census for 1851 shows John Hide, age 64 years, widower, fisherman, occupying the Post Office, Seaside and being head of the household. Living with him were John Head, son in law (fisherman), Ann Head (daughter of John Hide) and their two children John and Maria. Earlier records show that on 19th September 1840 Ann Head was appointed Post Mistress for 'Seahouses, East-Bourne' by Lord Lichfield. (Post Office archives ref.2570 applications 1839-1841). Then in 1855, Kelly's Post Office Directory lists John Head as Postmaster and owner of bathing machines, Seaside. John and Ann Head's daughter Maria later married Henry W. Keay who became a Mayor of Eastbourne.

Enterprising salvage reported in the Sussex Express 26th December 1840. It says:

'Eastbourne.

Brig Ashore - Early on Friday night a severe storm of wind and snow came on during which the brig 'Ino' of Shoreham, laden with coals came so near the shore as unfortunately to strike on the rocks at Cow Gap, near Beachy Head. The crew, thinking from her making water that her keel was knocked off, hastily left her in their large boat, but instead of landing they moved round the 'Head' and came in near Seaford. On the following morning, early, they came to look for the Brig, but

in the interim she had been discovered by our fishermen, who partly throwing the cargo overboard had lightened her, as at the next tide to be able to get her afloat again. No material damage was sustained and they got her safely into Newhaven Harbour. These hardy fellows are deserving of their good fortune for had not their Herculean labours been attended with success, the Brig and cargo must irretrievably have been lost. As it was about 50 tons of coals were thrown overboard and at low water our poor people were not slow in availing themselves of the means of providing the good fire which was thus placed in their power'.

The fishermen earned salvage money and the poor kept warm for Christmas and the New Year.

The 1841 census shows a total of 51 fishermen, but it must be borne in mind that this census book is short of at least 2 pages. The total population of Eastbourne for 1841 is given as 3,015 including a total of 131 Workhouse inmates.

Another salvage incident in 1845.

The report in the 'Brighton Guardian' 24th September, for that year records;

'On Saturday last, a vessel in a crippled condition, having lost her foremast, was seen by some of our fishermen of Seaside. They put off to her in a galley punt, boarded her and were taking her to Newhaven Harbour, when, rounding Beachy Head, she was struck by a sea that took away her gaff and did some other mischief. At this time the mate in letting the halyards go, also let go the rope to which the galley punt was attached. A lad named Erridge was in her on his own and being unable to make to the vessel, the galley's sails being used on the damaged vessel, hoisted his frock on an oar and steered for the land but when nearing Birling Gap, the boat upset, resting on the lad's neck. He was however providentially rescued from his perilous position by some coastguard men who had been anxiously watching his progress'.

Salvaging, not without its dangers!

The above incident is what was described as 'Hovelling' or to 'Hovel'. This practice had gone on among the coastal inhabitants since perhaps man first put to sea in boats.

To 'Hovel' - a chance to get an abandoned vessel at sea or to assist into a safe haven when a vessel is disabled, thereby obtaining payment or 'salvage money'. In those early days it often applied to a boatman who went out to wrecks, occasionally with a view to plunder, as no doubt they did and gave no assistance to the poor shipwrecked sailor. There were many instances of downright inhumanity where no attempt was made to rescue the poor souls.

'In the struggle to be first to plunder the wreck, the persons on the wreck were forgotten, the very Law encouraged the wreckers to forget them, or murder them, for it defined a wreck as anything from which 'no living creature came ashore alive'.

Even the ship's cat would be killed. This behaviour brought about the founding of the Lifeboat Institute with the innovation of the lifeboat to solely save life.

A definition of the above Hoveller derived from 'Hovelier' (hobble) signified a coastal watchman or lookout man who went by horse (hobble) or on foot to get assistance, or took a boat to assist for salvage money. (Hovelling, from 1805 Protest Notes of George Sims MP916 East Sussex Records Office, Lewes. The Galliot 'Ionge Zujnenga' 'A hoveller who gave information of this vessel in distress '*To Christopher Harryott, giving information of the vessel being in distress as customary. £2.2s.0d'*).

From a report in the Sussex County Magazine,

'It is said that in Victorian times c.1850 a very curious custom among Sussex fishermen was the 'Bending In' ceremony, which generally took place in April when the Luggers were preparing for the North Sea fishing.

The Luggers would be on the beach along with the fisher folk community (fishermen, their wives, children and the old fishermen no longer able to go to sea). The priest of the parish would hold a service on the beach giving a blessing to all present and to those going to sea and a blessing that their catches will be bountiful.

After the blessing the fishermen would take hold of the nets, which were in long rows on the beach, beside the Luggers. The Captain and mate would be in the boat at the bow and stern.

The net was lifted into the boat by the fishermen and laid down by the Captain and mate who 'bent it in' in careful folds, all to the accompanying chant which sounded like 'Holly haunch ho-o-o-o-o'

All the boats began and ended this ritual at the same time. The 'Bending In' done the fisher folk would then set into baskets of bread and cheese and stone bottles of beer with the Priest joining in the 'picnic'. Picnic over, the older fishermen and helpers would put shoulder to the Lugger sides and with a cry of 'Holly haunch ho-o-o-o-o' start the Luggers on their way on the greased 'trows' (wood planks) into the sea repeating the same until the Lugger was afloat with a final cry of 'Hi'.

A portrait of an Eastbourne Fisherman, Pleasure Boatman and Lifesaver.

George Hide (nickname Dot) was born in 1814, the year before the Battle of Waterloo. The only son of John and Ann, he followed in his father's footsteps and became a fisherman. At the age of 22 years in 1836 he married Mary Ann Knight (b.1816). Mary Ann being from the local family of fishermen and early lifeboat men.

George and Mary Ann had six children, John (b.1837), George Merrick (nickname Pincher, b.1840), Mary Ann (b.1842 she married fisherman Henry Hurd (b.1833), Samuel Beckett (b.1844), Benjamin Charles (b.1847) and Charles (nickname 'Bones', b.1849). All were fishermen and pleasure boatmen to a man, all their lives.

Nicknames were used quite a lot throughout the fishing fraternity in early times and up to the present day. It is said the fishermen to identify themselves when involved in smuggling activities against detection by the Excise and Coast Guard men used nicknames. As regards George Snr. he was anything but a 'Dot'. George Merrick was known as 'Pincher' and in later life in 1880's Eastbourne, was known as leader of the local fishermen. As for Charles 'Bones', he was said to have got his nickname because when born he was all 'skin and bone' and fitted into a pint pot. As he grew up he developed into a man of Herculean proportions. Like his father 'Bones' was a well-known lifesaver of persons from the perils of the sea.

George 'Dot' Hide became well known as a brave and accommodating person among the people of Eastbourne. First coming to notice as early as 1828 when as a 14-year-old lad, he along with cousins Frederick Hide 17 years, Richard Hide 13 years and James Hutchings 15 years were on the beach at Eastbourne when a large French Lugger laden with fish from the north of England came in at Eastbourne for water. The captain not being aware of the shallowness of the coast was detained on shore. The tide had fallen and the wind rose producing a swell and the vessel was listing heavily on the shore. The colours were hoisted for assistance, which the captain was unable to afford from the smallness of his boat. The local fishermen were unwilling to render aid (no love of the French in those days, the war being not long over and the never-ending problem with the French over poaching. Like today the fishing fraternity and the indigenous coastal inhabitants it is said, still have an inbuilt aversion to the French). Young George and the others volunteered to help and took the French captain off with his water. The anchor of the French Lugger was got up and the vessel went safely to sea.

In 1833, George was involved in the lifeboat rescue of the 'Isabella' along with his father John and uncle James 'Navarino'. Then at the age of 26 years George performed an outstanding act of bravery. It was on the night of Friday 13th November 1840, close by Martello Tower No.72 at Eastbourne when his actions saved the lives of the crew of the wreck 'Joseph' of Sunderland, a coal Brig en-route from Tynemouth to Southampton. The newspapers of the time gave dramatic and graphic accounts of the rescue.

'The Times' 17th November 1840.

EASTBOURNE. Nov. 14th. -'This place has been visited by awful winds and tides have run tremendously high, washing over the Parade, (Marine Parade) and filling the cellars of some houses. No material damage being done except to the old lodging house of this place, celebrated by the name of the 'Round House' where the late lamented Duke of Kent spent some of his juvenile days. So far on shore we have fared tolerably well, but it is my painful task to inform you that two Brigs have been wrecked - one to the eastward and one to the westward of the town. The former was coal laden from Newcastle to Southampton and came ashore on Friday night; the crew took to the rigging and waited the death which must have been their fate, had it not been for the humanity and daring intrepidity of one of our fishermen, who, amidst the gaing of the storm and the cheering of his comrades, dashed through the breakers at the peril of his life and conveyed a rope to the vessel, by means of which, I am happy to state all hands were safely landed. The name of the fisherman who has the enviable satisfaction of having performed this act of genuine nobility is George Hide. Every possible attention was paid to the shipwrecked crew. I regret to state the other vessel to the westward became a complete wreck. Not one was saved, so entirely was every chance of human aid cut off. The corpses of the captain and two men have been washed on shore, also a cow, but no traces have yet been discovered which may lead to the knowledge of what vessel she was. It is feared much mischief may be calculated on. Many sail are now passing up Channel, among them a large ship with loss of foremast'.

A more comprehensive account of George Hide's bravery was reported in the 'Sussex County Advertiser' Lewes 21st Nov. 1840. (There were no Eastbourne newspapers until c.1860).

EASTBOURNE. - The late Gales. - Two Wrecks. - We are enabled to give a more detailed report than we could receive before publication last week, of the wreck of the Brig ' Joseph' of Sunderland.

'Timothy Ashford, master, burthen 178 tons, coal laden, which took place on the 13th November, between Tower 72 and the Great Redoubt, in Eastbourne Bay. At about half past eleven o'clock, it blowing a heavy gale from west sou-west, a Brig was observed by the coastguard look out men of the Eastbourne station, coming from the west-wards under her two topsails, steering for the shore, which she reached in sinking state and grounded about midnight. Lieut. Conduit, the Chief officer and his crew proceeded immediately with Dennet's rocket apparatus and endeavoured to establish a communication with the Brig, when their attentions were frustrated by the bursting of the rocket and destroying the triangle. Heavy seas were breaking by this time over the hull of the vessel and the crew were obliged to secure themselves in the main rigging and the top and as the tide was flowing and she approached nearer, every lifting of the immense waves which broke over her, Cornelius Jones, a boatman of the Coastguard, boldly plunged into the surf with a small lead line, endeavouring to throw it over any part of the Brig, but after repeated attempts and in imminent danger of losing his life, he could not succeed; when George Hide, one of the fishermen of Eastbourne, most gallantly plunged in and was several times thrown back by the tremendous seas, but was providentially so fortunate as to succeed in throwing the lead line on board to the sufferers, who at

Copy of an original painting of the coal brig 'Joseph' wrecked by Tower 72 and the rescue of the crew. Eastbourne 13th November 1840.

this period collected on the weather side of the vessel, as she had fallen on her larboard broadside with her masts to seaward, lying parallel with the beach. Communication having been thus established by George Hide's gallant intrepidity, the whole crew, eight in number were successively enabled to let themselves down on the ropes round their bodies, connected with the shore and were rescued from a watery grave by the coastguard and fishermen plunging into the raging surf as the poor creatures were in turn thrown within reach of their grasp; in which service George Hide rendered himself again most conspicuously, amongst those who bravely assisted. The men were taken into Tower 72, where every attention was paid to them by Lieut. Conduit and his crew. The vessel (the coals having washed out) became a total wreck during the continuance of the storm, having nearly two hours rising of the tide breaking over her. It appears she sprung a leak off Shoreham, but finding it impossible to get in anywhere in safety, she continued with the water gaining upon her to run to Eastbourne Bay, with shore of which the Captain says he was acquainted, but the water was so completely washing over her that she must have sunk out of reach had not a blue light shown by the coastguard, who saw the vessel standing along the bay in distress, directed them to the nearest spot for safety and a sandy beach. Her cargo is totally lost and the wearing apparel and effects of the crew, except some of their clothes and bags, which were restored to them by the application of the officer of the coastguard here, to the stations to the east-wards, to secure any of the clothes or property which might be washed further along the bay.

On Sunday morning the shipwrecked seamen attended divine service at Trinity Chapel (Holy Trinity Church), to return thanks for their merciful preservation. After the evening service, a collection amongst the congregation was given to assist the poor men to their homes, (one of the men, a married man, of Sunderland had thus been saved from a watery grave for the fifth time). And others of the inhabitants added to this little fund the next day. Assistance was also given by that excellent institution, the Shipwrecked Fishermen's and Mariner's Benevolent Society, to which Lieut. Conduit, RN. of the coastguard station at Eastbourne, is honorary agent. The bodies of the crew of the other vessel, of which the wreck was washed in on the Eastbourne side of the Wish Tower on the awful night, have all been found (except one) on the shore between the Wish and Langney Point on the days succeeding the storms, one without clothes, as if stripped to swim and with a cut on his head; the others with their clothes on and a watch was washed ashore with the glass unbroken. The vessel is known to be the 'Friend' a Brig of Sunderland, Joseph Wright, master, 160 tons and 6 men laden with potatoes, &c, as the master of the 'Joseph' Brig, wrecked as above, was acquainted with the master of the 'Friend' and had spoken to her in the evening as they were both trying to run along the shore in distress'.

The following report from the 'Sussex Express' 28th Nov 1840 points out the fact that;

'Came George Hide and hurried away by enthusiasm and at imminent risk of his own life, sprang into the boiling surf and with the strength of a giant flung a rope across the vessel; it was immediately seized and one poor fellow was drawn safely on shore, but never will be forgotten the feeling of hopelessness which spread over all when it was discovered that nothing was fixed to the rope by which could be drawn back again to the vessel by the others; again did George Hide attempt

successfully, the same fearful experiment, when one after another the sailors were safely drawn on shore. Gallantry of conduct such as that above described is deserving and we are happy in hearing is likely to meet its due reward'

A report in the 'Sunderland & Durham County Herald' 27th Nov 1840 mentions the wreck and rescue, praising the bravery of George Hide.

His bravery was subsequently recognized when on 9th December 1840 a general meeting of subscribers to Lloyd's of London took place and it was decided to present him with a bronze medal and £10.0s.0d, for saving life. This meeting was followed up with a report in The Times 11th Dec 1840.

Lloyd's. - 'A general meeting of the subscribers to Lloyd's took place on Thursday, Mr. G.R. Robinson in the Chair. The honorary bronze medal of the institution and a vote of £10.0s.0d. were awarded to George Hide, a fisherman of Eastbourne, for saving at imminent personal risk, the crew of the 'Joseph' of Sunderland, wrecked near Eastbourne during a violent gale on the 13th ult'.

Lloyd's bronze life saving medal presented to George Hide.

The Lloyd's bronze medal for saving life (at sea) was instituted in 1836. George Hide's medal was the 10th to have been issued up to 1840. The medal is 2 7/8" in diameter and not for wearing. In 1896 a smaller medal, intended to be worn was issued. When and where the medal presentation took place is unknown.

An oil painting of the rescue was executed at the time. Later in 1872, a copy of the original was made. The painting depicts a dramatic scene and Martello Tower 72 is shown. Tower 72 is long gone into the sea. (It stood out on the beach, taking a line from Beach Road).

The great exertions used by George Hide in the rescue left him in ill health for some time after and for the rest of his life he was never a fit man, although he still went to sea. The remains of the wrecked Brigs 'Joseph' and 'Friend' were sold by public auction and later

C.1870. George Hide (1814-1882) with medal and painting.

divided into smaller lots and resold, thus affording to many of the poorer inhabitants of Eastbourne, an opportunity of firewood for the winter, at a reasonable rate. So out of the tragedies came some comfort.

Two years later George Hide was again involved in life saving at sea, when on the 25th October 1842 the barque 'Watts' of Plymouth 500 tons laden with a cargo of timber, having lost her rudder in a strong sou-westerly gale was driven on the rocks of the Boulder Bank (remember the 'Isabella'). After being battered for some time she lost her fore and main masts, drifted off the Bank and grounded opposite the Sea Houses. The lifeboat 'Samaritan' under the command of Samuel Knight brother in law to George Hide, pulled by a crew of ten, was launched and rescued six men and a boy. A week later she had her cargo taken off, was re-floated and

C.1870. George Hide's wife Mary Ann (nee Knight) (1816-1895).

towed by steam tug to Plymouth. The Lifeboat Institute made an award of £5.0s.0d to each member of the crew.

Fishermen of Eastbourne C.1870. The Hide family. Left to right. Father - George Snr. son - Samuel Beckett, grandson - John, son - George Merrick Jnr. son - John, seated on the family capstan. Background is now the site of 'Fusciardi's' Ice Cream Parlour, Marine Parade.

Fishing.

Brighton Fishing Museum, reference 13951 December 1843.

'Some fine codfish have lately been caught off Eastbourne in larger quantities than usual. We saw some on Saturday last, fresh caught and weighing 14lbs, sold for a shilling. Sprats also of most delicious flavour have been abundant and sold at a cheap rate'

A Good Fishing Season.

The local fishermen had a good summer fishing mackerel and from a report it shows that in July 1845, *'the mackerel fishing was prosperous, between thirty and forty thousand were brought on the beach in the last week in June in one morning. The boats had one to eight thousand each (ten boats) exceeded that number. Price averaged 11 shillings a hundred'*

September 1845 and a report shows that chalk was still being quarried from Holywell when a well laden chalk sloop owned by T Hurst, in a strong easterly wind, sank off Langney Point. The crew of two made it ashore in the ships boat. The sloop it is supposed *'started'* a plank, which caused her to fill immediately.

October 1845 The Sussex Advertiser reported an incident at Eastbourne beach when two coal brigs were getting off on the flood tide. But a considerable sea arose owing to a strong westerly wind and both finished up broadside on. Severe damage looked imminent. But the wind eased and owing to the aid given by the fishermen they succeeded in hauling the 'Ark' about and pulled her off. Not so lucky with the 'Bee'; she did sustain damage on contact with a groyne.

Another Shipwreck and Lifesaving.

On the night of December 27/28th 1845, a Dutch East Indiaman the 'Twee Cornelissen', 860 tons, during a south sou-west gale was driven aground in Pevensey Bay. She had a valuable cargo of sugar, coffee and indigo (a blue dye plant). Come dawn, 18 of the crew managed to reach the beach in their long boat but Captain H.D. Van Kyp, the mate and 9 of the crew were left on board and were forced to take to the rigging of the mizzen mast due to the huge seas breaking over her decks. The lifeboat 'Samaritan' under Cox'n Samuel Knight and her crew of ten pulled her down to Langney Point on her carriage and launched from there at 10.30am. She took off the captain and 9 of her crew by 11.00am. When they had landed safely it was seen that one of the crew was still in the rigging. Four coastguard men put out in a boat to the rescue but on reaching the 'Twee Cornelissen' he was found to be dead.

For the rescue the lifeboat crew received a silver medal and citation from the South Holland Institute. The crew also received 5 guineas from the Lifeboat Institute and 5 guineas from A.E Fuller M.P. the owner of the lifeboat.

A report in the Sussex Express 31st Dec 1845, states that the cargo was distributed among the shore families. No allegations of plundering as in 1833. In 1926, William 'Young Bollard' Hide reminiscing, recalled that his father William 'Old Bollard' told him that with the wreck of the 'Twee Cornelissen' the sea off Eastbourne remained 'indigo blue' for weeks afterwards.

Harbour of Refuge.

Back in 1840 a Commission was appointed to examine the Sussex Coast,

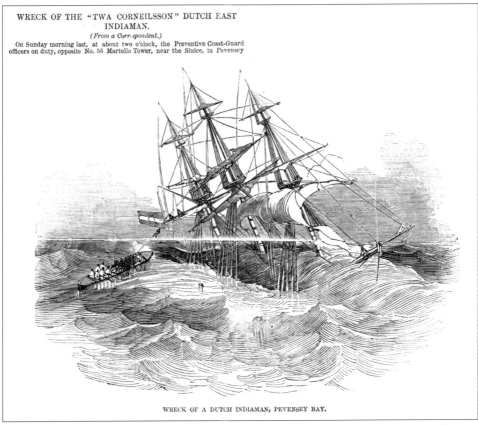

WRECK OF THE "TWA CORNEILSSON" DUTCH EAST INDIAMAN.
(From a Correspondent.)
On Sunday morning last, at about two o'clock, the Preventive Coast-Guard officers on duty, opposite No. 55 Martello Tower, near the Sluice, in Pevensey

WRECK OF A DUTCH INDIAMAN, PEVENSEY BAY.

Original Illustrated London News print 3rd January 1846 showing the first Eastbourne lifeboat 'Samaritan' and crew under Coxswain Samuel Knight rescuing the crew of Dutch East Indiaman 'Twee Cornelissen' wrecked at Pevensey Bay on the night of 27/28th December 1845.

Eastbourne Bay in particular, with a view to the construction of Harbours of Refuge. The east side of Eastbourne Bay was recommended as an advisable site for one. It wasn't until 1844 when the Commission caused a careful survey to be made of the Bay the result being unfavourable. There were patches of no less than 21 detached shoals of less than 5 fathoms of water. The report of a Captain Washington surveying officer pointed out the hazards, so the Commission decided against it.

Whatever else Eastbourne Bay was an admirable haven in a gale and still is, protected by Beachy Head and a bank that lies immediately under the Head that prevents the weight of the sea setting home into the Bay, where there is comparatively smooth water.

Silver medal presented for the 'Twee Cornelissen' rescue.

The Officer of the Coast guard and several fishermen who lived in Eastbourne assured Captain Washington that they were always able to beach their boats in a southwest gale.

1847 saw another proposal for a harbour at Eastbourne and Mr A.W. Brooks, Civil Engineer, drew up plans for the proposed harbour on the Royal Sovereign shoals, where the Royal Sovereign Light Tower now stands. It was to cover 1,000 acres with 6 to 8 fathoms in depth at low water during spring tides and be far enough off not to accumulate the shingle that travels along the south east coast and be a permanent deep harbour. Being built on the Royal Sovereign shoal it was also proposed to construct a Redoubt commanding the entrance to the proposed harbour as well as building an inner or high lighthouse to lead ships in. The harbour was to encompass a first rate Naval station and a harbour of refuge i.e. separate localities for the Queens ships and Merchant ships. The cost estimated at between £2.5 and £3.5 million, but as with the above proposal, not proceeded with.

In October 1886 yet another harbour at Eastbourne was proposed. The following report is from the Eastbourne Gazette.

'The proposal is to construct a harbour in Pevensey Bay, with a steam tramway skirting the sea, four miles in length, to or near the Redoubt. The promoters claimed for the scheme some of the following advantages: - a tidal harbour with deep water, building materials on hand and shingle in large quantities. A fishing and curing station might be established, plenty of land available. It is opposite the 'Diamonds' (fishing grounds) that the Eastbourne and Hastings boats fish. A safe anchorage is here found for vessels of all classes. The Newhaven steamers have sheltered here in

Colliers unloading at Eastbourne, Sept. 25, 1845.

rough weather when unable to enter Newhaven Harbour. Manure and town refuse for improving the soil might be conveyed cheaply over the proposed steam tramway The harbour would prove a great boon to yachtsmen, being more convenient than Newhaven'. About a hundred years later Eastbourne got its Harbour/Marina.

Back to the 1840's. Fishing.

The following is an example of some registered fishermen and mariners of Eastbourne listed between 1845 -.47 and issued with tickets from the General Register and Record Office of Seamen by the Collector and Comptroller of Customs of the Port of Rye.

Ticket No.	Name	Date of Birth	Mariner or Fisherman
167001	Samuel Lane	13.10.1804	Mariner
167002	William Coppard	11.12.1813	Fisherman
167003	William Head	02.12.1807	Fisherman
167004	John Head	20.01.1810	Fisherman
167005	William Clark Simpson	23.08.1802	Fisherman
167006	Joseph Waymark	29.09.1830 age 15yrs	Fisherman
167007	Paul Paul	--.08.1825	Fisherman
167008	Richard Hide	------------ age 28yrs	Fisherman
167009	John Wood	23.12.1791	Fisherman
167010	William Riddall	19.09.1782 born Aberdeen	Fisherman
167011	Henry Hurd	------------ boy	Fisherman
167012	William Knight	26.01.1826	Fisherman
167013	Henry Huggett	11.12.1812 age 34yrs	Fisherman
167014	George Young	21.09.1822 age 24yrs	Fisherman
167015	Edward Wickham	27.05.1813	Fisherman
167016	Daniel Waymark	14.06.1833	Fisherman
167017	Amos Betts	09.12.1830 age 16yrs	Fisherman
167018	Thomas Prodger	28.12.1821 age 25yrs	Fisherman
167019	George Prodger	05.03.1824 age 22yrs	Fisherman
167020	William Godden	23.03.1820	Fisherman
167021	Henry French	01.09.1827 age 19yrs	Fisherman
167022	Richard Wood	26.12.1829	Fisherman
167023	William Dudley	03.04.1815	Mariner

167024	George Erridge	11.12.1826	Fisherman
167025	Thomas Wood	07.04.1831 age 15yrs	Fisherman
167026	Phillip Swain	03.04.1822	Mariner
167027	Benjamin Goldsmith	16.11.1828	Fisherman
167028	Henry Huggett	26.08.1793	Seaman
167029	William Pumprey	17.03.1817	Fisherman
167030	Thomas Climpson	06.07.1819 born Westham	Seaman
167031	Charles Waymark	22.03.1831 age 15yrs	Fisherman
167032	Charles Wood	04.12.1831 age 16yrs	Fisherman
167033	Joseph Carter	13.03.1831	Fisherman
167034	James Huggett	24.06.1830 age 17yrs	Fisherman
167035	Samuel Wood	27.10.1830 age 17rs	Fisherman
167036	Samuel Knight	14.04.1815	Seaman
167038	Thomas Hook	30.06.1834	Fisherman
167039	Walter Wickham	04.10.1817	Fisherman
167040	Milton Carter	23.12.1847	Fisherman

Portrait of fisherman John Simpson C.1858.

The above information is held at Public Records Office, Kew, under reference BT113/84

John Simpson c.1858 (see portrait) was the son of John Simpson, boat builder, who was a member of the 'Samaritan' crew 1833. John Jnr. was born Eastbourne 1834 and became a fisherman dying at the young age of 26 yrs after falling from a groyne. His name appears in the General Register of Seamen, Rye dated 1858.

The Simpson family served in the lifeboat 'Samaritan' crew namely, John Simpson, William Simpson and George Simpson. Tragically George was drowned while fishing with his brother William in the Channel. The boat being suddenly upset William was saved but his brother sank and drowned. The report from the Brighton Gazette January 1843, tells of his body being washed ashore near Hastings, after going missing some two weeks. Sadly his family namesake George Simpson aged 24 yrs lost his life at sea off the island of Montserrat in 1896 when the sailing barque 'Grecian' foundered.

William, boat builder, sailmaker and fisherman was born in 1802, dying aged 71 years, in December 1873, whilst living at 16, Marine Drove. His death is reported in the Eastbourne Gazette and records his part in life saving from the shipwreck 'Isabella' in 1833. William 'Old Laddie' Simpson was responsible in 1869, for re-constituting the Eastbourne Fishermen's Compensation founded in 1839.

Brighton Museum reference 14116 June 1847.

'At Eastbourne. One of our small fishing boats was upset on Saturday, a short distance at sea by a sudden squall of wind and went down almost immediately, part of her sail and mast remaining above water. The crew John and William Head clung to it till assistance arrived. This was promptly rendered and they were taken off unhurt, but thoroughly ducked.

On Sunday afternoon a shoal of mackerel was observed close inshore and a net having been got out, the fishermen were fortunate enough to secure about 2,000 in one haul'.

Brighton Museum reference 14224 March 1850.

The 'Plymouth Times' speaks of the mackerel fishery. ' *On Monday many of the boats came in with their nets gone, having been carried away by the heavy 'strikes' of the fish. When the shoals are dense the fish in impelling themselves through the water come with considerable force against the nets laid to entrap them and damage to the latter, not infrequently ensues. This was the case on Saturday night. The 'George and William' (Swain) of Hastings, out of 101 nets saved only 19. 'Ellen Nancy' lost 72 out of 127. The 'Favourite' (William Brown) of Eastbourne, lost all 90 in number, as did 'Fame' (John Hide) of Eastbourne, but they were picked up and brought in by a Plymouth mackerel boat the 'Mary Ann' To make up for these losses however the catches of fish by those whose nets held were most extraordinary. The 'British Queen' (George Hutchins) Hastings, brought in 31,500 and the 'Friends' (James Swain) of Eastbourne had 24,000. Several boats brought in from 5,000 to 15,000.*

The Cornish boats never engage in the fishery on a Saturday night and always keep in harbour on that and the following day, so they do not break the Sabbath. When at sea on other days too, Cornish fishermen generally keep up a most commendable system of divine worship, morning and evening. Looking at the net losses that befell the boats on the Sunday morning it was great matter of consolation to the former that they did not break through their rule on that occasion.

Our readers may not be aware that the shoals of mackerel are caught only at night and even then when the moon shines forth, as at present the fish choose darkness rather than light and swim in deep water. The fishermen pretend that when caught on such occasions the mackerel are not of such good quality as at other times and that they have a watery flavour'.

Reference 10062 April 1850.

'Mackerel at Plymouth have been selling as low as 3s and 4s a hundred. On Friday one of the Brighton boats came home with about 12,000 fish, which sold at 6 and 8 a shilling. The whole local fleet from Hastings, Eastbourne, Shoreham and Brighton will shortly return from the Sound'.

Wreck of the 'Thames' East-Indiaman at Pevensey Bay. February 1822. (See page 27).

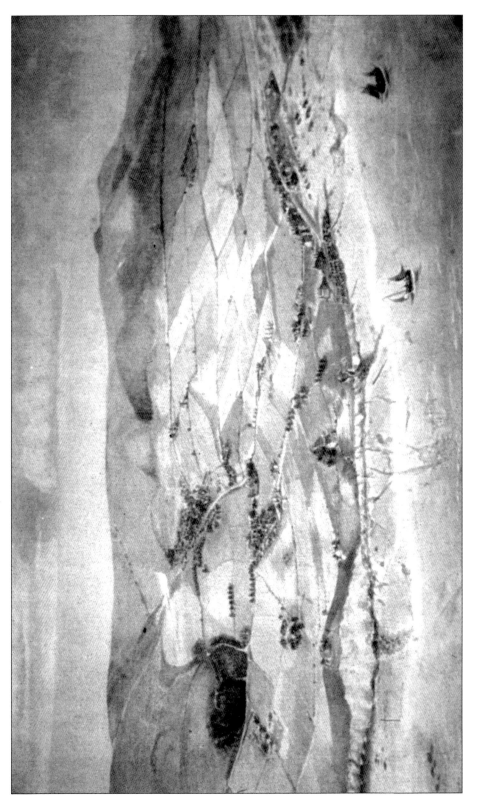

East-Bourn. C.1820 showing Sea Houses and original Fishing Station.

Chapter Two

Life at Sea and Ashore

1851.

The 1851 census shows a total of 65 fishermen of Eastbourne recorded in a total population of 3,432.

Through the 1850's summer months the fishing community mostly fished locally, kept home by an increase in the pleasure boating business, good money to be made, owing to the great number of visitors that arrived in town since the opening of the railway to Eastbourne in 1849. This also made it possible to dispatch locally caught fish by rail to the London market at Billingsgate. The line previously terminated at Polegate and branched off to Hastings.

With the development of the shoreline of low cliff between Field House (where the Queens Hotel now stands) and the Wish Tower, a sea wall was built and Grand Parade with the hotels finished around 1866. The beach area was put over to pleasure boating and bathing machines, becoming a busy bustling seafront with

Eastbourne Fishing Station 'Stade' 1852.

Oyster Dredgers C.1862.

hawkers, tinkers and minstrel troupe performances interrupted by the touting calls of the pleasure boatmen.

Moving on to 1861, the census shows that the fishermen and boatmen (now included) of Eastbourne numbered 68. The town's population had increased to 5,796.

1862.

The Mackerel season was not good. The local paper Eastbourne Gazette of February 18th reports: -

'The greater part of the boats engaged in the fishing have again taken their departure for the westward voyage. We hope they will be more successful than on the last voyage. In consequence of the unfavourable news from the fishing grounds off *Cornwall and Ireland, some of the boats appear very reluctant to make a start'.*

It is interesting to learn that Oysters were once gathered off Eastbourne. The season starting in September and the Eastbourne Gazette 15th September 1862 reported:-

'The Oyster season has commenced and there being a fine bed off Eastbourne, it has been occupied during the last week by a large fleet of Oyster smacks, besides small boats. It is gratifying to learn they have been successful and that the fish caught are in excellent condition'.

It was reckoned the Oyster beds were some twenty miles in length and seven or eight miles broad. At one time almost 20,000 tons of oysters were despatched down the coast from Shoreham railway station in a 12-month period. In those days the common man ate oysters but as in these days with over-fishing depleting stocks, they became scare thus the rise in price.

An interesting interview involving Reuben 'Old Screw' Wood about oysters is reported further on in the book.

November 1862.

'*A skate measuring some 5 feet across and weighing nearly 2cwt was brought ashore by fisherman 'Sayers' the fish being sent off to market'. The report goes on to say, 'A few good catches of herring have lately been made, but we are sorry to add that during the late gales several fishermen sustained heavy losses with their nets'. Also in the same report appeared, "We hear that a Club has been reformed to render assistance to such cases, the secretary being a William 'Old Laddie' Simpson, of Sea-side. He would be happy to receive any donation'.*

So the 'Fishermen's Compensation Fund' of 1839 was dormant but by 1869 it was formally re-constituted as previously mentioned.

Good catches of herring in November are shown by a report of the Allchorn boat catching 15,000. On this occasion they were sold at six score per 100. (i.e. one got 120 in total for the price of a 100)

Herring fishing off Eastbourne 1862.

December 1862.

The following incident was reported in the Eastbourne Gazette showing that life has not got any better regarding the carrying of knives.

'*Wed 10th Dec 1862.*

Stabbing: - 'An unfortunate occurrence happened on the Parade, fronting the sea, on Sunday evening last. The best information which we can glean is to this effect: - Some lads, amongst whom was Benjamin Hide residing at 4, Beach Cottages near

Tower Street, began teasing another named Wilkins, living at the Crown Inn, Old Town (son of the landlord, Walter Wilkins). Wilkins was the worse for liquor and getting irritated took a knife from his pocket and stabbed Hide in the chest. The wound inflicted was, it seems rather a serious one, it being at first uncertain whether the life of the sufferer would be spared; later accounts however, speak more favourably. Hide a fisherman, is stated to be about 18 years of age and Wilkins a year or so older'.

'Wed 17th Dec 1862. Walter Wilkins and another named Gibbs, were brought before R.J. Graham and F. Brodie Esqrs. on Saturday last at the Police Station, charged, the former with stabbing Benjamin Hide, the latter with aiding and abetting. It was stated that Gibbs gave Wilkins the knife, at the same time saying 'Give him that'. A certificate from Doctor Whitfield was read, stating that the young man was not in a fit state to be removed, the wound being of a serious character. After some consultation, the prisoners were remanded for a week, Mr Dempster, solicitor, attended on behalf of Wilkins and applied for him to be admitted bail. Bail was eventually accepted for both prisoners in two sureties each of 50 pounds and their own recognizance of £50 each'.

'Saturday 20th Dec 1862. Walter Wilkins, the younger and George Gibbs, the former charged with stabbing the lad Hide and the latter with being an accessory, were again brought up for further examination. Hide was sufficiently recovered to give evidence. The prisoners were committed for trial at the Quarter Sessions, bail being taken for their appearance. Later Wilkins and Gibbs were indicted for maliciously wounding Benjamin Charles Hide. Gibbs was acquitted of the charge and Wilkins found guilty, but recommended mercy. He was sentenced to three months hard labour'.

1863.

It was in the year 1863 that Eastbourne was visited by an epidemic of Scarlatina, which spread rapidly and invaded almost every house that contained young people. From the pulpit of Trinity Church the vicar, wishing to enforce a lesson as to the uncertainty of life, made mention of the destructive disease, which was stalking through the Parish. Next morning there was a 'stampede' of visitors to get out of town. The carriages on the railway were crowded irrespective of class and the Station Master was unable to supply the demand, so that there were families who took their departure in trucks. To allay the alarm, Eastbourne's leading doctor caused much amusement by writing to the 'Times' saying that the residents did not suffer from the fever, it only attacked new comers to the town. The epidemic however claimed many lives.

1863. Fishing.

June 1863 showed a good catch of mackerel.

'The mackerel that have been offered in Eastbourne up to the close of last week have been supplied mostly from Brighton and other adjoining places; on Sunday morning however, some little excitement was exhibited among our fishermen from some shoals of these fish having been seen a short distance from the beach. Boats were immediately put off, the fishermen straining every nerve to get 'a catch'. One boat came in minus everything except a few small fry, suitable only for baits to seduce larger shellfish. About half-past 12 another party set out and by a little

Mackerel Fishing at Eastbourne. Great excitement and a lifeline for many inhabitants of Eastbourne when the mackerel came through.

1863. Eastbourne Fishing Station. 'The Stade' with the brig 'Bee' of Scarborough discharging coal. (Now site of the Royal Parade, note the Luggers 'Bourners' laying ashore).

manoeuvring, succeeded in embracing a goodly number of the finny tribe, their loud hurrahs which beckoned the capture being distinctly heard on the beach. Many persons waited some time to witness the draught, but the fortunate occupants of these boats did not venture to land their spoils until four o'clock when the beach presented much the appearance of a fair, a striking contrast to the quiet, which usually prevails here on this day. This 'party' at the head of which is Mr George

Remains of Frap anchor used to haul off collier 'Bee' and other vessels. From original Fishing Station, now Royal Parade.

Hide, exhibited about 8,000 fish. Another party brought in near the same time about 700. The catch was larger, but a breakage occurring in some part of the fishing apparatus, thus prevented their landing what would otherwise have been an extraordinary catch. The 'Kettle' nets, too, were fully supplied as high a number as 20,000 being named as having been taken from them, but for this we can give no guarantee. Our fishermen having for some time been rather unfortunate, we are pleased to find that they at last have had a requital'

The Eastbourne Gazette in August 1863 reported: -

'At high water the coal brig 'Bee' was leaving Eastbourne beach, having unloaded her cargo and was in ballast when a hawser broke causing her to collide with a groyne, holing her below the water line, so in short time she sank. At low water she was plugged and taken to Newhaven for repairs'.

The 'Bee' was one of the last coal brigs to service Eastbourne as with the coming of the railway 1849, it took over completely the carriage of coal to the town.

In general 1863 was not a good year for the fishermen of Eastbourne - the catch of fish being poor. *'The catch of fish this season has not been at all remunerative to our poor fishermen, who daily risk their lives in the precarious calling. The herring fishery has been quite a failure. But sprats, although not brought in great numbers, have fetched good prices'.*

The herring fishing over on the French coast was the opposite, enormous catches were taken, so much so, that they were sold as manure. The cost of transport through France was so high that any price got inland would be swallowed up by rail fare.

The method of inshore mackerel fishing is described in the following article from the 'Penny Illustrated Paper' entitled 'Mackerel Fishing Off Eastbourne'

'Mackerel fishing is generally a most profitably employment to the fishermen who engage in it, while the season lasts, immense hauls being sometimes taken. A single cast of the net occasionally (particularly in the early part of the season) will realise as much as one hundred pounds. In many places, notable on the South Coast, the fish are caught in what are called 'seine- nets', as they approach the shore in large schools. Indeed they are sometimes so close in shore that the net is hauled upon the beach itself and its living freight of glittering silver fishes thrown thereon in a heap. Late spring or early summer is the most favourably season for the South Coast fishing; and at such times large groups of apparently idle men may be seen early in the morning lying upon the beach, talking, laughing and smoking sometimes hours together. They are only waiting for signs of a 'school', an indication of which is the splashing of the water in a long streak for a quarter of a mile or so seaward and extending in length some time half a mile. This can be seen however, only when the water is clear and moderately calm, as directly the water becomes thick the fish sink to the bottom.

On the sign the shoal is visible, bustle and tumult, shouting and excitement reign everywhere along the beach. Strong arms and vigorous pushes send the seine - boats from the shore into the sea and many yards on their way, towards the bubbling water ahead. Then every man grasps his oar, for now it is a race to the 'school' the first boat to reach it having the best chance of casting. The school of fish has in the

Kettle Net of the type used at Eastbourne C.1863. with acknowledgement to Roy Clark's book.
'The Longshoremen'

mean-while disappeared or gone further out to sea and the captain of each Boat Stands in the bows and looks for its reappearance and for the best place of casting. Two boats are used in this operation, one small the other large. The larger boat, which contains the nets, takes out four to six men besides the captain and the smaller boat takes out two or three. On coming within a convenient distance of the school, the captain orders the nets to be cast and the occupants of the smaller boat seize hold of the barrel, which is attached to a rope fastened to one end of the net and hold it fast. The men in the larger boat, in the meantime endeavouring to pay out the net as to enclose the whole or part of the shoal. The operation is done by the captain, while the others row. They cast the net somehow in the shape of a horseshoe and again on coming close to the small boat the ends of the net are drawn together and the hauling in is commenced. The nets used are sometimes more than half a mile in length and are fixed at each end to poles weighted with lead.

When the school is surrounded there commences a scene of excitement for the poor mackerel and great is the splashing and dashing of the water, in their endeavours to escape. But of no avail are their strenuous efforts; in the confusion they have not the sense to sink to the bottom and so escape the net, but try to break through it; their heads pass through the open meshes and then the expanding gills act as a hook and the fish are caught'.

The fishing boats used were open decked 'punts' and skiffs (row boats) Some local people of years gone by will recall seeing the mackerel schools coming close into the shore a frothing bubbling living mass of shining fish, so close one felt it would be easy to pick them out of the sea.

As reported above the 'Kettle nets' had a good catch and it was from the fisher folk that the saying 'A Pretty Kettle of Fish' could have its origins. The dictionary gives a fairly anonymous definition of the meaning of this saying as 'an awkward mess or situation' but it is not very forthcoming as to its origins. It is said among the fishing fraternity that it came into use during the 17th or 18th century, when static nets called "Kettle nets" were established round the coast of Britain.

See print of one that was in operation well over a hundred years ago, the principle being the same as that used at Eastbourne. Placed when the tide was out and as the tide came in, in came the fish, as the tide ebbs the fish swim with it and on meeting the obstruction of the net barrier which stretches away to the left almost to the shore, the fish naturally turn seaward and swim and are directed into

Gilbert Arms 1860. Scene of court case.

the pocket or 'Kettle'. When not quite low water the 'Kettle net' is entered and fish removed with a scoop net. This was an unselective method and a 'Kettle' captured all manner of fish, flounders, plaice, dabs, soles, whiting, codling, bass, mullet or anything that swam - *'an awkward mess of fish'* It's easy enough to imagine, one fisherman saying to the other *'That's a pretty kettle of fish we've got here'* Such an expression would not have remained just fishermen's talk for long, eventually being used by all and sundry. I am indebted to Roy Clark's excellent book 'The Longshoremen' for the above information.

1864.

The following year saw a dramatic drop in visitors to the town. This leads us into the next story regarding fishermen of Eastbourne. It tells a tale of assault on a drunk and abusive itinerant Irish sponge seller who came to Eastbourne and made uncomplimentary remarks about Eastbourne and its inhabitants.

'Wednesday 20th July 1864. A condensed report from the Eastbourne Gazette

Eastbourne Police Court - Monday before R.J. Graham Esq.

'In consequence of the Vestry Rooms being for polling the parish on the Church rate question and as the Police Station was deemed too small for the number of persons it was anticipated would attend in a case of interest set down for hearing this day, the large room of the Gilbert Arms, close by, a place we may say every way suited for the purpose, was taken by the Magistrates'. (See print of 'Gilbert Arms' which was situated at the corner of Grove Road and Terminus Road, across from the Library).

Cooper's Eastbourne Ales C.1860.

Headlines in the Local Paper. 'Serious Charges of Assault. Fishermen's Frolics and the Belligerent Irishman'.

'Arraigned before the Court on a charge of assault and affray were fishermen, John Cummins, Arthur Matthews, John Hide, George 'Pincher' Hide, Phillip Hide, Thomas Sayers and James Allchorn. The complainant being Daniel Regan, licensed sponge hawker.

The essence of the complaint was that, Regan being the worse for drink whilst on the seafront allegedly insulted a lady and made derogatory remarks about the Scarlatina epidemic of the previous year and quality of Eastbourne. Word spread round quickly of what Regan was alleged to have said and whilst he was in the Fishermen's Arms, Seaside, the defendants entered and challenged him. From evidence given by William Bradford, landlord, they offered Regan no violence but requested he leave town. He agreed to go with them

The defendants intended to get him out of town but not before they took him to the kitchen of the Railway Hotel (later Royal Hotel and now the site of Nat West Bank) Terminus Road. There they greased, buttered and covered him with rotten eggs and flour and were just about to dip him into a large water cistern when Police Sgt. Tobutt arrived on the scene and order was restored. Regan was given sanctuary in the Police Station and the defendants all arrested and summoned to appear before the Court.

After a long hearing in which it was found Regan after a good wash suffered no physical injury, the defendants with the exception of Phillip Hide were found guilty and committed on bail to appear at the next Assizes at Lewes.

The people of Eastbourne in sympathy with the fishermen raised a subscription and paid for Counsel to attend their defence at Lewes. The final outcome being they were all bound over in their own recognisance to be of good behaviour. So ended a sorry episode in the seafaring community of Eastbourne'.

Perhaps the following had something to do with the foregoing problem and they had all been drinking Cooper's Ales. Robert Cooper (born London 1819) came to Eastbourne as an orphan in 1830. He left for a short period and returned to Eastbourne in 1844, set up a Chemist shop in 1845, then took over a Brewery behind the New Inn, South Street and ran it until about 1870. This proved a profitable business. He died in London in 1909.

No doubt some of the fishermen quaffed quantities of Cooper Ales and no doubt sang to the advertising leaflets from the 1860's singing the praises of the quality of Cooper's Ales.

On 10th August 1864, a fisherman named Weller 'Garibaldi' Sayers reported an unusual 'catch'. Some two miles off Eastbourne he caught a large 'Sun Fish' lying asleep on top of the water. So great was the struggle to get it on board the fingers of 'Garibaldi' turned black with his exertions. The fish was perfectly oval in shape, weighing some 2cwt, the last one remembered being caught was back in 1838. The 'Sun Fish' was exhibited on the beach behind the Workman's Hall (Leaf Hall) and 'Garibaldi' hopefully made some money. Could this 'Garibaldi' Sayers, be the same Sayers, who caught the 2cwt skate back in November 1862?

July 1866.

George 'Dot' Hide, 52 years of age was not in good health and being unable to carry on his living of fishing, received the grand gift of a pleasure boat named 'Guardsman' and 20 gold sovereigns from the Shipwrecked Fishermen's and Mariners Society and Mr Herbert F Eaton. The presentation was fully reported in the local papers at the time and is covered in the record of 'The Pleasure Boatmen of Eastbourne'.

The photo of the Shipwrecked Fishermen's and Mariners Society subscription tokens are an example for the years 1862, 1873 and 1883. Tokens were issued by the Society on a yearly subscription basis and worn by fishermen and mariners round their necks, fastened with a tape when at sea. In the unfortunate event of subscriber's boats or gear being lost or damaged or loss of life, compensation was paid by the Society. Indeed all shipwrecked persons were instantly cared for on the spot, clothed and assisted to their homes. Widows and families of seafarers lost at sea were sought out, succoured and assisted by agents of the Society.

The Shipwrecked Fishermen's and Mariners Society was established in 1839 by John Rye, a philanthropic medical man of Bath assisted by Charles Gee Jones a former Bristol Pilot, as a result of the tragic loss of a fishing fleet with all hands off the north Devon coast in 1838.

From the outset the Society possessed eight lifeboats one of which was the Newhaven lifeboat but in 1854 all were transferred to the ownership of the National Lifeboat Institute. The Lifeboat Institute had from its inception also looked after the care and comfort of shipwrecked persons. This function was then passed over to the Society to manage, as is done to this very day. The first President of the Society Admiral Sir George Cockburn had the distinction of occupying Washington and

The Shipwrecked Fishermen and Mariners Society subscription tokens showing Lord Nelson and shipwreck.

Eastbourne Beach 1866 by W R Rogers. Towner Art Gallery.

burning the Capitol and White House in 1814, during Britain's brief war with the United States. Headquarters of the Society are currently based in Chichester, West Sussex. Information is that all original records are lost.

24th Oct 1866.

Narrow escape: - *'Two fishermen of Meads, named Collins, father and son both named Jacob, on their return from a prawning trip round Beachy Head and endeavouring to land at Holywell, unfortunately in trying to pass through the reef of rocks off that spot, the boat struck and immediately swamped, the men were at some distance from the shore, with deep water intervening but happily they both succeeded in getting to land. The elder Collins divested himself of his sea boots before making the attempt and was greatly aided by his son, otherwise it is doubtful if he could have overcome the obstacles that beset him. The boat was much injured and the poor fellows also lost most of its contents in gear'.*

The end of October saw *'good catches of herring off Eastbourne, near Langney Point and Pevensey Bay. The largest catches 900 and 600 respectively, were made by the crews of Phillip Swain's boats. The fish so captured were very fine and were purchased by Mr Thomas Vine, who at once turned them into bloaters- these being the first lot of herring dried in Eastbourne this season. The price from the boats was from 6s to 12s per hundred score'*

November 1866.

'The crew of Mr Mitchell's boat succeeded in obtaining four lasts of sprats. Other, though smaller catches, were also made'.

January 1867.

On 30th January 1867 the sailing ship 'Wave' went ashore at Cuckmere Haven and became a total wreck. She was followed a week later on 5th February by the Dutch Brig, 'Governeur Van Swieten' 300 tons, wrecked at Beachy Head, laden with hides, tallow and wool. She was bound from Buenos Aires to Antwerp. It was a Sunday when she was wrecked and many hundreds of Eastbourne inhabitants flocked to Beachy Head to view her. She broke up on the Monday and her cargo dispersed along the shore from above the Wish Tower downward. The beach being strewn with bales of wool. The presence of the wool brought many wool gatherers in the literal sense of the word. Many of the poorer class were seen coming home wet and heavily laden with 'sheep's clothing' and carts also well filled with the same stuff. A lot of Eastbourne's tradesmen also took the opportunity of a chance thrown their way. Two chronometers from the vessel valued at £100 each, were recovered from the ship and taken to Mr R Walker, watchmaker and jeweller, of Terminus Road, to be cleaned.

On Tuesday, after the town people's salvaging exploits, notices were placed along the shore prohibiting persons any more personal salvaging of the wreck's cargo. But on the other hand those who had rescued such property were informed that one third of the value of what they might reclaim would be available in salvage. One party succeeded in obtaining 50 bales of wool, another 30 bales and so on downwards in quantity till you came to the man, woman and child labouring under as much each could carry. Horses were employed to bring the booty ashore. With the wrecking of the Brig many a poor family could reap quite a harvest. The wrecked goods taken away on the Monday by private persons were left unmolested. Again on Wednesday fresh notices were issued warning people not to appropriate any of the cargo and warrants were issued by the Magistrates to search premises of persons failing to abide by the rules. Police Constable Gladman an Eastbourne policeman proved to be over zealous over this decree and a topical song was made up about him. One verse goes: -

> 'The policeman 'Gladman' he would be,
> Could he get on the right track?
> To enter every house and see
> Who had not taken their wool back'.

The real value of the Brig and cargo amounted to £30,000. The sale of the wreck of the Brig went for a knock down price of £67 to Messrs J Filder and G Adams.

March 1867. Salvage Money - Theft from the person.

Court 2nd March 1867.

John Packham on bail appeared under remand, charged with stealing £3 from the person of John Gausden, a labourer of Meads. It transpired that Gausden had been engaged in recovering cargo of the wreck 'Govenuer Van Swieten' and he was entitled to a certain amount of salvage money and that on Monday he went to Sea-side, where he sold his share of the profits to George 'Pincher' Hide for £6.10s.0d. Afterwards he went to a party and had a quantity of liquor, finishing up at the house of Mrs Packham in Leslie Street, (a poor area of Eastbourne, known at that time for its houses of ill repute) where he met a certain woman to whom it is alleged on the part of the defence, that he gave three sovereigns in mistake for three shillings. Gausden denied this stating he counted his money before getting into a bed after he had left the woman. Next day three sovereigns were missing from his pocket. John Packham was the only one that slept in the room with him for the rest of the night.

The next day Packham's wife was in possession of two sovereigns, but she denied they were Gausden's. In any event the Bench were satisfied that there was insufficient evidence to convict Packham of theft and dismissed the case. The Bench told Gausden he had only himself to blame for being drunk and getting himself into such company and such a house and must take the consequence.

May 1867.

A local report tells of the Eastbourne fishing fleet up off North Foreland taking large catches of mackerel.

June 1868. A Fishing Tragedy.

'On Wednesday 17th June 1868, two young men drowned in a boating accident. One being Walter Hide, age 17 yrs, fisherman, son of Richard Hide, fisherman. The other lad drowned was George Marshall, age 21 yrs, brother in law to Walter, his wife being Walter's sister Jane Rebecca - they had only been married a few weeks. George Marshall was employed by his father in the family Market garden at the rear of South Street.

The two deceased had gone out fishing for mackerel in Captain Ellis's boat the 'Pup'. She was about 16 - 17 feet long. Young Walter Hide was a very proficient seaman. Witnesses at sea reported seeing the 'Pup' suddenly veer and capsize. On getting to the scene all that was found was their caps, an oar and the backboard of the boat. A large black dog taken aboard the boat swam ashore after the accident. The bodies and boat were later recovered and at the inquest held at the Marine Hotel, Seaside, it was stated that Walter Hide was a very accomplished seaman for his age and a good swimmer, George Marshall however was not used to the management of a boat. A verdict of accidental death was brought in'.

Mackerel deep-sea fleet getting under way 1867.

May 1869.

On 26th May 1869, it was reported that *'a fisherman of Eastbourne, caught a lobster of unusual size, on the fishing grounds off Eastbourne (known as the 'Hoss' - well known for crab and lobster). 'The lobster weighed 9lbs and was 31inches long from tail to end of claw. The largest claw weighed 2 1/4 lbs, measuring in length 18 inches and in circumference 11 inches. The catch was exhibited for some time in the shop of Mr Waymark, fishmonger, of Inkerman Place'.*

September 1869.

Shortly after a Regatta in the middle of September 1869, a terrific gale was experienced for 3 days along the south coast. At Eastbourne it was severely felt and much damage caused throughout the town. This was nothing to what befell the schooner 'Oneida' 200 tons, commanded by Capt Morris, bound from Hull to Trieste with a cargo of railway iron. It was at midnight whilst off Beachy Head that her sails were blown to ribbons and at 4 o'clock in the morning she was driven ashore at Langney Point. Capt Morris and 3 of the crew were washed overboard and drowned. The remainder of the crew, 4 in number who had taken refuge in the main mast happily escaped to land, the mast having fallen towards the shore. The vessel broke up half an hour after going aground. The following morning a vessel the fishing smack 'Tamar' of Fowey was seen passing up channel flying a flag of distress. The lifeboat 'Mary Stirling' under Cox'n Joseph 'Joker' Huggett with a crew of eight men was promptly launched to assist. On getting to her the captain of the 'Tamar' refused to quit his vessel so the lifeboat put in at Bexhill, the crew returning by train and a few days later when the weather had abated sailed the lifeboat back to Eastbourne. On the occasion of this service the lifeboat behaved well in the heavy sea and wind that prevailed. The 'Tamar' evidently survived the storm.

The wreck of the schooner 'Oneida' was sold later at auction by Mr J C Towner, realising the sum of £64. The railway iron, which formed the cargo was got up and later sold for the benefit of the Underwriters.

Fishermen and Jolly Dogs - A tale of conflict between local fishermen, local artisans and visitors to Eastbourne.

Invading the town during the summer months, visitors rich and poor were a vital source of income to the hotel and pleasure boating industry. But the invasion of 'well to do' visitors caused bad blood between the young male 'toffs' and the young male working classes of Eastbourne. One can imagine the young well to do, known as 'Jolly Dogs' promenading along the parades and in 1869 a fracas occurred between them and the young men of Eastbourne resulting in assault and a general riot.

Disgraceful Disturbances.

'On Saturday evening 4th, September 1869, a scene took place on the Parades and in Terminus Road, which if repeated, as we sincerely hope not, would go far towards destroying the character Eastbourne has obtained as a quiet and fashionable watering place. We hardly know to whom to ascribe the origin of the affair, but it would seem for some time past an ill-feeling has been engendered between a set of some eight or nine young men here as visitors and the fishermen

and artisans of the town. The latter's ire has been aroused by the conduct of the former, who, affecting to be fast young men - 'jolly dogs' have for some time had it all their own way on the Parade, where strolling along arm in arm. So as to occupy the whole breadth of the walk, they have caused annoyance to ladies and others. The fishermen, boatmen, etc, however would not submit to this treatment.

The Vestry Hall, Grove Road, scene of court case. Built 1857 demolished 1902.

The first hostile encounter took place on the evening of the 2nd inst, a Thursday, when a single stick match was going on (sword fight with walking sticks) between two of the 'jolly dogs' Some rather unfair play was shown by one and a fisherman standing by remarking on this, was forthwith knocked down. An artisan coming to his rescue was treated in the same unceremonious manner, both left the Parade vowing vengeance against the 'jolly dogs'.

On Saturday it was pretty freely rumoured through the town that there would be a 'row' on the Parade and Police Sgt Verrall with commendable forethought, caused the policeman who was posted there to keep his post an hour later than usual. It seems the 'jolly dog' party had gained scent of the preparations on the opposite side, but kept on the Parade walking in their usual style. Some 'Christy minstrels' were performing at the time and a man named Hide Charles 'Bones' age 20 yrs, a fisherman, giving offence - either real or imaginary to one of the 'dogs', was forthwith knocked down with a thick walking cane and his head much injured. Police Constable Gladman standing close by immediately took the aggressor a young fellow named Stokes, into custody and it was as well that he was so secured.

He was taken to the Police Station followed by his friends and a large mob of fishermen and others.

On arriving at the top of Terminus Road (T J Hughes corner) stones were thrown and hooting commenced, but no serious rioting took place till the arrival of the mob opposite Sussex Gardens, (the precinct by Boots).

Active operations for a fight were commenced. A 'swell' of gigantic proportions offered to 'take on any three' of the fishermen. A short, but remarkably thick- set fisherman immediately accepted the challenge and got the best of the affair. The 'swells' then formed themselves in military order and being reinforced by an old gentleman, who possessed more pluck than discretion, showed a bold front. But the fishermen were undaunted and soon dispersed their opponents, marking their countenance in such a manner that their appearance was very grotesque. The 'swells' took refuge in neighbouring shops, from whence they afterwards proceeded home, when the road was clear'.

'A sequel to the affair took place at the Police Court on Monday, when Mr Henry Stokes after a lengthy examination was fined £5 for the assault on Hide. Hide and his witnesses got the full expenses allowed by law. We sincerely hope this may be the last of these disturbances, which must tend to throw discredit on the whole town and do it great injury'.

The background to the above incident was said to have been caused by the assailant Henry Stokes' family. The family were regular visitors to Eastbourne, residing at No.1 Grand Parade, the head of the family being a lawyer Mr Henry Stokes Snr. currently employed as Proctor to the Admiralty, who had represented the owner of the wrecked Dutch brig 'Govenuer Van Swieten' (February 1867) in a salvage claim by the Eastbourne fishermen. They had taken the owner to court to get a fair pay out for their salvage, the original offer being poor. Stokes Snr. was instrumental in them getting a lesser award and they had not forgiven him.

According to the defendant Stokes, his family had been given annoyance over the last couple of years from the Eastbourne fishermen and boatmen during their stays in Eastbourne. He maintained Hide was a main aggressor. 'Bones' Hide denied knowing anything about the fishermen being dissatisfied about the salvage award (That's hard to believe). Stokes alleged Hide had kicked him and he was defending himself so he cracked him over the head with his stick. This allegation proved to be untrue. Carpenter Mark Martin and bricklayer Henry Teague were with 'Bones' at the time. No proceedings were taken against either of them. The head injury to 'Bones' was quite serious according to the doctor who attended him.

As to the 'riot', this was serious according to reports and a lot of fighting took place. The fishermen and artisans were ready for a fight and so it seems were the gentlemen visitors.

Stokes Snr. took on a fisherman and came off worse receiving two black eyes and a damaged hand.

The case held in the Vestry building took some 5 hours to complete and on leaving there was another general melee resulting in the 'visitors' taking refuge in the 'Gilbert Inn' close by.

But things did quieten down and peace came over Eastbourne again. During the hearing a report states two men had a fight outside and one received a broken leg! It is well worth reading the full report of the hearing on 6th September 1869 in the Eastbourne Gazette.

1870.

Life continued and on the seafaring side we learn that in March 1870, the Eastbourne Boating (Rowing) Club was formed. At a meeting held at the Anchor Hotel, Marine Parade, under the chairmanship of Mr Cecil Long and Hon Sec. Mr C M Matthews, the committee decided to purchase a four-oared galley, two pair-oared boats and two single sculls. Frederick Bollard Hide was to build the pair-oared boats and they also engaged a retired Coastguardsman named Johns, to look after the boats. A member of the committee generously offered to build a boathouse and let it to the Club at a moderate rent.

The original Eastbourne Rowing Club premises were built on the beach to the rear

Eastbourne Rowing Club 1879. Left to Right Standing. J Vine, W Hill, W Dennis, ? Hubbard, Charles Haine. Seated. E Wood, William Allchorn, Unknown, J Morris, ? Payne. Seated in front. Sayers. (Cox.)

Eastbourne Rowing Club. Senior Coxed Four. Champions of the South Coast 1897-9. Left to right: F. Lewis, Stroke. C. Hookham, No. 3. F. Boorer, Cox. I. Allan, Bow. H. Sayers, No. 2.

Died at Helm of His Boat

Mr Harry Sayers, Famous Oarsman

TWO miles from the coast of Eastbourne, taking some friends out on a fishing trip, 75-years-old Mr Harry Sayers, of Latimer-road, died at the helm of his boat on Thursday morning. His sudden death has shocked the members of his well-known boating family and the many friends who had come to know him through his kindly nature.

His daughter, Mrs Jane Goddin, of Latimer-road, had yesterday (Friday) still to learn of her father's death. She is with her husband and child on a cycling tour of south-west England. A card posted at Weymouth was received from her yesterday and the police, who have been trying to contact Mrs Goddin, hope to find her at Southampton to-day.

Mr Sayers' nephew, Mr Alleyn N. Sayers, was on the beach on Thursday morning and helped launch his uncle's boat. His uncle had complained of pains in his chest but insisted on taking two friends on a fishing trip. Mr Alleyn Sayers went with him, and about two miles offshore Mr Sayers, who was at the helm, slumped sideways.

Mr Alleyn Sayers turned the

Continued on back page

Mr Harry Sayers

Died at Helm of His Boat

Continued from page 1

Continued from page 1

boat back to the beach and tried to revive his uncle, but Mr Sayers was dead.

With the passing of Mr Sayers, Eastbourne loses the last of the 1897 and 1898 Eastbourne Rowing Club senior team which at one time held seven challenge cups and came in first at 16 regattas along the south coast of England. The other members of the crew, Mr F. Lewis, Mr C. Hookham and Mr I. Allen, are all dead, but the remaining member, Mr F. Boorer, is now abroad.

Mr Sayers was also a member of the old Hornets football team. He leaves a daughter and one grandchild. A funeral service will be held at Christ Church on Tuesday at 2.30 p.m., and the interment will take place at Ocklynge in the family grave.

Private Fishing Parties catered for

Boat : Clarice Jane NN2
Stand : Next to Angling Club, Fishing Station, Eastbourne

HARRY SAYERS

FISHERMAN AND BOATMAN

Private Address
76 LATIMER ROAD ... EASTBOURNE

If you want a Good Day out FISHING, consult HARRY SAYERS

GUARD OF HONOUR FOR BOATMAN

FISHERMEN and boatmen formed a guard of honour at the entrance to Christ Church yesterday (Tuesday) afternoon at the funeral service for an old comrade, Mr Harold (Harry) Sayers, aged 75, of 76 Latimer-road, who died suddenly at the helm of his boat while taking two friends on a fishing trip last Thursday morning.

Mr Sayers was one of a very successful senior team of the Eastbourne Rowing Club which in 1897 and 1898 won many challenge cups and first prizes at south coast regattas. He was also a member of the old Eastbourne Hornets football team.

The service at Christ Church was conducted by the Rev. J. N. Marcon (vicar), in the presence of over 100 mourners. The hymn was "Praise my soul, the King of Heaven," and the Nunc Dimittis was sung as the coffin was carried out. Mr W. H. Mills was at the organ and played "Solemn Melody" (Walford Davies).

The chief mourners were: Mr and Mrs C. J. Godden (son-in-law and daughter), Mrs E. Hookham (sister), Mr Ernie Sayers (brother), Mr Ernie Sayers, Mr William Sayers and Mr Stan Sayers (nephews), Mr and Mrs H. Fuller (Piddinghoe), Mrs W. Fuller, Mrs W. Ramsden (niece) and Mr W. Ramsden.

GENERAL MOURNERS

Among the general mourners were :—

Mr J. Atherton, Mr M Andrews, Mr W. Ashdown, Mr R. Ashcroft, Mr M. A. Brown, Mrs E. Brown, Mr G. Boniface, Police Sergeant Burden, Mrs E. Bish, Mr and Mrs Horace Ball, Mrs E. Bushell, Mrs G. Bates, Mr Leslie B. Bristow, Mr L. Cottingham, Mr E. J. Carter, Mr and Mrs Andrew Chester, Mrs H. Clark, Mrs A. Chandler, Mr E. Catt, Mr H. Day, Mr J. Dryden, Mrs H. Day, Mr N. Dean, Mr H. Drewett, Mr A. J. Dunn (representing Eastbourne Angling Club), Mrs A. J. Dunn, Mrs M. L. Erridge Miss E. Egan, Mr W. Erridge, Mrs A. Fortescue, Mrs S. Farnell, Mrs J. Furbanks, Mrs G. Frere, Mrs Godwin, Mr A. W. Gallop, Mrs E. Gearing, Miss M. Green, Mrs H. Greenslade, Mr R. E. Green, Mr A. Gibbs, Mrs F. Gay, Mr O. Gurney, Mr J. Huggett, Mrs K. Hewitt, Miss Hewitt, Mr A. G. Hutchinson, Mrs E. Howe, Mrs P. Hide, Mrs E. A. Hewitt, Miss. C. Harffey, Mrs L. Head, Mr and Mrs C. B. Hide, Mr Ace Huggett, Mrs S. Hookham, Mrs K. A. Ingram, Mrs M. Jones Mr Eddie Knight, Mr W. Lavender, Mr A. Morris, Mr E. J. Mallard, Mr W. G. McKie, Miss G. McKie, Mr J. W. Martin, Mrs Harold Martin, Mrs M. G. Nicholls, Mr F. W. Novis, Mrs E. F. Pugh (niece), Mr A. Pitcher, Mrs J. Potter, Mr and Mrs A. R. Pocock, Mrs J. Percival, Mr and Mrs H. Plater, Mrs A. Paine, Mr Nelson Prodger, Miss S. Pollard, Mr. W. Prodger (second coxswain, Eastbourne lifeboat), Mr George Punyan, Mrs V. Pearce, Mrs E. A. Roadnight, Mr A. L. Remnant, Mr G. Stapleton, Mr A. C. Sayers, Mr A. M. Standen, Mrs A. Stanbury, Miss M. Smith, Mr and Mrs S. G. Sayers, Mr J. Sayers, Mr E. Sayers, Mr W. Sayers, Mr W. A. Sayers, Mr A. N. S. Sayers, Mr A. J. Sumner, Mr S. Sivers, Mrs E. N. A. Sayers, Mrs E. Sayers sen., Mr L. Stevens, Mr E. H. Sayers (nephew) Mr A. C. Staines, Mrs E. Shel... Mrs Ernie Sayers, Mrs W... Mr H. Thorogo... Thorpe, M... C... Wood, M... Mr J...

Harry Sayers C.1950.

---

of the Leaf Hall. In those early days the Club was very successful and for the years 1897-9 the senior coxed four were unbeaten regatta Champions along the coast from Weymouth round to Margate, at one time holding 7 Challenge cups. Rowing at No.2 fisherman and boatman Harry Sayers excelled. A member of the well known local family, Harry spent his life on Eastbourne's beach and fittingly died at the helm of his boat 'Clarice Jane' NN2, whilst at sea in August 1952 aged 75 years, taking friends out fishing. His family and friends knew him to be a person of a kindly disposition and well over a hundred mourners attended Harry's funeral. Born in 1876 he was the son of Alleyn 'Old Rig' Sayers.

Gun Running across the Channel. Eastbourne Fisherman involved.

Fisherman Henry Sayers, Gunsmith Benjamin Bates of Little North Street and Fruiterer Richard Willard of Pevensey Road, all of Eastbourne were involved in running arms to France.

At Eastbourne Magistrates Court on 7th November 1870 Bates was charged, that on 3rd October he illegally shipped 3 barrels of gunpowder and 2 cases of rifles from the beach at Eastbourne to Dieppe aboard Henry Sayers fishing boat 'Ocean Flower'.

In evidence it was said that Bates should have obtained a permit from the Board of Trade to export the arms and the boat must be licensed. Sayers was aware of this circumstance. But on the day in question the arms had been loaded on the 'Ocean

Flower' at Eastbourne and delivered along with a letter to a Frenchman named Menu on the quay at Dieppe. Sayers maintained he did not know what was in the barrels and the cases felt like they contained umbrellas.

Finding the case proved against Bates, he was fined £10. No action was taken against Sayers and Willard. Willard's part in the incident was never fully explained.

The war between France and Prussia started on 19th July 1870 when France under Napoleon III declared war on Prussia but finished up fighting against other German states as well. At the battle of Sedan, 2nd September 1870, France was defeated and Napoleon III captured. This did not end the war as the Third Republic was declared on 4th September in Paris. The battles continued and after a long siege from 19th September to 28th January 1871, the city of Paris fell. Peace was made on 10th May 1871. During the siege of Paris there was the bloody uprising of the left wing 'Paris Commune' against the Versailles government.

It would be interesting to know whether the arms were for the French government or the left wing insurgents of Paris. Fisherman Sayers would have had a problem if he had been stopped at sea by a Prussian warship. Is the above Ben Bates the Bates who became the owner and operator of the big sailing yacht 'Britannia' on Eastbourne seafront?

1871.

The census for 1871 shows there were some 113 fishermen/boatmen and associated trades. The population of Eastbourne stood at 10,342 a doubling since 1861.

A fine account of the Fishing Community, 1871.

'Further east than the Marine Parade is a gently sloping beach of shingle frequented by the fishermen. Here are hauled up the staunch Luggers, in which they do battle with the gales upon the open seas in quest of mackerel and herrings. For the most part these fishermen are of a fair complexion and of a frank and open countenance and hearing. Rigging and dressing their nets, tarring their boats, tanning their sail and apparel and oiling their dreadnoughts are the chief occupations of these men whilst ashore and they look with some disdain upon the smart boatmen who ply for hire on the smart parades. I have watched with interest their preparations for sea, the launching of their boats and their departure for mackerel fishing. I have seen about 80 of these men leave their homes for their perilous works, but as a rule the womenfolk do not come down to take leave of them. That is done quietly at home and there is no display of grief or affection upon the beach.

I noted however two exceptions. A very young mother with a baby boy only four months old, was sitting on the shingle near the 'Happy Return'. Whilst the Lugger was waiting on the beach for the tide to float it. One of the crew, a youth about twenty, the husband of the young mother, descended from the Lugger and sat down beside his wife, who without saying a word put the baby boy in his father's lap. There he sat looking with manly tenderness upon the child, but all he said was 'Ja-ack'. Each sailor that passed by put a great finger on the baby's fat cheek, exclaiming, 'Well, Ja-a-ck'. All seemed to know and love the baby of this young couple.

The other exception was a fair blue-eyed girl, who had the charge of four little brothers and sisters and who naturally thought it would amuse them to see the Luggers off, so she sat down with her young troops near the Lugger 'Dauntless'. Before this Lugger was afloat, a bright looking lad in a red woollen cap dropped over the Lugger's side and ran up the beach to the girl with the children. I turned aside my eyes and would not if I could, describe that sacred parting.

When the 'Dauntless' was off and her foresail hauled up and trimmed to the wind, I had a look at my little lady and saw that her face was hidden in her apron and she was sobbing. Probably this was the first voyage the youth had taken. I believe I wished almost as heartily as the girl for the safe return of that bright lad. Amongst these simple folk, their boats, their work and their affections, I have found that quietness which I sought for in vain amongst the pleasure seekers of Eastbourne '.

On Saturday evening of the 17th January 1872, 'in extremely bad weather, the brigantine 'Osprey' 150 tons with a cargo of coal ran aground on the shoal 'Sand Acre' at Holywell.

The lifeboat 'Mary Stirling' under Cox'n Joseph 'Joker' Huggett, could not be launched from the boat house beach, so she was hauled up to Holywell by horses and got down ready to launch when word was received that the crew had taken to the boat in the dark and had landed safely on the beach opposite Victoria Place. (Sea end of Terminus Road) In the dark an attempt was made using 17 horses, to haul the lifeboat back, but owing to the steep incline and weight the chains kept breaking. Things were left until Sunday morning when she was launched at Holywell and the crew rowed her back to the lifeboat house. The wreck broke up on Sunday becoming a complete loss. The shipwrecked crew after being attended to by the Shipwrecked Mariners' Society at the Workman's Hall, caught the train to London on that Sunday'.

October 1872. The capture of a Thrasher.

'Last week a fisherman named Prodger had a tremendous haul in his herring net, bringing ashore an immense fish known as a 'Thrasher' from the fact, as it is said, that its almost the king of fishes for strength and voracity. It measured 16 feet in length and had a powerful leather like tail. Prodger sold it to another fisherman named Carter, who made a pretty penny of it by exhibiting it under canvas on the beach'.

A near tragedy during the launching of a Lugger on April 30th 1873, happened when the Lugger was going off with a run, two fishermen Henry Novis and Reuben Wood who were assisting with the launch, were caught by the chain used for hauling the boat up, and dragged out to sea with her. As the boat rose and fell on the waves the poor fellows were ducked under the water, but holding on they were speedily rescued by Tom Bennett and others and brought ashore, unhurt and thankful for their escape.

James 'Jemmy' Knight, age 49 years, committed suicide at Newhaven in May 1873. He was captain of the Eastbourne fishing Lugger 'Band of Hope'. She was alongside at Newhaven Harbour, when he tied a rope with two half hitches round his neck and jumped over the side. A member of the crew, Samuel Beckett Hide in giving evidence at the inquest, held at the London & Paris Hotel tap, Newhaven, said, there had been no quarrelling on board or any miswords, but thought the deceased

LIFE AT SEA AND ASHORE

seemed rather strange lately. The boy cook, Charles Miles, saw Knight overboard with the jib-sheet line fastened round his neck. George French another crewmember of the boat stated that the deceased was very low-spirited. Dr F Dalton deposed on examination that Knight had drowned and a verdict of suicide was brought in.

August 1873. Rating.

Discussed in the Vestry at a Local board meeting the question of the difficulty in the collection of the rates on capstans, net shops and bathing machines from the seafaring fraternity arose. The rateable value in all cases only amounted to 1d and 2d in individual cases and at Hastings no rates were charged for these properties. Mr Hood stated, *'a former collector of taxes would pay the amounts himself as they were such trifling sums'*. In considering whether to drop these charges the Clerk said, *'We must rate all rateable property'*. The subject was then dropped.

A narrow escape from drowning happened on 28th December 1873, when an outward-bound steamer was passing down Channel when off Eastbourne she signalled for a boat to take her Pilot off and land him at Eastbourne. A fishing punt manned by four Erridges' put off into a fairly lumpy sea and after collecting the Pilot were some 50 yards from the beach when the punt shipped a couple of successive seas and immediately capsized. This was noticed from Marine Parade and a small boat manned by Henry Hurd and James Allchorn put off to assist. Tom Bennett and John Richard Mockett rushed into the sea and assisted in bringing the half drowned crew and Pilot ashore. By this timely action a tragedy was averted. Fisherman Hide swam out and got a line aboard the capsized punt and it was hauled ashore. A prime example of how the fishing fraternity go to assist colleagues when danger is afoot. As to the rescued Erridges thankful indeed as it was a good payday picking up a Pilot.

1874.

A report from 2nd September 1874 shows an Eastbourne fishing boat being run down.

'On 23rd August, a Lugger 'Five Brothers' belonging to William 'Old' Bollard Hide was run into while fishing off Eastbourne. Hide made the following statement ' On Sunday morning at 7 o'clock I was making for shore about six miles in a south-east direction off Eastbourne when I saw a steamer half mile away making the Channel course. She altered four points of her compass and came straight towards us, my mate Samuel Barnard, who was the only one aboard with me thought the steamer wanted to speak to us. As, however, they came so close to us I waved my hand for them to go under our lee, but they paid no attention and ran right into me, striking me right on the stern of the boat, turning me round and causing my bow to be right along the steamer's broadside. I was much frightened and called out to the man on the bridge of the steamer 'Lower your boat, we shall sink'

'On hearing this Samuel Barnard climbed up the side of the steamer and got aboard, upon which, notwithstanding my shouts for help, the steamer went away. Not a word was spoken by the man on the bridge. Samuel Barnard was taken away 3 miles and it was 2 hours before he reached my boat again being brought back by another Eastbourne Lugger coming from the direction of Brighton where it had been trawling'. Samuel Barnard related the following, 'When the vessel steamed

74

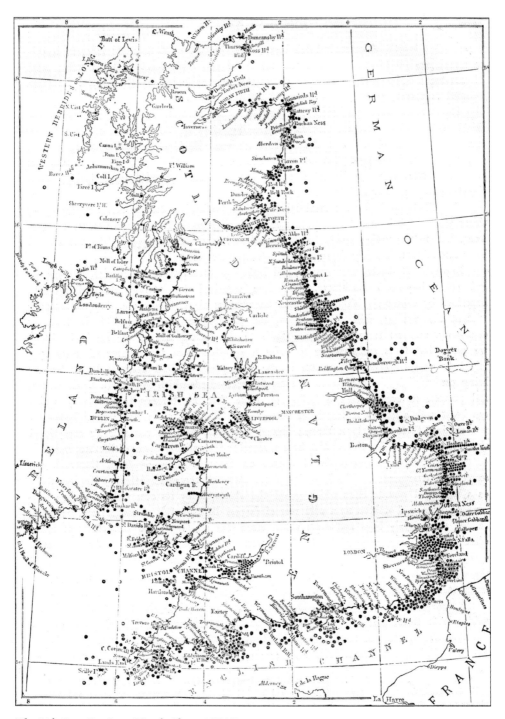

The Life-Boat Institute Wreck Chart 1876-7.

away I saw a boat coming from the direction of Brighton. 3 times I asked the officer on the bridge to hail it and let me get on board and go back to my Lugger, but he took no notice till my last request. He then offered me 50 shillings as recompense for the damage he caused, saying if I did not accept it he would take me abroad. Being much frightened I took the money'. Hide said. ' On advice I have not accepted the money. The damage to my boat is about £10'. Barnard added, the officer on the steamer said. ' This will be worse for me than for you'.

The Eastbourne Lugger 'Band of Hope' featured in what was first thought to be a tragic loss while at sea in September 1874.

'Considerable alarm was created in the town by a report that the 'Band of Hope', Charles Hide, Master, had been run down off the North Foreland, while engaged in a fishing expedition. From what has been gathered, it appears that a report reached Ramsgate, Kent, that the boat 'Band of Hope' had been run down, but that the crew had been saved. Benjamin Charles Hide, a brother of 'Bones' Hide, happened to be at Ramsgate with another boat and immediately forwarded the message to Eastbourne as nothing could be gleaned of 'Bones' and his crew at the Sailors Home at Dover. It was feared that not only had the boat been run down, but that all hands had perished. Yesterday morning, however, the telegraph wire conveyed the welcome intelligence that the 'Band of Hope' had just put into Ramsgate with a small take of about 400 fish. The receipt of the message may be better imagined than described. The mishap had happened to another boat of that name belonging to another town on the coast'

Fishing vessels and crews were regularly lost at sea. Ships of all size and trade being regularly lost within 10 miles of the coastline of the British Isles. The publishing of a wreck chart 1876-7 by the Life-Boat Institute brings this home. The lifeboats on the coast of Sussex were busy.

Back to Wrecks and Wrecking.

For many years folk living along the coast of our Country made a living from the salvage of shipwrecks and it could be said, what with Eastbourne's close proximity to Beachy Head and the rocky shore, it is a safe bet our Eastbourners did also. We all know the tales of the Cornish wreckers, enticing ships onto the rocks and plundering the wrecks. This could well have happened around Beachy Head. Consider the following lines from 'Congreve', which allude to the barbarous system of 'wrecking' once carried out on the wild Sussex coast.

'As Sussex men that dwell upon the shore,
Look-out when storms arise and billows roar,
Devoutly praying with uplifted hands,
That some well-laden ship may strike the sands,
To whose rich cargo they may make pretence'.

From a poem by E.M. after the wreck of the 'Caroline Dow'1909 the following words are very apt.

'Between Cuckmere and Beachy Head,
That rock bound coast that sailors dread,
Where scores have found a watery bed,
To sleep in death's long sleep'.

Beachy Head C.1820.

There would have been persons ready to wreck a ship when one considers that piracy occurred off Eastbourne and Hastings in the 18th century.

August 11th 1750, a Dutch ship 'Travil & Jacob' was stopped and boarded by the crews of two cutters, *'close in with Beachy Head'* the ship was taking a cargo of butter from Cork, Ireland to Bremen, Germany. The pirates stole 20 casks of butter. One of the pirate cutters was the 'Two Henrys' of Hastings. The master was later caught with one other member of the crew. Later tried in the High Court of Admiralty both were hanged at Execution Dock.

Another act of piracy happened off Hastings in 1768 and is how the Hastings inhabitants got the name of 'Chopbacks'. A Hastings gang boarded a Dutch ship in the English Channel and attacked the Captain by putting an axe in his back fatally injuring him, took control of the ship and stole the cargo. They were later all caught and eventually hanged for the crime. You rarely hear the term used today, but it still persists through local families with seafaring ancestors. The Hastings fishermen in turn call Eastbourne fishermen 'Willicks' or 'Willickers'. 'Willick' is the local Eastbourne term for a Guillemot, a sea bird that used to breed in large numbers on the cliff face at Beachy Head and was still being called 'Willick' by the local fishermen in the 1930's.

1876.

Returning to the question of legitimate salvage, as an example, George Hide with his 5 sons, John, George, Samuel, Benjamin and Charles, would have had a source of cheap labour when salvage incidents occurred.

An interesting salvage claim made in 1876 was when, bound for Antwerp from Buenos Aries, the single funnel, schooner-rigged 'Rubens' 1260 tons during thick fog ran ashore on 17th January at Birling Gap. The Coastguard was soon in attendance but there was no danger to the crew as the schooner settled on a smooth rocky bottom. Two tugs failed to pull her off so to lighten her, the crew and

Coastguards threw a quantity of the cargo of wool overboard, but it wasn't until 10 days later that the 'Rubens' was towed off and taken to Southampton for repairs.

The local fishermen having heard that the wool was being thrown overboard formed themselves into gangs, George Hide and his family one gang, Samuel John Allchorn and family another gang and the James Swain family another. They hired 3 carts with horses at a cost of £33 and went to the scene. They found bales of wool floating in the sea and amongst the rocks and in order to get the wool some of the gangs tied ropes round their bodies, being held by the others went into the sea and brought the wool ashore. Not without much difficulty with a sea running and the danger amongst the rocks. The bales of wool saved by the men in an ordinary condition weighed nearly half a ton, but in the wet conditions weighed nearly three-quarters of a ton. It took them three days to recover all that was available. They worked from daylight until dusk. This was quite an effort and very hard work as there was no shelter from the elements. In all fifty-four complete bales of wool and fifteen broken bales were recovered.

The value of the wool recovered by George Hide and gang was estimated at £1,316.12s 6d. Samuel Allchorn and his gang estimated at £466.17s 6d. James Swain and his gang estimated at £223. 2s 6d. They all subsequently put in a claim for salvage and were offered a total paltry sum of £281 for the wool valued at over £2,000. So they entered an action in the High Court of Justice to recover salvage money for the bales of wool recovered. Unfortunately they did not come out of it very well. The Judge decided although there had been a certain amount of danger attached to the recovery of the wool, he found that they had exaggerated the dangers to some extent. Considering the circumstance and the value of the property saved, his lordship was of the opinion that the offer of £281 was insufficient and he would increase it to £400 to include £33 for expenses. The distribution of the £367 would be in the following amounts - to George Hide - £237, to Samuel Allchorn - £75, and to James Swain - £55. They do not appear to have come out of that claim too well although the value of the pound in those days was far greater, although £400 against £2,000 doesn't seem a lot.

About a month later on 22nd February 1876, the barque 'Coonatto' 635 tons, ran ashore at Crowlink, just west of Birling Gap. She was laden with wool and copper ore en-route from Adelaide, South Australia to London. The lifeboat was in attendance and the steam tug, 'Victoria' from Newhaven attempted to get her off without success. This time the question of salvage of the cargo was put in the hands of Lloyd's agent from Newhaven, a Captain C.S. Knight. Hiring 100 men Knight organised the removal of the cargo taking it from the 'Coonatto' by boats and hauling it up the cliff by means of a steam engine and derrick. The cargo was recovered but the barque became a total loss. Part of her remains can still be seen to this day embedded in the rocks off Crowlink. The fishermen on this occasion other than perhaps being employed for labour did not get a share of the salvage.

Interestingly in Gowland's Directory for 1886 there was a house in Latimer Road, No.5 Addingham Terrace named 'Coonatto' the resident, a George Harmer. Did he make money working on her? Fisherman Samuel 'Doctor' Oliver lived next door at No.6. Fred 'Mucky' Erridge recalls 'Doctor' being from Wallsend (Pevensey Bay) a tall man who wore a high billycock hat and dabbled in homeopathic medicine (Hence the nickname).

The barque 'Coonatto' aground at Crowlink 22nd February 1876, she became a total loss.

A drowning two miles off Beachy Head on May 25th 1876.

Eastbourne fisherman Thomas Arthur Holman, 38years met with a watery grave. He was on board the Lugger 'Industry' skippered by James Boniface. The boat was fishing for mackerel at the time. The incident happened when Holman took a long stride on deck and the 'way' of the boat caused him to stumble and fall overboard. His comrades attempted to help him but the boat heeled away from where he fell and due to the wind and tide he was carried some considerable distance. After keeping his head up for some 15 minutes sadly he drowned and his body picked up by Hastings Lugger 'Young Harry'. The body was brought ashore about 8 o'clock that evening. He had lived in Seaside with his wife but had no children. The inquest was held at the original Kings Arms, Seaside. A member of the crew, Edward Brown said he saw Holman stumble and threw a spar to him in the water but it appeared he did not see it. Holman had a little beer but was not drunk. A verdict of 'accidentally drowned' was brought in with a recommendation that lifebelts be carried on all boats.

October 1876.

Misbehaviour as Bonfire night approached. Fishermen George Erridge, Charles Swain, James and Charles Hide had blackened their faces and on entering the Railway Hotel bar (now site of Nat West Bank) Terminus Road, no doubt full of ale, quaffed some more and broke into a series of bonfire songs. On and on they went and when requested to stop and leave the premises by the landlord Mr Ambler, they refused and sang louder. A constable was called and all four were ejected. The next day they appeared in Court charged with being disorderly. Charles Hide pleaded guilty, the others not guilty. Found guilty Erridge, Swain and James Hide were fined 1s with 10s costs. Charles Hide, because he had pleaded guilty was fined 1s with reduced costs of 5s. It paid to be honest!

Getting What's Owed.

Appearing at the Court in Eastbourne on 13th November 1876, William 'Young' Bollard Hide, a fisherman of Seaside was charged with assaulting William Nichols a hawker of fish, living at 6 Ashford Road. Nichols story was that on Saturday, 4th November, he was on the beach when Hide demanded of him 14 shillings that he owed him. He told Hide he hadn't the money in his pocket but he intended to pay him. Hide without any more to do laid hold of him and tried to throw him in a siver (a pile) of herring on the beach. Not being able to manage that, Hide got him down, knelt on him and rubbed a herring in his face covering him with blood. Hide said he wouldn't mind paying a sovereign for what he'd done and added *'this has outset a shilling of the 14s'*

Cross examined by Mr Mathews for Hide, Nichols denied he had made any offensive gesture to Hide when asked for the money. He had never shaken money in Hide's face. He told Hide he had the money but he would have to wait. He (Nichols) was unpopular on the beach at the moment because he owed money to 3 or 4 persons. He also had a judgement summons against him. Two witnesses were called for Nichols, one a man named Shoosmith and another was a bath chairman called William Reed. For Hide, John Mitchell, Joe Carter fish hawkers and John Clark Coastguardsman gave evidence, all said Nichols sneered at Hide and a tussle ensued, it was 'six of one and half a dozen of the other' and it was the custom with fishermen to throw fish at persons that owed them money.

The Bench found Hide guilty of assault and fined him £1.10s.0d. with costs of £1.6s.0d.

1877.

New Years day 1877, opened with a violent storm along the coast and Eastbourne was hit badly. The land end of the Pier was washed away. Pier master Mr Sawdie and two employees, Henry Barber and Caesar Mitchell made a very late escape from the collapsing Pier. Having to jump for it Barber broke a leg. Hundreds from the original Splash Point opposite the Queens Hotel watched the destruction of the Pier. Now Splash Point is known as down at the Great Redoubt. The debris from the Pier was swept down along the shore towards Langney Point, the report of this got to the ears of Henry Gardner, landlord of the 'Volunteer' Pub in Seaside Road (now demolished). Gardner with some fishermen made their way to Tower 72, where they knew the floating debris would come ashore and to collect what could be saved. On the warning of this wet, severe weather, the residents of Marine Parade and Mann's Row (now St. Aubyn's Road) and Seaside, began 'Pugging up' and boarding doorways and downstairs windows in anticipation of heavy rain bringing flooding. The seas would also come over the beach and sea wall by Marine Parade down through Mann's Row into Seaside. The residents called out 'Pug up' when inclement weather was expected. 'Pugging up' would mean sealing the doors with earth. Mann's Row at the time was an unmade road of dilapidated terraced fishermen's cottages built by a Mr Mann, local builder, who was also involved in the building of Martello Towers.

The great storm on that New Years day caused the following: -

'There was much damage all the way down east through the Fishing Station, fishing huts being carried away and broken up by contact with the Great Redoubt. The cottages in Mann's Row were flooded to an extent never known before, Hollingham's the baker's was flooded the Fisherman's Arms completely gutted, the water half way up the rooms. Three net huts washed away, the Lugger 'Susan's Pride' and fishing boat 'Champion' were partially stove in. The fishermen were badly hit by this storm, they lost ropes and nets, tackle and capstans were torn up. Mr Thompson, greengrocer of Seaside, nearly lost a score of pigs, their sty was flooded and great difficulty was had in saving them. They could have been lost, as it is well known that pigs in trying to swim cut their throats with their front feet. The flooding extended to opposite the Workmen's Hall (Leaf Hall) On the parades, a great hole was made in the promenade, wooden steps washed away and damage done by shingle. Men were employed in digging gullies in the road and this did save Mr Gilbert's shop at the bottom of Seaside Road'.

The end of January 1877 saw a discontented casual in the Workhouse, John Ellis, aged 64yrs, refuse to break up 2cwt of flints on the grounds of disability. A Doctor examined Ellis and declared him fit and able. Ellis said he could pick oakum (tarred rope) or do any light work but not break up flints. Subsequently he appeared at Eastbourne Court, was found guilty of malingering and given 14 days hard labour.

Back to the fishing and we learn that the inshore mackerel fishing in early October 1877 was good. An unprecedented catch of mackerel took place a short distance

At the mercy of the sea. Wreck of a fishing boat.

from the shore eastwards of the 'Crumbles' on Thursday morning. On the Tuesday previous a large shoal was seen off Pevensey Bay and several boats put off expecting a rich harvest, but returned minus the fish. On Thursday however they were successful and during that day little short of 200,000 were brought on shore near the lifeboat house. They were sold at 12 for a shilling on the beach and a great number of men were engaged all the day and through the night packing them in boxes for removal by train to London. Mr Tom Bennett of Seaside and Mr Bourne of Meads, their united number being a little over 70,000, owned the boats that brought in the greatest quantity of fish.

The herring fishing in November brought about the loss of an Eastbourne fishing boat. It was on the 16th November 1877, that the Lugger 'Industrious' left Eastbourne for Ramsgate for the purpose of herring fishing. The owners were, James Allchorn, Edward Allchorn, James Allchorn Jnr. William Jackson and Walter Welfare, the crew being George Cummings, W Hobby, James Adams, and J Goldsmith. Jeffery Allchorn was in command.

The boat reached Ramsgate and went to sea on the morning of the 25th proceeding to the 'Nock' fishing ground, which lay some considerable distance seaward of North Foreland. Returning in the evening it anchored a short distance from the shore between North Foreland and Margate. It was a dark evening about eight o'clock when, while the sea was running high, the anchor dragged and with the rope stranding they were obliged to cut themselves adrift. Another anchor was thrown over and the Lugger again brought up. The rope however, again stranding and they were compelled to cut themselves adrift a second time. They then attempted to run for Margate, but the boat became unmanageable and they struck the East Foreland sands within a short distance of Margate and about 200 yards from the shore. They then used lights and showed signals of distress. These were seen from the shore and the Margate lifeboat put off to their assistance and succeeded in rescuing the whole crew and landing them safely at Margate. The following day the whole of the gear and nets were recovered and it was discovered that the 'Industrious' had been stove-in in several places during the night, through coming in contact with the immense quantity of wreckage that strewed the beach and she became a complete wreck. The loss to the Allchorn family and Jackson was considerable, the boat being uninsured.

The night of the above storm some twenty-five vessels were wrecked and sunk off Margate with great loss of life. Only sterling work by the Margate lifeboat and crew prevented more loss of life. Fishing then as now is a dangerous occupation and has a high death rate. As an example the following report from the Eastbourne Chronicle March 1877 shows that in that month alone, due to the dreadful gales in the North Sea there were: - 39 vessels lost. Men and boys lost 215. Dependent relatives left - Widows 96, children 184 and aged parents 15. Isaac Adams, fishmonger of 1, Lewes Place, made a plea in the paper for urgent donations to assist the dependants.

30th November, saw *'a 4 foot octopus, in perfect condition stranded on the beach at Marine Parade, it was captured and after display in Adams Fishmongers, a communication was made to the Brighton Aquarium Company, who said they would take it and it was then sent in an iron tub kept for the purpose, by train to*

Brighton. It is said octopus are often seen some seven miles off on the 'Horseshoe rocks' but difficult to take without injury'.

Back on the 19th November, the Local Board met at a special meeting to discuss the foreshore question. A proposal was put that the Commissioners of the Levels be approached to give up their rights over the foreshore between Marine Parade and the Great Redoubt, in effect the 'Stade' Fishing Station. The proposal was raised because of sea encroachment and continual damage caused at neap tides and stormy times - the worse area being Marine Parade through to the Great Redoubt.

The Commissioners of the Levels were a body that had responsibility for the Coastal foreshore, including the drainage and defence and to levy taxes and rates covering the Pevensey and Hastings Rapes.

It was pointed out at the meeting that the foreshore between Marine Parade and Holywell had already been taken over by the Local Board and the Parades built. Marine Parade built to protect the Sea Houses in the early 1800's, then in c.1849 the start of the building of Grand Parade sea wall and promenade, finishing at the Wish Tower 1864, then the completion between the Wish Tower and Holywell by c.1878. The question was whether to build four groynes at a cost of £1,000 each. This it was thought would stop the encroachment of the sea over the shingle into Seaside. The Board were prepared to take care of the costs with the aid of the ratepayer. The Grand Parade area had benefited from the sea wall and promenade, properties having increased in value.

The object of this meeting was to get the groynes erected and it was stated to build a great work like a sea wall would drive the fishermen east of the Great Redoubt. So at this stage there was no push for a sea wall. The coming of the December gales and long tides was mentioned and became an important factor.

Marine Parade with furze groynes C.1870.

Monday 26th November 1877.

Mr G F Chambers, spokesman for the Local Board, met the Commissioners for the Levels at the Castle Hotel, Hastings. The Commissioners agreed something needed to be done as soon as possible and declared their intention to put down two new groynes and to put down furze to protect the road and give consideration to the Board taking over the foreshore. Complaints about flooding were being received from the residents of that area. Again the question was whether to build groynes or a sea wall. As previously stated a sea wall would drive the fishermen off their ancient Fishing Station (Stade) and push them further east to the other side of the Great Redoubt and of course with the building of a sea wall it would be a prime area to develop commercially. The Fishing Station covered about 200 yards of the foreshore. The 'writing was on the wall' for the fishermen!

The land (Crumbles/Waste) up to the foreshore in question was now since 1850 jointly owned and controlled by the Duke of Devonshire and Mr Gilbert and the area covering the site of the Great Redoubt by the Admiralty. They would have to be approached about the taking over of the foreshore by the Board.

It had been the great storm and floods of January, the year before, that caused such a problem that the local businessmen and inhabitants of Seaside stirred up the Local Board to take action. As mentioned before, letters were written and a petition signed.

December 1st 1877.

A *'foreshore' letter to the local paper from a resident, laid out the idea of 'a sea wall, proposing it ran from the Anchor Hotel (Albermarle) on Marine Parade through to the glacis (sloping smooth flint stone foundation) of the Great Redoubt, with upper and lower parades and the addition of a terrace of fine houses'.*

A Poets Plea sent to the Local Paper:

> **A cry for help from Seaside.**
> What will become of Eastbourne East?
> Will land or water be increased?
> Before the 'merry month of May
> We may be drenched or washed away.
> The question rests with those who ought.
> To give this eastern question thought.
> Perchance the Duke and 'Local Board'.
> Will time and money both afford?
> So that our grievance may fade
> And merge into Grand Parade.

The pressure on the Local Board sowed the seed as mentioned above to move the fisher folk from where they had settled and fished for centuries. This was to be the start of great problems for them.

December 15th 1877.

A Local Board report shows member Mr Cable, criticising the work of the Commissioners of the Levels over their work done with regard to the simple pegging down of furze. In his opinion it was quite inadequate. It was also stated that Mr

Streatfield had vacated his house (Sea Beach House) owing to the danger from the sea. It was said he had spent £1,000 some years back protecting it. From all the foregoing problems, something would have to be done - groynes or a sea wall? Positive action would come within another year.

August 28th 1878.

'On Monday morning and Eastbourne fisherman, John Prodger, when about 5 miles off, recovered the body of a man and deposited it in the Dead house, Ordnance yard, Seaside. It was greatly decomposed and it was believed the deceased was one of the crew of the 'Grosser Kurfurst', which foundered off Folkestone on 31st May'.

October 1878.

Rough weather at the end of October saw a wreck and lifesaving involving local fishermen and damage again to the foreshore, Marine Parade. From a report at the time: -

'The barge 'Charles' known as a 'dandy' of Rochester, official number at Lloyd's No.46. tonnage 110, bound from Portland to London with a cargo of Portland stone, brought up off the Pier on Wednesday, 27th October, at about 8.30pm. At nearly high water with the wind freshening from the S.W. and a moderate rolling sea running. Her crew consisted of Captain John Collins, who is now in delicate state of health, his son John, aged 14 years and the mate John Coney. Owing to having fallen in with squalls, during the early part of the day, which coursed from N.W to S.W. all hands were doubtless fagged out and glad to shelter within reach of assistance if required.

With the flowing morning's tide, (Thursday) which set in about 3.30am the wind increased in force from S.S.W and by 8.00am was a gale, yet still the barge remained anchored off the Pier which gave rise to much comment from the fishermen who were anxiously watching for any signal that might be given from her, as they concluded it was impossible for her to weather the gale there. At this time it also appears that the Captain began to fear for the safety of his barge and crew. As the increasing heavy swell began to sweep his decks with terrible warning, this led him to hoist the ensign, but this of course is no signal of distress, or any other proper signal, therefore his hoisting served only to confuse every one.

One asked, had he hoisted the flag to indicate confidence in his craft to ride the gale? Or did he wish it to be understood that he wanted a man or two to assist him weigh anchor and navigate her to some other place of shelter? If the latter, his knowledge of the sea should have told him that none but the lifeboat could live through the heavy breakers then dashing on the shore and surely every Captain and sailor knows how to make a distress signal in the absence of correct distress signal flags, by hoisting anything in the shape of a ball, to wit a rolled up jacket, a bundle of rags, or a coil of ropes; but this man made no such signals of distress. Now if he wanted assistance, such as could only be rendered by a lifeboat and at the same wish to avoid the claim of salvage for services rendered and risk taken, had the lifeboat put to sea and saved his crew and craft under his no signal flag, he would have had the power to even refuse to thank them, hence it is that the regulations of the call to duty of 'the lifeboat' shall be the sign of distress. I make these remarks because I heard some wise-acres talking very largely and denouncing the fishermen *as cowards for not putting off the life-boat, prior to the distress signal being given. But doubtless the fishermen will forgive such wondrously intelligent demonstrators of what they do not understand.*

Long before the Captain hoisted the flag in question, the coxswain of the lifeboat, Joseph 'Joker' Huggett and her crew were on the beach ready and waiting to obey the summons to their self-elected duty of risking their lives to save others, but it was not until 8.45 am, three quarters of an hour since he first hoisted the ensign, as he lowered and reversed it, running it up with the union downwards, this, though not a correct signal of distress, was answered as such from the shore, at the same time there was a rush for the lifeboat, but such was the violence of the waves beating the only door of the boathouse, through which the boat can be taken, owing to the beach being washed away, that is was with considerable danger and necessary delay before the boat could be got out, but this accomplished, away she sped with horses and men to be launched at the Wish Tower end of the parade, for it would have been impossible for any crew to have rowed her from her station against the surf and flowing tide to windward.

During this time the sea made considerably, sweeping the decks of the 'Charles' and great anxiety was manifested by the large concourse of spectators for the safety of the lives in jeopardy. It being evident that she might founder at any moment. The lifeboat had now reached the end of the parade and when about to be launched the cry was raised that the barge has parted her cables and is drifting. This changed the course of action; several of the boats crew and coastguardsmen seized a Cab at hand and drove with all speed to the foreshore, to which she was then drifting, the remainder of the fishermen endeavouring to keep pace with them. By this time the barge had set a 'trysail' by which she was enabled to keep steerage way and made for the shore near the Coast Guard Station, (between Marine Parade and the Great Redoubt). A flag being hoisted there for directing the Captain for the best goal. The excitement now was beyond description, yet calm and courageous stood the brave fishermen with lifeline in hand ready to plunge into the angry billows and at the risk of their own lives to rescue the crew instantly on her touching the beach. On came the unfortunate barge on this her last voyage, the sea ever and anon breaking over her decks each moment appearing her last, while her brave and gallant little crew handled their ill fated craft with that courageous skill and caution which the circumstances demanded.

The barge 'Charles' took the beach on the west side of the west groyne from the Coast Guard Station and instantly she grounded, the fishermen with life lines plunged into the raging surf and landed the mate, next the boy and lastly the Captain. During this last act three of the fishermen thus engaged nearly lost their lives through the groynes not being planked up, as a tremendous sea caught them and dashed them against the groyne piles and swept them through, by which all their lines got entangled, subjecting them for a brief period to imminent peril as they lay in the wake of the sea. The screams of the women, shouts of the multitude, with the rush of other fishermen to their rescue cannot be depicted; it was but for an instant then they struggled to their feet and were rescued by their brethren as a sea broke over that would have swept them into eternity. The injuries that they had received were such that only strong powerful men as they could have borne to escape with life, for Charles Hide received a severe scalp wound and a bruised leg, his brother Ben Hide, bruised arm and leg, cousin Philip Hide, bruised thigh and cousin Jesse Huggett escaped injury. Thus these three brave men are injured for their humanity by the unprotected state of the groynes, rendering the possibility of reaching the shore exceedingly dangerous.

It was touching to see the veteran saver of human life in Eastbourne, the renowned George Hide who holds medals for saving 50 lives, though old and infirm yet courageous as ever, standing on the beach encouraging others to deeds of human kindness and in answer to his wife's (Mary Ann) scream as she saw her two sons (Charles and Ben) swept through the groyne, George Hide said, 'Be calm, mother, it will be alright'. Words only that can flow from the lips of a hero of the first magnitude.

Doctors' Hayman and Brown were quickly on the spot rendering every assistance to the injured. The crew of the 'Charles' were taken to the Workmen's Hall where they were well cared for'.

November 1878.

Later a collection was made for the rescuers and the following report from the Hove Mercury 8th November 1878, sums up the character of the Eastbourne fishermen.

'The brothers Hide, who with the two Huggetts and others rendered such good and gallant service in rescuing the crew of the 'Charles' from the vengeful waves, appear disposed with true hero-modesty to hide their light under a bushel. They object to money being collected on their behalf and have handed over the amount already received to the Shipwrecked Mariners' Society. They are brave fellows and as unobtrusive as they are brave'.

Praise indeed from along the coast at Hove.

C1870. Rough seas at Agony (Splash) Point showing Field House now site of Queens Hotel.

Sea-side Houses. Eastbourne c1820.

Chapter Three

The Forced Removal of the Fishermen
from their Ancient Fishing Station

'With regard to the foreshore, the gale had reaped terrible havoc, sweeping away thousands of tons of shingle, leaving bare, undermining and destroying the foundations of what were once dwelling houses for the Coastguard officers. The lifeboat house nearly washed away. Another gale will do the job, the lifeboat being kept out for safety. The coastguard and rocket apparatus house swept to its foundations and the footing of the signal mast almost washed away. Boats had been dragged into the roadway for safety, fishing gear etc, also moved for safety. The Club boathouse (Rowing club) was also washed to its foundations, the rowing boats had to be removed. The sea overflowed a wall of shingle to the east of Marine Parade, poured in torrents down through Mann's Row into Seaside tearing up the road and surcharging the drains in Pevensey Road, driving the sewer gas before it. There were several complaints of violent headaches one of the first symptoms of a dreadful epidemic produced by sewer gas'.

So the problem of the foreshore between Marine Parade and the Great Redoubt arose again. Attention had been paid to this area by the addition of six groynes being erected, two built by the Commissioners, four of them at the expense of the

View to the east showing original 'Stade' Fishing Station, now Royal Parade C.1870.

Plan of original Fishing Station and area before Royal Parade built. Reproduced from the Ordnance Survey Map of 1875.

Duke of Devonshire and Mr Gilbert. For some reason the Commissioners for the Levels had refused to let the groynes be planked in and this failure brought about the devastation and nearly the deaths of the fishermen. It was after many meetings of the Local Board over the problem of the foreshore, that the full Board meeting of the 25th November 1878, decided to raise a Bill, the Eastbourne Improvement Act (1879) for the building of a sea wall, a Town Hall and sanitary improvements.

The Local Board were to take over responsibility for the sea wall and foreshore from the Commissioners of the Levels. A provision was made in the proposed Bill for an Embankment and Breakwater (the breakwater would be of concrete construction and reach out from the shore just west of the Great Redoubt, some 1000 yards or 1 furlong, 3 chains and 3 yards, quite a construction). This was put in as a sop to those against the sea wall and never seriously considered by the Local Board. The Breakwater plan was supported by the fishermen. It was never built.

The copy of the 1878 plan shows all premises and Net shops numbered and occupants of the same, listed. It is of great interest to know just where the fishermen families and tradesmen were situated. Mann's Row also known as York Buildings (now the site of St Aubyns Road) is an example. All Nets shops, capstans and buildings within the sea wall perimeter would be gone and lost forever.

January 6th 1879.

At a special meeting of the Local Board the propriety of the promotion of the Bill was confirmed by an absolute majority. As result the Local Board was represented by Doctor G A Geoffrey, Board Chairman and Mr O'Hara Q.C. when the Bill was petitioned before a Committee at Parliament for permission to proceed.

This hearing took place in March 1879. Evidence of cost, acquisition of land and property and development of the foreshore was put and the Local Board representatives were stringently questioned by the Committee as to the reasons and motives. An interesting point to emerge from this was the fact that the Local Board made no mention to the Committee that the fishermen were incumbent on the foreshore and had been so for hundreds of years. Interestingly Mr John Streatfield of Sea Beach House, who had complained of the encroachment of the

Fishermen's cottages. Mann's Row (York buildings, now St Aubyn's Road), view from beach to Seaside C.1880.

sea on his property, actually petitioned against the Bill, but as the minutes of the March hearing of evidence stated, no Counsel appeared for him against the Board's petition, so it was not considered.

The Breakwater scheme was also never seriously put forward by the Local Board as an alternative to the sea wall. The Parliamentary Committee duly sanctioned the proposal for a sea wall. So the Local Board had succeeded in their aims to develop the foreshore not only as a sea defence but to develop commercially.

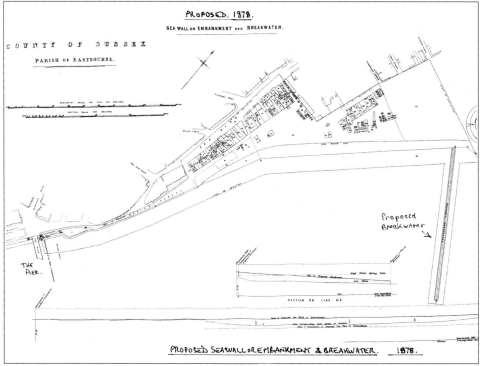

Plan of proposed Sea Wall and Breakwater 1878.

EASTBOURNE LOCAL BOARD.

Sea Wall or Embankment and Breakwater.

Parish of EASTBOURNE, in the County of Sussex.

No. on Plan.	Description of Property.	Owners or Reputed Owners.	Lessees or Reputed Lessees.	Occupiers.
1	Railed enclosure	Thomas Henry Wyatt, James Beattie, Charles Manby, Harriot Barbara Davis Manby, Arthur Robert Hood	George Ambrose Wallis, William Lumb Wallis, George Ellwood	George Ambrose Wallis, William Lumb Wallis, George Ellwood
2	Marine parade, approaches, and sea wall	Eastbourne District Local Board		
3	House, shop, covered yard, and premises	Duke of Devonshire	John Vine, senior (Seaside)	James Vine
4	House, shop, yard, and premises	Duke of Devonshire	John Vine, senior (Seaside)	John Vine, junior
5	House, shop, yard, and premises	Duke of Devonshire	John Vine, senior (Seaside), Samuel Holmes	Samuel Holmes
6	House, garden, and premises	Duke of Devonshire	— —	Mary Ann Rason
7	House, garden, and premises	Duke of Devonshire	— —	John Head
8	House, shop, yard, and premises	Duke of Devonshire	— —	Simpson Head
9	House, shop, yards, and premises	Duke of Devonshire	— —	Richard Hide
10	Bathhouse, baths, yard, and premises	Duke of Devonshire	— —	Thomas Bennett
11	Occupation road	Duke of Devonshire, Henry Parsons, Sarah Knight	— —	Simpson Head, Richard Hide, Thomas Bennett, George Head, James Fry, William Gibbard Judge, Frederick Comber

Schedule 1878.

Eastbourne Local Board.

Parish of Eastbourne—*continued*.

No. on Plan.	Description of Property.	Owners or Reputed Owners.	Lessees or Reputed Lessees.	Occupiers.
12	House, yard, and premises	Sarah Knight	— —	George Head
13	House, yard, and premises	Sarah Knight	— —	James Fry
14	House, yard, and premises	Henry Parsons	— —	William Gibbard Judge
15	House, yard, and premises	Henry Parsons	— —	Frederick Comber
16	Public road, gas and water pipes, and sewers	Eastbourne District Local Board Eastbourne Gas Company Eastbourne Waterworks Company		
17	Net house	Duke of Devonshire	John Streatfield	William Mitchell
18	Store house and premises	Duke of Devonshire	John Streatfield	Edwin Barker
19	House and premises	Duke of Devonshire	John Streatfield	James Hide, senior
20	House, shop, bakehouse, yard, and premises	Duke of Devonshire	John Streatfield	Edwin Barker
21	Shop, workshop, yard, and premises	Duke of Devonshire	John Streatfield Charlotte Parsons	Henry Graham Alfred Graham
22	Shop, yard, and premises	Duke of Devonshire	John Streatfield Charlotte Parsons	Leonard Stevens
23	Court or path	Duke of Devonshire	John Streatfield Charlotte Parsons	Leonard Stevens Arthur John Whitaker John Streatfield
24	House, shop, and premises	Duke of Devonshire	John Streatfield	Arthur John Whitaker
25	House, shop, yard, and premises	Duke of Devonshire	John Streatfield Henry Parsons Samuel Holmes	Samuel Holmes Henry Parsons
26	House, yard, and premises	Duke of Devonshire	John Streatfield	William Brown
27	House, yard, and premises	Duke of Devonshire	Sarah Knight	William Reid
28	House, shop, stabling, outbuildings, yards, and premises	Duke of Devonshire	Charles Simmons	Henry Mandy Simmons Charles Henry Simmons
29	Offices, stores, stabling, yard, and premises	Duke of Devonshire	Matthias Mockett, junior	Norton Stevenson George Stevenson

Eastbourne Local Board.

Parish of Eastbourne—continued.

No. on Plan.	Description of Property.	Owners or Reputed Owners.	Lessees or Reputed Lessees.	Occupiers.
30	House, outbuildings, yard, and premises	Duke of Devonshire	— —	Eastbourne Waterworks Company Thomas Allum
31	Livery stables, coach-houses, yard, and premises	Duke of Devonshire	Ebenezer William Robins John Newman	John Newman
32	"The Workmen's Hall," yard, and premises	Trustees of "The Workmen's Hall," viz.: Charles Leaf Julia Leaf Jane Leaf	— —	Trustees of "The Workmen's Hall," viz.: Charles Leaf Julia Leaf Jane Leaf
33	Public road, gas and water pipes, and sewers	Eastbourne District Local Board Eastbourne Gas Company Eastbourne Waterworks Company		
34	Public road, gas and water pipes, and sewers	Eastbourne District Local Board Eastbourne Gas Company Eastbourne Waterworks Company		
34a	Public road, gas and water pipes, and sewers	Eastbourne District Local Board Eastbourne Gas Company Eastbourne Waterworks Company		
35	Storehouse and yard	Duke of Devonshire	John Streatfield	Thomas Bennett
36	House, garden, and premises	Duke of Devonshire	John Streatfield	John Streatfield
37	House, yard, and premises	Duke of Devonshire	John Streatfield Charles Verrell	William Allchorn
38	House, yard, and premises	Duke of Devonshire	John Streatfield	Henry Chatfield
39	Public road, gas and water pipes, and sewers	Eastbourne District Local Board Eastbourne Gas Company Eastbourne Waterworks Company		
40	Foreshore	Duke of Devonshire	John Streatfield	John Streatfield
41	Net shop	Duke of Devonshire	— —	James Hide
42	Cottage and premises	Duke of Devonshire	— —	James Hide
43	Bakehouse	Duke of Devonshire	— —	Unoccupied

Eastbourne Local Board.

Parish of Eastbourne—*continued.*

No. on Plan.	Description of Property.	Owners or Reputed Owners.	Lessees or Reputed Lessees.	Occupiers.
44	Net shop	Duke of Devonshire	— —	William Hide
45	Foreshore	Duke of Devonshire Right Honourable Lords Commissioners of the Admiralty Commissioners of Levels Carew Davies Gilbert		
46	Foreshore	Duke of Devonshire		
47	House, shop, work-shops, garden, yards, and premises	Carew Davies Gilbert	James Parks	James Parks
48	House, shop, work-shops, yard, and premises	Carew Davies Gilbert	James Daws	James Daws
49	Lifeboat house	Carew Davies Gilbert	— —	Royal National Lifeboat Institution
50	Toolhouse	Carew Davies Gilbert	— —	Commissioners of Levels
51	Boathouse	Carew Davies Gilbert	John Newman	Eastbourne Rowing Club
52	"Marine hotel," garden, and premises	Carew Davies Gilbert	Alfred Hillman	Sidney William Gearing
53	House, garden, and premises	Carew Davies Gilbert	— —	William Esam
54	Public road	Eastbourne District Local Board Eastbourne Gas Company Eastbourne Waterworks Company		
55	House, yard, and pre-mises	Carew Davies Gilbert	John Stretton	Edmund Stretton
56	House, yard, and pre-mises	Carew Davies Gilbert	John Stretton	William Barnard
57	Yard	Carew Davies Gilbert	John Stretton	Edmund Stretton William Barnard
58	Cottage, yard, and pre-mises	Carew Davies Gilbert	John Stretton	James Sawyer
59	Cottage and premises	Carew Davies Gilbert	John Stretton	Elizabeth Hide
60	Cottage and premises	Carew Davies Gilbert	John Stretton	John Lister
61	Cottage and premises	Carew Davies Gilbert	John Stretton	William Mitchell
62	Yard, outbuildings, and premises	Carew Davies Gilbert	John Stretton	Elizabeth Hide William Mitchell John Lister

Eastbourne Local Board.

Parish of Eastbourne—continued.

No. on Plan.	Description of Property.	Owners or Reputed Owners.	Lessees or Reputed Lessees.	Occupiers.
63	House, garden, yard, and premises	Carew Davies Gilbert	Reuben Climpson	Eli Waymark
64	House, shop, yard, and premises	Carew Davies Gilbert	John Vine (Grand Parade)	Martha Bates
65	Cottage, yard, and premises	Carew Davies Gilbert	John Vine (Grand Parade)	Edward Kenyon
66	Stores and premises	Carew Davies Gilbert	John Vine (Grand Parade)	Norton Stevenson George Stevenson
67	Public footpath	Carew Davies Gilbert		
68	"Brewer's Arms" beershop, stable, yard, and premises	Carew Davies Gilbert	— —	Alexander Hurst Arthur Matthews
69	Yard	Carew Davies Gilbert	— —	Alexander Hurst Arthur Matthews Edward Bignell William Bassett Henry Mason
69a	Shed	Carew Davies Gilbert	— —	Alexander Hurst Arthur Matthews William Bassett
69b	Shed	Carew Davies Gilbert	— —	Alexander Hurst Arthur Matthews Edward Bignell
70	Stable and yard	Carew Davies Gilbert	— —	Alexander Hurst Arthur Matthews Joshua Hatton
71	Workshop	Carew Davies Gilbert	— —	Alexander Hurst Arthur Matthews Henry Mason
72	Oil store	Carew Davies Gilbert	— —	Alexander Hurst Arthur Matthews Edward Bignell
74	Stores, net houses, stable, and premises	Carew Davies Gilbert	— —	Carew Davies Gilbert Arthur Matthews William Moon John Erridge Weller Sayers George Sayers George Parks
75	Workshop, premises, and approach	Carew Davies Gilbert	Reuben Climpson	Joshua Hatton
76	House, shop, bakehouse, yard, and premises	Carew Davies Gilbert	— —	John Hollingham

Eastbourne Local Board.

Parish of Eastbourne—*continued.*

No on Plan.	Description of Property.	Owners or Reputed Owners	Lessees or Reputed Lessees.	Occupiers.
77	Cottage and premises	Carew Davies Gilbert	— —	James Vine
78	Workshop and premises	Carew Davies Gilbert	— —	Mary Verrall
79	House, shop, and premises	Carew Davies Gilbert	— —	Solomon Christian
80	Cottage and premises	Carew Davies Gilbert	— —	James Huggett
81	Cottage and premises	Carew Davies Gilbert	— —	George Erridge
82	Cottage, net shop, and premises	Carew Davies Gilbert	— —	Edward Wood
83	Store, net shop, and premises	Carew Davies Gilbert	— —	Frederick French
84	Cottage and premises	Carew Davies Gilbert	— —	Weller Sayers
85	Cottage and premises	Carew Davies Gilbert	— —	John Erridge
86	Cottage and premises	Carew Davies Gilbert	— —	Richard Hurd
87	Cottage and premises	Carew Davies Gilbert	— —	William Packham
88	Cottage and premises	Carew Davies Gilbert	— —	Henry Matthews
89	Yard	Carew Davies Gilbert	— —	Henry Matthews
90	Court, called " York Buildings "	Carew Davies Gilbert	— —	Solomon Christian James Huggett George Erridge Edward Wood Frederick French Weller Sayers John Erridge Richard Hurd William Packham Henry Matthews Spencer Goodsell George Erridge, junior George French Thomas Knight William Verrall Mary Verrall James Vine
91	Cottage and premises	Carew Davies Gilbert	— —	Spencer Goodsell
92	Cottage and premises	Carew Davies Gilbert	— —	George Erridge, junior
93	Cottage and premises	Carew Davies Gilbert	— —	George French
94	Cottage and premises	Carew Davies Gilbert	— —	Frederick French

Eastbourne Local Board.

Parish of Eastbourne—*continued*.

No. on Plan.	Description of Property.	Owners or Reputed Owners.	Lessees or Reputed Lessees.	Occupiers.
95	Cottage, store, and premises	Carew Davies Gilbert	— —	Thomas Knight
96	Outbuildings and premises	Carew Davies Gilbert	— —	James Huggett George Erridge Edward Wood Frederick French Weller Sayers John Erridge Richard Hurd William Packham Henry Matthews Spencer Goodsell George Erridge, junior George French Thomas Knight William Verrall Mary Verrall
97	Workshop and premises	Carew Davies Gilbert	— —	William Parks
98	Cottage and premises	Carew Davies Gilbert	— —	William Verrall
99	Workshop, cottage, and premises	Carew Davies Gilbert	— —	James Huggett Mary Verrall
100	Yard	Carew Davies Gilbert	— —	John Hollingham William Parks John Erridge Weller Sayers George Sayers George Parks
101	Chaise House	Carew Davies Gilbert	— —	Richard Harris
102	Yard and premises	Carew Davies Gilbert	— —	William Mitchell William Taylor Sarah Knight
103	Net shop	Carew Davies Gilbert	— --	James Allchorn George Hide
104	Net shop	Carew Davies Gilbert	— —	John Head Thomas Bennett
105	Net shop	Carew Davies Gilbert	— —	James Allchorn, senior
106	Net shop	Carew Davies Gilbert	— —	William Brown
107	Net shop	Carew Davies Gilbert	— —	William Allchorn Samuel Allchorn
108	Workshop and premises	Carew Davies Gilbert	— —	James Allchorn William Allchorn

Eastbourne Local Board.

Parish of Eastbourne—*continued.*

No. on Plan.	Description of Property.	Owners or Reputed Owners.	Lessees or Reputed Lessees.		Occupiers.
109	Herring dees, yard, and premises	Carew Davies Gilbert	—	—	Sarah Knight William Reed
110	Net shop	Carew Davies Gilbert	—	—	Sarah Knight James Allchorn, senior Samuel Tutt
111	Herring dees	Carew Davies Gilbert	—	—	Henry Longhurst Daniel Dunbrell Joseph Carter
112	Stabling and premises	Carew Davies Gilbert	—	—	Henry Longhurst Daniel Dunbrell John Moss
113	Foreshore	Carew Davies Gilbert			
115	Cottage and premises	Carew Davies Gilbert	—	—	Thomas Prodger
116	Coastguard station	Carew Davies Gilbert	—	—	Lords Commissioners of the Admiralty
117	Coastguard, boathouse, and premises	Carew Davies Gilbert	—	—	Lords Commissioners of the Admiralty
118	Stable, coachhouse, loft, and premises	Carew Davies Gilbert	—	—	Carew Davies Gilbert
119	Net shop	Carew Davies Gilbert	—	—	George Hide, junior
120	Net shop	Carew Davies Gilbert	—	—	George Hide, senior
121	Stable, coachhouse, loft, and premises	Carew Davies Gilbert	—	—	Charles Barnes William Bradford
122	Herring dees	Carew Davies Gilbert	—	—	John Thomas Mitchell
123	Stable, coachhouse, loft, and premises	Carew Davies Gilbert	—	—	Norton Stevenson George Stevenson
124	Cottage, yard, workshop, herring dees, stabling, and premises	Carew Davies Gilbert	—	—	William Pearson
125	Workshop, yard, and premises	Carew Davies Gilbert	—	—	Thomas Samby
126	Workshop, stabling, yard, and premises	Carew Davies Gilbert	—	—	Thomas Bennett
127	Stabling, coachhouses, yard, and premises	Carew Davies Gilbert	—	—	Freeman Amos

Eastbourne Local Board.

Parish of Eastbourne—*continued*.

No. on Plan.	Description of Property.	Owners or Reputed Owners.	Lessees or Reputed Lessees.		Occupiers.
128	Workshop, yard, and premises	Carew Davies Gilbert	—	—	James Humby
129	Smithy, yard, and premises	Carew Davies Gilbert	—	—	William Bannister
130	Workshop, yard, and premises	Carew Davies Gilbert	—	—	Edwin Butcher
131	Cottage, workshop, stabling, yard, and premises	Carew Davies Gilbert	—	—	Charles Teucher
132	Stable, coachhouse, yard, and premises	Carew Davies Gilbert	—	—	Charles Teucher Henry Wariner
133	Herring dees, yard, and premises	Carew Davies Gilbert	—	—	Charles Teucher Henry Longhurst
134	Stabling, yard, and premises	Carew Davies Gilbert	—	—	Charles Teucher John Stubberfield
135	Cottage, garden, yard, and premises	Carew Davies Gilbert	—	—	James Wymark
136	Cottage, garden, yard, and premises	Carew Davies Gilbert	—	—	Ceasar Mitchell
137	Cottage, garden, yard, and premises	Carew Davies Gilbert	—	—	James Allchorn
138	Cottage, garden, yard, and premises	Carew Davies Gilbert	—	—	George Hide
139	Net shop	Carew Davies Gilbert	—	—	Reuben Wood
140	Net shop	Carew Davies Gilbert	—	—	Samuel Wood
141	Stables and premises	Carew Davies Gilbert	—	—	Charles Banks
142	Net shop	Carew Davies Gilbert	—	—	William Waymark
143	Net shop	Carew Davies Gilbert	—	—	Richard Hide
144	Net shop	Carew Davies Gilbert	—	—	Daniel Waymark
145	Net shop	Carew Davies Gilbert	—	—	Samuel Carter
146	Net shop	Carew Davies Gilbert	—	—	James Collins
147	Net shop	Carew Davies Gilbert	—	—	William Waymark
148	Net shop	Carew Davies Gilbert	—	—	Thomas Sayer
149	Net shop	Carew Davies Gilbert	—	—	William Moon
150	Net shop	Carew Davies Gilbert	—	—	Harry Hurd

Eastbourne Local Board.

Parish of Eastbourne—*continued*.

No. on Plan.	Description of Property.	Owners or Reputed Owners.	Lessees or Reputed Lessees.		Occupiers.
151	Net shop	Carew Davies Gilbert	—	—	William Jackson
15!	Net shop	Carew Davies Gilbert	—	—	George Gausden
153	Net shop	Carew Davies Gilbert	—	—	John Reed
154	Boathouse	Carew Davies Gilbert	—	—	George Gausden
155	Net shop	Carew Davies Gilbert	—	—	Joseph Huggett
156	Net shop	Carew Davies Gilbert	—	—	George Parks
157	Net shop	Carew Davies Gilbert	—	—	Allen Sayers
158	Herring dees	Carew Davies Gilbert	—	—	John Collins
159	Net shop	Carew Davies Gilbert	..	—	George Parks
160	Net shop	Carew Davies Gilbert	—	—	James Swain
161	Net shop	Carew Davies Gilbert	—	—	William Erridge
162	Net shop	Carew Davies Gilbert	—	—	Dennis Breach
163	Net shop	Carew Davies Gilbert	—	—	Joseph Mockett
164	Net shop	Carew Davies Gilbert	—	—	James Allchorn
165	Net shop	Carew Davies Gilbert	—	—	James Bonniface
166	Net shop	Carew Davies Gilbert	—	—	Samuel Olive
167	Net shop	Carew Davies Gilbert	—	—	George Waymark
168	Net shop	Carew Davies Gilbert	—	—	Richard Wood
169	Net shop	War Department Duke of Devonshire Carew Davies Gilbert	—	—	James Bonniface
170	Net shop	War Department Duke of Devonshire Carew Davies Gilbert	—	—	Benjamin Hide
171	Foreshore	War Department Duke of Devonshire			

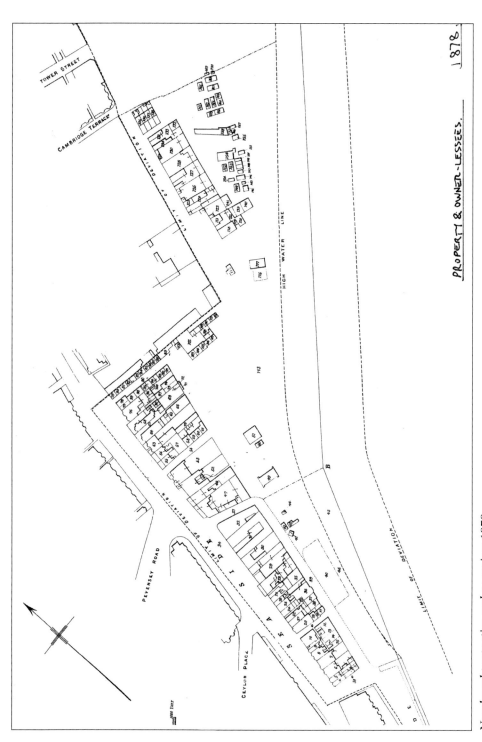

Numbered properties and occupiers 1878.

The Bill would include, amongst other powers, the power to evict persons from the foreshore. Was this the fishermen's lot? Not without a fight. The fishermen organised themselves under the leadership of George 'Pincher' Hide, a public subscription being raised. Mr Granville Somerset, Queens Counsel and Mr Trust, Civil Engineer would represent them, giving their services free.

June 1879.

At the hearing at the House of Lords on Tuesday 17th June 1879, the 'Eastbourne Improvement Bill' came before a Select Committee made up of Lords of the Realm with Earl Bellmore as Chairman.

Mr O' Hara Q.C. and Mr Littler Q.C. represented the Local Board, supported by Mr G A Wallis C.E. and Mr Ingleman C.E. Representing the fishermen were Mr Granville Somerset Q.C. and George 'Dot' Hide along with his son George Merrick 'Pincher' Hide, they fought the corner for the Eastbourne fishermen, on a principle that they be allowed to stay on the 'Stade' Fishing Station where the fishermen of Eastbourne had been settled for centuries.

Mr Littler Q.C. opened the case on behalf of the Local Board and objected to the 'locus standi' of the fishermen. Mr Granville Somerset was then heard in support of the 'locus standi' of the Eastbourne fishermen. Their Lordships having consulted, agreed the fishermen had a 'locus standi'.

Mr G.A Wallis, Civil Engineer, for the Local Board said he had designed and built the sea wall west of the pier (Grand Parade) for the Duke of Devonshire and that the eastern end could only be properly protected by a sea wall. When there was a high tide with strong winds there was a great danger of flooding to the east end. The Waterworks were situated about three quarters of a mile away and he believed a flooding of sea would seriously pollute the well. He thought the land to the east of the Great Redoubt would be quite suitable for the fishermen. In the last 2 years the land to the east of the Great Redoubt had commenced to be laid out by the Duke of Devonshire and Mr Gilbert. Some of the fishermen had purchased some of the sites and built houses there. So they would be ideally placed for the Fishing Station east of the Great Redoubt.

Cross examined by Mr Granville Somerset Q.C. Mr Wallis said, it was proposed to build a sea wall in continuation from the present Marine Parade in a curve to the Great Redoubt. The part in the centre was occupied by the fishermen. Now with the encroachment of the sea the fishermen were placed in difficulty with getting their boats in and out. Twenty years ago the fishermen were fairly well placed but now with the encroachment they had been obliged to move their capstans inland to make their boats safe. He added that he had never been told whether the fishermen paid rent to Mr Gilbert and he had never been told they did not. The fishermen had never applied for land east of the Great Redoubt, but he supposed they would have the same power as where they were now. He continued to say, the local residents had petitioned the Local Board time and time again to protect them from the sea. He said it was not true the Local Board in taking power to build a sea wall were carrying out a building scheme. To develop would recoup the cost of building the sea wall.

For the fishermen Mr Granville Somerset called Mr Trust, Civil Engineer, who said he had considerable experience in construction of sea works, but he had always acted rather as a consulting than practical engineer. He thought there was no good anchorage east of the Great Redoubt and if boats had to land there they would be in great danger. He had come there to give evidence without a fee or reward, and had formed his opinion only after mature consideration. He was well known in his profession and had a number of clients. He went on to say, while the sea had made encroachments, at the same time large portions of the beach had been carted away to build with and to make roads. The idea was to make a Grand Parade to the east. If done it would deprive the fishermen of their livelihood. In his opinion the sea wall was not necessary, good groynes would protect the foreshore. The Grand Parade to the west was not necessary to keep the sea at bay, but built to the advantage of the Duke of Devonshire and his tenants. It was an ornamental cliff faced with a sea wall and not built because there was necessity for it.

George Hide, fisherman of Eastbourne for the petitioner, said he had saved 50 persons from drowning and was the father of a large family having 26 grandchildren. He did not pay either rent or tithe and hoped he would not have to do so. All the people in his own trade of fisherman were of the same opinion and did not want to move. About £30,000 was invested in the fishing trade and the annual yield was about £20,000. This was divided among about 400 hands. He remembered the putting down of groynes but they had not done their duty. They had however, done some good as they had recovered a sufficiency of ground to build a town on. There was nothing but certain destruction ahead for fishermen if they must come east of the Great Redoubt.

Cross-examined; he said he had no landlord but Mr Gilbert gave permission to keep his nets in a house on the beach. There were 200 owners of boats in Eastbourne, but he could not say why only 60 owners had signed the petition against the Bill, perhaps some were away fishing. It was quite true that most of them got their living by fishing on the coast and sometimes a long way from Eastbourne. It was certainly unsafe to anchor boats east of the Great Redoubt. If they went to the east of the Great Redoubt it would be certain death as the sea breakers there were 3 times heavier than the place now occupied. Their forefathers selected the place they now occupied because it was more sheltered than any other by Beachy Head.

George 'Pincher' Hide son of the last witness agreeing with the statement of his father, said that long experience had confirmed him in the impression that landing beyond the Great Redoubt would be dangerous. Mr Granville Somerset Q.C. then addressed the Committee on behalf of the petitioners. Then Mr Littler Q.C. for the promoters of the Bill.

Earl Bellmore summing up said the Committee approved the Bill on the understanding that on clauses being brought up tomorrow, the case of the fishermen would be considered.

The next day, the case of the petitioners was further considered and ultimately dismissed. So that was that, after centuries the fisher folk of Eastbourne would have to leave the ancient 'Stade'.

A letter to the Eastbourne Chronicle 21st June, 1879, pleaded for the fishermen, after the passing of the 'Eastbourne Improvement Act' of the effect it will have on them, some of the oldest and hard working of the inhabitants.

'Hundreds of years before Eastbourne was thought of as a 'Watering' place they made the 'Stade' there own and now were being thrown off, losing their ancient rights'.

The editorial of the above paper stated it

'thought the case for the fishermen was not put well by the fishermen's legal representatives. Praises were sung of George Hide Snr. and George Jnr. as two good representatives of their class, 'toilers of the sea'. It was a feather in the cap of Eastbourne that its fishermen can be represented before a House of Lords Committee'.

The newspaper hoped the move would not be too bad and the land east of the Great Redoubt would be well adapted for them. The foreshore and land east of the Great Redoubt belonged to the Duke of Devonshire, Mr Gilbert and the Government.

28th June 1879.

A letter called for the fishermen to be compensated and assisted in their moving to another site. The fishermen had lost the day, but how else could it have gone at the House of Lords the Duke of Devonshire being an incumbent and a senior Duke?

Mr Gilbert was the biggest landowner of the proposed sea wall site at that time. George and Mary Ann Hide and others would lose their homes on the shingle beach as a result of the new sea wall. The development no doubt hastened the death of 'Dot' putting him in an early grave. He died in 1882, aged 68 years, two years before the sea wall was completed.

Extract from 'Eastbourne Recollections'. By R J Graham, J P. (Lived in Eastbourne from 1825, book written in 1888).

'Major (that's his Christian name) Vidler, in the 1800's, superintended the building of the Martello Towers on the coast and in later life held office under the Commissioners of Levels, looking after the drainage and protection of the Pevensey levels. In discharge of his duty he thought little of the town of Eastbourne in comparison with the safety of the Levels and he carried out a theory, which was very destructive to the town. In my recollection there was an extent of beach in front of the Sea

To _Mr John Hide_

of _____

Eastbourne in the County of Sussex.

Take Notice, that the Eastbourne Local Board hereby require you to remove forthwith the boats, tackle, and all other effects belonging to you now being upon the beach land situate at or near the Marine Parade, in the parish of Eastbourne, in the County of Sussex, and which said land the said Local Board are authorized by the Eastbourne Improvement Act, 1879, to take for the purpose of constructing a Sea wall, public road, and for other purposes.

And further Take Notice, that if your boats, tackle or other effects whatsoever remain upon the said beach land after the expiration of twenty-four hours from the service of this notice upon you, the said Local Board will remove the same, and will not hold themselves responsible for any damage that may be thereby occasioned.

Dated this ____ day of May, 1880.

D V Campion Coles.

Clerk to the Eastbourne Local Board.

John Hide's notice to quit original Fishing Station, June 1880.

August 1880, the 'William and Mary' replaced the 'Mary Stirling' lifeboat and is seen here laying across the Sea Wall contractor's rail track with the following crew aboard. Left to right, Cox'n. Joseph 'Joker' Huggett, Sailor Mitchell, Tom Sayers, John Reed, Edwin 'Lord' Matthews, Billy Stanbridge, 'Smuggler' Erridge, Billy Matthews, Alleyn Sayers, Jimmy Swain, Jesse Huggett, John Hurd, Bowman, Charles 'Bones' Hide.

1879 Fishing Station area before the Sea Wall and Royal Parade built. To left is Marine Parade. In the centre can be seen the Lifeboat house with spired turret, now much altered in Marine Road.

Houses, now called Marine Parade, over which the sea never broke, boats laid up there and capstans stood in security. At that place there were well planked up groynes. These planks Vidler persisted in removing on the plea that the beach shingle should be allowed to travel on to make an embankment at the Levels. The natural result has been a continuous encroachment of the sea upon the town till at length, it has been necessary to build a sea wall'. (So Major Vidler was the cause of the problem?)

The 'Eastbourne Improvement Act'. became enacted on 3rd July 1879.

The Local Board employed a Glasgow contractor John Jackson, to build the new sea wall at a cost of £19,000, and promised to have the ground ready for him in June 1880.

April 1880.

Preliminary work of a general nature started in April 1880, but the fishermen were in no hurry to vacate from a place that had been theirs for centuries. Capstans, boats, tackle, nets and all kinds of gear requisite of their trade had to be got up and moved. Indeed their lack of haste brought about the issuing of an order on 8th June, from the Local Board through their Clerk, Mr Campion Coles, against the fishermen, to remove their boats, tackle etc, forthwith or face the consequences of the Board removing same without responsibility. John Hide, eldest son of George 'Dot' Hide, received such an order. The document has survived. The Local Board were also involved in an action with Mr Gilbert who was claiming £100,000 for his rights to land on the foreshore. The arbitration to which the matter had been referred reduced the claim to £13,000.

The fishermen were in no hurry to move and on 5th July 1880, a memorial was presented to the Local Board by boat owners, net owners and fishermen, stating they were under 24 hours notice to quit the foreshore with their tackle and boats to make way for the sea wall. They stated they had had the right to use the foreshore for generations and they were in humble circumstances and asked the Board if it could see its way to granting them compensation towards their enforced move. Mr Simmons, a Board member said, as it was the Boards action that caused the removal of the fishermen from their quarters, the Board ought to consider what could be done. John Hide who received his order to quit on 8th June obviously had ignored the order, hoping for compensation?

August 1880.

The Eastbourne lifeboat 'Mary Stirling' was replaced by a new boat the 'William and Mary' and housed in the Boathouse (Marine Road).

As work progressed on the new sea wall antagonism grew between the fishermen and the contractor's workers. The contractors had laid a railway track from Marine Parade out to the Crumbles some 1½ miles in length. It was to enable a steam locomotive pulling trucks filled with shingle to build up the foreshore as foundation for the sea wall. (Today one can see the definite slope of the Royal Parade down to Seaside, Cambridge and St Aubyns roads as examples).

Whilst the contractors were on site the fishermen continued fishing off the beach and laying up their boats over and around the railway track causing problems to the contractor. The usual course of events was, the contractor told the fishermen what time the steam locomotive would be coming through, and to move their boats accordingly. This worked after a fashion, but was an inconvenience for the fishermen and everybody. Imagine when the tide was wrong for going off fishing, or weather inclement. Obviously the fishermen did not want to move. It brings to mind again, the old Sussex saying 'we wont be druv'.

November 1880.

Work progressed slowly during the summer and into the autumn with things coming to head on Monday 15th November when the fishing Lugger 'Little Mackerel' owned by James Boniface was laying across the railway track and was run into by the locomotive.

At 7.00am that day the fishermen were told by the Clerk of the Works, a Mr Wilkinson to move the boat off the track. (The week before the Town Crier had in fact been summoned by the Local Board to declare to the fishermen that their boats must be kept off the track at all times). With much forbearance Mr Wilkinson delayed the start of the locomotive until 9.00am. No effort was made to move the boat. Mr Wilkinson on the instructions of Mr Tomes the Local Board's surveyor, then gave the order to the driver of the locomotive to start up and run the boat down. This was done, but just prior to this fisherman James Boniface was alleged to have thrown a piece of timber across the track in front of the locomotive. It was pushed to one side by the locomotive that continued and ran into the boat damaging it. It was alleged that Boniface then jumped up on the locomotive and assaulted Mr Wilkinson. Then other fishermen there began tearing up the rail track, some 70 yards in length. Boniface was arrested and held in custody and on 20th November, he appeared before the Magistrates charged with 'Obstructing a Railway' (a serious offence, life imprisonment maximum) and assault on Wilkinson. Mr Campion Coles prosecuted with Mr Edgeworth defending. After some 2 hours of legal argument and hearing the alleged facts, Boniface was committed on bail to appear at the next Assizes.

January 1881.

On Wednesday 26th January 1881, at Lewes Assizes before Judge Justice Lindley, James Boniface appeared on the two indictments. Mr Merrifield Q.C. prosecuting, Mr Gill Q.C. for Boniface. It was only a short time after Mr Merrifield had been outlining the case against Boniface that the Judge stopped the case and said, he felt the prosecution should never have been brought and directed the jury to bring in a Not Guilty verdict. He said it was a case in which both parties had extreme views of their rights. The contractor had no right to run into the boat, but it did not follow that the fisherman was justified in placing an obstruction on the track. Boniface was accordingly released.

James Boniface later sued the Local Board and the contractor for false imprisonment, and in July 1881, at Lewes Assizes, Boniface was awarded £70 plus costs against the Local Board and £80 against the contractor for damage to his boat. One imagines James Boniface really did have a 'Bonny' face!

Because of all the problems, the contractor John Jackson made a claim for compensation against the Local Board. He blamed the Board for failing to clear the site as promised prior to his commencing work on the new sea wall and this failure

Edward Boniface. (1862-1915)

Possibly, James Boniface (1818- 1919) Wife Sarah (nee Shoesmith) (1837-1908) with daughter Frances Margaret (born 1864).

had brought about increased costs. The fishermen should have been moved, but they were not. The Board had not agreed for them to use the foreshore east of the Redoubt and of course the fishermen were very reluctant to do so and had requested compensation to move. The Local Board had promised the site would be cleared ready for the contractor, a lot of sympathy lay with the fishermen.

February 1881.

On Thursday 24th February 1881 at the Vestry, the claim went to arbitration and was heard by Mr Lloyd, Civil Engineer. 'Jackson v Local Board' Mr Jackson was claiming £3,000. At the hearing Mr Wilkinson, Clerk of the Works, gave an account of how the contractor had been obstructed by capstans and chains for drawing boats over the railway track. He had told Mr Tomes the Board's surveyor, who in turn advised him on several occasions to 'run into the boats'. Mr Tomes came down on one occasion with some horses and men and cleared the boats off the track. Mr Tomes had offered Hide, a fisherman, £10 to remove, but Hide said he wouldn't take less than £100. It was through Mr Tomes' advice that he did eventually run into a boat. Three witnesses Fred Bollard Hide, William Bollard Hide and William Reed a ginger beer seller, said they had heard Mr Tomes tell Mr Wilkinson to run into the boat.

Mr Jackson gave evidence that he pressed the Board to enable him to take possession of the site to start the sea wall in April 1880. Mr Tomes told him to start and to get his plant on site. It had originally been planned to build up the site with chalk from the west end at Holywell, but he was told by the Board that this would cause too much damage to the road, so eventually it was decided to infill with shingle, hence the railway track, but at much greater cost, 3 times in fact. But all this time without full possession of the site the work could not be done. Mr Jackson claimed compensation for having to pay wages when work could not be done. He could not estimate the cost to a £1 but can safely say the labour has cost half as much again than it would have done under normal conditions. There were Christy Minstrels about the site along with a Banjo man and Red Indians.

The hearing continued next day and the facts arose again about the fishermen being on the site. While the fishermen now had no legal right to be on their old Fishing Station public sympathy was with them. It was said that in July 1879, 500 feet of foreshore had been cleared for them east of the Great Redoubt but no fishing boats had landed there. In reply the fishermen said that no date had ever been made available to them by the Duke of Devonshire or Mr Gilbert to move, so they had continued using their old ground.

George 'Dot' Hide was called and stated that when the Eastbourne men went out fishing they landed their fish at Eastbourne not at Hasting. (Someone had suggested they land at Hastings thus leaving the Eastbourne fishing station clear). He said he had an interest in 5 or 6 capstans. The walled in one, at present was used for pleasure boats and he paid a small rent to the Duke of Devonshire for that one, but nothing for the others. He had lived on the Fishing Station all his life. He had attended the hearing by subpoena. Yes, notice had been served on him by the Board for the removal of his boats and capstans. He had paid a ground rent to Mr Gilbert for his Net shops. It was then agreed that in the case of Net shop holders' compensation was an entitlement.

On through Saturday the hearing continued, the Board saying that Mr Jackson had sufficient room on the foreshore with the fishermen also there and work should not have got behind. Local Board witness Mr Schmidt, said he was on the beach when possession of the western end was given to the contractor on 1st June 1880. Mr Tomes was also there. He saw two boats removed. Mr Tomes and himself asked Mr Wilkinson whether that place was satisfactorily cleared Wilkinson had replied, 'Entirely so'. Wilkinson was also asked if he wished Hide's capstans removed. He said not. He did not want any other boats removed being satisfied with the space he had.

With the fishing boats away at sea during the good weather work could continue, but later in October- November there were more boats ashore due to the bad weather and poor fishing conditions. (No wonder Boniface and the other fishermen did not want to move their boats)

Giving evidence Mr G A Wallis Civil Engineer, Local Board member, gave his opinion on building the sea wall, stating he had carried out the whole of the sea wall work to the Wish Tower stating he had done satisfactory work himself in reclamation of land, indeed the houses on the way to the Devonshire Park being built on land reclaimed by himself.

Mr Wills for Jackson, asked Wallis about the fishermen having no place to go. Wallis said they, the fishermen, had been negotiating for a site east of the Great Redoubt, the land belonging to Mr Gilbert and the Duke of Devonshire. The Local Board had taken no action to find the fishermen a place. In further questioning of Mr Wallis it transpired that the Local Board had bought the land of Mr Gilbert's outright so Mr Jackson could have been given uninterrupted possession. Mr Wallis considered he had, but added the public also had access to the sea and when work

Construction work on the Sea wall and Royal Parade C.1880.

is finished the public will have the right to access. Asked if the fishermen would also, he replied, they would find it more advantageous to go elsewhere.

Mr Wills for Jackson criticised the Local Board for not clearing the land for Mr Jackson and for not dealing with the difficulties of the fishermen who had to get off the land. Wallis said it was not their business to do so, going on to say it was Mr Gilbert's place to do so.

View from the Great Redoubt of Royal Parade development C.1880. Note the laundry drying on the beach. Laundry was a big industry at that end of the town among the fisher folk women. The light coloured building just right of centre is 'The Victoria Hotel'.

(So it transpires that the fishermen were ignored by the Local Board and had to make their own arrangements for land east of the Great Redoubt. It was the Board that raised the 'Improvements Act', knowing full well that fishermen would have to go) The hearing finished that Saturday evening.

March 1881.

On 30th March 1881, the Eastbourne Gazette published the result of the arbitration case. It found for Mr Jackson and the Local Board had to pay him a total of £1,074. 10s 0d. made up of loss of wages, plant laying idle etc.

The Arbitrator, Mr Lloyd, was very critical of the Local Board in regard to the local fishermen saying,

'They (the Board) knew that if such a sea wall were erected at that particular place the fishermen who had been using the place since time immemorial, whose fathers before them were there in undisturbed and unmolested possession at the time when Eastbourne was a fishing village, would be obliged to quit and build their huts elsewhere. The Local Board saw all this, but they had not have the spirit to tell the fishermen to go away, in a craven hearted manner, a manner justly termed undignified and unworthy of a Board like that of Eastbourne. They said, let the contractor deal with the fishermen. Let him bear the onus of clearing the ground. Say nothing to him about the fishermen at all. Let him find it all out for himself. Let him do our dirty work, for we do not want to be too hard on our friends, the fishermen, or to be put to too much expense by them' and so Mr Lloyd went on, and because of the Board's attitude the piscatorial fraternity (fishermen) had become firm friends of the contractor, after being sworn enemies.

(One could consider that the Local Board being made up of gentlemen of private means, professional, business men and landowners they felt that the Fishing Station did not fit in with their image of an Eastbourne that was known as the 'Empress of Watering Places'? Indeed at a Vestry meeting in 1879 the minutes show the following comment *'The east end was an inferior part of the Town and being such a fine place the east end needed bringing up to status').*

A 'monumental' telling off and so it should have been. It was quite disgusting the way the fishermen were treated. Stories have come through of being done out of their rights and property. Maybe one can see that there is some truth in the stories. George Hide had said he had *'no landlord and paid no tithes'* points to the fact that the waste where the fishermen lived and fished was 'Waste' until being 'shared' between the Duke of Devonshire and Mr Gilbert and even after the Waste was taken over in 1850, George Hide and the fishermen with cottages on the Waste, paid no rents or tithes for them. The Net shops and capstans were built by the fishermen themselves and a rent was paid to Mr Gilbert after 1850 for some of them. In fact no charges had ever been made for the use of those capstans built on the ancient Stade by the Lords of the Manors of Eastbourne back in the 1700's. From those days it would appear that the fishermen and certainly George Hide had built their own capstans and Net shops and as we know paid no rents nor tithes.

The 1881 census shows a total of 98 Fishermen, Boatmen and associated occupations.

Claims for compensation were made by the fishermen whose families had occupied the Fishing Station (ancient Stade) for many years before the Duke and Mr Gilbert had shared out the Waste/Crumbles between themselves and were not returned as lessees or occupiers of Mr Gilbert's land (they had never paid rent nor tithe). The list of claims gives the names of fishermen, description of property and amount claimed. Research to date does not show whether Mr Gilbert or the Board met claims. Another interesting claim was that of Joseph Mockett, landlord of the 'Ocean Wave' Pub. A plan shows where he had undisturbed possession of an area of beach for his big pleasure sailing yacht 'Skylark' and other boats and capstan for some 20 years, 1861 - 1881 and possibly back to 1830.

It would be in the interest of Mr Gilbert and the Duke to cede land east of the Great Redoubt if no compensation were to be paid to the fishermen, this would surely be a softener?

April 1881.

In April 1881, the Local Board offered the fishermen a total of £600 to move 'bag and baggage' off the Fishing Station foreshore required for the sea wall. The Board had been reluctant to offer any compensation as they felt since the House of Lords case when the fishermen lost the day, that if they offered the fishermen any compensation to move they (the Board) would be acknowledging the fishermen had rights to the foreshore.

Late April 1881 saw the fishermen moving with all possible speed. Mr Insoll the Duke of Devonshire's agent was down on the beach arranging new quarters for the fishermen east of the Great Redoubt. The Duke and Mr Gilbert having agreed to let the fishermen have the land and in May agreements of tenancy were drawn up by Mr Gilbert with the fishermen.

The Eastbourne Improvement Act 1879

A List of Claims by parties not returned as Lessees or Occupiers by C. D. Gilbert Esquire.

Name	Description of Property		Amount of Claim £ d
Allchorn, James	Large Capstan and Prop .. 200	Shop 50	250
ditto	Large Capstan and Prop .. 200	Shop 100	300
Allchorn, Samuel	Shop, Net		40
Allchorn, Samuel & Henry	Small Capstan and Prop		30
Bennett, Thomas	Capstan and Prop		30
Boniface, James	Large Capstan and Prop . 200	Small ditto 25 / Shop, Net 50 / Shop, Rope 10	285
Breach, Dennis	Capstan and Prop 30	Shop 50	80
Brown, William	Shop		140
Dennis, Alfred & Waymark, Daniel	Shop, Net 200	Small Shop in rear 10	210
Gausden, George	Two Capstans and Prop 250	Shop, Net 120 / Shop, Boat-building 150 / Removal of Boats & Gear 50	550
Hide, George, Senior	Capstan and Prop, Shops share in, Ship "Excel" 3 small Boats Nets Tackle and Gear		1500
Hide, George	Shop 20	Capstan and Prop 30 / Shop 25 / Capstan and Prop 30	105
Hide, Benjamin, and Charles & Hide John	Large Capstan and Prop	Small ditto 30 / Shop 20	250
Huggett, Joseph	Shop 100	Capstan Chain and 3 Props 100 / Boats, 2 sets of Sails & Anchor, Herring Nets, 16 Mackerel Nets, Ropes, Drew Net, Ropes, Oyster bridges Ropes & Crank Drew Net, Sea Boat Nets £4224	4224
		Carried forward £	4524

Fishermen's compensation claims against Mr Gilbert C.1880.

Name	Description of Property		Brought forward £ 4524
Jackson, William	Capstan and Prop 30	Shop 35	65
Knight, Sarah	Two Shops, Herring etc, Selinghurst Tanhouse & Yard		350
Parkes, George	Large Capstan and Prop 200	Shop, Net 40	240
Reed, John	Shop		50
Sayers, Walter	Capstan and Prop, Removal of Boats, Nets & Gear		135
Swann, James	Capstan and Shop		60
Waymark, William	Capstan and Prop		30
Waymark, George	Shop		100
Waymark, Daniel & Wood, Richard	Large Capstan and Prop		200
Wood, Reuben	Net shop, drying-house Stable	Capstan and two Props	300
Wood, Richard	Shop		100
Wood, Samuel	Capstan and Prop		30
		£	6184

So the move was made to the new Fishing Station, the Net shops and capstans again being built by the fishermen themselves and in 1885 when another Eastbourne Improvement Act came into being all future tenancy agreements would be with the Town Council.

Some of the fishermen of Eastbourne said that the Duke and Mr Gilbert gave the present Fishing Station land to the fishermen forever but, the land was conveyed to the Town Council at the time. This extract is from 'Municipal Eastbourne' by H W Fovargue, Town Clerk stated:

Fishing Station. - 'The extension of the Royal Parade which was necessary in connection with the reclamation of the foreshore and the construction of the sea wall, involved the removal of the original Fishing Station. The Duke of Devonshire and Mr Gilbert conveyed the site of the present Fishing Station east of the Great Redoubt, to the Corporation for the use of the Fishermen at the respective price of 10s 0d and £100'.

Further research into the question of the fishermen's rights revealed that on Monday May 4th 1885, a meeting of the Town Council took place at the New Hall, Seaside Road, (the Town Hall not yet completed) with regard to the Fishing Station. Items discussed were the draft agreement to be signed by the Duke of Devonshire, Mr Gilbert and the Corporation, an agreement related

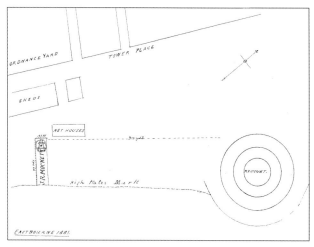

Joseph R Mockett's capstan and his 'Skylark' pleasure yacht stand. 1830-1900.

to sums of money (previously shown) and an agreement, which gave the Corporation the Fishing Station land for ever. A good agreement in favour of the Corporation. The Duke of Devonshire and Mr Gilbert undertook to give the land east of the Redoubt to the Corporation, and agreed to pay one third of the costs for erection of groynes and to protect and maintain the groynes for up to 5 years after agreement. They also undertook to give £1,000 each.

The land/foreshore was granted with the condition it was to be used as a Fishing Station only. The land and money was given to the Corporation in order that the fishermen should have a fishing site forever. No sea wall should ever be built there and such provision should be entered in the agreement in black and white. The land was to be granted to the Corporation so long as it was occupied by fishermen.

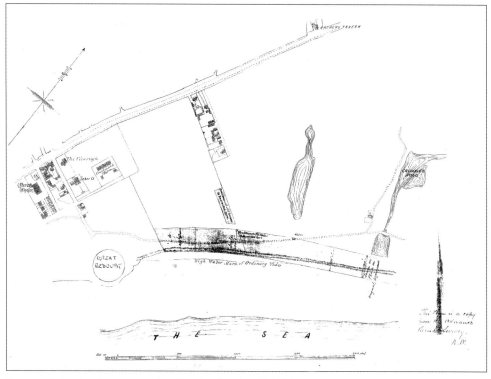

Proposed site for the present day Fishing Station C.1880.

The chairman of the meeting the Mayor, G.A. Wallis, said, *'The object is to protect the fishermen, and so long as Eastbourne is by the sea, there will always be fishermen here in Eastbourne'*. (That is a different approach from him after all he did to get the fishermen thrown off their ancient site)

The agreement would state that the Corporation could not erect any buildings on the land other than capstans, boathouses or places of reception for storage of nets and other fishing gear. The agreement to be included in the Eastbourne Improvements Bill 1885. Mr G Wallis also said, *'While there is a single fishermen left, the land cannot be used for any other purpose than a Fishing Station'*.

It was felt the Duke and Mr Gilbert wanted to see a major fishing industry established in Eastbourne and in later years of the 1880's it did seem this might happen.

Eastbourne Gazette 19th August 1885.

'On Friday, 14th August 1885, at the Marine Hotel, Seaside, there took place a ceremony long remembered by those engaged in the fishing industry of Eastbourne. There was a large attendance of fishermen who had assembled to receive from Mr W. Kirkland, Mr Gausden, Mr J Vine, Mr J Hurst, and other members of the Town committee connected with the Eastbourne Improvement Act, the legal documents, plans etc, conveying to them from the Duke of Devonshire and Mr Gilbert, the ground now occupied by them, to be used as a Fishing Station for ever. William Brown, one of the oldest fishermen presided. Mr Kirkland explained the legal points contained in the documents in question and expressed the great pleasure etc in

Eastbourne Fishermen and Boatmen. William Brown is seen on extreme right. Others left to right, ? Brown, Richard John Erridge, ? Erridge.

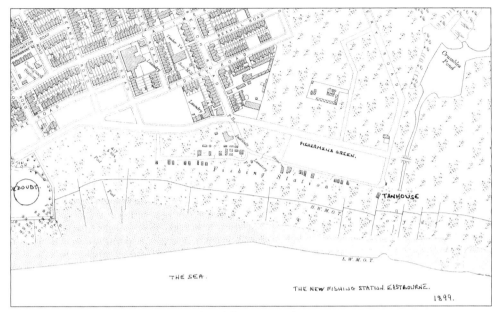

Plan of Fishing Station 1899. Reproduced from an Ordnance Survey map 1899.

performing this duty. William Brown acknowledged the great benefit bestowed on the fishermen and thanked everyone concerned, with a special thanks to the Mayor Mr Wallis, who had exerted his influence on behalf of the fishermen'.

The Eastbourne Improvement Act 1885, received the Royal Assent on 6th August 1885.

'Schedule 3 of the above Act deals with the granting of land by the Duke and Mr Gilbert to the Eastbourne Corporation for the use of a Fishing Station for the fishermen of Eastbourne and the Corporation to have the power to let the land to the fishermen at such rent and on such terms and conditions as they from time to time think fit. If at any time the land shall cease to be used for the purposes of fishing it shall revert back to grantors (Duke of Devonshire and Mr Gilbert) or their respective sequels in estate.

The Corporation shall not, except with the written consent of the grantors or their respective sequels in estate, at any time erect any building on the Fishing Station other than capstans, boathouses sheds or places of reception and storage of nets and other fishing gear.

The Corporation shall not, except with the consent of the grantors or their respective sequels in estate, construct a sea wall or any works on the foreshore other than groynes'.

So we see all that was discussed at the meeting on 4th May, come to be and the fishermen would have a Fishing Station for as long as fishermen fished from the Fishing Station. The land for the Fishing Station was never given to the fishermen but to the Corporation for the use of the fishermen and is still the case today. Obviously as fishing has decreased over the years, so has the land for its use. Land sites previously used by the fishermen for net drying, net repairs, boat maintenance etc, now controlled by the Council are, the Redoubt bowling green, Treasure Island pleasure ground and car park. The Putting green, and land across the road now part of a row of gabled terraced houses. The tennis courts area and adjacent car park, which used to be 'Fisherman's Green' once a playing field for the use of the fishermen.

Building their own Net shops and capstans and paying only a nominal rent to the Council the constructions lasted many years until c.1960-70 when the Fishing Station had fallen into a somewhat dilapidated state and the Council with the agreement of the then fishermen, pulled down the Net shops and erected the present day Net shops, a few which today are functioning as in days of old. With the Marina/Harbour being fully operational and accommodating fishing boats, the day may well come when the Fishing Station is no more.

So back to the year 1881 and a report that the last capstan had been removed on Friday 29th April. The Net shops had been valued and Mr Jackson stated he would be ready to continue when the area was fully cleared.

7th May 1881.

A meeting of the Local Board stated £620 had been paid to the fishermen for removal of the capstans. But not shared fairly - as the 'battle' in the 'Ocean Wave', on 17th May, suggests.

14th May 1881.

The Local Board anxious in the interests of the Parish to get some return for the money laid out on the sea wall, proposed to erect 80 houses on the land, reckoning on a ground rent of £12 each. The Board would be in receipt of nearly £1,000 per annum, so that after a period of 25 years the Parish would have recompensed their outlay.

9th July 1881.

Mr Jackson causes concern by saying he was going to charge the Board for deterioration of Plant caused by the action of salt spray and for damage done to the Sea wall by the action of the sea.

6th August 1881.

The Local Board borrows £8,000 for the completion of the Sea wall.

The wrangling continued between the Local Board and Mr Jackson over the sea wall and finally Jackson ceased work on the sea wall towards the end of 1882 before the work was completed. 900 feet of the wall had been washed away. Jackson claimed insufficient protection had been afforded him blaming the lack of groynes, which should have been erected by the Board.

The Local Board on the other hand maintained that there was a breach of contract and that unless Mr Jackson proceeded with the work, they would complete the job themselves.

This threat was carried out wherein Jackson entered an action against the Board for damages. The case was taken before an Arbitrator, who awarded Jackson the sum of £1,600 subject to a point of law. The case was finally taken to the House of Lords, where judgement was given in favour of the Local Board, Mr Jackson having to pay all costs.

'Ocean Wave' Tower Place (now Latimer Road).

The Local Board which ran the Town lasted until November 1883, when it was superceded by a Mayor and Corporation - in other words by a Town Council under the 'Municipal Corporation Act. 1882'. The keystone of the new parade (Royal Parade) was laid by the first Mayor of Eastbourne Mr G A Wallis on 4th January 1884. The sea wall was finally completed on 11th February 1884 under the supervision of Mr Tomes Corporation surveyor.

Having moved to the east side of the Great Redoubt the fishermen were not happy and sent a memorial to the Council requesting it to consider the serious inconvenience they experienced in landing their boats east of the Great Redoubt, the beach there was also being used as bathing ground for gentlemen. They begged to be allowed to land their boats west of the Great Redoubt. But to no avail, they had to stay, so they quickly built their own Net shops and capstans and the area developed into a fine example of self-endeavour.

Battle in the 'Ocean Wave'.

1879. Original 'Stade' Fishing Station with Lugger 'XL' NN13 ashore. Centre group of fishermen shows George 'Pincher' Hide to the fore in dark clothes.

The building of the sea wall and Royal Parade only partly stopped the flooding of Seaside, as it flooded well into the 20th century and the loss of shingle beach increased especially on Marine Parade. We are told by a report of 1896 of the great loss there and up at Holywell, where some ten years previously (1886) there were great swathes of shingle all gone by 1896.

The interesting photograph of the original fishing station scene dated 1879, taken by G Row before the building of the Royal Parade, shows George 'Pincher' Hide. He is the dominant fisherman with the beard standing with the bow of Lugger NN13 behind. NN13 was owned by 'Pincher' and named 'X L'. She was built in 1877 and made her first voyage in 1878. A 1st class 20 ton Lugger by George Gausden, it can be seen she was a fine vessel and equipped to sail up to the North Sea after herring and cod and down Channel following the mackerel through to Ireland. It took a fair bit of finance to operate these Luggers being crewed by up to 7 men. The crew was paid by results. They all had a share of the catch and as understood the system was as follows, the owner had three shares the skipper two and the crew a share each. No fish no money!

The following is a report of the drowning of a crewmember of the Lugger "X L" in January 1880.

'The fishing community at Seaside were somewhat startled by the intelligence that George Cummins was drowned. It appears that about a quarter past six in the evening the "X L" NN.13 belonging to the Eastbourne fleet of fishing Luggers left the beach with the intention of proceeding to the Isle of Wight for the purpose of

mackerel fishing. There were seven hands on board, including the deceased and the skipper, Milton Carter. The boat was under sail and by twenty minutes to seven she had got a little on the other side of the Boulder bank to the west of the Pier, when Cummings came up from the fore cabin to take his watch.

It is thought he placed his foot on the gunwale and slipping he fell backwards into the water.

The skipper who was on deck at the time observed his disappearance, and speedily called the crew on deck. All looked for the body for some time, and although the boat was nearly becalmed, all endeavours to sight the unfortunate man were in vain. After the search had continued for some time the Lugger returned to the beach at Seaside, and the sad news was communicated to those on shore. The next morning several boats went out and the crew of one the 'Georgie', found the body floating near the place where he fell in. The crew in the 'Georgie' (Jones, Erridge, Simmons and Longley) had just shot their lines, when they observed something floating in the water, which turned out to be the body of the deceased.

The body was landed about a quarter to ten and at once conveyed to his home. The deceased was a widower, about 38 years of age, and leaves several children. The 'X L' is owned by George 'Pincher' Hide. It is thought by some the deceased had a fit and this idea is strengthened by the fact that the body had not sunk'.

At the inquest held at the Marine Inn, Seaside, the following evidence was forthcoming.

'*Richard Cummins brother to the deceased said, 'George was aged 40 years. He was a fisherman working on the Lugger 'X L'. I last saw him alive at 10 minutes to five on the Thursday evening'. Richard had come to bid him goodbye before he went to join his Lugger. George seemed alright and expected to be at sea for 14 days'.*

George Huggett a member of the crew, 'At ten to six in the evening I went on board and the deceased was already aboard. He was in good spirits when below and was laughing and talking as usual. After having his tea the deceased went up on deck and shortly after he heard the alarm from the Captain and went immediately on deck to be told that Cummins had gone overboard. They lit up some torches and searched for him. They were about a mile from the Pier the sea was dead calm'

Milton Carter, the captain of the 'X L' said, '*The deceased was on deck from the time the boat 'fleeted' until about half past six when he went below for his tea. On coming on deck later to take up first watch. He came along and was just going to sit beside me when he fell overboard. There was no noise. I sounded the alarm and lit the 'flares'. We searched for some ½ hour there was hardly a ripple on the sea. Cummins was not the worse for drink'.*

Joseph William Jones, a fisherman of 4, Marine Drove said, '*I went out in the 'Georgie' to search for the body of the deceased and found it about a mile from the Pier. It was after the Coastguard boat had been dragging. The body was floating head downwards. I do not know whether the sea boots filled with air would have the tendency to keep the head down and feet up*' Dennis Breach a member of the jury said, '*I have been overboard in sea boots and came up head first*'. A verdict of accidental drowning was brought in.

The deceased left 3 motherless children. A subscription was raised among the townsfolk to aid the orphans. Later that month a report appeared in the Eastbourne Gazette as result of an enquiry made by a person interested in the welfare of the orphaned children. It is as follows:

'They had since the death of their mother 11 years ago, been living with their grandparents 14, Manns Row, Seaside, Grandma being 66 years and Grandad 70 years. The late George Cummins had contributed to the household as best as he could but being away for weeks at a time fishing, meant he was unable to raise the children. It had been a struggle and would be more so now with his death. Manns Row was a very poor part of the town and the buildings in disrepair. They were inhabited mostly by fishing families. Of the three orphans Ada age 14 years had just been placed in service. George age 11 years had now moved to live with relatives in Croydon and 13-year-old Joseph was crippled and still lived with his grandparents'.

May 1879.

The construction of the promenade round the Wish Tower was completed and opened to the public.

An Outlet for Fish.

May 1880 saw the opening of possibly the first Fish and Chip shop in Eastbourne. The copy of an advert in the Eastbourne Gazette for that year shows J (Jesse) Gilbert owning such a shop then called a Fried Fish & Potato shop at 180 Seaside. There was a Fish & Chip and fishmonger shop there for many years afterwards, namely Bustons, and more recently Chester's the local fishing family. Now closed, the premises are situated close by what was the White Hart pub, opposite Christ Church.

John 'Trunky' Colstick, brother-in-law to Jesse Gilbert, managed the Fish shop from its opening. A lifeboatman from the 1883 Birling Gap rescue and a drinking pal of 'Bones' Hide. The tale goes that he along with 'Bones' and others in 1882 hired a horse cab belonging to Joseph Mockett of the 'Ocean Wave' pub on a Sunday and went for a booze up in the country. Finishing up at the Corporation Arms, Pevensey, where problems ensued and they were all locked up in the cell at the Town Hall in the High Street. Quite a day out. See a fuller report of the incident under the year 1882.

'Trunky' led an interesting life. Born in Old Town Eastbourne in 1854 he went to sea at the age of 12 and had several voyages before the mast to the West Indies and South America. He went from ship's boy to Captain's servant in 3 trips. He survived a hurricane in 1869 and told of one voyage to South America when in Bueos Aires the crew went down with yellow fever with the result that local Negroes were signed on articles to sail the ship back to England. In his prime he was a bare fist prize fighter and one local fight was against his lifeboat mate William 'Nick' Jackson whom he fought for a wager down by the Crumble pond (Princes Park Lake). He beat 'Nick' by knocking him into the pond.

His wife was born in Prentice Street, Eastbourne. Her birthplace cottage stood on the site of Sir Alfred Dent's Carlisle Road residence, the cottage being knocked down in 1887. As a child she remembered seeing a man locked in the Stocks at 'Stocks Bank'.

June 1937. John 'Trunky' Colstick and wife both in their 82nd Year.

'Trunky' died 21st December 1937 aged 83 years. At his funeral two of his old crewmates from the 1883 lifeboat, Alfred 'Tuppy' Sayers and William 'Kilcraft' Erridge saw him off. Also present were local fishermen, boatmen and lifeboatmen, Andrew Chester, Jack Tuxford, Mike Hardy, Fred Allchorn, William Allchorn and Eddie Hardy. Coffin bearers were Jesse Huggett, Tom Allchorn, Fred 'Tinker' Novis and Henry Thomas. 'Trunky's wife died in 1938.

OPENING OF A
Fried Fish and Potatoe Shop
(Opposite "Ye Rising Sun" Coffee Tavern)
180, SEASIDE, EASTBOURNE.
PROPRIETOR—J. GILBERT, FISHMONGER

Hot Fish and Potatoes every Evening, 2d; othe Fish daily,

Possibly Eastbourne's first Fish and Chip shop May, 1880.

Despite the gallant efforts of Eastbourne fishermen and boatmen Samuel Allchorn, John Erridge and Caesar Mitchell the tragic drowning of a Hastings fisherman James Tyrrell took place on a late November evening 1880, off the beach west of the Wish Tower. Having been blown in heavy seas along the coast from Hastings Tyrrell was alone in his boat just a few yards from the beach when the above Eastbourne men rushed into the sea to attempt to reach him but were driven back by the heavy seas and Tyrrell was washed out to sea out of sight, only for his body to be discovered next day ashore at Holywell. At the inquest Samuel Allchorn and John Erridge spoke of how they and Mitchell having stripped off their guernseys, boots and hats tried with ropes about their waists, to swim out to Tyrrell but the seas were too strong. Erridge had shouted to Tyrrell ' Keep your heart up and try to get ashore'. They were so close to Tyrrell. He had jumped out of the boat and Mitchell nearly grabbed him but then a heavy sea came over them and Tyrrell was washed away. Criticism was made over the fact that the red fisherman's light at the Fishing Station had been removed due to the building of the Royal Parade on the site. The Hastings man could have possibly come ashore there, as it was the best place to land a boat during heavy weather. Tyrrell left a widow and 5 children.

1881 and at midnight 5th February a Net shop on the beach opposite the Workmen's Hall, belonging to Thomas Sayers caught fire and was completely destroyed along with gear to the value of £100. A lightning strike was thought to be the cause.

Mr Gowland of the Library. Upsetting the Fishermen.

On 8th March 1881 Frederick Bollard Hide, fisherman, was charged with being drunk and disorderly.

'*Mr Thomas Gowland, of the Library, Marine Parade, said - about half past six on Monday evening he was in his house, upstairs, when he was called down as someone (Hide) wanted to see him. Gowland, however, expecting mischief, kept out of the way until Hide left. Gowland afterwards went for a policeman and while he was gone, Hide and another person returned and wanted to get upstairs and were violent towards Gowland's wife and sister. Hide expressed his intention of strangling Gowland and dragging him round town. When Gowland returned with a policeman they found Hide again in the shop at Marine Parade. Pc Plumb, (later Eastbourne's Chief Constable) said, as a result of what Gowland told him he went with him to the Library and found Hide there. Pc Plumb requested Hide to leave, which he did, but remained outside on the pavement and refused to go away. He was drunk so Pc Plumb removed him to the lock-up. Hide complained that something derogatory about the fishermen had appeared in the 'Courier' (newspaper) and he had had just a little difference with Gowland as a result. Mr Gowland said he did not wish to press charges but he did not see why he should be subjected to annoyance by people like Hide, who when he (Gowland) appeared on the parade howled and hooted after him as if he was a mad dog. Hide was fined 1s and costs of 7s. 9d*'.

Down West.

The Eastbourne fishing Luggers 'Industry' and 'Young Harry' were berthed at Plymouth Devon when the 1881 census took place on 3rd April. Thomas Swain is shown as master of the 'Industry' and crew as Thomas Sayers 45yrs, Edward Hobby 57yrs, James Huggett 45yrs Henry Tutt 36yrs and Jeffrey Shamrock Allchorn 19yrs. The Lugger 'Young Harry' showed master as James Allchorn 64yrs, and crew Thomas Swain 66yrs, Samuel Allchorn 38yrs, Henry Allchorn 30yrs, Robert Simmons 27yrs, William French 23yrs and Frederick French 18yrs. Further local boats in Plymouth that day were 'Providence' George Waymark 62yrs master, crew William Wood 44yrs, Frederick Dyer 70 yrs, Henry Cummins 33 yrs, Charles Waymark 28 yrs, Charles Boniface 18 yrs and Charles Hurd 17 yrs. Also 'Pride' Peter Waymark 32yrs master, Henry Matthews 32 yrs, Jasper Marquick 41 yrs, John Harris 43yrs and Richard Adams 21yrs. 'XL' Milton Carter 49 yrs master, John Hurd 59 yrs, Thomas Welch 38 yrs, William Lane 39 yrs, William Matthews 30 yrs, Alfred Smith 18 yrs and William Erridge 20 yrs.

John Hide fisherman, boatman and publican born 1837, eldest son of George 'Dot' Hide kept records and accounts of his fishing business from 1868 and some of them up to 1899 have survived. They make interesting reading.

For December 1868, we see his share in his Lugger with total outgoings for the whole year amounting to £11.13s.4d. The outgoings on the Lugger gives an insight into what was required to keep a Lugger seaworthy in those days with materials and names of the tradesmen of Eastbourne, one name that still persists through to this day is Caffyns, the motor dealing company. Another name being Parks, a basket making business in 1868, which continued through to the 1990's, when it traded as a Leather goods shop in Cornfield Road. Simpson the boat builder and sailmaker is shown.

John Hide fished along with his brothers George Merrick 'Pincher', Samuel Beckett, Benjamin Charles and Charles 'Bones' and shown is the photograph of John Hide's Lugger 3NN her name 'Four Sisters' on the beach at Eastbourne, c.1880. John, wearing a bowler is standing aft at the tiller and on the deck can be seen his three sons, John, Dennis and Edward 'Ted'. The Lugger 'Four Sisters' was a fine vessel built in Eastbourne by William Simpson at his boat yard on part of what is now St.Aubyns Road. A 'Bourner 'as the Eastbourne Luggers were known, she was about 40 feet in length, Lugger sail rigged, of 14 tons, crewed by up to 7 men and boy, she drift netted and long lined for fish,

John Hide's Fishing accounts from 1868-70

Pen and Ink drawing of 5-year-old John Hide, Fisherman's son. Drawn by S B Gregory 1842.

John Hide's Fishing accounts 1875.

Fisherman John Hide on board (at tiller) his fishing Lugger 3NN 'Four Sisters' on Eastbourne beach C.1880, with sons John, Edward, and Dennis on board.

first registered 1868. The 3NN prefix on her bow indicated she was a class 2 Lugger. NN followed by a number indicated a class 1 Lugger. This practice ceased in 1892 and all classes began NN thereafter.

'As to tonnage for ships and vessels a brief definition is as follows: Gross tons are not a measurement of weight, but of volume - 1 gross ton equals 100 cubic feet.

John Hide aged 75 years 'Scotting the nets' on Eastbourne beach.

1868 Took up for Nets	£	1 1
Dec 12 Herring Nets	8	10 0
1869		
Feby 25 Mackerel Nets	22	10 0
May 4 Mackerel Nets	6	15 0
Oct 9 Mackerel Nets	5	2 6
Dec 6 Herring Nets	11	2 6
1870		
Oct 3 Mackerel Nets	0	8 9
Dec 4 Herring Nets	13	4 0
1871		
May 8 Mackerel Nets	2	19 6
May 8 Mackerel Nets Parks	3	6 6
June 13 Mackerel Nets	9	14 0
July Mackerel Nets Parks	3	10 0
August Mackerel Nets	0	10 0
Oct 9 Mackerel Nets	5	16 6
Oct Mackerel Nets Parks	2	10 0
Dec Herring Nets	4	6 4
1872		
April Mackerel Nets	3	1 10
April Mackerel Nets Hobby	1	18 0
May Mackerel Nets	3	0 0
May Mackerel Nets Hobby	0	12 6
June Mackerel Nets	3	6 8
June Mackerel Nets Hobby	0	18 0
July Mackerel Nets Hobby	0	1 3
Oct Mackerel Nets	14	14 0
Oct Mackerel Nets Hobby	3	0 0
Dec Herring Nets	3	0 0

John Hide's Fishing accounts 1868.

Ton being a corruption of tun. Ships were first measured by how many tuns of wine they could carry'. Captain D Thomas R D, Hull.

The 'Four Sisters' looks well able to deal with voyages up to the North Sea and down the English Channel across to Ireland. She would have worked off the old and new Fishing Stations, it being quite a task hauling up and launching her off the beach and been involved when fishing from Eastbourne was productive in the late 1880's when the fishing fleet increased considerably.

The prefix 'NN' seen on the Eastbourne fishing boats indicates they are registered at Newhaven the nearest Port with a Customs Station. All Eastbourne registered fishing boats are still registered as such. Fishing boats are registered with the first and last letter of the nearest Customs Station port, but there are exceptions i.e. Hastings boats bear the letters RX. indicating Rye, they can't have RE because Ramsgate has a Customs Station and is a Fishing port, and takes precedence hence RE. Brighton boats bear SM, for Shoreham their nearest Customs port. Originally Hastings and Eastbourne did have RE (Rye) as registration letters but this changed in 1869.

Back to 1881.

On Tuesday, 18th January 1881, another shipwreck tragedy occurred when during a gale force heavy snowstorm at 9 o'clock in the morning a German brigantine 'Aphrodite' of Hanover 300 tons with a cargo of coal struck a reef of rocks about 300 yards off Holywell and immediately began to break up. The crew took to the rigging and their cries for help could be heard above the storm. But alas the ship broke up and due to the intense cold there was only one survivor - four men and a boy drowning. The survivor was saved by brave Henry Boniface who went into the sea at peril to his own life and got him ashore. He was taken to the family cottage of James Boniface and when recovered asked in German for 'a pipe of tobacco'.

During the above rescue, the Eastbourne lifeboat was being launched when she took a heavy sea and was knocked from her carriage, damaged and unable to proceed. As a result the Hastings lifeboat was summoned by telegraph and she launched. With the intense cold, snow and gale force wind they had a miserable time making

No. 42.

Borough of Eastbourne.

In Agreement made the 28th day of April 1892 between the Corporation of Eastbourne, and John and Benjamin Hide, of in the Borough of Eastbourne, Fisherman, hereinafter called the said tenant, whereby the Corporation agrees to allow the Capstan erected by the said tenant, to remain on the portion of the Fishing Station in the said Borough, more particularly shewn on the plan lying in the Borough Surveyor's Office, and thereon numbered 42.

In consideration whereof the said tenant undertakes and agrees :—

(1) To pay to the Corporation the sum of Two Shillings and Sixpence on the first day of January, in each year, in advance.

(2) If default is made in payment of the said sum to remove the said Capstan at any time when required by the Corporation so to do, or on his failure to do so the Corporation may remove the same and if necessary recover the expenses of so doing by action at law, or otherwise.

AND the Corporation further agree that in consideration of the said tenant paying the foregoing rent he shall be undisturbed in his possession of the land and premises included in this agreement and shall be at liberty to transfer his interest in the same under this Agreement to any party or parties connected with the fishing industry, subject to the approval in writing of the Corporation.

As witness the hands of the said Henry West Fovargue, Town Clerk of the said Borough duly authorised by the Corporation in that behalf, and

Signed John Hide

Witness Jesse Huggett
Fishman   Signed
Witness Simon Brown   Town Clerk.

Fishing Station capstan licence issued to John Hide 1892. Witnessed by Jesse Huggett (Lifeboat Cox'n)

Harriet Ogle, del.

THE FIRST LUGGER BUILT AT EAST-BOURNE.
(By P. & J. Simpson, 1844.)

N.B. registration letters RE. an early Rye registration pre-1869.

headway, she was launched at 1.30pm and reached the scene at 4.00pm. (no engine in those days) much too late alas, as the 'Aphrodite' had broken up. In tempestuous seas the Hastings lifeboat and crew came ashore at Eastbourne and spent the night at the Leaf Hall. The following day the lifeboat could not be returned to Hastings by train as intended because snowdrifts had blocked the line. So they returned by sea and that proved a problem, the bitter cold affecting the crew to a great degree.

The inquest into the loss of the 'Aphrodite' was held at the Ship Hotel in Meads. There was criticism that there was no rocket apparatus on hand to get a line to the wreck and the possible saving of life. The inquest was told rocket apparatus was only held at Birling Gap and Pevensey. (There had been a rocket apparatus 2 miles east of Holywell, placed there in 1848 but in 30 years no service was rendered so it was withdrawn in 1878). The ship had broken up within ¾ of an hour there being no hope for the crew. The Hastings lifeboat crew were commended for their seamanship.

Back to June 1880 saw the foundering of the brig 'Harvest Home' some 3 miles off Eastbourne, she sprang a leak off Shoreham and all efforts to keep her afloat failed, she was 42 years old and so un-seaworthy that her timbers gave way. Fisherman Edwin 'Lord' Matthews saw her sinking and her crew take to the ship's boat. He had a fishing boat launched (no time for the lifeboat) and towed the boat and crew ashore. The crew having nothing other than what they wore. After being suitably looked after by the Shipwrecked Mariner's Society they left by train for London

The above Edwin 'Lord' Matthews in October 1880, was involved in a 'set to' in the Ocean Wave pub with fishermen James and Edward Boniface. The story goes, that on a very stormy night in October the Eastbourne fishing fleet landed at Eastbourne except the Boniface boat. She was actually driven down to Wallsend, as Pevensey Bay was then called. Meanwhile Matthews being concerned had searched the beach with a lantern endeavouring to find the Bonifaces, but to no avail. Next day it was discovered they had come ashore at Wallsend, and the landlord of the Ocean Wave, Joseph Mockett went and collected them in his cart. On their arrival in the Ocean Wave, Matthews chaffed them about their seamanship. The Bonifaces' took exception to that and both attacked Matthews, a kick from Edward Boniface the son of James dislocated Matthews right kneecap and being in agony was assisted home where he lay for 16 weeks. It was 20 weeks before he could go to sea again.

In May 1881, Matthews took the Bonifaces' to the County Court at Lewes claiming £30 damages for his injuries. The case was heard before a Judge and jury. Fishermen John Colstick and John Mockett gave evidence for Matthews. Harry Boniface a brother of Edward gave evidence to the effect that he had seen Matthews knock his knee in a fishing boat previous to the assault. Harry Boniface went on to say the family were 'of exemplary teetotalism, some of them being teetotallers with respect to beer, but not to the short stuff (spirits)' this brought much laughter in the court.

The jury found for Matthews and the Judge awarded Matthews £10 plus costs, commenting that Matthews contributed partly to the assault because of his behaviour. Could it be the same James Boniface that punched Mr Wilkinson over the locomotive incident in November 1880?

But it was the same James Boniface who along with his wife Sarah that had a 'set to' with Ben Hide back in September 1875. It started in the 'Ocean Wave' pub when Boniface had come in to pay his men. He owed Ben Hide money and Ben called him a 'bloody rogue and a thief'. Boniface pulled Ben's whiskers and a fight started. It went on outside the Pub and along comes Sarah Boniface and joins in. Ben gives her a punch and puts her down. The police arrive and the outcome was that Ben was arrested, taken to Court and fined on two counts of assault a total of £1.6s.6d. In mitigation he said he hit Sarah Boniface because she interfered.

Before we finish with the Bonifaces, Elizabeth Boniface was fined 1s and 13s costs for using obscene language outside the 'Ocean Wave' at 10pm on an evening in January 1877. She had on seeing her teetotal husband in the bar, hammered on the window. Landlord Joseph Mockett remonstrated with her and was met with bad language, she wouldn't stop and Mockett manhandled her off the pavement. The police attended and summoned both. Mockett was fined 10s for assaulting Mrs 'Bonny' as one witness called her.

In those days the 'Ocean Wave' and 'Victoria Tavern' pubs were opposite each other and faced the open shingle beach, which was part of the Fishing Station. The area running along in front of the pubs being known as Tower Place and later changed to Latimer Road.

Going back to that stormy night in October 1880 did prove a problem to the fishermen of Eastbourne as the Shipwrecked Mariners Society report in November showed through the honorary local agent Mr S Hall of Seaside road. *'An amount of £7.7s.0d was awarded to the fishermen of Eastbourne for losses sustained to*

boats in the gale of October. There are eighty five fishermen and others connected with sea duties who subscribe to the Society, but as in the need of public help to keep pace with the calls, subscriptions would gratefully be received by Mr Hall'.

The hauling up the beach of boats was and is always fraught with danger. In November 1881 fishermen Nicholas Jackson, Walter Wickham and landlord of the 'Ocean Wave' Joseph Mockett were engaged in hauling up a heavy boat by the aid of a horse and two capstans. A chain suddenly snapped due to the strain and the wooden spar of one of the capstans struck Jackson and Mockett, seriously injuring Jackson. His left arm was broken and his lower ribs driven in. Mockett received a severe cut to the head. Wickham was only slightly hurt. Jackson aged 68 years, was carried insensible to his home 6, Cambridge Place.

1882. A Sunday in the Country.

Some Eastbourne fishermen pals had a trip in the country on a Sunday in April and finished up being arrested for being drunk and failing to quit licensed premises.

The Town Hall, High Street, Pevensey, (now a Museum) was the venue for the Court case.

The report reads.

'A powerfully built man named Charles Hide a well known fisherman at Eastbourne, was charged with refusing to quit licensed premises and being concerned in the attack on the Police at the Corporation Arms, Pevensey. On the same charge was John 'Trunkey'

B. PUTTOCK,

FAMILY & COMMERCIAL HOTEL,

PEVENSEY STATION, near EASTBOURNE.

Close to the Ancient Ruins of Pevensey Castle & about one mile from the Beach.

LICENSED TO LET HORSES AND CARRIAGES.

'Corporation Arms' C.1880.

Colstick, George Sayers, James Hide and Jesse Gilbert. All were brought up before the Justices. Mrs Puttock, the landlady stated the defendants arrived at her house in a drunken state saying they were travellers. She refused to serve them and they used foul language to her and would not leave her house. Pc Reed attended and a fight occurred, all men eventually being placed in custody in the Town Hall cell. Confirmation of the facts was given by Mr. Geary, the Parish Constable. On behalf of the defendants, John Pilbeam landlord of the 'The Lamb' Hooe said they had been to Bexhill and when at his Public house they were not drunk. Joseph Mockett, landlord of the 'Ocean Wave' also deposed they were not drunk on the day in question. The Justices found the facts proved and all were fined £2 each and 18s 8d costs. Fisherman Charles Swain who had been with them had been dealt with earlier and sent to prison'

'Bones' and his mates had obviously hired a carriage and been on a 'beer run' into the country being well 'oiled' before they arrived at Pevensey. They all finished up with the dubious honour of being probably the last 'prisoners' to appear at the Pevensey Court House. It ceased to function soon after in the same year 1882.

It was about the time of the above happening that the father of 'Bones', George 'Dot' Hide passed away on 27th April 1882 aged 68 years. His death was reported in the Eastbourne Chronicle. A Well- Merited Tribute. - Speaking of the decease of Mr George Hide, fisherman of Seaside,

'Eastbourne has lost in the person of Mr George Hide one of the bravest of her citizens. He used his great strength and knowledge of the seas so effectively that he either saved at great risk of his own life, or assisted others in saving, the lives of no less than 50 persons. Mr Hide was rewarded with medals and testimonials by those who appreciated brave deeds. His name will not soon be forgotten in Eastbourne and he leaves behind him sons whose chief ambition is to follow in their father's footsteps'.

Reports of his death also appeared in the Eastbourne Gazette and the East Sussex Journal. Described by people who knew him as *'one of nature's gentlemen'*

Finally for 1882 problems arose with fishing, this time about the price and method of selling and buying. A report in the Eastbourne Gazette for September tells of a private meeting in the parlour of one of the fishmongers, where the method of selling and buying was discussed. It was understood that there was a desire on behalf of the fish buyers to adopt what is known as a 'Dutch auction' instead of the present mode of disposing of the catch by the mode of increased biddings. The 'Dutch' mode is for the seller to name a price and gradually lower it until some one is found to buy the fish.

March 1883.

Fisherman James Collins of 10 York Buildings, Manns Row was accused of stealing 100 herring the property of Joseph Carter fish dealer. The herring had been stolen from his herring deeze (dees) shed on the Fishing Station at the back of the Ordnance yard. The herring had been drying on sticks in the deeze. Collins was seen walking away from the deeze with a large basket, later recovered from a cow lodge in Compton Place meadow with the herring in it. Collins was also charged with the theft a shrimp net the property of William Erridge. The result of the above has not been ascertained.

A Royal Honour.

Fisherman James Allchorn, of 1 Beach Cottages was selected to represent the Eastbourne fishermen at the International Fisheries Exhibition held at Kensington London, in May 1883. He was among 400 representatives of fishermen from all over the world. Queen Victoria invited the fishermen to Windsor Castle to meet her and the Prince of Wales also received them at Marlborough House. A very proud time for James Allchorn and the fishermen of Eastbourne, indeed for the whole town. James was for many years a Fisheries Officer for the Sussex District along with George 'Pincher' Hide. When James died in 1897 his Fisheries position was taken by 'Pincher's' son Albert.

August 1883.

On Saturday 31st August 1883, James Allchorn had the opportunity to see the Prince of Wales again when he and the Princess made an official visit to Eastbourne to open Princess Alice Hospital, the new Pumping Station and dedicate the new Western Parade. Eastbourne was dressed over all in flags and bunting, ceremonial arches and floral tributes.

'The Royal couple arrived by train at the Railway Station and went by horse carriage round the town, in a grand procession. 'Bones' Hide Coxswain and the full crew of 15 men were aboard the lifeboat 'William and Mary' which stood on its carriage on the Grand Parade opposite the Cavendish Hotel. They gave three hearty cheers for the passing Royal couple and were acknowledged with a bow from both their Highnesses.

Prior to that the Royal carriage had been down the east end of town. The procession went down Seaside Road into Seaside and turned right, through the Ordnance yard, where gaps had been specially made. On turning right out of the Ordnance yard, just opposite was an old cottage with only the roof on which was covered in British Ensigns, this cottage was the last remnant of the ancient fishing village. (The building of the sea wall and Royal Parade was taking place). At the start of the Marine Parade the Royal eyes lit on a long row of Bathing machines drawn up and hung with flags and banners of a nondescript character. The idea and taste of the fishermen and their wives was not of a very high class order, but at any rate they did their best and displayed their loyalty'.

Eastbourne Fishermen and Boatmen Arch. Visit of Prince and Princess of Wales. 31st August 1883.

On Marine Parade, just to the east of the Anchor Hotel, (now Albermarle) was the 'Fishermen's Arch', composed of boats, nets and various tackle. A novel idea at the Arch was that of fixing all over the nets fresh caught mackerel. The fishermen in their blue guernseys and white trousers, either manned their boats or were hanging on the framework of their arch as though clinging to the rigging of a ship at sea. Underneath, on either side of the road other fishermen were standing with upturned oars in true nautical style, ready to salute their Royal Highnesses. Immediately under the Arch, in the centre of the line of men one of the oldest representatives of his class was ready with bouquet in hand, which he had received permission to present to the Princess. The old veterans name was James 'Navarino' Hide aged 85 years. He looks somewhat weather beaten, but is hale and hearty yet. When the advance guard of Dragoons had gone by the old salt pushed his way up to the Royal carriage and handed the bouquet to the Princess amidst the lusty cheers of his comrades, given in a fashion only known to fishermen. 'Navarino' was well satisfied when Her Royal Highness gave him a cordial recognition and thanked him with a few words and a kindly smile'. 'Navarino' died just three weeks later on September 21st.

'The launch' by H J Rhodes. 1886.

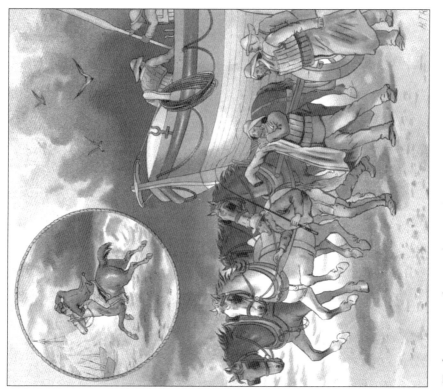

'To the rescue' a drawing by H J Rhodes. 1886.

Chapter Four

The Lifeboat and The 'New Brunswick' Rescue.
The Era of the Deep-Sea Lugger

In 1880, the Eastbourne Lifeboat 'Mary Stirling' having been on station since 1863 was replaced by a new boat the 'William and Mary'

With the re-forming of the local branch of the National Lifeboat Institute at the Vestry Hall, on 7th March 1881, Charles 'Bones' Hide at the age of 32 years was appointed Coxswain of the 'William and Mary' in succession to Joseph 'Joker' Huggett. 'Bones' was highly thought of by the new committee, his seamanship and bravery being second to none.

Quote 'A first Coxswain was the responsible person in the boat and the services of Charles Hide have been secured. He is thoroughly competent to satisfactorily discharge the duties'.

Fisherman Charles 'Bones' Hide was a well known character in Eastbourne and along the South coast so when it came to a trial of life saving sea going garments who else to demonstrate them but 'Bones' before a crowd of some 5,000.

Quote 'A public trial of life saving garments invented by Wentworth & Co, took place in the sea in front of the Burlington Hotel on August, 30th 1883 this trial attracted a very large crowd of spectators who lined the beach for some considerable extent. It is calculated that fully 5,000 persons were present. In the first instance, Charles Hide, Coxswain of the lifeboat and another of the crew, dressed themselves in a vest such as worn by a yachtsman or traveller, and fell into the sea. They immediately rose to the surface and floated thereon without the slightest exertion. As they were lying in the water they caused considerable amusement by quietly smoking pipes handed to them. They then donned an ordinary tarpaulin fishermen's suit fitted with the apparatus, and the experiment was equally successful. Charles Hide then donned a pair of heavy fishermen's boots in which he floated with great ease.

Hide reported that he found the new jacket garment far more buoyant than the cork lined jackets ordinarily worn by the life boatmen when on duty. The buoyant garment is a preparation of compressed cork which feels soft to the touch'

Whether this garment was adopted by the Lifeboat Institute is not known. It was evidently of a commercial/retail nature as it was advertised and on show in the shop of Mr Nevill Strang, Terminus Road.

'Bones's first recorded service as Coxswain of the 'William and Mary' was the afternoon of Monday 24th September 1883 when she went to the rescue of the Norwegian barque 'Isabella' 300 tons, sailing from Frederikstad to Honfluer,

France. Laden with timber, she missed her stays and failed to come about in a gale and was driven ashore at Bexhill just west of the Coastguard Station. The coastguardsmen quickly arrived on the spot bringing the rocket apparatus and after several futile endeavours got a line aboard, but no rescue was made via the line. The 'William and Mary' then arrived after battling with heavy seas, having experienced an hour's delay in getting her launched from the inconvenient position of where the boathouse was situated. The lifeboat anchored westward of the stricken vessel and ran under the stern from which the crew of eight dropped into her, and were safely landed through the heavy surf amidst the hearty cheers of the large crowd watching. The barque 'Isabella' by this time was in a very disabled condition and breaking up. Having safely landed the crew. 'Bones' launched again through the very rough and blinding surf and took the Captain back to the stricken vessel and stood by alongside whilst the ships papers and crews possession were recovered. A fine bit a seamanship by 'Bones' and his crew, again landing the lifeboat through the heavy surf at Bexhill. The lifeboat and crew later returned to Eastbourne by train.

The cause of the delay to the launching was as a consequence of the new sea wall (Royal Parade) being constructed between the boathouse and the shore.

September 1883.

Joseph Mockett applied for an off beer licence for his shop at the east end of town in consequence of the removal of the fishermen due to the new sea wall works. It was pointed out the fishermen went out and came in from sea at all hours and weathers and often wanted refreshments, not now obtainable. The application was refused.

October 1883.

The local paper reported a drunk and disorderly charge against fisherman, James Fly in Pevensey Road, Norway, (now Seaside and the north way out of town). Fly had been brandishing a poker and wanted to take on anybody. Found guilty he was fined 5s with 10s costs. Involved in the same incident was fisherman Charles Figg who had been thrown out of the Alexandra Arms beer shop by the landlord. He had stripped off and wanted to fight. Fined 5s with 14s. 6d costs or in default, 14 days hard labour.

November 1883. The 'William and Mary' to the Rescue.

The start of November 1883, saw tremendous seas and gales along the south coast, and on the 5th, fishing boats at the Fishing Station were destroyed and damaged. This weather continued through the month and Sunday 25th saw the most famous rescue by the Eastbourne lifeboat in its history, under the command of Coxswain Charles 'Bones' Hide. The day had opened with torrential rain and storm force gales from the Sou'Sou' West.

From first hand reports at the time the epic goes thus,

It was the first Mayor's Sunday procession to take place in Eastbourne. Mr G A Wallis having the honour of being Eastbourne's number one citizen. (The Local Board, which ran the Town, lasted until November 1883, when a Mayor and Corporation superceded it)

'William and Mary' to the rescue, 25th November 1883, Birling Gap. Drawn by Mr H Emary.

It was approximately 10.30am just as the Mayor and Corporation had robed up in the Vestry Hall, Grove Road in preparation for the procession to the Parish Church of St. Mary's, Old Town. The weather as said, was very inclement. They were due to leave when a report came from the Coastguard on Beachy Head, with a messenger announcing a vessel, the Norwegian barque 'New Brunswick' was in distress off Beachy Head. Councillor Tom Bennett sub-agent for Lloyds immediately left the procession, which had just been formed and after a hurried consultation with Alderman Rudd who was the Eastbourne Lloyd's agent. He hastened to the Telegraph office and wired the information through to Newhaven as it was thought their lifeboat could probably arrive at the scene of the wreck well before the Eastbourne boat could get there, there was a gale blowing from the Sou' Sou' West, and the Eastbourne lifeboat would be going directly into the teeth of that gale.

A wire came back from Newhaven that the seas were too rough for the lifeboat to be launched and it would take an hour for the Tug to raise steam so no help was forthcoming from Newhaven. But the vessel could not be left to its fate. Mr Emary, local secretary of the Eastbourne Lifeboat Institute, questioned whether it was advisable

'Old Lifeboat House' 1933. Marine Road.

Present day view of 'Old Lifeboat House' Marine Road.

to launch the Eastbourne boat but after consultation at the Lifeboat Station (which was situated in what is now Marine Road at the rear of the Leaf Hall) with Coxswain Hide it was determined to take her overland and launch at Birling Gap.

It was fortunate that this decision was arrived at, as it will subsequently be seen the Newhaven lifeboat never left harbour. The whole credit for the affair devolved upon the Eastbourne crew. No doubt 'Bones' put to Mr Rudd and Mr Emary, the fact that when he had been 2nd Coxswain on the old boat 'Mary Stirling' on 17th January, 1872, under Coxswain Joseph Huggett in similar diabolical weather, the brigantine 'Osprey' had driven ashore at Holywell and they could not launch at the Station. So the lifeboat was hauled to Holywell by horses and got down to the Flats, there to be launched. (This incident must have swayed it 'Bones's way, also with the new road to Beachy Head having recently been built)

Whilst this consultation was going on the Eastbourne crew mustered at their post and received the announcement with hearty cheers. They pulled the boat manually as far as South Street before six horses were attached. These six horses were owned by Mr Newman of the 'Anchor Hotel' and were then added to at a later stage by another four horses at Meads from Mr Matthias Mockett of Meads House.

The pull up the new road to Beachy Head was a terrible struggle and it required the full power of ten horses with the crew and a host of volunteers of all classes of Eastbourne residents. They worked with a will to push the heavy boat up the steep ascent rendered ten times more difficult by the drenching rain and the gale, which blew straight in their faces.

On they went and in two hours reached Birling Gap.

At that time the stricken vessel could be dimly seen amid the drifting squalls some three quarters of a mile from the shore, with the sea at times breaking over it. The crew were lashed to the rigging waving signals of distress. It was now 1.30pm and the weather had every appearance of increasing in violence as the tide was on the turn. There was difficulty in getting the lifeboat down onto the beach, as the gap was too narrow for the carriage. The boat was taken off and with endeavour and hard work the gap was widened by physical labour. All the time spurred on by the voice of 'Bones', fishermen, gentlemen, coastguardsmen and visitor set to work with a will. An Englishman does not know what impossible means. Timbers were used to make a slipway down the gap and the lifeboat was lowered down reaching the waters edge. A perfect hurricane prevailed and the waves rolled in mountains high. A dense black cloud came drifting in from the ocean and just as the lifeboat was launched, burst with terrific fury on one and all. The rain did not descend in ordinary drops but in 'bucketfuls' yet undeterred the gallant lifeboat crew stood their posts trusting themselves to the judgement of 'Bones' Hide their Coxswain. Every eye was fixed on him. Watching for a favourable moment, *'Now pull, lads'* was his cry and the first great danger was overcome. One last wave of the hand and 'Bones's voice is heard above the raging of the sea, *'Wish us God speed, and a safe return'*. They were 'on their way to save' pulling on their oars into the teeth of the gale.

Crew members Fred 'Coggy' Hide and 'Nick' Jackson later related, *'as the lifeboat was being lowered down the Gap she was holed through the hull side, this proved to be a blessing in disguise as on her way to the wreck, sea water taken in kept her down and stable in the heavy seas'*.

To those watching from the shore it seemed that the lifeboat would never reach the wreck, again and again it appeared to be overwhelmed by the tremendous seas and disappeared in the heavy squalls. Slowly but surely Charles Hide and his gallant crew approached the vessel. At times they were forced back their boat filling with water, but she rose clear and for fully one hour did the struggle continue, it seemed almost beyond endurance but British pluck prevailed and the wreck was reached.

It was impossible to take the lifeboat alongside so a rope was made fast and the lifeboat allowed to drop astern of the wreck. One by one the crew of ten with the Captain were dropped and transferred by line through the sea into the lifeboat, but one poor fellow got his ribs crushed in the transfer but all were saved and the lifeboat turned for shore. This was no easy passage but in gallant style 'Bones' Hide beached the 'William and Mary' close to where she launched. The shore was reached about 4.30pm and ready hands drew it and its live cargo out of the water. The injured man and his shipmates were taken away to the cottages on the Gap and received aid.

The work of the lifeboat crew and helpers was not over as it took much strenuous work to get the lifeboat back up from the beach. This was eventually done and before the long journey back to Eastbourne, refreshments were taken by the crew and helpers, food and drink having been brought over on the instructions of Mr Tom Bennett, by Henry Gardner, landlord of the 'Devonshire Hotel' Seaside Road, brother in law of two members of the lifeboat crew William and Frederick Bollard Hide, cousins of 'Bones'.

The lifeboat was eventually on station in the boathouse at 7.00pm, a long tiring day. The rescued seamen received the very best in hospitality.

The distressed vessel was the barque 'New Brunswick' 480 tons with a cargo of timber en-route from Quebec, Canada to West Hartlepool. On approaching the English Channel they were caught in terrific gales that prevailed on them for days and approaching Beachy Head her main-topmast and fore-topmast were carried away with the principal sails. They attempted to weather the Head on Saturday/Sunday night. Early Sunday morning saw them driven unmanageably towards the Head and had to put down anchors, which at first dragged and they hoisted signals of distress. Their anchors eventually held and the Coastguard on Beachy Head having seen their plight telegraphed Eastbourne for assistance. The events then unfolded as described.

The crew of the "William and Mary" were as follows.

Left to right in the photograph.

Standing back row: Richard 'Dick' Swain, William 'Young' Bollard Hide, John 'Trunky' Colstick, Jim 'Snob' Merritt, George 'Smuggler' Erridge, 2nd Coxswain Edwin 'Lord' Matthews, John 'Kruger' Prodger, Will 'Nick' Jackson, William 'Kilcraft' Erridge, William 'Alligator' Erridge.

Seated centre: Frederick 'Coggy' Bollard Hide, William 'Billy' Stanbridge, Coxswain Charles 'Bones' Hide, Albert 'Tuppy' Sayers, Reuben 'Cassy' Reed.

Seated front: Thomas 'Tommy Ruin' Swain.

The photo of the crew taken alongside the Lifeboat house showing the flags of the 'New Brunswick' was taken by George Churchill of Cornfield Road, Eastbourne.

The next day, Monday, praises were sung round Eastbourne as people became aware of the gallant rescue by the Eastbourne lifeboat crew and while they rested after their Herculean effort there happened an incident that was to sour the efforts of the Eastbourne crew and be the cause of much acrimony which has lasted to this day. During the millpond calm weather of the Monday, the Newhaven lifeboat 'Michael Henry' under Coxswain Richard Lower and crew put to sea having acquired the services of the Tug 'Tipper'. They took possession of the abandoned 'New Brunswick' claiming her as salvage and towed her into Newhaven Harbour duly claiming in the first instance £1,000. A fortune!

```
LLOYD'S WEEKLY SHIPPING INDEX – November 30, 1883.

New Brunswick – Newhaven; November 26,– The New Brunswick, Norwegian barque
Tobiason, from Quebec for West Hartlepool, brought up yesterday,
about 11 a.m., one mile off Birling Gap during a south gale. The master
cut away fore and main topmasts and brought the ship upmast two anchors,
giving her all the chain hex had on board, and hoisting a distress flag.
The crew were landed at 5 p.m. by the lifeboat. After two unsuccessful
attempts today some men were put on board by a tug and the lifeboat,
and the vessel is now being towed towards this port by the tug. No agree-
ment. Later:– vessel towed in November 27.

New Brunswick, Newhaven, November 27, 2 15 p.m.–Salvors asking 1,000l.
Think, with your authority, might settle with them, if done at once, for
between 500L and 600L. Captain states he is will to settle with salvors
for 500L, if you are agreeable. Advise settling as soon as possible.
Wire me instructions, LLOYD'S AGENT.
```

£1,000 salvage claim by Newhaven lifeboat crew and others for 'New Brunswick'

Within days a subscription fund was raised in the Eastbourne Gazette in recognition of the brave action of the 'William and Mary' crew. The rescue was applauded country wide, reports appearing in the national press. The poet, Herman Merivale on learning of the heroism of Coxswain Hide and the crew of the 'William and Mary' wrote a poem 'The Lay of the Lifeboat' 'singing' their praises.

Crew of the 'William and Mary' November 1883. Photograph taken against the Lifeboat house in Marine Road, showing flags of the 'New Brunswick'. Photograph by George Churchill.

Crew members, standing back row left to right, Richard 'Dick' Swain, William 'Young' Bollard Hide, John 'Trunky' Colstick, Jim 'Snob' Merritt, George 'Smuggler' Erridge, 2nd Coxswain Edwin 'Lord' Matthews, John 'Kruger' Prodger, Will 'Nick' Jackson, William 'Kilcraft' Erridge, William 'Alligator' Erridge,

Seated centre, Frederick 'Coggy' Hide, William 'Billy' Stanbridge, Coxswain Charles 'Bones' Hide, Albert 'Tuppy' Sayers, Reuben 'Cassy' Reed.

Seated front Thomas 'Tommy Ruin' Swain.

Throughout December, 'Bones' and the crew were feted, attending many dinners given in their honour. All told they had accomplished a famous rescue. At a ceremony just before Christmas 1883, at the Leaf Hall, Seaside, 'Bones' and the crew were presented with a money reward of £4 each, and the Town's appreciation expressed by the Mayor Mr G Wallis.

A Lifeboat evening was held and monies were raised for the Lifeboat Institute.

December 1883. Spud Less.

The December gales caused hunger to the crew of an Eastbourne Lugger, which put off during an afternoon to fish for a few hours off Eastbourne. They took no food aboard. The wind freshened to a gale and despite their endeavours they were driven off the land. Finding they were likely to be at sea all night they cooked the few potatoes they did have on board. The cook went to the boat's side to drain away the water when to his dismay the saucepan parted from the handle and their small supply of food disappeared into the depths. For two days and two nights the poor fishermen had to subsist on a few herring roughly cooked on the embers of their fire. At length, however, the wind shifted a point or two and they were able to make landfall at Eastbourne. Their townsfolk had been extremely worried for their safety owing to their prolonged absence and feared they had met a watery grave. Not so, and the returned Lugger's crew enjoyed a hearty meal. Who these fishermen were is not known. This tale appeared in the local paper December 1883.

Towards the end of December, two local fishermen brought ashore with difficulty, a monster skate measuring 8 feet long from tip of nose to end of tail, 6 feet across and weighing some 2 hundredweight.

1884.

It was on Friday 4th January 1884, at the Anchor Hotel, that silver medals, presented by the Mayor Mr Wallis and the people of Eastbourne, were pinned on the chests of 'Bones' and his crew by the Mayoress Mrs Wallis. To the married members of the crew Dr. Cunningham presented beautifully bound books for their wives and told the assembly he would be in Eastbourne this coming summer with his yacht and would like to see his old crew again and give a beating to all along the coast in the coming season, with his present boat 'Maria'. After a good repast the cloth was removed from the table, (after the Mayor and Mayoress had retired) tobacco, pipes etc were introduced and the company settled down to a 'free & easy'. There were toasts aplenty and songs sung by 'Snob' Merritt and 'Kruger' Prodger. Altogether a very convivial evening was had.

With all the euphoria of the event the Town Council at a meeting in January 1884, accordingly passed a motion to subscribe the sum of 21 guineas annually to the Lifeboat Institute.

In February 1884, a member of the Devonshire Club, Hartington Place, wrote a poem celebrating the 'New Brunswick' rescue, which was published in the Eastbourne Gazette.

Coxswain 'Bones' Hide and crew went from strength to strength with regard to their seamanship. It was on Tuesday 12th February 1884, that they showed their skill in handling a lifeboat in a competition. The following says it all.

Lifeboat Competition at Brighton.

'The contest took place at Brighton yesterday and resulted in the Eastbourne lifeboat crew, who manned the centre board boat furnished by Messrs Forrest & Son, Limehouse, London, proving victorious. In addition to the boat manned by the Eastbourne men there was what was described as a patent raft and a National Institution lifeboat managed by a Brighton crew. According to the regulations, which governed the contest, the start was to be made from an even line on the beach, the crew to pull out to a flag placed some distance out to sea. Admirals' McDowel and Courbet were the judges.

The start was made at five minutes to two o' clock the signal being the lowering of the flag on the Pier head. The Eastbourne crew were the first to get away in fact they launched their boat and were off as soon as the flag was down. Their boat experienced three heavy seas shortly after the start. But they succeeded in rounding the distant flag some considerable distance ahead of the other two boats, both of which appeared to have experienced some difficulty in getting away, although it is only fair to say, that with regard to the patent craft it's rudder unshipped as soon as it was launched. Arriving at the flag the boats had to make sail and beat windward, and to pass the tug 'Mistletoe' lying some distance to windward. The Eastbourne boat passed it some ten minutes ahead of the raft, and then made for the shore. The National Institutes boat appeared not to have complied with the sailing regulations and to have pulled the whole of the distance out to the 'Mistletoe'. 'Bones' and his crew landed amidst great enthusiasm, thousands of people having congregated on the beach'.

Well done 'Bones' and crew, but this was not the result that was wanted. The National Lifeboat Institutes boat was expected and required to win. There was a

'Lifeboat Competition'.

£600 prize for the best boat. Unfortunately for 'Bones' and crew and Messrs Forrest, the judges declared a no contest as the sea was too calm. It was not to be until another contest held in December 1886, when the Lifeboat Institute's self- righting boat 'The Rescue' won the prize.

Salvage Furore.

Whilst all the aforementioned were going on there was an acrimonious undercurrent of discontent between the Eastbourne lifeboat crew and that of Newhaven.

When 'Bones' and the crew of the 'William and Mary' heard of the recovery of the 'New Brunswick' and the subsequent astronomical salvage claim put in by Coxswain Lower of Newhaven, they were quite rightly peeved, if that's the right word to use. They were furious. Were the Newhaven Cox'n and crew within their rights to do what they did? Their morality could be questioned. As it is recalled they declined to put to sea on the Sunday in question the sea being too rough and were quite happy to leave the 'New Brunswick's crew to their fate. They were wired about the incident and requested to launch. As is known, they declined and they further stated it would take one hour for the Tug to raise steam to get them out of the Harbour but no effort was made to do this. Consider they knew of the distressed vessel at approximately 10.30am the morning in question. If they had requested the Tug to raise steam they could have got to the 'New Brunswick'. They would have had a following wind, given it was gale force, but it would have taken them down to her. It took 'Bones' and his crew two hours to get to Birling Gap before they could launch and then about an hour in the teeth of the gale to get alongside the 'New Brunswick'. If the Newhaven lifeboat had launched she would have reached her well before the Eastbourne lifeboat.

There can be no doubt that words were exchanged between 'Bones' on behalf of his crew and the Newhaven Cox'n Lower, was it sharp practice by Newhaven?

The Eastbourne crew had risked their lives in the rescue and while resting up on Monday, Newhaven had put out in calm, placid weather and got rich pickings, which they were going to keep for themselves. There was nothing in law that could be done by Eastbourne. So it was decided, 'Bones' with the full backing of his crew then made a claim for life salvage from the owners of the 'New Brunswick'. This claim went against the rules of the Lifeboat Institute. There was no way they would ever accept 'Bones' making this claim but 'Bones' had the full backing of his crew who were so incensed by the Newhaven action their fury overruled their heads. '*We wont be druv*' that old Sussex saying coming to the fore. All this took place while 'Bones' and the crew were being feted by the people of Eastbourne and indeed the country. 'Bones' was counselled by the local Lifeboat Institute committee and his many learned friends and others, to drop the life salvage claim, indeed it is known that cousin William Bollard Hide a crew member had strong words with him, but 'Bones' and other crew members crew would only do so if Newhaven dropped their salvage claim. Newhaven would not. Being of the poorer classes the claim represented a fortune that they were not prepared to forego. So it was stalemate.

In May 1884, 'Bones' and 2nd coxswain 'Lord' Matthews were summoned before the local branch of the Lifeboat Institute. 'Bones' and Matthews would not budge over their life salvage claim and accordingly both resigned stating they would not enlist under the National Lifeboat Institute's rules again. (Said in the heat of the moment, they did serve again) pre-empting any decision by the National Institute.

The National Lifeboat Institute could not let things rest there. (The life salvage claim by 'Bones' and the crew went through and they received a total of £105, about £5 each). After a meeting in London of the Royal Lifeboat Institute's Directors, in early June 1884, a letter was sent to the local committee, stating it was their wishes that the Eastbourne crew as at present constituted be dismissed and a new crew be appointed. ('Bones' and Matthews as is known, had already resigned). 'Bones' and his crew were very popular in Eastbourne and the action of the Lifeboat Institute, was locally much regretted.

The local committee told 'Bones' and the crew they must cease forthwith and have nothing more to do with the lifeboat. 'Bones' and the crew of course accepted this, but they stressed if there was ever a need they would be proud to serve again if called upon.

Of course there were lots of reports in the local press. To give the local papers of the time credit, most printed the facts and were dismayed because they had a high regard for 'Bones' and his crew. They stated that the Newhaven crew were to be awarded a good sum of salvage money for doing next to nothing. Although this had happened nothing could take away the heroic rescue of the 25th November 1883. The public's considerable sympathy being with 'Bones' and the crew, it was moved amongst a number of influential gentlemen of the Town that another lifeboat be purchased for 'Bones' and his crew independent of the Lifeboat Institute. This idea was very seriously considered for some months but in the end 'Bones' himself squashed the idea. On the day of the letter of dismissal 'Bones' and the crew were paraded in a carriage flying the flag of the 'New Brunswick' round the Town accompanied by a Band and given a rapturous reception by the townsfolk.

The Newhaven coxswain Richard Lower and crew after the outlandish salvage claim of £1,000, had to settle for £300 even then this was no mean sum. Questions still remain to be answered.

1. Who gave permission for the Newhaven lifeboat to be launched and take the 'New Brunswick' as salvage?

2. Could the lifeboat launch at any time just to take salvage other than save life? (Lifeboat Institute rules at the time banned the use of a lifeboat to be launched solely to take salvage).

There is no record to date of any condemnation of Newhaven by the Lifeboat Institute.

The 'Lifeboat Journal' for August 1884 gave a full account of the reasons for the dismissal of the Eastbourne lifeboat crew and it further stated,

'A boathouse keeper had been appointed to take charge of the station with instructions that in the event of a wreck or vessel being in distress, he was to give the key to any reputable seafaring or otherwise competent body of men demanding them' Further quote 'should such an eventuality occur, the old lifeboat crew would be found willing to take their old places in the boat, in spite of the unfortunate differences which led to their dismissal'.

The above statement gives the appearance that healing process was taking place between 'Bones', the crew and the Lifeboat Institute. Not a 'lock out' as reported some 90 odd years later 1978, in the Eastbourne Gazette.

September 1884.

The first Royal Parade Regatta and many of the late Lifeboat crew were involved. They even had a special race for the old Lifeboat crew.

October 1884.

The local Lifeboat Institute had a meeting in the Vestry Hall, Grove Road and decided on a new Coxswain and crew for the lifeboat. Jesse Huggett, cousin to 'Bones' was made Coxswain, and Tom Boniface 2nd Coxswain. They were formally appointed in November 1884. A double crew was also appointed, 'Bones' and the old crew among them. So all was well between 'Bones' and the Institute and there had never been any problems between 'Bones' and the crew and the rest of the fishing/boating community. 'Bones' had always been given full support from them and was very highly thought of.

One comment made by the local Lifeboat Institute committee was '*both Coxswain Huggett and 2nd Coxswain Boniface were teetotal?*'

After all the foregoing, things did quieten down and life went on. Although one must recall that, that was the time when the fishermen were being thrown off their ancient Fishing Station and forced to move east, a time of great turmoil among the fishing fraternity.

In 1978 an article on the 'New Brunswick' incident was published in the Eastbourne Gazette and is somewhat misleading.

It states '*The lifeboat house was locked for 3 long bitter years and bad feeling was the order of the day between 'Bones' his crew and every one else*'.

Not so, 'Bones' and crew were always highly thought of, then and ever after. A replacement crew was found in four months. The boathouse was not locked up for three long years. There were regular lifeboat practices and on the first service in 1887 since the incident the new Coxswain Jesse Huggett launched with 'Bones' and several of the old crew in his crew.

The Gazette states, '*November 1883, was the first time the lifeboat 'William and Mary' had been seen in the streets of Eastbourne*'. Not so, it would have been seen regularly each year on Lifeboat day when it was pulled through the streets and in July 1882. With Coxswain and crew it was dressed over all in Devonshire Place for the visit of Princess Christian of Schleswig-Holstein who laid the foundation stone for Princess Alice Hospital.

The Gazette states. '*Bones' aged about 45 years*'. 'Bones' was 34 years old at the time.

It states. '*The lifeboat was being pulled along Upper South Street, where it was met by an astonished Mayor and Corporation procession*'. Not so, they were aware of the incident prior to the start of the procession to the Church. The route would have been from the Vestry in Grove Road (where they en-robed and procession started from) up Water Lane (Southfields Road) to the Parish Church of St. Mary's.

The Gazette states. *'The discussion over what action to take, between Mr Emary the local secretary of the Lifeboat Institute and 'Bones' took place outside the Wish Tower Lifeboat house, which is now the Lifeboat Museum'*. Not so, that Lifeboat house was not built until 1899, 16 years after the rescue. It later became the Lifeboat Museum in 1937.

The Gazette states. *'After the presentation of the medals and an entertaining lunch, it was to be the last time that harmony in public prevailed. There would be no more adulation'*.

Not so, as already stressed 'Bones' and crew were always highly thought of whilst not agreeing with their claim for life salvage, the public always admired what had been done by 'Bones' and the crew. They were not vilified, as the Gazette would have us believe.

The Gazette states. *'The local committee stalled in taking action against 'Bones'*. Not so, in May at a Committee meeting 'Bones' and 2nd Cox'n Matthews resigned over the issue. It was some fortnight later that the National Institute sent a letter dismissing 'Bones' and the crew.

The Gazette states. *'Jesse Huggett appointed Coxswain of the Eastbourne Lifeboat in 1887'*. Not so, Jesse was appointed in October 1884.

The Gazette states. *'Late in 1887, was the first service of the 'William and Mary' under Cox'n Jesse Huggett and there are no details of the rescue'*. Not so, that first service was in January 1887, and was fully reported and mentioned 'Bones' and several of the old crew who were aboard the lifeboat.

As well as the Eastbourne Gazette articles there are other published reports of the 'New Brunswick' rescue and subsequent dismissal of the lifeboat crew over their claim for 'life salvage'. The statements give an impression 'Bones' and the crew were greedy. It is a pity they do not give the full facts of the rescue and the (non) involvement of the Newhaven lifeboat, Coxswain and crew and their subsequent salvage claim.

Whilst there is no excuse for the claiming of 'life salvage' against the Institutes rules, the facts and reasons why should be reported. History should not be hidden.

You couldn't' keep a man like 'Bones' down for long, something soon turned up that would give him the opportunity to show his seamanship and it was on August 26th 1885, that a schooner 'Dinawi' of Carnarvon, from Port Madoc bound for Bremen, grounded on the sands at Eastbourne.

'Several local fishermen led by 'Bones' Hide, James Hide, Charles Hurd, William Sayers, Richard Mockett and George Waymark went to the assistance of the crew and through their endeavours the schooner was re-floated. Had it not been for their assistance the schooner would have suffered considerably from the force of the sea'.

January 2nd 1884.

The Mayor gave a dinner for the poor and aged folk of Eastbourne at the Leaf Hall, commencing at midday. A full house feasted on prime joints of roast beef, boiled legs of mutton, with plenty of vegetables, followed by plum puddings and tarts with oranges and apples for dessert, finishing up with tea and coffee. Afterwards three hearty cheers were given for the Mayor Mr G A Wallis.

January 9th 1884.

It was proposed to extend Cambridge Terrace to join Royal Parade, the Terrace later becoming Cambridge Road. Later that month a report appeared in the local press regarding Mann's Row, a terrace of run down fishermen's cottages owned by Mr Gilbert. Notice to quit in two weeks had been served upon the unfortunate dwellers. Mr Gilbert was taken to task for calling upon these poor people to quit with nowhere to go. Some had lived there for nearly half a century.

'If you had not seen the place, you would scarcely believe elegant Eastbourne could boast so unsavoury a locality. Early demolition was their doom under any circumstances. Destitute of proper sanitary arrangements, the buildings are also in a rickety tumbledown condition, and the aromatic scents emitting into the main thoroughfare, saluting the nostrils of passers by, lead one to wonder why Mann's Row has been so long free from an outbreak of disease. Mr Gilbert requires the ground to make room for a new road through to the Royal Parade'.

He made a lot of money re-developing the site and did indeed build what is now known as St Aubyns Road, but not with houses for the poorer classes, Boarding houses were the order of the day. Where did the fishing families of Mann's Row go? To lodge with relations or go to the Workhouse? The planned housing for them east of the Redoubt had not yet been built.

March 1884.

The month of March mackerel fishing shows good reports for the Eastbourne fleet.

'We are glad to hear that the principal fishing Luggers belonging to Eastbourne, who are now engaged on the mackerel fishing ground off Plymouth have during the last week been very successful. One boat landed as many as 4,000 at a time, others scarcely a tenth of that quantity. This being the season of Lent there is a great demand for fresh fish, and the prices at Plymouth have been remarkably high. The greater part of the fish has been sent to the continental market. The news of the approach of the mackerel shoals was instantly telegraphed to all the fishing ports, and on Sunday some scores of fishing vessels from Lowestoft, Yarmouth and other ports on the East coast were to be seen sailing off Eastbourne away down the Channel in hot haste to take part in the mackerel harvest. If they are successful prices will soon fall. Fishing not so good locally just a few odd mackerel have been caught in our Bay'.

Down off Plymouth.

'Several of the Eastbourne Luggers engaged in the mackerel fishing in the western part of the Channel have been unusually successful during the past week. Some of the boats have landed over £50 worth of fish, and it is stated that one boat has realised nearly twice that amount'.

From a Hide fishing document it shows Ben Hide c/o Mr Paddon, Fish salesman, Barburn Quay, Plymouth. This was a calling address for fisherman Ben Hide a younger brother of John, when down at Plymouth with the fishing fleet.

April 1884.

Come the beginning of April the news was not so good,

'*Owing to the prevalence of strong easterly winds, our fishermen engaged in the mackerel fishing have not been very successful during the last week. When the wind changed on Saturday, one boat ventured out of Plymouth Harbour, and had one cast, bringing up 700 fish which sold at £2 per hundred.*

Most of the Eastbourne boats have now gone further westward, and are cruising off Falmouth, some of the larger Luggers have ventured across the Channel to the Irish coast and are engaged with the mackerel fleet off Kinsale. One consignment of mackerel has at present reached the English market, which realised £6 per hundred'.

Steamboat fish carriers would take catches at speed to homeports, prior to markets.

A local report 2nd April 1884, announced that fisherman Alleyn Sayers

'*though he was promised £2 for bringing four shipwrecked fishermen from on board an American barque and landing them at Eastbourne last week, he has not yet been able to obtain payment*'. (Fishing boat probably run down by the barque)

September 1884.

A further local report, which is as follows:

'*What about those new cottages for the poor? Fishermen's families had to turn out of their dilapidated homes last winter at Mann's Row amid great domestic inconvenience to poor women and children. We were told that the Lord of the Manor would put up some moderately rented houses for those who had been his humble tenants for over twenty years, I see no outwards and visible signs of any new cottages for the poor in this town, and the winter is close upon us. I hold too good an opinion of the Lord of the Manor, Mr Gilbert to believe that he will allow his agents to overlook the claims of the fishermen's families of whom he has always spoken so respectfully*'.

October 1884.

Henry Bollard Hide, the youngest of the 'Bollards', brought to the attention of the Authorities the fact that there was no 'Fishermen's Light' at the new Fishing Station. There had been one at the old Fishing Station, which had been very satisfactory. He further stated that every sea faring town had a red light for the use of the seafaring community. The light was needed to guide the fishermen safely ashore on a dark night and was imperative during stormy weather. His views were directed at the new Town Council.

In March 1885 the Council finally erected a light on the Beach Hotel. All winter there had been no light.

Whilst fishing for herring off Beachy Head in November, rough weather and a wind from the south-east forced the Eastbourne Lugger 'Dauntless' master Jeffrey Shamrock Allchorn, to make port into Newhaven Harbour.

Well known fisherman and boatman Alleyne 'Old Rig' Sayers, Eastbourne born and bred, passed over to 'the majority' in June 1885. Held in great respect by all who knew him, he was formally in charge of Mr H P Hughes yacht and won many races. All the boats on the beach had their flags at half-mast for the funeral.

Eastbourne Fishing Station C.1900. To the right can be seen the Rocket Apparatus House and Fishermen's Light pole.

July 1885.

A report issued by the Board of Trade told that the London, Brighton and South Coast Railway conveyed to London from Eastbourne no less than 82 tons of fish.

This was of course, in addition to the large quantity of fish caught by Eastbourne fishermen consumed in the town and neighbouring villages. These figures show the great importance of the fishing trade to the town, which would be considerably further developed on completion of the new fishing station.

The year 1885 finally saw the establishment of the Fishing Station at its new permanent site east of the Great Redoubt and in February of that year Councillor George Gausden, boat builder and fishing boat owner made a statement to the Town Council;

'The fishing industry which now numbers some 200 fishermen and families reside mainly in housing for the working classes being built at the east end of the town.

View to the west of Fishing Station taken from Tan House groyne C.1910.

They have over the last two years generated £11,000 per annum. This constitutes a staple trade and ought to be further encouraged by the Council. Improved facilities at the Fishing Station would greatly increase profit and add to the income of the Town'

There was a need for a Fish Market, as fish was still being sold on the beach when the catch was landed by 'dutch auction' in the old way. The fishermen did not always get a fair price for their catch. Mr Gausden considered the Council to be Trustees of the Fishing Station for the fishermen. He went on to talk about the Eastbourne fishing fleet drifting for mackerel and herring off Kinsale and Baltimore, Ireland and explained the system for provisioning the Luggers for these voyages was that the cost goes in with the general expenses, and is taken out of the earnings. Salt meat is used for long voyages, supplemented by fresh caught fish and fresh meat got from Ports along the way. Fish caught, was sold off at those Ports. Fish caught off Ireland was sent to England by steamboat.

Gausden went into partnership with a Mr F W Leyborne Popham, Gausden building the Luggers and Popham supplying most of the finance. They built up a fair sized fleet of Luggers over 30 feet in length. Most were skippered and crewed by local men and some men brought down from Lowestoft. There were of course the local fishermen with their own Luggers and smaller punts. The Eastbourne fishing fleet would drift for mainly mackerel all the year round, with herring and scallops (pronunciation 'scollops') also taken. The local boats used as pleasure boats in the summer, (not the Luggers) would also trawl locally for flat fish.

C.1890 On the beach at Eastbourne Fishing Station, George Gausden's Lugger 'Little Florence' 45NN (named after his daughter) under original lugger sail rig. 'Little Florence' was later lengthened to a 'Shinaman' with Dandy rig sail.

Eastbourne Fishing Station C.1892. Sailing luggers from left,
'Little Florence' the 'Rover' of Worthing and 'Lady Eleanor'.

Popham and Gausden fell out and in 1891 Popham moved to the Southampton area with his boats.

George Gausden was interviewed October 1891, and the following observations recorded; 'Fears were expressed locally of the moving of some of the big Luggers owned by Popham from Eastbourne. At the time local fishing was anything but prosperous. It could not be accounted for, for the last 25 years the autumn fishing had never failed but the last 3 years it had completely failed. Gausden owned five of the large Luggers, over 30 feet, working out of Eastbourne. They were away at sea namely 'Providence' 5 men plus 1 boy, 'Little Florence' 5 men plus 1 boy, 'Lady Eleanor' 5 men plus 1 boy, 'Happy Thought' 6 men plus 1 boy and 'Nautilus' 4 men plus 1 boy. The first four were fishing between Ramsgate and Lowestoft and the other down at Plymouth. They go no further north now.

The Irish mackerel fishing was the best now, having been down at Kinsale and Baltimore since 1885. Quote from Gausden ' I like the Irish very much. They are a little distant to you at first but when they know you they will do anything for you. Their failing is they are too fond of whiskey, but I don't blame them, they don't have our home comforts'.

'Most of the boats drawn up at the Fishing Station are longshore boats run by their owners. They do a bit of trawling for flat fish and drifting for herring, though 1891 has been a bad year. They mostly catch mackerel all year round except in mid winter when scallops are taken. The majority of our longshoremen are pleasure boatmen during the summer months. After Christmas there is very little fish about and it's hard times for them. They are honourable and independent. Their nature and calling gives them a feeling of independence. A man on the sea cares and fears for no one. That seems to be the spirit of most of them. Sooner than beg they would rather lie down and die'

Another report from back in July 1892 on the mackerel fishing off Ireland is as follows;

'The mackerel fishing off the coast of Ireland began very indifferently, but towards the close it very much improved. Prices have been fairly good, but Mr George Gausden who has just returned to Eastbourne, found unexpected difficulties to contend with, not from the Irish but from others. Gausden had five fishing Luggers at work the 'Lady Eleanor', 'Little Florence', 'Bird o' Freedom', 'Happy Thought' and 'Impulse'. When he set out he had hoped to send the fish by the new railway but the line had not been completed (from Baltimore to Cork, then by steamer to England). Finding it necessary to find other means of transit he endeavoured to send the fish direct from Baltimore by steamer, but was met by point blank denial from Liverpool and Lowestoft companies who seem to have thought it would suit their interest to refuse. They also limited a Yarmouth smack owner to two hundred boxes (half hundred) a day. Gausden naturally was indignant, and, in conjunction with the Yarmouth man he chartered the steamers 'Talisman' and 'Norseman' at a cost of £380 per month, also paying for the fuel. Gausden said his boats were 'shadowed' and he had to take proceedings against the offending parties at Skibbereen, where they were bound over to keep the peace and also ordered to pay Gausden's expenses. Whilst he was in Ireland, Gausden stayed at Baltimore a sea-coast port about 50 to 60 miles from Cork and 9 miles from the railway at Skibbereen'.

Could Popham have been one of those behind the obvious aggravation Gausden's boats experienced?

August 1886.

A destructive fire at the Fishing Station cost local fishermen dearly. Two Net shops belonging to William Climpson and Alfred Erridge caught fire and caused damage to others. Two boats and gear was destroyed in all, those that suffered loss were,

Steel boiler salvaged from cargo of SS Elephant lost in the English Channel 1884. Boiler recovered 1886.

Wreck of the 'Tally Ho' 26th December, 1886.

A. Erridge, Jesse Huggett, Joseph Huggett, W. Climpson, George Adams and George Gausden. A total of £358.11s damage was caused. Mr Harry Stevens of 67, Tideswell Road of the Fishermen's Mutual Association caused a fund to be raised and an evening of entertainment produced at the Devonshire Park Pavilion. The programme included a service of song known as 'Jack and the Lifeboat' sung by a choir of local fishermen.

The same month a seaman, James Forrester of the steamer 'Kingdom' fell overboard whilst the vessel was off Beachy Head at night and was fortunate to be picked up an hour later by the sailing schooner 'Rasmus' its crew having heard his cries for help, and put him ashore at Dover. A very lucky man.

October 1886.

A manufactured large steel boiler, part cargo of the steamer 'Elephant' which sank without trace in the Channel February 1884, was recovered in October 1886 by fisherman Jacob Collins with others and beached at Eastbourne. A claim was submitted to the Court of Admiralty, but it was not until November 1890 that the claim was dealt with, the boiler being on Eastbourne beach for some 4 years. A total of £26 salvage money was paid to Jacob Collins and others. But the tale didn't end there; the boiler lay on the beach at Eastbourne until December 1902, a plaything for children, before it was towed away by traction engine to Birmingham. Some journey, considering the size of the boiler. 18ft long, breadth 8ft 4 inches, weight 22 tons. According to a report the boiler was in excellent condition and bore scarcely any trace of having been derelict on Eastbourne beach for some 16 years.

November 1886.

The fishing was good, herring plentiful 130 for 9d.

Boxing Day 1886.

11.00pm Boxing Day, 1886, saw the tragic wrecking of the brig 'Tally Ho' about 100 yards east of the Redoubt by the Fishing Station, during extreme weather conditions. Four members of the crew were saved but sadly four were drowned just yards from the beach. She grounded right on the beach and was only yards from land yet such was the storm that it was impossible to get a line aboard. The survivors were luckily washed ashore through the heavy surf. Others not so lucky failed to survive the bitter cold. An interesting tale from an eyewitness, a Mr F Cooke a friend of 'Bones' Hide told of standing on the beach with 'Bones' and hearing the cries for help coming from the crew of the 'Tally Ho'.

Cooke relates that 'Bones' at risk to his life plunged into the boiling surf and threw a lead heaving line aboard. The idea being to make it fast and pull a heavier line aboard and bring the crew ashore with a breech buoy. A signal tug was felt and the men on shore pulled the line but sadly hauled the dead body of a sailor ashore who had tied the rope round his waist.

At danger to himself 'Bones' again entered the surf and threw a line aboard only for another dead sailor to be pulled ashore. There were no more takers when 'Bones' put another line aboard. Sadly bodies were later found down at Langney Point. If a line could have been got aboard by rocket early on when the 'Tally Ho' first went aground then perhaps more lives would have been saved?

An inquest held at the Hartington Hotel, Cavendish Place disclosed that there was no rocket apparatus on hand, recalling the tragedy of the 'Aphrodite' in 1880, had there been it was felt lives could have been saved. Another point raised was that the Fishermen's light had been completely inadequate and had blown out. A rider was added that the Town Council be petitioned to erect a light at high water mark and the Board of Trade be appealed to for rocket apparatus. It transpired that the Fishermen's light erected on the Beach Hotel apart from not being lit at the time in question was not high enough. If the light would have been visible the Captain of the 'Tally Ho' could well have beached where the fishing boats came ashore. Henry Bollard Hide wrote to the local paper criticising the fact that the light was out and the need for a substantial light to be erected near the Net shops at the Fishing Station.

The hull of the 'Tally Ho' was sold for £22 while her cargo of coal was purchased by the Steam Laundry Company, Latimer Road, Eastbourne, for £125

January 1887.

Within a few days of the 'Tally Ho' disaster, on Tuesday January 4th, the barque 'Sjadranninger' (Queen of the Sea) 858 tons, bound from New York to Hamburg, with a cargo of petroleum was wrecked off the 'Gun Gardens' Beachy Head. The lifeboat 'William and Mary' was launched in a blinding snowstorm from the Wish Tower under Coxswain Jesse Huggett. 'Bones' and several of the old lifeboat crew were in this crew. After 1½ hours hard pulling she reached the wreck and took off the crew of 16. Returning in about the same time the lifeboat beached at the Wish Tower. Hot tea and coffee was handed to the rescued sailors and the almost exhausted crew of the lifeboat. The shipwrecked sailors were lodged locally and entrained for London on Thursday. Mr and Mrs Harry Stevens of the Fishermen's Mutual Association entertained the gallant Cox'n and crew of the 'William and Mary' after the rescue to a hearty lunch. It was a particularly hazardous rescue operation due to the extreme weather conditions, a gale force wind in blinding snowstorms. The 'Sjadranninger' struck fast on the rocks and broke her back, the crew taking to the rigging until the lifeboat arrived. Altogether a first class service and rescue by the lifeboat and crew. An interesting occurrence was that the Newhaven lifeboat had also been launched and reached

Wreck of the 'Sjadranninger' Beachy Head 1887.

the wreck some two hours after the 'William and Mary' had effected the rescue.

The wreck had a cat aboard which could not be found at the time of the disaster. A week later the cat was found and brought ashore, lucky cat. The 'Sjadranninger' became a total loss. This was Eastbourne's first oil disaster, evidently some of the barrelled cargo was removed but the rest became impracticable to recover. The wreck lay on the rocks until September 1887, when another severe storm broke her up and drove the hulk along the shore where it damaged the Pier before being driven out to sea where she sank.

April 1887.

Thomas Prodger, an old fisherman living at 13, Bexhill Road was convicted of assaulting his wife, on 18th April 1887 and was sentenced to one month's hard labour. The magistrates pronounced a decree of judicial separation

In April another disaster at sea. A collision between German steamer 'Australia' and Deep Sea Mission boat 'Breeze' occurred off Beachy Head. The 'Breeze' sank with the loss of 5 hands except seaman John White. The 55ton yacht 'Breeze' had only just been presented to the Mission and was on her way from Fowey to Great Yarmouth for fitting out for her work amongst deep-sea fishermen. 'The Mission to Deep Sea Fishermen' a fine charitable institution was founded in 1881 to give pastoral and medical care at sea as the 'lot' of British fishermen around the British Isles was terrible.

Willickers, trying to kill a Willick!

A 'Willick' being a sea bird the 'Guillemot' that once inhabited the cliffs and sea in great numbers at Eastbourne. Eastbourne fishermen were known as 'Willicks' or 'Willickers'.

It was in May 1887 that local fishermen Henry Matthews and William Morris were fined for attempting to take and kill a 'Guillemot' during the close season. Both pleaded guilty. The prosecution was brought by the RSPCA. The facts of the case were that a dear lady, Connie Robinson was on the Parade when she saw the fishermen in a boat, throwing stones and attempting to hit the Guillemot, which was diving and attempting to elude them. She tried to stop them by shouting that it was 'close season'. She then took herself off to look for a policeman, told him, but he wasn't interested. So off she went back to the Parade, rowed out in a boat to the fishermen and told them she was going to report them to the RSPCA. She did with the resulting fines of 5/- and 8/6d costs being imposed on Matthews and Morris. Miss Robinson was a persistent lady who won the day. As regards the 'Willicks', Guillemots it could be they took too much fish. The Guillemot had not always been protected by a 'close season'. In John Heatherly's 'Guide to East- Born' 1819 it is reported that;

'they and other sea birds offered good sport, but on being shot were no good for the table, their flesh having a strong fishy flavour, but the fishermen of East- Bourn used them to bait their shell - fish pots, being very thankful for them'

June 1887.

The Regatta for June that year showed an exhibition of diving off the Pier head by E Climpson, T Gowland and R Vidler.

October 1887.

A Fishermen's light to replace the one previously fixed to the Beach Hotel was erected in October by the Council and sited near the centre of the Fishing Station. Being a lantern fixed to a spar 50 feet above the level of the beach and the light to be kept burning from sunset to sunrise. Oil to be used in the masthead lamp, placed in a copper lantern, which could be lowered and raised. The pine spar was constructed by Alfred Erridge father of Fred 'Mucky' Erridge.

March 1888.

The launching of several Eastbourne Luggers of over 40 tons at a cost of some

Original 'Pilot Inn' Meads C.1880.

'Pilot Inn' after extension C.1890 with proprietor John Hide, Fisherman and Boatman.

A fisherman of Holywell at the 'Pilot'.

£1,000 each, built by George Gausden for himself and Mr Popham for the fishing in the West and off Ireland.

The fishing fraternity of Meads and Holywell, and also other fishermen used the Pilot Inn, Meads as this tale informs us. It was in January 1990, at the funeral of Eastbourne fisherman, lifeboatman and bathing machine man, Fred 'Mucky' Erridge, that Andrew Basil Chester, local fisherman and fishmonger, recalled his Grandfather Andrew telling him that back in the 1890's he used to keep a boat at Birling Gap, walk there from Eastbourne, go lobstering, and walk back with his catch, stop off at the 'Pilot' for a pint and sell his lobsters there. You can't get fresher than that and alive! As opposed to a daily journey to Birling Gap, a fisherman Tom Reed in his short personal history 'The Fishermen and Boatmen of Eastbourne' relates;

'It was the practice for some who were lobster and crab fishing at Birling Gap to remain the whole week there, going round on Monday, laying their pots each day and sleeping at night in an old concrete hut on the cliff top. The Birling Gap Hotel did good business. A pony and trap from Cave Austin, fishmonger, South Street would collect the catches.

Tom Reed's personal history is well worth a read.

July 1888.

William 'Young Bollard' Hide, whilst fishing some 2½ miles off Beachy Head recovered the body of a seaman aged about 30 years. At the inquest the body was not identified and a verdict of 'drowned' brought in. Interestingly a juryman Joshua Whaley failed to attend the inquest and was fined 10 shillings by the Coroner.

November 1888.

Sadness descended over the fishing community of Eastbourne in November, when James 'Bird' Francis and Richard Wood were drowned whilst line fishing (hooking) only about a mile off shore, at midday, to the east of Beachy Head. They were in a small pleasure boat the 'Palatine'. There were also several other boats 'hooking'.

The 'Palatine' was seen to be making her way back when a terrific squall descended on all the boats and after the squall had passed the 'Palatine' was missing. The boat 'Elaine' owned by William Allchorn and crewed by William French and Joseph Jones came ashore and broke the sad news. There was still a tremendous sea running but at this news three fishermen Tom Swain, Albert 'Tuppy' Sayers and Richard Hide immediately launched the sailing Lugger, 'Lord Randolph' and made their way through the heavy seas to where the 'Palatine' was last seen but there was no trace of her or Francis and Wood.

The lifeboat was launched from down at the Wish Tower in less than 20 minutes with Jesse Huggett, Cox'n, Tom Boniface. 2nd Cox'n, and crew of Richard Hurd, *William Erridge, John Hurd, *'Bones' Hide, *Fred 'Bollard' Hide, Richard Wood, *Richard Swain, Tom Sayers, Cummings, Boniface, Carter and *William 'Billy' Stanbridge. (*Crew of the 1883 lifeboat 'New Brunswick' rescue)

The sailing qualities of the lifeboat were described at the time;

'she scudded before the wind like an arrow, tacking, fetching or running close to the wind, she sped like a feather. Her progress was watched from the shore by hundreds of people on the promenade as she was seen bearing down on a fishing boat which for some time had been trying to fetch to the shore and was in great difficulties, throwing off the foam from her bows she bore down on the unfortunate fishing boat with rapidity and graceful movements of a sea bird. It was Allchorn's boat the 'Golden City' her mizenmast had been carried away and she lay with bare poles, her head to the wind. The lifeboat took her in tow and soon ran her in to safety off the Crumbles'. ('Golden City' was used during the summer months by the Allchorns as a pleasuring sailboat then reverted to her fishing role come winter)

The lifeboat then made her way to where the 'Palatine' foundered and the Cox'n spoke to a steam Tug 'hove to' in the heavy weather, the Captain of the tug said an upturned boat had been seen some 1¹/₂ miles off Beachy Head but the weather was too rough to take it in tow. After a fruitless search the lifeboat returned to Eastbourne where she was quickly hauled up the beach by an assortment of well to do, working people and fishermen's wives with shawls on their heads. The bodies of Wood and Francis were recovered respectively late December 1888 and early January 1889.

Although the lifeboat was launched very quickly the question of a Lifeboat House at the Fishing Station was soon raised and on December 10th, a meeting of lifeboat men and fishermen proposed to petition the Council requesting them to approach the Lifeboat Institute for the Lifeboat House to be transferred from its site in Marine Road to the beach where the fishermen lived and worked.

December 1888.

After the failure of the herring fishing along the Channel, the Hastings fishermen and their families were in a very sad plight along with the rest of the poor in the Old Town of Hastings. How bad it was can be imagined by the fact that the Workhouse could not contain the amount of paupers seeking admission and arrangement had to be made for Battle Workhouse to take the surplus.

A local appeal for assistance was made on behalf of the Hastings fishermen who were in great distress. The lot of the Eastbourne fishermen was no better their families suffering much privation, and to quote a report at the time *'they would sooner starve than cry for help'*. Hard times indeed. The winter months of October, November, December 1888, and January, February, March of 1889 showed a great lack of fish of all species, so times were hard for the fisher folk.

May 1889.

A report on the Eastbourne fishing industry stated that a total of 20 Luggers left Eastbourne for Scarborough in the north and some for Kinsale, Ireland in the west. They carried crews of 5 to 8 hands each and their registered tonnage ranged from 14 to 40 tons. It was hoped the voyages would prove successful after a bad winter. Some local Luggers and punts had been off in search of mackerel and the few fish caught had not been landed at Eastbourne but at Newhaven, which offered better harbouring facilities. The local fishermen did this more in a way of protest as it was felt there was a need for a harbour at Eastbourne but that was nearly a hundred years away from fruition.

At last in May rocket apparatus was installed by the Board of Trade in a specially built Rocket house at the Fishing Station. So after the tragedies of the 'Aphrodite' and 'Tally Ho' the means of saving life was at hand in charge of the local Coastguard.

Theft of Lobsters.

May 2nd saw Hugh McCluskey a Scot aged 70 years, appear in court charged with the theft of 3 lobsters, the property of Charles Wood fisherman (for some 45 years) of Meads. McCluskey had stolen the lobsters from a box used to store them, on the beach at Holywell and sold them to fishmonger Isaac Adams for 10p per lb. Found guilty he was fined 4/7d or 10 days in prison. The court was told McCluskey gained a living by picking up beach pebbles and selling them to charitable ladies.

Eastbourne Naval Volunteer Cadets. HMS Inverclyde C.1910.

February 1890.

Fisherman's son Fred Huggett age 17 years was charged with damaging a boat belonging to George Gausden at the Fishing Station. Three holes had been smashed in the hull. Pleading guilty he was sentenced to two months hard labour. Two small boys who took part in the offence were called forward and told if Mr Gausden had prosecuted them they would have been liable to imprisonment and flogging.

Further pressure was put on the Council by a petition for a Fish Market to be established at the east end of town at the top end of Beach Road, especially as there was an injunction on the sale of fish on the foreshore, but this obviously did not cover the Fishing Station. In former times boats would and could sell their catch on the beach in front of the Parades. It was stressed that boats from Hastings, Rye, Brighton etc, would land their catches regularly at Eastbourne if there was a custom built Market.

The month of February saw the local Juvenile Naval Brigade give a display of various drills and evolutions at the Theatre Royal under Commanding Officer Tuxford. The previous evening the lads gave a march past on Grand Parade. Chief Officer of the Coastguard Mr Teeling founded the Eastbourne branch in 1888. Details of the Volunteer Cadets, locally under the command of Sub-Lieut. A J Fellows, Headquarters HMS Inverclyde, Eastbourne Company at No 2, Colonnade Gardens can be found in Gowland's Directory 1912.

April 1890.

Peter Prescoe, a fisherman, 35 years, fell from a yacht in Gausden's boat yard and broke his right leg and was taken to Princess Alice Hospital. He fell from a height of 25 feet.

View of the Missions to Seamen's (Fishermen's) Institute from Royal Parade Bowling Club.

Chapter Five

The Fishermen's Club

An article on the founding of the Fishermen's Club is contained in the book 'The Pleasure Boatmen of Eastbourne' and for continuity it is repeated here and expanded on.

In 1885 thanks to the generosity of the principal landowners of Eastbourne, Mr Gilbert and the Duke of Devonshire donating land east of the Great Redoubt, a new Fishing Station was established. Then with the development of housing for the working classes at the east end, many fishermen moved there to be closer to their daily occupation.

Alcohol for many fishermen was a release from the rigours of their hard life with the result that some families suffered, the wives especially. Drunkenness and wife beating being not uncommon with the result that the local religious factions felt there was a need for spiritual recreation for the fishermen when not at sea.

In January 1886 there were two Fishermen's Missions (Institutes) in Eastbourne. One called 'The Fishermen's Mutual Association' occupied rooms with premises in Fairlight Road, near Sea Beach Lane, (Beach Road) founded by Mr Harry Stevens. Fishermen and lifeboat men Cox'n Jesse Huggett and 2nd Cox'n Tom Boniface were on the committee, Huggett being treasurer, Boniface, caretaker. At a meeting April 1886 it was agreed by some fishermen, as far as possible, not to fish on a Sunday.

The other, a Mission Hall had been built in 1881, in Sea Beach Lane (probably sited where the Royal Naval Old Comrades Club is today) under the control of the Vicar of Christ Church, the Rev. Robert Allen. It had been opened for 'navvies and fishermen' and called 'The Fishermen's Institute'. Christ Church built in 1859 was known as the 'Fishermen's Church'.

As well as the above 'Missions' the Misses Bell of Eastbourne ran a small 'Mission' hut on the beach at the Fishing Station, this being removed by 1887.

By December, 1888, the above 'Fishermen's Missions' (Institutes) ' appear not to have been what the fishermen needed for their social and spiritual needs, perhaps the 'Beach Hotel' was still drawing many members! As a result a meeting was held in the New Temperance Hall on the night of Monday 10th, attended by a large number of fishermen, boatmen and the representative of the Missions to Seamen, Rev. C.P. Cooper. Rev. Cooper presided over the meeting. The proposal was to build a 'Missions to Seamen's Institute' at the Fishing Station and the proceedings were conducted in the orthodox mission style.

Present at that meeting were Mr Kensett, Richard Wood, William Wood, Charles

Members of the Missions to Seamen's Institute C.1900. Back row, left to right: 1 Mark Hookham, 2 George Allchorn, ------ 5 Time Erridge, ------ 7 Sam Hurd. Middle row, left to right: 1 Ted Sayers, 2 Joe Prodger, ------ 4 Samuel Oliver, ------ 9 T. Huggett, 10 Harry Boniface. Front row, left to right: Richard John Erridge, 2 William Godden, 3 Tom Boniface, 4 T. Clayton, ------ 6 Jack ELms, 7 'Irish Mick', 8 Henry Boniface, 9 Jack Mockett. Seated front centre, on left: William Boniface.

Hide, John Mockett, Nick Jackson, Jesse Huggett, George Erridge, William Allchorn, Samuel Tutt, Edwin Matthews, Samuel Oliver, George French, Fred Huggett, Reuben Reed, John Erridge, John Hurd Snr. and Jnr. D. Foster, D. Matthews, S. Dyer, Edward Wood, Thomas Knight, H Tutt, William Hobby, William Godden, and others. After discussion it was agreed to build the Mission. The following committee was then put to the meeting and accepted. Messrs. Jesse Huggett, Richard Wood, Peter Waymark, Fred Huggett, Thomas Boniface, Mr Chandler (coast guardsman), Mr Yepp (missionary), Mr Couchman (colporteur), Mr Coleman, Mr Kensett, the Misses Bell and Miss Seward.

The committee was formed to carry out the project and raise funds. This they did by advertising an appeal for subscriptions from the people of Eastbourne. In response to an application made to Mr Gilbert, he kindly gave a piece of ground on the beach. By April 1890, an iron building had been erected and was in active operation, painted on the roof in large letters for all to see were 'The Missions to Seamen's Institute'. At the start meetings were held on Sunday afternoons and evenings and also Thursday evenings. All helpers and officers of the Mission gave their services free so there were no maintenance expenses other than lighting and heating.

The Mission building became known locally as the 'Bethel' perhaps in deference to the 'Institute' in Sea Beach Lane (Beach Road). It was a teetotal, social and spiritual meeting place for the seafaring fraternity.

By 1892, it appeared that the 'Bethel' was not functioning too well, as a report in the Christ Church magazine for December of that year showed; *It is with great pleasure that the church has secured the 'Mission to Seamen's Bethel', renting it from the Rev. C B Cooper and his committee. A 'Reader' Mr D Giddens is coming to devote his whole time amongst the boating and fishing families'*. The Vicar of Christ Church was appointed Honorary Chaplain to the 'Bethel'. Fund raising continued and within a few months a coffee and reading room were added.

There were local people willing to work on behalf of the boatmen and fishermen and their families, apart from the Misses Bell, Seward and Moginie there was Miss Laura Adams, the daughter of Rev. Samuel Adams of St. Mary's Parish Church, who would journey down daily to the 'Bethel' in those days being conducted on a religious basis. Miss Adams conducted the prayers and hymns for many years and was in charge of the coffee bar and organized concerts, she also visited the boatmen and fishermen's wives and children in their homes.

By March 1893 some 20-30 men and boys were attending the 'Bethel' nightly.

A Christ Church report on the 'Bethel' disclosed that a service of thanksgiving was held for the local fishermen, remembering the terrible stormy night of 19th November. In December Jesse Huggett took a party out in his boat to take good cheer to the Lightship at Christmas. By 1894 it was announced that 20 men had signed the pledge (abstinence from alcohol) and come May 1896, an enlarged Mission's to Seamen 'Bethel' was opened to a grateful membership of fishermen and boatmen and their families.

The 'Bethel' evolved in later years under the stewardship of Albert 'Sam' Allchorn and Arthur Sayers into what is known today as the 'Eastbourne Fishermen's & Boatmen's Protection Society Club' the 'Fishermen's Club'.

An interesting gathering to celebrate the Queen's Jubilee year, took place at the Seamen's Institute 'Bethel' in November 1897 when at 6.30pm between 60 - 70 fishermen and boatmen sat down to a substantial tea. The tables presided over by the Misses Moginie, Adams, Hildyard and Mrs Hewett. After tea, half an hours smoking was enjoyed by the men and at 8pm a concert was begun and carried on with great spirit until 10pm. The following programme was carried out and the men contributed with a number of Songs, 'Nancy Lee' and 'The Little Hero' by William Godden. 'Sailors on the Sea' by Ted Sayers. 'The Boys of the Old Brigade' by Harry Godden. 'Under the Burning Sun' by Jack Elms. 'The Sailor Boy' by Jack Mockett. 'The Ship I Love' by Jack Sayers. 'The Wedding Bells' by William Godden Jnr. 'Mona' by Ben Erridge. 'The Fusiliers' by Charles Hide Jnr. Mouth organ pieces were played by Ted Sayers and Jack Dove. Miss Adams sang 'Herring are in the Bay'. With the singing of the National Anthem the proceedings closed, each man carrying away with him a silver pencil case as a memento of the occasion.

In 1898 at a meeting presided over by the Vicar of Christ Church it was decided that a Slate Club be started for the fishermen and boatmen. Mr Jesse Huggett Jnr. and Mr Ernest Sayers consented to act as stewards

December 1902 and lanternslide pictures were shown with the subjects being 'Jim, the Boatman's Yarn' and 'Christie's Old Organ'. The lantern was controlled by Ted Sayers and readings given by Miss Adams.

The same month saw a report on the Institute as follows,

'The Institute, open daily from 5.00am to 9.30pm. The well-conducted coffee bar is much appreciated. The prevalence of Sunday work among both fishermen and pleasure boatmen is the chief obstacle in the way of religious growth among them and that God and the Holy Spirit may open the eyes of these men to see the evil of this disregard of God's sacred day, a habit inherited from past generations. Sympathy, however, must be felt for them when it is remembered that the uncertain earnings of a precarious means of livelihood make the temptation to use Sunday as a day of work very strong.

Miss Adams would thankfully receive gifts of old and new clothing for the fishermen and their families. Statistics November 1901 to November 1902: -
Daily attendances at the Institute - 7,297.
Attendances at services - 293
At Bible class - 284
Visits to homes - 713
Bibles and New Testaments sold - 14
Prayer Book - 1'

In 1903 the 'Eastbourne Fishermen's Compensation Fund Society' ceased to function, leaving the fishermen and boatmen with no Society to represent them. Nevertheless, gatherings at the 'Seamen's Institute' at the Fishing Station appeared to suffice for their needs over the next few years until January 1914, saw a meeting of solidarity among the fishing/boating fraternity over a potential problem for the boatmen.

It was on Tuesday night 27th January, when a meeting of pleasure boat owners took place in the Beach Hotel to consider the proposal of the Town Council to alter the Boat Stands on the Grand Parade. Among those present were boat builder, Mr George Gausden. Messrs Ted Sayers, William Allchorn, John Hide Snr. and Jnr. William Simpson, Alleyn Sayers, Tom Swain, Ted Allchorn, John Hurd, Mike Hardy Snr. and Jnr. Tim Erridge, Henry Matthews, William Boniface, Penfold and others.

Mr Gausden was voted to the chair and he told the meeting, the local Watch Committee had been advised that more room was needed on the Grand Parade for deck chairs and in order to obtain the space required it was suggested the pleasure boats would have to move further east. On a motion proposed by Alleyn Sayers and seconded by William Allchorn a resolution was passed to the effect that the pleasure boat owners did not want to be removed from their stands on the Grand Parade. A petition embodying the terms of the resolution was agreed by all present and a committee was appointed. It was further decided to form the 'Eastbourne Fishermen's and Boatmen's Protection Society ' (E.F.B.P.Society). It was duly formed and is still in existence to this day.

The day was won on this occasion, no boat owners being moved. Officers of the Society elected at that first meeting were President Mr Charles Jewell, Chairman. Arthur Sayers, Hon. Secretary, J Godden, Hon. Treasurer. Henry Boniface. Later that year came the start of the Great War seriously affecting the Society with many members of the Society leaving to enlist and give their lives for the cause.

The first annual general meeting of the Eastbourne Fishermen's and Boatmen's

Protection Society was held on Thursday 3rd July 1915 at the Fishermen's Institute. About 20 members were present. Hon. Treasurer. Henry Boniface, being absent, having enlisted. The Hon Secretary J. Godden presented the first statement of accounts, which was adopted, with a balance in hand of £22.11s.3d. Mr Godden also announced that several members were away on active service. On a proposition of Ted Sayers, the members who were away serving their country were to be considered fully paid up members of the Society. The motion was passed unanimously. President Charles Jewell was re-elected for the ensuing year.

With the Eastbourne Fishermen's and Boatmen's Protection Society meeting in the Institute's premises we see their coming together for the first time, a marriage that lasts through to this day. The premises were teetotal and remained so for many years. For both to survive it turned out they needed each other. Those early dedicated fishermen and boatmen and Institute members were the bedrock of what we know today as the 'Fishermen's Club'.

Records are somewhat sparse but a report from the local paper of January 1916 shows the Society were active in protecting their rights. The case was over a person other than a fisherman and boatman attempting to take over a Net shop at the Fishing Station. The Society successfully fought this and brought the local Watch committee into line over their rights. Over the years many battles have been fought with the Council, some won, some lost. The year 1885 had seen the Fishing Station land granted to the Eastbourne Council who as Trustees held the land for the fishermen and boatman for their sole use in perpetuity, so long as fishing and boating was taking place. But as these occupations declined so the Council took over areas of the Fishing Station.

The first ground lost was an extension to the Redoubt bowling green in 1923. That same year the Tennis courts were opened on 'Fishermen's Green' and so it went on.

The original net repair and drying beach now a car park and children's 'Treasure Island' pleasure grounds, Royal Parade.

In later years net drying ground gave way to 'Treasure Island'. All was hard fought over by the Society, but having to give way to the law that was clearly on the Council's side as the land had fallen into disuse. Interestingly the old Marine Club, Eastbourne Angling Association building only occupied their original site on the Fishing Station by agreement with the Society. This building was also used by the local R.N.V.R. until 1914. Most fishermen and boatmen will say the dealings with the Council generally have over the years been very amicable.

For the years 1920-21 Mr J. R Siezmur was elected President and Mr Arthur Sayers, Secretary. At the A.G.M. held in the premises of the Institute in August 1922, accounts presented showed funds in hand of £70 with no expenditure for the year. Mr Montague Mayor was re-elected President, Mr Siezmur, Chairman and Arthur Sayers, Secretary.

By 1930 the Society was flourishing having 147 full members and 50 honorary members. At their annual dinner held at the York House Hotel that year the dinner was presided over by Dr A. Crook the President, Mr Faulkner being absent abroad on business. The loyal toasts were given and replying to the toast to the Corporation, Councillor G. West replied saying, it was the fishermen and boatmen of Eastbourne who first enabled him to enter public life and he was proud to be dubbed the 'boatmen's councillor'. Members giving toasts that evening were Henry Morgan Boniface, Fred Hurd, Ernest Sayers Snr. the Toastmaster being Tom Swain. Chairman Arthur Sayers spoke of the Corporation having been good to the Society in many ways and that there was no finer fleet of boats or better men along the South Coast.

The Hon. Secretary, Albert 'Sam' Allchorn spoke, saying, *'We are a very old Society and yet we are coming to the conclusion that we are now doing things we ought to have done years ago. For a start we held our own regatta last year and there are other things to do which the committee have in mind'.*

A presentation of a half hunter watch was made during the evening to the retiring Parade Inspector Luck. Badges were also presented to Albert 'Sam' Allchorn and Arthur Sayers for services to the Society.

The 'things' the committee had in mind were for the Society to convert to a Club and purchase the Fishermen's Institute premises. Discussions at that time by the principal movers of the idea, namely Alec Huggett, Arthur Sayers and Albert 'Sam' Allchorn, were held in the kitchen at the home of 'Sam' Allchorn. So it was that on 5th June 1930, members of the Eastbourne Fishermen's and Boatmen's Protection Society under the Chairmanship of Arthur Sayers met in the Victoria Hotel, Latimer Road, when it was proposed and unanimously passed, that the Society should purchase the 'Fishermen's Institute' premises, to convert into a Club. Quite an undertaking, but this they did and from then on the title 'The Eastbourne Fishermen's and Boatmen's Protection Society & Club' came into being. Albert 'Sam' Allchorn, Alec Huggett and Arthur Sayers were elected Trustees. The management committee being made up of Society and Associate club members, who are known today as "A" and "B" class. Thanks to those forward thinking and dedicated members, the complete joining of the Society with the Institute premises came about, but not without problems.

The Society had to expend its last penny on the Institute to get it out of the state it was in. A tale tells of corruption and prejudice from some quarters but this was overcome and indeed at one point the Society was legally bankrupt. In spite of all, they found their feet with the backing of the friendship of many prominent Eastbourne people and their own endeavour. An alcohol licence was obtained. The Club free of all political thought survived on an industry of co-operation and the old adage 'Charity begins at home'.

So through the years to the present day the dedication of the Club's officers and members have made it a flourishing enterprise, the envy of many, but not without occasional problems.

To develop the social side of the newly founded Club a series of concerts were held through 1931, the first being in the Club premises in February, A report shows that an enjoyable evening was spent, the scenery being made and designed by Club members, admission was free. Members contributed to the programme. Billy Knight and company gave two sketches, 'Two in a Bar' and 'Cat & Canary'. Jack Huggett led the way with Sea shanties and chorus songs. Dick Lacey with 'Coster' impersonations and Fred Hurd (a star turn) with humour and dramatic monologues. Other acts coming from D Brennan, Miss W Newman, Nelson Sayers, Alec Huggett and Arthur 'Brownie' Brown.

1931 was a busy year, socially for the Club.

On 21st February, the annual dinner was held in the York House Hotel, President Dr A. Crook was unable to attend so the mantle fell on the shoulders of the Rev. R. Fenning, Vicar of Christ Church, who had a keen interest in the Club and the fishing and boating community. An interesting reply for the guests that evening came from Mr Alexander Robertson the local Hon Secretary for the Lifeboat Institute. It had a slant on the nicknames and characters of some of the fishing and boating fraternity. He recalled some of the leading lights;

'Ernest 'Chinaman' Sayers, Albert 'Tuppy' Sayers (in the crew of the famous Eastbourne lifeboat rescue of 1883), Fred 'Donkey' and 'Early Doors' Allchorn, and the Bonifaces'. Then there are the Prodgers, they are a large family and their weather beaten faces reminded him of pirates, Will is the clown. We have a fine family of Huggetts' including Jesse, Jack, Alec and their father. Next come the Erridges' two or three of them, Coxswains of the lifeboat in earlier days. Then to the Hardys' Jim, Jack, Eddie and Mike the Cox'n who has a habit of phoning him at 2.a.m. saying, 'Mike, speaking' to tell him of an S.O.S. Let me tell you are a good lot of fellows and I include in that 'Old Tinker' Novis (Henry, the father of Fred ' Tinker')'.Old Dusty' Matthews, 'Tishy', 'Old Foot' Jack Prodger, 'Squarty' Little 'Mucky' Fred Erridge, and 'Ratty Jack' (laughter)

'Old Dusty' Matthews created a minor sensation by interjecting during the speech, saying *'I got my name 70 years ago by being blown into Harwich'*.

Chairman Arthur Sayers' speech recalled the Society was one of the oldest in the Town having existed through from 1839. It guarded the interests of the men, their wives and families. Eclipsed during the Great War it had now reached a point where it was once more worthy of its name.

Speaking in general terms the building up of the Society had been up against the

Fishermen's Club Annual Dinner 1932.

darkness of ignorance, a result of the lack of education to some degree, but it had been surmounted. He thanked the Corporation and expressed the Society's appreciation for all it did. Theirs was the oldest section of the community in Eastbourne. They were proud of what they had achieved, because without fishing and boating they could say no other Town through humble ownership had so fine a fleet of boats. They claimed their share in giving the Town publicity and it was a fact without the Society there would have been no Regatta over the last few years. They had cost the Council nothing financially, last year though the Society had a deficit of £10. The Council should look to help out in the future. Of the fishing and boating community some 99 per cent were members of the Society. Arthur Sayers concluded his speech by thanking the Reverend Fenning of Christ Church, for all he had done over the years in helping them to acquire the Institute premises and had supported the suggestion that an alcohol licence be obtained; he was a true champion of the Society and its members. The evening finished with songs and harmony.

Henry 'Dusty' Matthews and Jack Elms sing 'Hearts of Oak' at the Annual Dinner, 1934.

The annual dinners certainly were enjoyable occasions attended by prominent people of Eastbourne. So much so that a second dinner

Members in the Institute C.1935.

in 1931, was held at the York House Hotel on 12th December, attended by his Worship the Mayor, Mr Maclachlan, John Slater. M.P. Local brewer Mr Ronald Cardwell and Dr A Crook and others. Fine things were said about the Society and fun prevailed. Mr Cardwell in proposing the toast to the Club said *'Yours is a dangerous and chilly occupation, you have shown yourselves to be brave men because from time to time you drink my beer (Star Brewery) (laughter). I now have the privilege of saying five little words that make the world run smoothly, 'have a drink with me' (laughter and cheers).*

Replying Mr Arthur Sayers said he did not think there had been a time when he had worn the jersey of a fisherman and been so honoured. He had special words of praise for Dr Crook who had stepped into the breach in the past and had the welfare and interest of the Club at heart. For the Club, Mr Sayers said they were now in a position to provide fishermen with their nets, a cup of tea in the mornings and even cigarettes and it was all British. (Applause) Community singing then set the ball rolling with Alec Newman at the piano and Sid French leading the way, the fishermen and boatmen joined in with gusto. Old Henry 'Dusty' Matthews 84 years got up and sang and was cheered for his effort. Others who contributed with songs and recitation were, Jack Elms, Jack Sayers, Jack Huggett, Nelson Sayers, Alec Huggett, Fred Hurd, Jack Davey, Jim Knight, Jack Sayers Jnr. but fisherman 'Brownie' Brown got tired of waiting to sing and went home. In all though, a good time had by all.

1932 saw a new Club Chairman. Mr R. Pike, Dr. Crook continuing as President. The Council were after more ground at the Fishing Station, talks evidently were amicable with the Council promising to make some improvements at the Fishing Station with the proviso that should they be made the fishermen should play their part for the good of the Town. That year the Club was indebted to the local Star Brewery and brewer Mr Ronald Cardwell for assistance with finance and the fitting of a bar and a tea/coffee bar in the Club premises.

1933 and the newly elected Club President Mr Ronald Cardwell presided at the annual Club dinner held at the Gildredge Hotel. The gathering included five club members with a total age of at least 387 years. George Prodger, Henry 'Dusty' Matthews, William 'Kilcraft' Erridge Mike Hardy and Jack Mockett, the youngest a mere 70 years. The evening was concluded with a musical programme by F and S Smith, piano J Davy, J Huggett and Mike Hardy. Community singing was led by 'Chum' French with such shanties as 'Fire down below' 'What shall we do with the drunken sailor' and 'Hearts of Oak', all going with a nautical swing.

Coal fires for heating was the order of the day in 1934, best Welsh steam cobbles at 38/- a ton and a 12/6d monthly bill for Ronuk polish. The newspaper 'Daily Express' was bought daily for members and two teapots purchased to satisfy the need for tea during the day. A joint wage of £3.10s per week was paid to the steward and stewardess, a deposit of £20 being required from them on obtaining the post. Members' mothers were allowed into the Club free.

250 members and guests at 2/6d a head attended the annual dinner held at the R.N.V.R. Depot, adjacent to the Club premises on 12th October 1934. The Club was on a sound footing financially and that night, vocally, the tradition of cheeriness was maintained by lusty voiced fishermen and boatmen, the musical tit-bit of the evening being a duet 'Hearts of Oak' sung by Henry 'Dusty' Matthews aged 86 and Jack Elms a mere 67.

Mr Ashcroft gave up the Chairmanship of the Club in 1935 and was succeeded by Mr Ernest 'Chinaman' Sayers. Through 1936 improvements to the Club premises included the installation of central heating. Winter socials and musical evenings were re-introduced with success and children given a Christmas party, which became a great success for many years. Chairs from the Pier Company were bought for Club use and a wireless set purchased for £6, £2 was got for the old one. George Erridge Jnr. was allowed 10/- compensation for loss of work caused by burning his leg on the electric fire in the Billiard room. Two members were spoken to for singing in the Bar.

For the very first time the 1938 annual dinner was held on the Club premises, the function filling the main room. The Club had been extended with a new wing added that year but a comment from the Chairman showed all members did not like it. He commented at the dinner 'We as a fishermen's club are as good as any in Town and the success of any club is unity, not backbiting'. Strong words indeed. Guests attending that dinner were the Mayor- elect. A E, Rush, Sir Robert Dodd, Charles Taylor. MP, Mr Ronald Cardwell and Bishop Walter Carey, a champion of the working classes of Eastbourne and a great friend of the Club for many years. (Naval Chaplain at the Battle of Jutland and Chaplain to Eastbourne College, his portrait hangs in the Club) Speaking at the dinner he criticised the rent rises on the poorer classes of Eastbourne. Another guest at that dinner was a former club member, Henry Morgan Boniface at that time Chief Fisheries Officer for the Sussex coastal area.

Boatmens Ran Dan Race. Sept. 1935. Winning crew: Cox; Time Errodge, Burt Addington, Nelson Sayers and Bill Andrews.

120 children attended the Christmas party for 1938 at the Club premises with a giant Christmas tree for all to see, a happy time was had. The Mayor attended, and after food and songs, presented each child with a bag of fruit and a new penny. Thanks were extended to the Ladies section consisting of Mrs. Huggett, Mrs. Andrews, Mrs. Wood, Mrs. Chester and Mrs. Parker for their

EASTBOURNE CARNIVAL. AUGUST. 1937. THE FISHERMEN'S CLUB ENTRY.
A YARMOUTH FISHING TRAWLER.

services. Further thanks were extended to the Clifton and Wenyoke Hotels for their contributions of crackers, balloons and decorations. The Christmas party 1939 also entertained 120 children.

For a time during the 1930's the Club obtained revenue by hiring out the premises for certain hours during the day for use as a private school to the Misses Westrop and Gamble for mixed 5-11 year olds. An ex pupil, Mrs Joyce Purshouse (nee Morris) recalled the fee being 1s.6d a week with 38 children in the class using tables as desks. A vivid memory that stayed with her all her days was of the rat trap in the lavatory. It terrified her.

GUESTS OF FISHERMEN.—The Mayor-elect (Councillor A. E. Rush), Bishop Carey, Sir Robert Dodd, Mr Charles Taylor, M.P., and Mr Ronald Cardwell were dinner guests at the Fishermen's Institute on Saturday. The dinner was held by the Fishermen's and Boatmen's Protection Society and Club.

With the outbreak of the World War 2 a resolution was passed that members in H.M. Forces retain their membership free during hostilities and all members of H.M. Forces be admitted as temporary members for a fee of 1/-. But, still no women to be served drinks at the bar. The Sports committee was abandoned for the duration.

The A.G.M. February 1940 elected a War committee. Chairman. Ernest 'Chinaman' Sayers. Society Committee members. Albert 'Sam' Allchorn, William Allchorn, William Boniface, Jesse Huggett, Harry Erridge Snr. Edwin' Ned' Sayers and Mike 'Jersey' Hardy. Co-opted club members. Bill Andrews, T Mills, B Mepham and R Austen. Blackout measures were put in hand, silver cups placed in the Bank and enquiries put in hand regarding moving of the Club premises to St Anne's School during the war years in case of emergency. A stirrup pump was purchased for use in the event of a fire and £500 invested in War Bonds.

The Club premises suffered slight war damage and in July 1944 received a cheque for £217 to effect repairs. Net shop No.37 at the Fishing Station received war damage. This war 'damage' was caused when two dogs reputedly coupling, set off a mine, parts of the poor animals being blown as far as the Beach Hotel.

Eastbourne itself suffered heavily from enemy action being the most bombed resort on the South coast. With the war coming to an end in 1945 there were complaints of overcrowding of the Club at weekends with the result that members were restricted to bring in their wife and one friend only.

After the war, fishing and pleasure boating gradually went into decline and by the mid 1960's only Allchorn Bros continued to operate their pleasure boats. The Club

CLUB OUTING. C. 1947.

SOME CLUB MEMBERS IN THE OLD CLUB . C. 1960

under various dedicated Society class members went from strength to strength but only with hard work. Society 'A' class member being defined as, a Fisherman *'one chiefly earning his living by fishing on the sea, and a Boatman as one chiefly earning his living as a licenced boatman plying for hire on the sea'*.

The Associate 'B' class membership grew and helped sustain the Club and membership most years had a waiting list. Children's parties were legendary.

The old traditional fishing and boating families gave sterling service to the Club. Hardy, Chester, Andrews, Wood, Allchorn, Huggett, Sayers, Erridge to name but some. The Club was their inheritance and a great sense of purpose and stability flowed through the club during those years. As before the war, so after, the Club regularly entered the local Carnival and most years won their section. Annual dinners were always fully attended, the Club booking the Winter Gardens, Pier, Grand and Cavendish hotels being among the venues.

1946 saw the Club asked to pay £40, a big sum in those days, for the re installation of the fishermen's red lamp that had shone from a mast close by the old rocket house. A most important aid to fishermen the light had been maintained by the Council for 50 years but they now refused and Trinity House bore no responsibility. A letter was sent by the Club to Charles Taylor (later Sir Charles) M.P. Eastbourne, a long serving club member, asking him to assist in the question as to who should bear responsibility for maintaining the lamp. Shortly after this the Council accepted responsibility and the lamp remained operational until 1970/71 when the mast was taken down and the lamp was finally erected onto Allchorn Bros No.5 Net shop where it remains (inoperative) to this day.

Times were indeed hard in those early post war years and in 1947 with rationing and a general shortage of food and materials, a Club rule was made that when whisky was received from the Brewers, members only were to be served with a second nip! The Society class members certainly had their work cut out contending with proposed schemes and financial impositions by the Council. A Solicitor was retained to represent the Club and safeguard the fishermen and boatmen rights.

The people of Eastbourne were reminded of the war years when in January 1948 a mine was set off by a stray dog on the beach at the Fishing Station and damage was caused to the pleasure boats of the Allchorn and Sayers boating families. Compensation was paid and the advantages of being a Society member came through. Snippets from the committee minutes for those post war years, show a member was asked to stop letting his dog drink from his beer glass, another asked to wash his hands before playing cards and the Club steward refused to take 'Fretting' money due to its dirty condition.

The A.G.M of 1951 saw Albert 'Sam' Allchorn propose that all Committee members and not just Society class members elect a Club Chairman but this was defeated. In those days Club Chairman was always a Society class member.

Management that year was: President. Mr Ronald Cardwell, Chairman. A J Chester, Hon. Secretary, A Andrews.

Committee: Society class. M. Hardy Snr. M Hardy Jnr. W Sayers. A Huggett. R Hegarty. E Sayers. W Wood. T Allchorn. Brian Allchorn. Associate class. E Vernon, E Gearing and F Culver.

The Sports committee and others backed up the above. It wasn't until 1964 that the Chairman could be either a Society or Associate class member.

By 1954 a waiting list had to be introduced for new members. Mr Eric Owen, Managing Director of the local Star Brewery became Club President in 1955.

During the 1950's some Club dinners were held at the Pier Hotel, always fully attended, eventually the venue finished up at the Grand Hotel catering for 500 persons. The dinners continued for many years fully supported by members, happy days for all concerned thanks to the enthusiasm of committee members.

In 1957 with the fabric of the old original tin built Institute failing and good money being spent on maintenance, the idea of a new Club building was mooted. Plans were drawn up at this stage but put on hold possibly because the Council were considering developments at the Fishing Station. A repaint of the Club took place to keep it up to standard and new electrical central heating was installed to replace the old coke fired system. On the social side an interesting Tombola prize was a barrel of beer won by the Strudwick family.

The first jukebox was installed in the Club in 1960 and that year the Carnival float entry was 'The Royal Sovereign Lightship'. The following years saw the decorated float entries of 'Moby Dick' his waterspout being provided by a bucket of water and a 2nd World War stirrup pump. A 'Viking' ship, with the 'Vikings' sporting beards made from plumbers hemp. The pirate ship 'Hispanola' the bloodthirsty crew of Club members sporting that year 'home grown beards'. Big George Cole as 'Blackbeard' was ideal for the part. Member Dave Nicholls kept his beard for many a year. 'HMS Amethyst' was another worthy entry. It was fun but hard work by members involved in the construction of the floats in particular from Colin Allchorn who also gave many years service as treasurer and committee member.

1961 saw the introduction of two sixpenny fruit machines installed and a 3-piece band hired for dancing. February 1963, women were admitted to the Club as associate members on payment of 2/- subscription and entitled only to the Club amenities, no vote nor able to become officials of the Club. This was the year that the Council proposed to replace the existing Net shops and redevelop the Fishing Station site.

The fact that the Club would have to give up some of their ground and re-site the Club premises was of great importance to the Club, especially the Society class members. A sub committee of 'Sam' Allchorn, Dick Hegarty, Fred 'Mucky' Erridge and Andrew Chester was formed to liaise with the Council over the proposed redevelopment plans. It was hard work from 1964 onwards for those Club officials, the Council to be dealt with and the question of raising finance for what would be a new built Club. Thanks to the benevolence of some local people, come November the Bank was prepared to advance finance for the new building. Legal advice was for the Club to become a Limited Company. So duly at the A.G.M in 1965 it was proposed and passed for the Club to become a Limited Company and by April the new building contract was signed for work to commence from May to October.

The A.G.M. on 9th May, saw the proposal for the Club's assets to be transferred to the 'Eastbourne Fishermen's and Boatmen's Protection Society and Club Limited'. This was carried and the first meeting of the Club as a Limited Company

The Vikings.

H.M.S. Amethyst. Outside the old Club premises.

DEMOLITION OF THE ORIGINAL CLUB BUILDING. 1966.

took place. There were 94 members present and Trustee 'Sam' Allchorn aptly chaired that first meeting. It was at this meeting that Society members were designated 'A' class and Associate members 'B' class. At an extraordinary meeting held on 12th September 1966 the assets of the old Club were transferred to the new Club Company. The completion of the new Club premises overran into 1967 and were finalised by the end of February. The official opening took place on 9th March at 8.00pm. Mr Eric Owen, Club President performed the opening ceremony to a packed Club. Through hard work by all concerned, members were now the proud owners of an up to date 1st class purpose built Club. But there was more hard work ahead as the finance loan had to be paid off. From a total cost of £34,375.15s.0d. some £7,000 was outstanding.

With the opening of the new Club and increasing membership it became apparent that the long serving dedicated sports secretary Ted Barber who ran the entertainment side needed assistance, so an entertainments committee was formed consisting of Bob West, Vic Hunnisett, Norman Hope, Roy Fillery and Brian Allchorn. Meeting on Monday evenings, plans and proposals were discussed to raise the level of entertainment. The Ted Crouch Trio were engaged for the Saturday night summer months, the jukebox having been got rid of in November 1966. Fancy dress parties on Christmas Eve were popular and a tradition was established that all participants visited the 'Angling Club' for a drink and a skylark! They in their turn similarly visited the Club on New Years Eve, Halloween. Darts and 40's evenings were likewise a great success. In those days before 'in house catering' potatoes were left to bake in various members homes and collected during the evening and served up with beans, sausages and the like cooked on a mobile unit in the corner of the ballroom by real life Chef, club member George Cole.

April 1967 saw the membership limited to 750. By 1971 this had risen to well over 1,000. April also saw the building overdraft down to £6,000, which was paid off over the next 2 years - a great effort.

By February 1972, membership was up to 1,300. That year a Miss Fishermen's competition was held in May and became a long-standing event. Good coverage was given by the local press to this event in common with most of the Club's special events. The Club held a 'Fishermen's Ball' dance in February 1973, at the Winter Gardens, with the Cyril Stapleton Band providing the music. It was a sell out, with two visiting coach loads of Hastings fishermen and their wives attending. These 'Balls' proved very successful for some years with Grand draw prizes held with values of £500, a considerable sum in those days, washing machines, bicycles and sheepskin coats as an example. Other top class bands providing music were Edmundo Ross and Syd Lawrence.

There became a need to extend the Club area to accommodate the increased membership and one way was to go up! Again the hard work of the committees from the President through to members was brought into force and as a result a new upper bar extension was built and officially opened in February 1975. Thanks in particular went to members, the Strudwick brothers. They undertook and operated the building of the new extension, saving the Club thousands of pounds and for their devoted work they were made life members and presented with inscribed watches and grateful thanks. A fine effort by dedicated Club members. A modern lounge bar where the wearing of working clothes was banned, built for members to get away from the bustle and noise of the downstairs bar, a haven of peace for a drink and conversation.

Sadly on the day of the opening of the new bar the funeral took place of Albert 'Sam' Allchorn, fisherman and boatman, who devoted his life to the benefit of the Society and Club serving as Trustee, President, Chairman, Hon Secretary, committee member and guiding the Club through to see the new premises built carrying on a tradition that started with his forbears back in 1839. 'Sam's' memorial is surely the fine Club premises and thriving membership.

In 1932 as a Trustee he was prominent in the purchase of the original premises, and in 1967 to become a Limited Company and building of the new premises. His sons Brian and Colin in keeping with family tradition have served the Club well. Brian in particular has held the offices of President, Chairman and committee member.

By 1977 the secretary's workload had trebled, a thriving Club had by then membership approaching 2,000. Come 1981 it had indeed passed that mark with 2,328 and 473 lady members. That year saw the first Wedding reception held at the Club and on 19th November, an Amateur Boxing night was held in the Ballroom.

In 1982 the country was at war with Argentina in the Falkland Islands and members showed their support for the servicemen and women by holding a Falklands Party night to raise funds. A successful evening was held, £590 being raised. Extensions to the Children room, Cracker bar and Snooker room took place in November 1984 the Cracker bar being completely renovated. That year also saw the start of the Football section, a success from the start and still thriving. A successful Bowls section came along in 1985. These sports sections having been preceded by the Golf section in 1977.

1985 - 86 saw an extended Snooker room with a third table, maintaining the excellent reputation enjoyed by the Club throughout the local Snooker fraternity, plus a kitchen extension and restaurant added to the upper bar area. So restaurant facilities became available and over the years improved until today the Club has a first class restaurant. February 1988 and the sale of wine by the glass became available at the bar. The 1980's nevertheless were not without their problems on the financial side but thanks to the dedication of treasurer Roy Morris who kept a tight rein on finance in conjunction with secretary John Kirkpatrick the Club got through this uncertain period.

A Club institution on Friday nights was the 'Tontine'. Run for so many years by club stalwart the late Bill 'Booner' Wood and latterly by his wife Rose. Bill a lifetime member of the Club, having given sterling service over the years in various offices. Being noted for being 'agin it' so much that on one occasion he voted against a proposition only to be reminded by the Chairman that it was himself that had proposed it!

Through the 1990's to the Millennium and into the 21st century the Club continued under the leadership of Club President, the late Bob West.

With challenges in the new century, the Club will surely surmount these and maintain the title of a premier membership club of the South, whilst the "A" Society members diligently protect their rights against the rising and continuing problems of the Fishing Industry.

	PRESIDENT	CHAIRMAN	TREASURER
1934-35	R.M.CARDWELL	H.P.ASHCROFT	E.SAYERS JR.
1936-40	R.M.CARDWELL	E.SAYERS SR.	E.SAYERS JR.
1941	R.M.CARDWELL	E.SAYERS SR.	H.ERRIDGE
1942	R.M.CARDWELL	E.SAYERS SR.	F.ALLCHORN
		H.ERRIDGE	
1943-46	R.M.CARDWELL	E.SAYERS SR.	F.ALLCHORN
1947	R.M.CARDWELL	G.BONIFACE	M.HARDY
1948	R.M.CARDWELL	A.J.CHESTER	S.G.SAYERS
1949-50	R.M.CARDWELL	A.J.CHESTER	J.HUGGETT
1951-52	R.M.CARDWELL	A.J.CHESTER	A.W.ANDREWS
1953	R.M.CARDWELL	E.H.SAYERS	A.W.ANDREWS
1954	H.N.SCLATER	E.H.SAYERS	A.W.ANDREWS
1955-56	E.R.OWEN	A.E.ALLCHORN	A.W.ANDREWS
1957-58	E.R.OWEN	R.A.HEGARTY	A.W.ANDREWS
1959-60	E.R.OWEN	B.E.ALLCHORN	R.A.HEGARTY
1961-62	E.R.OWEN	A.E.ALLCHORN	A.B.CHESTER
1963-64	E.R.OWEN	B.E.ALLCHORN	A.B.CHESTER
1965-66	E.R.OWEN	A.E.ALLCHORN	A.B.CHESTER
1967-68	E.R.OWEN	R.A.HEGARTY	A.B.CHESTER
1969-70	R.G.ATKINS	W.G.T.WOOD	R.A.HEGARTY
1971	A.E.ALLCHORN	R.C.CLARKE	R.A.HEGARTY
1972	A.E.ALLCHORN	R.C.CLARKE	C.A.ALLCHORN
1973-74	A.E.ALLCHORN	R.W.WEST	C.A.ALLCHORN
1975-76	R.G.ATKINS	R.W.MORRIS	C.A.ALLCHORN
1977	R.G.ATKINS	R.W.WEST	C.A.ALLCHORN
			M.BAILEY
1978	R.G.ATKINS	R.W.WEST	R.E.ANDREWS
1979	R.G.ATKINS	B.E.ALLCHORN	R.W.WEST
1980	R.G.ATKINS	B.E.ALLCHORN	R.W.MORRIS
1981-82	R.W.WEST	J.W.EASTES	R.W.MORRIS
1983-84	R.W.WEST	N.R.HOPE	R.W.MORRIS
1985-86	R.W.WEST	R.A.WOOTTEN	R.W.MORRIS
1987-88	R.W.WEST	B.E.ALLCHORN	R.W.MORRIS
1989	R.W.WEST	P.J.BOWKER	R.W.MORRIS
1990	R.W.WEST	P.J.BOWKER	R.W.MORRIS
1991	R.W.WEST	B.E.ALLCHORN	P.J.BOWKER
1992	R.W.WEST	B.E.ALLCHORN	P.J.BOWKER
1993	R.W.WEST	D.PRATER	P.J.BOWKER
1994	R.W.WEST	D.PRATER	P.J.BOWKER
1995	R.W.WEST	M.R.SPOKES	P.J.BOWKER
1996	R.W.WEST	M.R.SPOKES	C.J.HEATH
1997	R.W.WEST	B.S.BANKS	C.J.HEATH
1998	R.W.WEST	B.S.BANKS	K.T.NEWSON
1999	R.W.WEST	M.R.SPOKES	K.T.NEWSON

Officers of the Fishermen's Club 1934-1999.

Chapter Six

Tragedy and Survival at Sea - Fishermen Reminiscences

Back to the year 1890 and the month of June saw the launching of another racing yacht, the 'White Slave' built by George Gausden at his yard in Beach Road for Mr Popham. She was Lugger rigged as the previous yacht 'Paradox'. Designed by W Fife Jnr. She was 60 feet long and had a 14 ft beam, 40 ton, no centreboard but a keel of 30 tons 5 cwt. She had a foremast of 31 feet, mizzen 77 feet, the sail area being 4,000 square feet. A crew of 11 skippered by Captain Tonkins of Penzance. The 'White Slave' launched off the beach, was christened by Miss Florence Gausden aged 11 years, the daughter of the builder. Like the 'Paradox 'the 'White

The 'White Slave' built by George Gausden 1890.

Slave' failed to impress as a racer and within a year or two she was converted to cutter rig.

July 1890.

Unusually stormy weather later in July caused the grounding of the barge 'Eureka' 73 tons, with a cargo of linseed cake and oats, at Langney Point. She dragged her anchor when off the Redoubt, known as the 'roads' where the local boats anchored. The lifeboat 'William and Mary' Cox'n Jesse Huggett and crew launched quickly

'William and Mary' lifeboat practice launch at the Wish Tower under Cox'n Jesse Huggett 1890.

The 'William and Mary' at sea 1890.

at the Wish Tower having been towed on her carriage along Grand Parade from Marine Road. They rowed to the 'Eureka' taking off the Captain, his wife and two men landing them east of the Redoubt. Shortly after this the cables of the 'Eureka' parted and it was then she grounded. The 'Nautilus' a fishing Lugger belonging to Popham and Gausden had the greatest difficulty coming ashore at that time having a catch of some 1600 mackerel on board. The grounded 'Eureka' brought much work to the local fishermen and labourers, as she had to be unloaded in 'situ' on the beach when the storm abated. All under the direction of Councillor Tom Bennett, acting on behalf of Lloyd's of London. The 'Eureka' was later got off by Tug and taken to Newhaven for repairs. The lifeboat crew were commended for their prompt actions.

September 1890.

The death of fisherman William 'Old Bollard' Hide age 71 years. The father of William 'Young' Bollard, Frederick Bollard, Jesse Bollard, Arthur Bollard, Henry Bollard and daughters Sara Bollard and Elizabeth Bollard. The 'Bollard' name in this particular branch of the Hide family is said to come from when 'Old Bollard' had a French fisherman friend named Boillard who was his smuggling compatriot, subsequently naming his children so. Sons, fishermen William and Frederick were members of the lifeboat 'William and Mary' at the 1883 'New Brunswick' rescue. Jesse and Arthur became accomplished Sussex County cricketers. Jesse was for the year's 1878-1883 curator (grounds man) and player/coach for South Australia Cricket Club, laying the original Adelaide Oval cricket ground.

William 'Young Bollard' Hide (1851-1936) wearing his Eastbourne 1883 lifesaving medal.

December 1890.

Just prior to Christmas, Auctioneer C. Edgar Horn offered for sale on the direction of fisherman James Boniface, his fishing boats 'Cecilia' which fetched £6. 10s. 0d. 'Little Jim' £18.10s.0d and 'Little Mackerel' £47. 10s. 0d. The boat 'Wonder' was bought in. A number of nets and a Net shop were also offered for £15.

1891.

It was in 1891 that the Prince and Princess of Wales paid another visit to Eastbourne and as in 1883 the fishermen and boatmen erected an Arch in their honour. During the month of March that year the Council discussed the proposal of a Sea Fishery District, under the Sea Fisheries Act 1888, covering the South Coast in sections i.e. Rye to Newhaven, which concerned Eastbourne. It would mean an Inspector of Fishing being appointed to safeguard the size of fish caught and other management of the coastline and fishing. In 1888 with the passing of the Sea Fisheries Act, an original district was established running from a line south east of Dungeness Lighthouse to Hayling Island. As today, they were conservation conscious. In any

Fishermen's and Boatmen's Arch, Marine Parade erected for the visit of the Prince of Wales, 20th June 1891.

event at a later period an Inspector of Fisheries was appointed and George 'Pincher' Hide was elected a committee member of the Sussex Fisheries representing Eastbourne, a post he held for many years.

At the same meeting the Council were still discussing the proposed Fish Market for the Fishing Station. A Fish Market was eventually built for the fishermen by 1900.

The report of George 'Pincher' Hide Inspector of Fisheries for the year 1890 was issued and for Eastbourne it showed an improvement on the years 1888/9. There were ten deep sea Luggers employed in trawling for plaice from March to May with good catches. In drift net fishing for herring, some forty boats engaged from 15th October to 16th November with good catches. Line (hooking) fishing for cod, whiting and ray was followed with five boats (punts) with fairly good results. Pots for whelks employed six boats (punts) from October to January, again good results. Spratting with drift nets was poor. Overall the season was fairly good. The report also published the value of fish caught £1,518 and brought ashore at Eastbourne for the past year 1890. But it should be remembered that the large fleet of Eastbourne Luggers fished away down to Ireland and up the north selling their catches as they went. It wouldn't do to over fish our local stocks. The report went on to say that some twenty years ago (1870's) and before there were huge oyster beds off Eastbourne but trawlers in large numbers came and in a very short time the operation known as 'killing the goose that lays the golden eggs' was performed, the beds being dredged empty. (See Reuben 'Old Screw' Wood's interview reported later in the book)

Early September saw the wrecking of fishing boat 'Owl' owned by Jesse Goldsmith. She was on her way from Eastbourne to Newhaven, her sail split off Beachy Head and she foundered on the rocks becoming a total loss. Goldsmith was lucky to escape with his life. The 'Owl' was 30 feet long and valued at £100 and had only just been purchased from the West Country but being unsuitable for beach landing was on her way to Newhaven to be converted. Goldsmith had invested all his money in her and was now destitute. A collection was raised for him by the Mayor and a good sum collected.

The 1891 census shows a total of 100 fishermen, boatmen and associated occupations, running on par with the 1881 census. It is felt the 'microfisch' of the 1891 census is not complete.

June 1891.

A sea drama took place when the Newhaven to Dieppe ferry the steamer 'Normandy' went aground on the rocks at Holywell, in thick fog at 5.35am on Friday 26th June. She was only 150 yards from the shore. No immediate danger was anticipated and a steam tug was sent round from Newhaven to pull her off. The Eastbourne lifeboat was launched and rowed up to the scene under Cox'n 'Old Lad' Jesse Huggett his crew being 2nd Cox'n Tom Boniface, Frederick Bollard Hide, Alfred, John and William Erridge, Reuben Wood, Harry Boniface and George 'Gruff' Hide Jnr. Lloyd's deputy agent Mr Tom Bennett also sent his boat 'Elizabeth' to Holywell, skippered by James Allchorn Snr. with a crew of Daniel and William Waymark and Samuel Beckett Hide. 11.00am saw high tide and the 'Normandy' pulled off the rocks without damage, to the cheers of many onlookers at Holywell.

December 1891.

The debate over the site of the Lifeboat house again came to the fore when a distress signal was seen coming from the Royal Sovereign lightship at 1.30am on a day in December 1891.

Jesse Huggett, Coxswain living at 1, Marina Terrace, Beach Road, rang the alarm bell, which was attached to his house. The crew and volunteers quickly attended the lifeboat house situated in Marine Road behind the hotel buildings of Royal Parade and 5 horses were got ready. The lifeboat was then launched off the beach at the Fishing Station as opposed to the other launch site at the Wish Tower. It took 1 hour to get to sea. The lifeboat then took off an injured seaman from the Lightship. Jesse Huggett was of the opinion the lifeboat house should be at the Fishing Station where the rocket apparatus was kept. What with most of the fishing fraternity living within the area of the Fishing Station that must be the best site. There would be no need for a carriage and cradle for it to be hauled along the road this took a lot of time. The debate continued and a year later a suggestion was made for an iron boathouse with a slipway to be built where George Gausden used to launch his newly built boats and yachts. This eventually came into being in 1903. It is still there to this day but now only used to house the inshore lifeboat as the lifeboat is now moored in the Harbour basin where the new lifeboat house stands. The other lifeboat house at the Wish Tower was built in 1899, but launching off the beach there proved to be unsuitable, the building later becoming the Lifeboat museum.

The value of fish landed at Eastbourne for the season 1891 was £1,716, £200 up on the previous year. The value of fish landed at Eastbourne in 1892 was £2,963. Total weight 5,565 cwt. These statistics were started in 1885.

March 1893.

Arthur Matthews, landlord of the Beach Hotel and fishing and pleasure boat owner died aged 48 years, March 1893. He would be remembered for his yacht racing against Alleyne 'Old Rig' Sayers

June 1893.

The drowning of an Eastbourne fisherman marred the month of June. It was between 2-3.00pm on the afternoon of Monday 5th when the fishing Lugger belonging to George 'Pincher' Hide, named the 'Albert and Alfred' but better known among the fishermen as the 'Gruff' the nickname of 'Pincher's son George Jnr. was run into by the steamer 'Ogmore' of Dundee, en-route to Falmouth. The 'Gruff' was about 1 mile Sou' Sou' East of Belle Tout lighthouse. She was in company with the Lugger 'Little Stranger' owned by Charles Boniface. Their intention was to fish the mackerel grounds off Newhaven. The 'Gruff' was crewed by Harry Cummings (Skipper), Henry Novis, Percy Catt, Alfred Tulliford and William Marchant. The 'Gruff' was smashed to pieces and sunk immediately, the crew suddenly finding themselves struggling in the water. Novis who was a powerful swimmer swam about until picked up by the Lugger 'Little Stranger'. He was exhausted and was going down for the third time. The other four men clung to the bow chain of the steamer 'Ogmore' until a rope was thrown to them. Three of them seized it and were hauled aboard, but Skipper Harry Cummings was too exhausted to catch it and drowned. The three men were transferred to the 'Little Stranger' who took all four rescued men ashore and the steamer 'Ogmore' continued her voyage. It was apparent the fault lay with the 'Ogmore' as a Board of Trade inquiry later established. The body of Harry Cummings aged 50 years, was recovered some 10 days later. He left a widow and young son. The 'Albert and Alfred' (the 'Gruff') was valued at £400 but was not insured, a big loss but surely recovered through a claim against the 'Ogmore' owners? The nets were later recovered.

November 1893.

Said to be one of the most disastrous gales ever to visit the shore of Great Britain, sprang up on the weekend of Saturday/Sunday 18th/19th November 1893, with great loss of life at sea said to be some 200 persons. At Eastbourne effects were less bad than some places. The local herring Luggers had much difficulty getting ashore on the Saturday evening and two were not heard of until Monday morning. One Lugger 'Little Mackerel' and crew returned to Eastbourne at 8.00am, telling of the fearful time they had experienced of a terrific battering of the wind, snow and waves. At the same time news was received of the loss of the Eastbourne Lugger 'Thistle', but good news of her crew having been saved by a French fishing smack, the dandy rigged 'Avenir' of Boulogne.

During the storm that weekend, Sunday morning 19th saw the Eastbourne lifeboat under Cox'n Jesse Huggett launched to the rescue of Hastings fishing boat 'Bantam' adrift in stormy seas 2 miles off the Great Redoubt. It had been during Saturday afternoon that she experienced the fierce gale force wind and snow whilst fishing for herring in Pevensey Bay and had taken her nets in and reefed her sails, putting down two anchors. 'Bantam' rode out the gale until Sunday morning when it became too much and she dragged her anchors. The lifeboat 'William and Mary' took ½ hour to reach her, taking off the Skipper and 3 men. Then began a struggle to get back to the beach at Eastbourne. It took some 3 hours against the wind and tide, but make it they did landing near the Wish Tower.

The tale of Lugger 'Little Mackerel' was that with her Skipper Charles Boniface and one crew of just a boy named Huggett, set off on Saturday afternoon to fish for herring in Pevensey Bay. With the coming of the storm she took her nets in and reefed her sails down to the minimum and virtually drifted and was driven out off Beachy Head till the storm abated coming ashore on Monday morning, with Boniface and the boy Huggett cold and exhausted.

Rescue of the crew of 'The Thistle'

The Lugger 'Thistle' owned by Joseph Mockett and crewed by skipper Charles Hurd, Tom Simmons, Harry Novis and Curley Gibbs had also put off Saturday afternoon after herring in Pevensey Bay. As the storm took hold she lost her nets. Her sails were blown away and she was blown up off Beachy Head spending all Saturday night in darkness with gale force winds and snow to contend with. On Sunday morning at 5.00am she lay some 6 miles off the Head completely disabled when the French boat 'Avenir' under Captain Papin and crew got alongside in the heavy sea. Hurd and Novis jumped aboard but Simmons and Gibbs failed to do so. The weather being so bad contact was then lost between the 'Thistle ' and 'Avenir'. Hurd and Novis were well looked after by the Frenchmen while Captain Papin endeavoured to find the 'Thistle'. In all she was some 11 hours searching to 4.00pm Sunday afternoon, before she came upon the 'Thistle' some 28 miles off Beachy Head. Captain Papin was then able to take off Simmons and Gibbs and took the 'Thistle' under tow. Due to heavy seas the cable parted and 'Thistle' sank. The 'Avenir' made her way to Newhaven where she put the crew of the 'Thistle' ashore and after repair of the damage sustained to her the 'Avenir' sailed for Boulogne. Captain Papin refused to take any money as thanks for his heroic rescue. What a wonderful effort by Captain Papin and his crew from the way they behaved in saving the lives of the crew of the 'Thistle' as there was every chance they would not have survived. It was so good to see this act of bravery and kindness from the French fishermen.

The Mayor and people of Eastbourne sang the praises of the brave French fishermen and a memorial was got up as a way of saying thanks to them. It was learnt in December that year that the Board of Trade awarded Captain Papin a gold medal and his crew, silver medals and £2 each for their humanity and bravery.

On the 28th March, 1894, the Mayor of Eastbourne Alderman Keay accompanied by his wife and several members of the Council went to Boulogne, where in the presence of its Mayor, he presented to Captain Papin and crew on behalf of the people of Eastbourne their heart felt thanks with 'Illuminated Addresses' and purses of money for saving the lives of the Eastbourne fishermen. A great day for the entente cordiale.

On Thursday, 27th September the same year the gallant Captain Papin and his crew paid a visit in his vessel 'Avenir' to Eastbourne. The report of the visit goes on to say;

'Early in the morning the two masted fishing vessel was seen in the offing. Our longshoremen are a keen sighted lot and the news spread quickly amongst them. Two of the rescued men, Charles Hurd and Henry Novis are licensed boatmen and as might be expected they seized the earliest opportunity of coming athwart the

Frenchmen and welcoming them to Eastbourne. The Frenchmen had some fine fish for sale - turbot, brill, soles and gurnets and 'Bones' Hide sold the catch for them realising £4. 8s clear. At first the Frenchmen were at a loss for an interpreter, but a lady living on the Royal Parade came to their aid. Soon after they fell in with George Austin (a well known photographer in the east end of town) George could speak French and he was at one time a local fisherman.

Captain Guillaume Papin was about 34 years of age, with black hair and eyes, a pleasant face. He wears no beard or moustache but having been 8 days at sea had a strong dark stubble. He was of middle height, thin and well proportioned. Wearing a blue/black cap, a very short brown jacket and blue trousers tucked into Wellington boots. Although they had sold their fish they retained one fine turbot for presentation to the Mayoress. The Town Hall keeper, Kennard arranged for them to visit the Town Hall and on their way there they called at the home of Councillor Tom Bennett, who had visited Boulogne, but Tom was laid up with gout hard to imagine a Radical such as him being stricken by the aristocratic complaint. In the Mayor's Parlour the Mayor and Mrs Keay greeted the Frenchmen; and the turbot was presented with a great deal of 'impressement'. Alderman Morrison was able to relieve George Austin of his interpreter duties. Among those present as well as some fishermen was the Town Clerk. Bottles of champagne were uncorked and refreshment laid on. Good wishes toasted. "Your health, gentleman all," exclaimed Henry Novis quaffing his glass of champagne. (A lucky man Henry 'Harry' Novis, twice surviving a watery grave in 1893) Outside the Town Hall a group photograph was taken by Mr Atkinson of Grove Road. The Frenchmen were then taken around the town by Austin, Hurd, Novis, Hide and other fishermen. Captain Papin set sail from Eastbourne in the evening and so ended a pleasant day for all involved'.

So back to 1893, and on the 23rd day of November during a sudden squall off Eastbourne, there was another act of bravery and seamanship by the Captain and crew of the Rye schooner 'Forester'. The lives of another two Eastbourne fishermen, the brothers Phillip and Charles Huggett were saved when their fishing punt 'Duke of Norfolk' capsized off Beachy Head. The Captain of the 'Forester' Richard Johns wrote the following letter, dated 28th November 1893, from Great Yarmouth to the Chief Coastguard at Eastbourne;

'Dear Sir, - On my arrival here (Great Yarmouth) I looked at the papers to see if the two men we saved off Beachy Head last Thursday, about a quarter to three p.m. had reported it, but I cannot see any report of it, and my ship's husband at Rye J. Bowen, tells me he has not seen anything of it in the papers. If true, I think it is a great neglect of them and not doing justice to me nor my crew, neither to the public at large. I had double reef mainsail on my vessel at the time the accident occurred. We were nearly at the pitch of the Head, going east, when, about a quarter to three p.m. a sudden gust of wind capsized the Eastbourne boat. We saw it and also heard their cries for help, and, having saved many in my lifetime, I feel equal to such cases. I said, "Out boat men" and began to let go the lashing of gripes of the boat. I said, "Cut, be quick". We got the boat up weather side. I put my helm hard down, let the ship came come around, all aback, out goes our boat at once, in jumps all my crew except myself, and away they went, the Eastbourne men calling out, "Make haste, or we cannot hold on any longer". Now their boat had sunk and my men just got to them in the nick of time to save them from a watery grave. When safe,

Captain Papin (centre) with his crew of the French fishing boat 'Avenir' who in November 1893 in the English Channel rescued four crew members of the Eastbourne Lugger 'Thistle' during tempestuous weather. Seated left is skipper of the 'Thistle' Charles Hurd. Seated right is Henry William Novis a crew member.

two Eastbourne boats were in sight. They asked if my men would wait and put them on board one of them, as they would rather go as one had a fire. They did so and the boat took them, and I expect saved their nets for them, poor fellows. I hope they have, but the boat I fear the tide would sweep away. Had I got them on board they would have had every kindness shown to them, both clothes and food, etc and would have been landed either at Newhaven or Eastbourne. I thought that not seeing any report of it the boat we put them on board of might claim the credit for saving them, as they were not in sight when the accident occurred. They ought to have reported it and let the credit of prompt and smart action be given to those whom it is due, to encourage others to be to be watchful at such stormy times when on deck, not knowing what may take place and what help we can render to each other. Neither me, nor my crew want any fee or reward, but, thank God, he used us to save their lives. I have saved many in my time jumping overboard after them and other ways as well. I have three medals for it and presents in money from the Humane Society as well, also from Lloyds, also from the Government, by risking my life for it. To encourage my crew, they ought to have the credit, for, you know sir, a little praise goes a good way with poor Jack as well as people on shore'.

Yours obediently,
Richard Johns,
Master of the schooner "Forester," of Rye.

A brave mariner indeed. It is strange no report of the incident can be found in the local newspapers. It is to be sure the Huggett brothers would have been eternally grateful to Captain Johns and his crew. An excellent piece of seamanship involved in the whole operation especially Captain Johns handling the schooner single-handed. No mean task to manoeuvre a sailboat. As mentioned above Richard Johns saved many lives from the perils of the sea during his maritime career. One such act of bravery is recorded in the book 'Lloyds Medals 1836-1989' by Jim Gawler. From Lloyds General Minute Book 4th June 1856 it states that on 6th May 1856 mariner Richard Johns was instrumental in saving life from the shipwreck 'Endeavour' of Ipswich, off Fowey, Cornwall and presented with Lloyds bronze medal.

December 1893.

Another life saving incident happened on Christmas Eve 1893, with entirely different circumstances.

'Meads Fisherman, Jacob Collins of Coppards Cottages, close by the 'Pilot Inn', was walking along the cliff between Holywell and Beachy Head during the morning when he saw a body floating in the sea. Looking over the cliff he saw three lads-Arthur and Edward Plummer and Samuel Bradford- not far away, and soon succeeded in directing their attention to what he had seen in the water. The boys with great pluck and thoughtfulness, at once dashed through the waves, and on reaching the body, found it was that of a girl, still alive. They held her head above water until Collins was able to get down to the beach, and the party between them carried her to a cottage at Holywell, where the kindest treatment was extended to the young woman, whose name was May Weston, aged 19 years. She had only been in the town a few weeks, having been employed at a local business establishment as a dressmaker. She had left her apartments suddenly that morning on receipt of a letter. She was taken by the Police to Princes Alice Hospital and after treatment is to appear before the Magistrates on a charge of Attempt Suicide'.

At the court hearing it transpired that the young lady had lost her job through no fault of her own, being employed as a 'second hand'. Having no income and losing her home she decided to end it all and at Christmas time too. She was committed to the Quarter Sessions to stand trial and in the meantime put in the care of a Miss Bell who offered to take care of her.

June 1894. Midnight Chorus.

About 12.15am on a Sunday fishermen Harry Tutt, Alfred Erridge, Frederick Huggett and Arthur Huggett were singing and using bad language in the vicinity of 2 Hydnye Street, the home of Sarah the wife of fisherman Samuel Beckett Hide. Due to the noise Police attended with the result that the above were all fined 5s and allowed 3 days to pay.

October 1894.

The Fishermen's light on the beach at the Fishing Station was remounted on a new 60 ft long pitch pine pole, due to a stay being rotten on the previous light. The supplying and fitting was done by Alfred, father to Fred 'Mucky' Erridge. Alfred Erridge was also an amateur painter having some of his work held by the Towner Art Gallery.

On the fishing front, Eastbourne returns of fish caught and value for the year 1894 exceeded 1892/93. The methods of fishing for these periods were trawl fishing (deep sea), drift nets, lines and pots. The types of fish caught were, brill, cod, herring, lobster, plaice, sole, sprats, turbot, whiting, crab and whelks. The total number of each class of vessel working out of the Fishing Station were; all Sail, 1st class = 6, 2nd class = 33, 3rd class = 3. Generally the catches and weather had been fairly good but the inshore fishing for herring and mackerel had been poor

November 1894.

Late November saw the Annual Lifeboat day when the custom of pulling the Lifeboat through the principal streets of Eastbourne took place. This custom had been so from earlier days but was discontinued in 1900.

1895.

The fish catches for 1895 out of the Fishing Station and landed was a quantity of 3696 hundredweight; all types of fish total £3,307. This exceeded landings at Newhaven, which came to the value of £2,944.

A further fuller report on the Sea Fisheries of England 1895, showed there were 600 steam fishing vessels, 3,000 Sailing boats and Rowing boats making a total capital investment of £3,536,000 in Fisheries.

The harvest for 1895 amounted to value of £5,129,000. In the Sussex district the bad season was blamed on the Naval and Military experiments in the area. The number of sailing fishing boats working on the Eastbourne Fishing Station was 1st class = 8, 2nd class = 26, 3rd class = 10. Herring catches were above average. Other fish caught being plaice, sprats, cod, whiting, ray, whelks, crab and lobster.

February 1896. A Gang of Gamblers.

Philip Huggett of 14 Sidley Road, Fred Huggett of 6, Bexhill Road, William French of 28, Eshton Road, J Peach of 9, Popular Row and John Knott of 10, Eshton Terrace on 26th February, were summoned for gambling on the foreshore at the Fishing Station. They were seen by the Police to be playing cards for money seated between two boats. F Huggett who stated his name was plain Fred was fined 12s and the others 6s including costs.

1896. Watch Committee minutes.

July. The Borough Surveyor submitted a report to the Committee containing a plan of the Fishing Station showing Net shops erected and requesting a check be made with existing agreements and on proposed agreements not already entered into with the fishermen. Mr A Erridge was given permission to repair the late Mr C Hide's Net shop at the Fishing Station for storing his boats. On the pleasure boating side Mr J R Mockett complained to the Committee of persons getting into and sitting on his boats during performances of entertainers on the beach of Grand Parade.

August. An application by Mr A Matthews to occupy a Net shop and take possession of a capstan on a site immediately west of the hauling post of the Lifeboat was granted.

September. A report showed that all Net shop licence fees had been paid in full for the previous year 1895 and a bonus of 3 guineas was paid to Parade Inspector Burr.

October. Fisherman J P Huggett was granted a licence for a vacant capstan.

November. An application by Charles Hide for the use of a piece of land to erect a capstan and office at the Fishing Station was granted for a capstan only.

September 1896.

The end of September saw a stormy period when hundreds of tons of shingle was swept away and a sight to see was some 200 fishing vessels anchored off Eastbourne, sheltering during the heavy weather.

December 1896.

George Simpson, aged 24 years was drowned at sea. The report from the Eastbourne Gazette December 16th is as follows;

'An Eastbourner drowned. - About a fortnight ago the relatives of George Simpson, aged 24 years, formerly a boatman and fisherman here, and a son of Mr Simpson, boat builder of Archery Terrace, were much exercised on reading in an evening paper that the iron barque 'Grecian' of Glasgow, had been totally lost off the island of Montserrat, in the West Indies, and it was feared there was serious loss of life. As their relative was known to be serving in this ship they immediately telegraphed to the owners, who replied that they themselves knew nothing further than what had been reported in the paper. Since then they have been in great suspense and their worst fears have been realised, as a day or two ago they received positive information that the only survivor of the 'Grecian' was the third officer, who has, no doubt sent word home of the sad fate of his shipmates. Much sympathy is felt by the friends of the family of their bereavement, and sorrow for the untimely end

C. 1890 Eastbourne fishermen about to embark on fishing expedition in Irish waters. Front row, left to right: Tom Welch, George 'Storey' Adams, Reuben 'Cassy' Reed, George Simpson, unknown, Dick Barnard, Jack 'Kruger' Prodger. Back row, left to right: unknown, William 'Laddie' Simpson, unknown, unknown.

of the young sailor, who was a favourite among his acquaintances. In his last letter home he said that he expected to spend his Christmas in Eastbourne'.

Sadly this George shared the same fate as his namesake ancestor George Simpson who drowned at sea in 1843.

February 1897.

The death took place of Richard Hide, fisherman of Eastbourne, aged 80 years. Born 1816 he was a first cousin of George 'Dot' Hide and served in the first lifeboat alongside him. This Richard Hide's lifesaving medals used to be displayed in the Lifeboat Museum. He was well respected by the townsfolk of Eastbourne and regularly attended Christ Church (The Fishermen's Church). Some of the mourners were his widow, Mr & Mrs Richard Hide (son & daughter in law), Richard Hide and Miss Carrie Hide, (Grandchildren) Mrs William Bollard Hide, Mrs Elizabeth Gardner and Mr & Mrs Jesse Huggett (nephew & niece, Jesse being Cox'n of the lifeboat).

The above Richard Hide in 1888 gave a reminiscence of his life and times in Eastbourne, age 71 years. He had given up fishing but was pleasure boating near the Wish Tower. He lived at 77, Seaside from where he gave his reminiscences.

'I remember a strange incident, it happened about 20 years ago (1868). We had been mackerel fishing off Cornwall. There was a bit of a breeze blowing and we were near the 'Deadman' a huge granite headland something like Beachy Head only more rugged, but not so high- when we saw a dark mass off the shore. We approached and found it was a boat in which there a man was lying. We threw a rope to him and dragged him on board, but he could not speak, he was deaf and dumb, and could not write. The poor fellow was nearly done for; another day would have been too late. It seems that he had drifted in the open boat from St Agnes, on the north side of Cornwall in the Bristol Channel. He had been in the boat four days and nights without any food. His friends wrote us a letter thanking us for saving him and sending a paper with the account, but they said they were too poor to give us a reward. However, the Royal Humane Society gave us 28/-'.

'Of the smuggling, I do remember, although it was a bit before my time and I did a little of it myself. We used to bring over silks, satins, wines and tobacco. I remember seeing a cargo of £20,000 worth landed near where the Pier now stands. The owners had arranged so as to have carts in readiness and they got all away without being interfered with by the Preventive men. The next voyage (would have been 1824, when Richard Hide was aged 8 years old) that same boat was used however they were chased by a Man-o-War. They put on all the sail they could, but the warship was gaining on them, and they began to throw their cargo overboard. The government ship opened fire and shot through the sails, and so, the smugglers, one of who was my uncle James 'Navarino' Hide had to lay to. They had just thrown the last bale overboard, but in their hurry they did not weight it property, and so it did not sink. It was picked up and the contents being contraband the crew were arrested and sent to sea for five years aboard a Man-o-War. I also saw the wrecking of a West Indiaman under the lighthouse 'Belle Tout', with a cargo of sugar. On going there I picked up 70 yards of silk and 70 yards of very expensive lace. The smugglers were very daring men. A man named Samuel Knight, he was a

member of the first lifeboat crew in 1833 engaged in the rescue of the 'Isabella, was warned by the Custom House officers, but he went off in broad daylight and tried to smuggle a cargo ashore. He was taken into custody, however and sent to prison.

The smugglers Luggers could carry something like a 100 tons, had no names, and no one of coarse knew who their owners were'.

'I have seen a good many gales. The worse I remember occurred when I was five or six years old (1821-2). The gale came on top of a spring tide. The Martello Towers were further back from the sea then than they are now, being more than a stone's throw from the highest tide. But that day the sea came over and flooded the country, and washed against the walls of Pevensey Castle. A great many cattle were drowned. All the wells in the neighbourhood were spoilt for months afterwards'. 'There was a very heavy gale in 1845 when the 'Twee Cornelissen' was wrecked in Langney Bay. We got out the lifeboat given us by Mr Fuller and we pulled her over hedges and ditches and got her down to Langney Point and launched her. We saved her crew and my, it did blow. You could not keep a hat or coat on and I had to walk home in my shirt and trousers. We all got a silver medal and a testimonial. We had to do something to get a medal those days, we gave our services for nothing'.

'I was present in 1840, when my cousin George Hide swam out to the coal Brig 'Joseph of Sunderland' aground on the Crumbles, and saved the lives of the crew. He threw a line aboard and the first man off brought the rope with him so he had to swim out again but we got them all ashore. He helped them ashore having a rope round his waist and I pulled him in each time. He was nigh done up by the time the last one was brought ashore'.

'Some fifty years ago I went fishing to the Cornish coast for mackerel, year after year for 30 years. The first year we went there (1830's) the Cornish fishermen were terribly jealous of us and cut our nets. However one day we had a splendid catch and went into Plymouth. The Cornish boats had caught nothing and the men were as savage as could be. We were detained there a fortnight due to bad weather and as the men of two of the Cornish boats were nearly starving we made a collection and gave half- a- crown a head and the owner, who was aboard put down £1. They never molested us after that, although before they would sink our nets and give us as much trouble as they could. But the people who gave us most trouble were the Frenchmen when we fished off Yarmouth. They would sail right through our nets and cut them to pieces. Some of the English fishermen used to revenge themselves and cut up their nets. We met with a tremendous gale up in the North Sea once. We battened down our hatchways and ran to Lowestoft. Several of the fishing vessels three times our size went down, and we could render them no help. We were up to our waists in water. A Hastings Lugger, made like us for Bakewell Bay, near Lowestoft. There was a tremendous surf running and as we were crossing the bar we saw the Hastings vessel go down with all hands. We could not help her and expected any minute to go down ourselves. It was a mercy we were saved, but we weathered it all right'.

'I remember a severe winter in 1822 or 1823 when the Thames was frozen over we had snow here in Eastbourne some 18 feet deep, people had to be dug out of their houses, it lasted 13 weeks. In the time of the Crimean War it was terribly cold. The sails and masts of our fishing boat were covered with ice. We went into Portsmouth

Harbour and I never saw a prettier sight. The Men- o -War in the Harbour were all covered with ice. Icicles hung from the rigging and all the sides were frozen, it was like the Arctic Regions. We caught tons and tons of conger eels, the coast all round looked like a wall of ice'

'I hate the smell of beer, No, I never could drink. I smoke and began when I was 13 years old. I got a great fright one day and so became subject to fits. The doctor said if I smoked I should get rid of them, and I have never had a fit since. I was very weak as a boy and no one expected me to live to be a man'.

'Sixty-five years ago Eastbourne was only a small fishing village. There weren't many people in it and the boys were so few that when two or three stayed indoors we used to get the girls to join in our games, as we could not get enough to play cricket. There used to be a 'Well' where North Street now is, and many, many times I've had a drink out of it'.

'About 30 - 34 years ago (1854 - 58) the barque 'William' I think she was called was driven ashore under the Belle Tout Lighthouse. She was laden with wine. We put off in a boat from Birling Gap and were almost alongside when a tremendous wave washed over us and strangely enough a cask of wine came with it and knocked our oars out of our hands. All we could do was to get safe back to shore. The wine cask came ashore too, and several of the crew got drunk from it. The crew of the 'William' were saved'.

So ends the reminiscences of Richard Hide.

1897. Watch Committee minutes.

May. Fishing Station. An application by George M Hide for use of a piece of land immediately west of Mr Hoad's sail making shop was granted. The Chief Constable reported that three fishing boats lying on the foreshore without permission had been removed.

December. Ben Erridge's application to take over the Boat Stand of the late Arthur Matthews at the Fishing Station was granted.

August 1897.

Great sympathy was expressed for fisherman Joseph Mockett of 55, Latimer Road, who in losing his fishing boat 'Industry' was deprived of his principal means of earning a living. The 3-ton sailing vessel used for fishing and pleasuring had been left anchored off, to the west of the Pier. Unfortunately the pleasure steamer 'Alexandra' ran into it about 9.00pm and cut out her stern quarters and part of her bow. With the help of the crew of the sailing yacht 'Britannia', Mockett succeeded in getting the damaged boat ashore, but she was not worth repairing. The loss was put at £60. This is the time when pleasure boats were in request and early next month the herring fishing began. A hard time ahead for Mockett. A subscription was set up by the Mayor to enable Mockett to get a new boat. It was Mockett that back in November 1893 lost his boat 'Thistle'.

October 1897.

Another death for 1897 was that of young 28-year-old Arthur William Matthews, fisherman and boatman, with the funeral at Ocklynge Cemetery taking place in

October. He was the son of Arthur Matthews, landlord of the Beach Hotel who died in 1893. The cortege started from the house of the deceased, Jubilee Laundry Sidley Road, in a glass hearse followed by eleven carriages. The coffin was carried to the graveside by six fishermen. There were about 200 people present at the burial, proof of the esteem and regard in which the deceased was held.

Reuben 'Old Screw' Wood came to the notice of a reporter for the Eastbourne Gazette in October 1897 and was a forerunner of a later interview with 'Old Screw' in 1905 documented in the book 'The Pleasure Boatmen of Eastbourne'. This interview gives an interesting insight about Eastbourne and fishing ways. It describes Reuben as being short and white haired with a skin hue resembling mahogany and having a permanent smile which gave him a most engaging air of innocence. Reuben related that his mother's father was an Allchorn and his grandfather, a Wood, lived some time in Prentice Street, Eastbourne.

To quote; *'I went to school at old Peter Brown's. It was a Free School in those days. Peter Brown's sons Randall and Tom were regular chummies of mine. My grandmother burnt to death in a little house right opposite the Town Hall. She went to put the old gentleman's shirt before the fire and her clothes catche'd alight. After I left Peter Brown's school I went to Johnny Duke's school at Marine Drove in those days. Johnny Duke was a butcher by trade. His father lived in Simmons' lower shop opposite the Windsor Tavern. Johnny was a beautiful writer he was. He could write the Lord's Prayer on the size of a sixpence. I learned reading writing and spelling. I was very good at reckoning. I lay I could reckon in my head as fast as any. I don't want a pencil. Philip Swain, he went to school with me. He wears a brown 'frock' and went to sea for many years he's a pal of mine. (Swain lived to the age of 94 years) My father was drowned when he was washed overboard from his Lugger the 'Favourite' a brand new boat. I took his place as master of the 'Favourite'.*

Do I remember the oyster fishery? I was the very man who found them at first and catched them. We drudged (dredged) for them. Swain and I discovered them first off Langney Point. Some will say that is a lie, but it is the truth. They were not as big as half-a-crown when we found them. You know what pap oysters be like? There was always an old bed in Pevensey Bay, what they called 'clomps'. I catched 7,000 oysters in one day once, a beautiful oyster better than e'er a one you can get in Eastbourne now. It happened in the wintertime and there came on a heavy frost. I sold them for 6d a hundred small'uns and 1s a hundred for the best.

The 'Telegraph' was one of the first vessels from Whitstable to catch Eastbourne oysters. The 'Leader' I think was there too. Bless you, there were a hundred sail here nearly at one time. At one time we used to get four or five shilling a hundred for the oysters. Afterwards thay came down to 1s and 6d. I'll tell you a bit of a story. We went to sell them round the streets. Dexter the chemist, in his shop, wanted fifty and wanted us to open them for a shilling. We were not going to cut our hands for a shilling in opening half a hundred oysters.

The oysters lasted fourteen or fifteen years. It was four or five years before the smacks came, they tore the beds right up. I have two of my 'drudges' (dredges) at home now. Now a days they can only catch a few clump oysters.

I go fishing myself sometimes now. I've gone for long lines and for hooking whiting and codfish. I have not gone much since the Royal Parade has been built- twelve or fourteen years. I have been up to Beachy Head fishing for bass when there used to be a lot. Some of them up to 14lbs. We never got much above 2/6 or 3/- for them.

As for pleasure boating, I've been off to sea today with some ladies nearly to Bexhill. I will sail a boat with e'er a man in town now. I don't care who he is. What do you think I did two years ago? Rowed from here right round Cuckmere, up the haven to Litlington Gardens, and right to Curlings. I started at quarter past eight. I had sold the boat and delivered her. I was at Berwick with Mr Dumbrell looking at his bullocks, then got home by train by dinnertime.

As to fishing, I've been in our boats to the North Sea and as far as Lands End. When we first went fishing we never made very much. Afterwards it was better. I sailed out of Brighton on the 'Kitty' along with Tommy Winchester. The boat belonged to Mr Chessman, he built Osborne House, (Isle of Wight). We got £50 a man, six men. The owners had their shares.

The 'Fanny' 23 tons was built here (Eastbourne). I used to go to the North Sea in her. I used to go away for 3 months. We put into Yarmouth and Lowestoft. I have been up as far as Scarborough.

I have often sailed and rowed in regattas. I have rowed in four- oared galleys and paired -oar matches. I have known a regatta 50 years ago. My son Edward got £42 worth of prizes in one year, and has them at his house on Marine Parade'.

Old Screw' then went on to relate about life as a pleasure boatman on Eastbourne seafront.

'We didn't go pleasuring till we had done our fishing season. I was on the Marine Parade at first. No Grand Parade was built. This season has been the worst I have known in my life. There are too many of us. The steamers take hundreds, they have broke Brighton. I am the oldest. Dennis Breach and Johnny Hide have been here a long time.

Next May 1898 Reuben will be 74 years of age. He lives at 106 Tideswell Road. Twice married at Eastbourne Parish Church by Canon Pitman, he has four sons and three daughters. The summer has gone, the winter is close upon us, the sea front is no longer crowded, but if you stroll along the Parade you will find Reuben and his smile is still there'.

Altogether an interesting personal picture of a longshoreman's life in Eastbourne.

November 1897.

Next month on 3rd November an anonymous letter appeared in the Gazette, which referred to the interview with Reuben 'Old Screw' Wood and his claim that he was the first to find the oyster beds off Eastbourne. The writer stated;

'I deny it. And to cut an argument short, I would refer you to the original Eastbourne Gazette published about the year 1859 where you will find a report that fisherman Caesar Mitchell borrowed a dredge from a person at Newhaven and caught the first oysters.

The reason for trying if an oyster bed lay off Eastbourne was that in long line fishing

he occasionally drew up oysters caught by the hooks. Also a bed off Langney Point was known to Mitchell, twelve months before he dredged it.

When the first large oyster smack arrived, many local fishermen were interested in a rumour that some person, for a sum of money, showed the marks in which direction the oyster beds lay, to the smacksmen. It would no doubt be interesting to some, at the present day, to know what sum was received and by whom?'

Chapter Seven

A Fish Market - The 'Pride and Envy' Tragedy

January 1898.

Henry Fox's request for the Net shop and capstan at the Fishing Station that had belonged to the late Mr Arthur Matthews was granted.

1898 was the year that it was decided to build the 'Terris Memorial Lifeboat House' at the Wish Tower (Now the Lifeboat Museum). The Daily Telegraph in memory of actor William Terris raised a subscription.

In June of that year a new slipway had been constructed for the lifeboat at the Wish Tower and the current lifeboat 'William and Mary' with difficulty was launched from there. The building of the Royal Parade obstructed the old lifeboat house in Marine Road and made it impossible to launch anywhere along its length and it had been a time consuming pull along the seafront to the Wish Tower. The new boathouse at the Wish Tower was built 1899, but the slipway proved not to be amenable to launching, so it wasn't to be long before another lifeboat house was built at the Fishing Station in 1903.

July 1898.

July saw the sad drowning off the Wish Tower of two young Italian male waiters from the Grand Hotel, their bodies being recovered later by fishermen William French, William Stanbridge, Fred Huggett and Leonard Langford.

September 1898.

The SS. 'International' on September 30th whilst in tow from London to Cherbourg, France, to be broken up ran aground at Birling Gap. Her crew of ten were saved by the towing tug. She could not be pulled off and became a total loss being sold as she lay for £225. The 'International' a former cable laying ship had laid the cable that ran from Birling Gap to Dieppe, France, and strangely she severed the very cable she had been engaged in laying.

1899. Watch Committee minutes.

March. Boat builder George Gausden wished to be relieved of his tenancy of a piece of shingle land at the Fishing Station. Mr Joseph Hope applied to build a Net shop on this piece of shingle. Applications were granted.

April. It was agreed that a boathouse and capstan on plots Nos.61 & 54 at the Fishing Station belonging to Harry J Tyrell be sold to Mr C Southgate.

May. A capstan at the Fishing Station between stands occupied by Ben Erridge and

Eastbourne Lifeboat 'William and Mary' 1899. The crew is identified as follows, left to right: Tom Boniface 2nd Cox'n, Coastguards, Jessie Huggett 1st Cox'n. Boniface, Erridge, Erridge, Erridge, 'Bones' Hide, Tim Erridge, John 'Jack' Mockett, Erridge, Andrew William Chester, Andrew Jesse Chester.

Harry Tyrell was granted to John Erridge.

October 1899. Two Lifeboat Houses.

The 'William Terris Lifeboat House' at the Wish Tower was completed with the new lifeboat 'James Stevens No.6' in occupation. The old lifeboat house at Marine Road was no longer in use and the old lifeboat 'William and Mary' 1880-1899 was removed to the Lifeboat Institute store at Poplar, London.

March 1900.

No chance for the new lifeboat to be called out. In the early hours, 2.00am Friday 16th March, ten miles off Beachy Head, a collision between two ships took place, the steamer 'Stanhope' and an unknown schooner. The 'Stanhope' sank within minutes her crew took to the boats but the ships mascot, a black retriever went down with the ship. No one knew of the incident until the boats containing the crew beached east of the Pier at 5.00am to be met by fisherman Jack Hurd. On learning of their plight, he took them to the Prince of Wales Pub, Seaside Road, where the landlord Mr A Dumbrill fitted them out with extra clothes and gave them refreshments through the good services of the Shipwrecked Mariners Society agent, Chief Petty Officer Pelly of the Coastguard. The crew proceeded to London by train at noon.

June 1900.

Again there was much discussion by the lifeboat crew about the need for a lifeboat house at the Fishing Station where they all resided. All this after the building of the William Terris Memorial lifeboat house at the Wish Tower, but there remained

The family of Jesse and Emily Huggett. C. 1890.

problems with the slipway. A custom built one was needed for the lifeboat and was not forthcoming, great difficulty being experienced with launching at the Wish Tower.

In the year 1900 Coxswain Jesse Huggett died and new Coxswain Ben Erridge took his place in charge of the lifeboat.

Fisherman and Lifeboat Coxwain, Jesse Huggett (1849-1900).

From the report in the local paper Jesse proved to be a big loss to the fishing fraternity;

'By the death of Jesse Huggett the Eastbourne fishermen have lost one who had won and had for many years deservedly retained their respect and confidence. They recognised in him a man of sterling merit. Upright and straightforward, kindly and sincere, he was looked up to by his friends and neighbours and as the trusty coxswain of the Lifeboat. Like his father before him, he became a fisherman and made voyages to Plymouth, Lowestoft and other places during the mackerel and herring seasons. Of late years he devoted much of his time catching lobsters and crabs. He has suffered lately from the octopus, which invades the lobster pot and leaves nothing but the shell of its prey. A year or two ago he ruptured himself and had not been well since. At 3.00am on Tuesday last week he went off in his boat, the Nona, with his youngest son Archie. After hauling in the nets and pots Jesse fell back in the boat in great pain. Archie had to bring the boat back single handed against a head wind and it was close on 3 hours before he landed. Once ashore, being in dreadful agony the doctor was called and he was taken to Princess Alice Hospital. After great suffering Jesse passed away on Friday.

Mr Huggett spoken of as 'Jess' was one of few men who are able to exercise a marked influence for good on those around him. A great friend of temperance, he was a member of the Independent Order of Total Abstinent Sons of the Phoenix and a frequenter of the Fishermen's Institute.

The late Mr Huggett succeeded cousin 'Bones' Hide as coxswain of the Eastbourne lifeboat, rendering good service on several occasions. He leaves a widow, sons, Jess, Harry and Archie and daughters, Mrs Chester, Mrs French, Kate and Jessica. Every Christmas Mr Huggett made a trip to the Royal Sovereign lightship taking with him gifts for the crew contributed by the local people'

August 1900.

The two masted schooner 'Caroline' 140-tons was driven ashore near Langney Point during gale force winds. The pleasure yacht 'Britannia' with crew of Thomas Huggett, Ben Erridge, Tom Erridge, Thomas Boniface and John Mockett launched and went to her assistance. On getting alongside the 'Caroline' her skipper and crew refused to leave her. With the weather increasing in fury the lifeboat 'James Stevens No.6' was launched and took off the crew of 3 but the skipper stayed aboard. Eventually as heavy seas were breaking over the 'Caroline' the Life Saving Apparatus volunteers in attendance on the beach shot a rocket line across the grounded 'Caroline' and her skipper left his ship via the line. Broadside to the seas the 'Caroline' became a total loss.

The Fishing Industry.

June 1900. The Beach Hotel to open early.

Friday at the Police Court, Mr F. Lewis Lawson applied on behalf of Mr Charles Tanner the tenant of the Beach Hotel for permission to open at 5.00am, an hour before the usual time. He said the house was situated almost at the very point where the fishing boats arrived and where the market for the sale of fish was held. The fishermen went to their work certainly in hours, which were almost unknown to members of his profession, and he believed their work was finished at an exceedingly early hour in the morning. As a rule the boats from fishing trips arrived back from 4.00am to 4.30am in the morning. On their arrival they had to be anchored and otherwise attended to. The catches were brought ashore and the fish was sent to London by the early morning train at 6.30am. Not only the Eastbourne men but also great numbers of Hastings fishermen used the water around

Wreck of the 'Caroline' at Langney Point August 1900.

Eastbourne. They had to rely on such accommodation as they could get here and they were often without shelter from 5.00am to 6.00am.

Mr Tanner who gave evidence said the fishermen came here from Hastings, Brighton and Lowestoft. Sometimes there might be a dozen boats at a time. There were generally three or four crew in each boat. They said they would like to have the same facilities in Eastbourne as in other places where they could get refreshment at 5.00am in the morning so they might get their fish sold and go to sea again. There could be some 50 to 60 persons attending the market. The exemption licence would be for the majority of the fishermen who brought the fish ashore.

John 'Kruger' Prodger, of 49, Beach Road said, he had been a fisherman all his life, some 40 years. It would be a convenience for the men to have a place open earlier than 6 o'clock.

Sometimes twelve or thirteen boats arrived with thirty to forty men coming ashore.

Chief Constable Plumb stated he had made enquiries at other towns. At Hastings 3 public houses opened at 5.00am, at Portsmouth several opened at 4.00am and at Brighton several houses at the fruit and vegetable market opened early and were used by the fishermen.

Mr Lawson Lewis said, and I can speak for Boston and Grimsby.

The Magistrates granted an exemption order for some 3 months. Early opening weekdays only.

So the fishermen got their early pint but there were many fishermen who were teetotal and religious and early hours drinking would not have been popular. From this report we learn that the Fish Market was up and running but dependant upon keeping busy by fish being plentiful and boats using the Eastbourne Market. Interestingly in those days local caught fish was sent by train to the London fish market, Billingsgate. Plenty of work and business for the associated trades of Eastbourne.

September 1900.

Application for renewal of the exemption licence for the Beach Hotel and a fight to keep the Early Hours 5.00am opening was heard at the Police Court.

Again Mr Lawson Lewis represented the landlord of the Beach Hotel, Mr Tanner. The Town Clerk Mr Fovargue appeared for the Police and Watch Committee and in addressing the Bench he said, he felt that it was quite unnecessary for the place to open at 5.00am. There was no market going on down there at that time. Up to the present, the house had not been used by many fishermen in the early morning but had been used mainly by labourers and workers on their way to their employment.

Police enquiries for eleven days in August had shown the number of boatmen who visited the house between 5 and 6.00am was 31, an average of 3 a day. The other persons taking advantage of the early opening were 176 males and 6 females and the market was held at 7.00am and 3.00pm on those days.

Mr Tanner said, although the exemption order was granted in June up to the present it had not been an advantage to the fishermen because it had been a bad fishing season.

Charles Hide, a well-known inhabitant known as 'Bones' said, '*I live in Sidley Road and have been a fisherman here for thirty-six years. If the weather had been finer we should have had a better season. Speaking roughly there are 50 fishermen and 64 boatmen, and the majority of the boatmen will go fishing when they leave off boating on the Parades.*

The catches will increase during October, November, December and January, fish has to be packed up and sent off by the 6.30am train. I still go fishing myself. If the boats come in at 2.00am it takes them two or three hours to get the fish out. Blow high or low, rain or snow, the fishermen have to be there'.

Town Clerk, '*Couldn't they take some refreshment with them*'?

'Bones' Hide, '*It would not be very nice having a drop of beer 'sloshing' about in a fishing boat*'.

The Town Clerk suggested that the boats that had stoves could boil coffee.

'Bones' Hide, '*Of course they could if they had a drop of rum to put in it. (Laughter) The herring are caught and sold at all hours of the night*'.

The Town Clerk, '*They don't carry on the market at all hours of the night*'.

'Bones' Hide, '*I tell you they do*'.

John 'Trunky' Colstick, a wholesale fish dealer living at 252, Seaside, confirmed Hide's evidence.

The Rev Allen (Vicar of Christ Church and honorary chaplain to the Fishermen's Institute, 'Bethel') put in a petition signed by 37 fishermen who expressed their opinion that the exemption applied for was quite unnecessary

After hearing all the foregoing the Bench decided to grant the exemption certificate to run from 1st October to 31st January. The market would be tested during that time, but they felt that there was not a need for the exemption to run for the full year. The original exemption had been granted with the full backing of the Watch Committee and the Police.

Well, 'Bones' had given 'expert' evidence of the need backed up by 'Trunky' Colstick an old lifeboat crewmember of 1883. The earlier application being supported by 'expert' evidence from another crewmember of 1883, 'Kruger' Prodger.

How long this early opening exemption licence lasted is not known, but from the above we do know the Beach Hotel opened normally at 6.00am but not on Sundays, probably from the time when the Fishing Station was developed at its site in c.1884 east of the Great Redoubt.

November 1900.

An application by Bathchairman Thomas Eager for permission to erect a Net shop at the Fishing Station, was refused.

One can assume that the early 1900's saw about 100 fishermen plus associated trades employed at the Fishing Station. An example from past census records for fishermen; totals only, show the following:

Year	Total
1841	51 not complete
1851	74
1861	68
1871	113
1881	88
1891	100

January 1901.

With the Fish Market having been set up at the Fishing Station it was thought there would be no problems of selling of fish. This was not the case though and in January at a meeting of the Watch Committee a letter was received from fishermen, John 'Kruger' Prodger, Joseph Mockett and Charles 'Bones' Hide stating they had been requested by several fishermen to complain of fishing boats landing at the Royal Parade and selling fish off the beach. It is most unfair as there was a Fish Market at the East End. The Parade Inspector stated there was a Byelaw banning the selling of fish from the Parades. He had received no complaints from residents. Result by the Committee, no action to be taken.

Who those maverick fishermen were is not known. (37 fishermen teetotallers that signed the petition in September 1900, and presented it by the Vicar of Christ Church?)

1901. Watch Committee minutes.

August. A letter from Henry Bollard Hide complained of a nuisance caused by gypsies being allowed to camp on vacant land to the rear of Belmore Road. It was agreed that the land be fenced off.

October. Mr R Jones was given permission to erect a small shed to house a boat at the east side of the Fishing Station so long as the land not required by the fishermen.

December. An application by Benjamin and Samuel Beckett Hide to erect a Net shop in place of two old Bathing machines at present on the site was granted.

December 1901.

Friday 13th December was an unlucky day for Eastbourne fishermen. It was in the forenoon that the lives of many Eastbourne fishermen were put in peril by the storm that developed while the men were out at sea with their boats. News spread that danger was imminent, owing to the freshening wind and growing agitation of the sea. Many hundreds gathered along the seafront and great anxiety was felt for the fate of the men and their boats most of which were small and frail craft in heavy weather.

'That morning some ten boats had gone off either 'hooking' or 'spratting' and when they had been launched between 9-10 o'clock the sea was calm with little breeze. The boats duly reached the fishing grounds about 3-4 miles out, all went well for an hour or so then the wind freshened and a gale set in from the south and the seas became heavy. All haste was made by the boats to get ashore. The crews experiencing great difficulty in the management of their boats, which were shipping heavy seas. An early accident befell one of the boats coming ashore, captained by the redoubtable 'Bones' Hide, a complete capsize occurring before the boat could

get through the surf, with result that the burly 'Bones' became 'cooped', in other words imprisoned under his boat. With some difficulty the boat, which sustained considerable damage was righted and 'Bones' assisted ashore. It was found he was little the worse for the experience.

The perilous position of the fishermen induced the Coxswain of the lifeboat Ben Erridge to assemble his crew and to bring the boat from the Wish Tower to the Fishing Station. This operation occupied a deplorable long time, due be it said, to no fault of the crew, but to difficulties inseparable to such an undertaking. The Cox'n and his crew assembled very quickly. The Coxswain said that with a proper slipway at the Wish Tower he could have got afloat in a very short space of time, although a heavy sea was running and the tide was high. Under the existing circumstances speedy launching was

Fisherman George 'John' Erridge, Skipper of the 'Jenny Lind'.

out of the question and the lifeboat could not have been got off to render effective service, if the necessity had really arisen. Overall it took over 1 hour to get to the Fishing Station. As it was all the boats got ashore but not without much drama. One by one the fishing boats reached the shore, all with two exceptions making for the Fishing Station where a large band of fisher-comrades were on the beach to assist them. Fred Huggett's boat went ashore at Pevensey Bay. Richard 'Dick' Swain, who had been doing a bit of 'spratting' contrived to get on the Royal Parade, but in the neighbourhood of the Redoubt he had a very rough time and said afterwards he had never before had such a time in getting ashore. John Erridge's Lugger 'Jenny Lind' with a crew of three was almost dragged out of the water by willing hands to get her ashore. The others beached at intervals, but in two instances they were knocked about in the broken water. Andrew Chester's craft capsized and the crew saved themselves with difficulty. Archibald Huggett was knocked insensible but he 'came to' quickly. Both Chester's and Huggett's boats were damaged the masts being broken and some tackle lost. The last of the boats got ashore at 1.00pm and a cheer went up as the gallant helpers went into the surf waist deep to haul the boat up the beach. Praise is due to those who voluntarily assisted in getting the boats ashore namely the following; Jack Allchorn, Harry Erridge, Tom Prodger, Alfred Hurd, John Mockett, Edwin 'Lord' Matthews, Henry 'Dusty' Matthews, Jesse Huggett Jnr. John 'Kruger' Prodger, J Parter, William 'Laddie' Simpson, 'Pincher' Hide, Ben Hide, Samuel Beckett Hide, Tom Huggett, Philip Huggett, Nelson Sayers, Frank Buckland, Tom and Harry Boniface, George Sayers and Ben Erridge'.

The sequel to this potentially fatal incident was the wholesale condemnation by the fishermen of the existing lifeboat arrangements. Their views being, either a suitable slipway is built at the Wish Tower, or that, during the winter months the lifeboat should be housed at the Fishing Station. The above article shows the great skill required by the fishermen whose boats had no engines to assist them at sea, just their sailing seamanship and knowledge of the sea.

February 1902.

February 6th saw the death of Richard 'Dick' Swain, Eastbourne fisherman and boatman, a full report appears in the book 'The Pleasure Boatmen of Eastbourne' page 68.

A Fisherman of Holywell.

At No.1, Coppards Cottages (81, Meads Street) lived fisherman Jacob Collins and his family. Jacob and his family had lived there from c.1871. Jacob was born in Meads 1835 and lived to the ripe age of 91 years, dying in 1926. He outlived his wife Anne 86years and a daughter Edith 64 years, both dying within a week of each other in 1924.

Interestingly son William who had been educated at the elementary school in Meads had such a talent in the Science field that he became head of the Scientific Instruments Company, Cambridge. His advice being sought by Universities, electrical and mechanical firms in Europe and the United States. He married a Miss Thorpe sister to Mr Stewart Thorpe of

Fisherman of Holywell, Meads, Jacob Collins (1835-1926).

Meads. Old Jacob when asked how long he had lived in Eastbourne replied, 'I've never lived in Eastbourne, I've always lived in Meads'.

February 1902.

At a meeting of the local Lifeboat Institute committee it was disclosed that the lifeboat had been on hand on the beach, covered in canvas at the Fishing Station during the winter months. This left the Terris Memorial Lifeboat House at the Wish Tower empty and the crew were threatening to resign en-bloc over the issue. Being led by their Cox'n Ben Erridge they were most determined. A new House was needed at the east end and there could be a need for two boats if the Terris House was still to be used. In April and another meeting disclosed the fact that there was going to be a 2nd boat and a new Lifeboat house to be built at the east end. It all made sense as launching from the Fishing Station was conducive with the lay of the beach and of course the crew all lived close by.

Eastbourne Fishermen's Feast. February 1902.

In order to celebrate the completion of the building of a new boathouse Alleyne Sayers entertained about 20 friends to a 'novel' supper, consisting of boiled 'willicks' pork, vegetables and Christmas puddings. The food was prepared and cooked on a stove in the boathouse by Mr George Hookham. Arthur Sayers, presided, Ted Sayers vice chair. Full justice was done to Mr Hookham's viands and with a few drinks singing ensued. Songs and singers were 'Do a good turn when you can' by Alleyne

Sayers, 'Jack the handy man' by L Cottingham, 'Soldiers of the Queen' by A Baker, 'Cabin on the railway line' by F Uphill, 'Queen of the earth' by S Quested, 'Dear hearts are waiting' by R Downs and 'The Anglo-Saxon race' by E Sayers. Toasts were drunk and finally the National Anthem was sung. A good time had by all. ('Willicks' nickname for Eastbourne fishermen. 'Viands' foods)

1902. Watch Committee minutes.

March. Alleyne Sayers was ordered to remove an advert painted on his Net shop at the Fishing Station.

December. Mr Gausden Jnr. appeared before the Committee regarding his father, boat builder George Gausden's ownership of 5 capstans and a condemned Net shop at the Fishing Station. He agreed his father would pull down the Net shop and give up tenancy of 3 capstans. This was approved by the Committee.

It was brought to the attention of the Committee that a Net shop at the Fishing Station was being used as a stable with no provision for drainage and manure disposal. This practice was to immediately stop.

A letter from Mr William Allchorn asking that his Net shop remain in its present position until next spring, then same to be removed to a new site free of charge. This was granted.

A similar application for the above was made by Samuel Oliver and granted.

Mr H Meadows was granted permission to place a small box and erect a small shed at the Fishing Station.

December 1902. Boots for Christmas.

Christmas saw the Mayor's gift of boots to those bootless children of Eastbourne. Selected from the poor of Eastbourne 52 boys and girls attended the Town Hall on Christmas Eve. *'It really was pitiable to see the wretched foot coverings cast aside. Soles with holes worn through them. Some little ones had no boots, and in some instances bits of rag supplied the place of stockings. Each child also received a mug of milk and bun'.*

1903.

The Eastbourne Fishermen's Compensation fund (from 1839 and 1869) was disbanded and £250 monies given to charity.

January 1903.

A sub committee of the Highway Committee dealt with an application to erect a screen on the sea side of the Fish market cost £22 and subject to the agreement of Mr Gilbert. The screen was approved and work executed.

1903. Watch Committee minutes.

February. Fishing Station. Alfred Erridge applied to build a boathouse on the site of the old wall. Committee were not prepared to sanction building on that site.

An application to build a Net shop by Charles Hide was granted.

May. The Marine Club (forerunner of the Eastbourne Angling Club?) were given permission to erect a building at the Fishing Station, 50ft deep, 36ft across and create a 10ft passage next to Samuel Oliver's Net shop.

June. Borough Surveyor was to prepare up to date plans of the Fishing Station numbering each Net shop and capstan. (This was done by February 1904. Unfortunately these plans are missing and should have been passed to the Records Office at Lewes)

July. The Marine Club building was erected at the Fishing Station.

August. William Allchorn and George 'Gospel' Hall to remove their old Net shops from the west end of the Fishing Station, forthwith.

October. Benjamin Hide applied to take over Richard Hide's capstan. Granted.

November. George Chester was granted a capstan at the Fishing Station.

The fishermen had a grievance over the proposal of the local Watch committee to let a piece of ground on the Fishing Station to a Mr Dutton to erect a boathouse. The fishermen took exception to this as the Fishing Station was for the benefit of the fishermen and should be non-profit making from letting or sub-letting. As Mr Dutton was not a fisherman nor had any connection with the fishing industry the Committee were breaking the covenants in the agreement. It was pointed out that bathing machine owners had been compelled to remove their machines and their shops, if not connected with fishing although they had been on site for years. The above protest was in the form of a letter signed by: Thomas Hide, Tom Swain, Albert Sayers, T A Sayers, William B Hide, William Allchorn, John Mockett, S W Allchorn, Charles Hide, Alleyn Sayers, George M Hide and Ben Erridge. The fishermen won the day; Dutton did not build his boathouse. (With the sale of Ratton Estate in 1918 the catalogue and estate plan disclosed bathing machine owners John and Thomas Hounsom and William Erridge had been allowed to store their machines during winter months on the beach west of Langney Point next to the Eastbourne Aviation factory and boat builder John Gowland, sites being on land owned by Lord Willingdon, Ratton Estate)

April 1903.

Fishing Lugger sunk. Fishermen in peril,

'On Tuesday, 7th April, 1903, two well known Eastbourne fishermen- Jesse Huggett Jnr. of Seaford Road, and John 'Foot' Prodger of Latimer Road, had a narrow escape from drowning owing to the sinking of the Lugger 'Sunbeam' about 6½ miles off, a little to the east of the 'Royal Sovereign' lightship. Huggett is the owner of the 'Sunbeam', which put off about 4.00am to haul some lobster pots that had previously been set near the 'Sovereign' rocks. Two other boats left at the same time, the 'Nona' with Andrew Chester and Archibald Huggett, and the 'Hildergarde' with William Bollard Hide and Thomas Hide.

The work on raising the pots had just commenced when suddenly a huge wave struck the 'Sunbeam'. Seeing she was about to sink, Prodger seized the oars, Huggett in the hope she would right herself, stuck to the tiller. Seizing the outrigger Prodger had just time to throw an oar to Huggett when the next wave to hit the boat swamped her and she quickly sank. While Prodger was able to get his sea boots off after being thrown into the water, Huggett was unable to do so and was in great

'Our Lassie' built in 1903 by Tom Sisk in the Boatyard, Beach Road. In the boat are Sisk's two daughters. Standing aft in the boat is Jesse Huggett. Among those standing in the yard are Roland Pragnell, Tom Sisk and Charlie Clark.

'Our Lassie' at sea under lugger sail rig. 1st registered as 2nd class boat, 15th December, 1903. 3.75 tons.

difficulty and but for the assistance of Prodger would have drowned.

Fortunately the boat 'Nona' was not far off, and the two men aboard Andrew Chester and Archibald Huggett, rescued Prodger and Huggett, who were picked up in an exhausted condition. The 'Nona' made all speed for land and the hapless fishermen proceeded to their homes. The sinking of the boat and loss of gear amounted to a loss of £80 not covered by insurance. The Mayor Councillor O'Brien opened a subscription list for Huggett and Prodger. A report of the time said both were hard working fishermen of exemplary character

The 'Sunbeam' had sailed in several regattas, was a 20ft Lugger and in excellent trim'. Monies donated by the townsfolk enabled Tom Sisk to build a fishing boat for the Huggetts and she was named 'Our Lassie'.

June 1903.

1903 saw the building of the Lifeboat house at the Fishing Station and on Wednesday, 17th June, a new lifeboat named 'Olive' arrived at Eastbourne Railway Station and was collected by Cox'n Ben Erridge and crew. She was a surfboat pulling 12 oars, lighter than the 'James Stevens No.6' and was provided with a sail and drop keel. She was not self-righting and had no water ballast tanks. Being light greatly aided the launching and her build was in accordance with the wishes of Cox'n Erridge and the crew. A winch was provided at the new Lifeboat house at the Fishing Station for the purpose of hauling her up the beach. So for a period Eastbourne had two lifeboats on Station.

Theft of a Fog bell from the fishing boat 'Pride and Envy'.

Appearing at the local court on a charge of theft of the bell value 10s was Charles Massey. The bell, the property of George 'Pincher' Hide was kept in a secure locker on board. The bell, thought to made of brass was in fact was like other bells, made of monk's metal. Massey admitted the theft and was sentenced to 1 month's imprisonment.

1904.

A general decline in the fishing industry was discussed among the fishing fraternity along the South Coast. Some blamed the foreigner encroaching on the English fishing grounds, an age-old problem, but some blamed the shortage of fish stocks in the Channel. Whilst the East and North East coasts had progressed the South coast declined. Hastings, Eastbourne, Brighton and Worthing markets all felt the decline.

From Hastings three of the largest fish buyers who for many years exported fish to

A view of the Fishing Station 1904 and a fine body of military men after a mass bathe. N.B. Top of picture: extreme left is the Rocket house, centre shows Fish Market roof and Net shops then extreme right the Lifeboat House, built 1903.

the Paris market had gone bankrupt. The French Government putting extra duty on fish sent to France from England did not help. Another reason for the decline was the loss and damage to fishing gear, a great deal caused by sunken wrecks of recent years, all making a living from fishing more difficult.

In Hastings in particular the Fishermen's Society had in the last 5 years paid out large sums for loss of gear and damage to boats. Those fishermen that did not subscribe to the Shipwrecked Mariners Society or a local Fund certainly had a problem when they lost fishing gear or sustained damage to boats. The usual case was to locally raise a fund for them if the loss was great.

Fishing gear, sails, ropes etc, showed costs rising and nearly all the material for manufactured gear a fisherman had to get his living from now came from abroad. While some was imported from Empire countries, the greater part came from the following: Flax for sails from Russia, cotton from America for herring and mackerel nets, linseed oil for curing, from the Baltic, cutch for tanning nets, from India, cork from Spain, lines and twine made from Russian and Italian hemp, the trawl warps, bridles, and shoot ropes made from manila, from the Philippine Islands, the tar in making these ropes from Stockholm. All the foregoing materials were needed by the fishing industry. A call was made to increase the import tax but this only made costs higher for the fisherman. All told though the problem went back to a lack of fish in the Channel.

The above information came from Mr G H Simmons, who in 1904 was the Hon. treasurer for Hastings Fishermen's Society. Starting his career as a boy in one of the large Luggers that used to spend nine months of the year fishing in the North Sea and off the Isle of Wight, he passed through all grades to the position of Lugger owner and until 1903 was the owner of a ship chandler's store. So he knew what he was talking about.

1904. Watch Committee minutes.

April. It was brought before the committee that some capstan rents at the Fishing Station stood in arrears. Agreements to be terminated if not paid within one month.

June. It was established that Net shops could be sub-let by owners only to bona fide fishermen.

May 1904.

The year 1904 was a tragic and perilous one for the local fishermen. Starting in May when a severe gale sprang up during a Sunday night while several local boats were out in the Channel mackerel fishing. The boats and crews that had a narrow escape were 'Willing Boy', crew Ben Erridge, Cox'n of the lifeboat and Harry Erridge, 'Maud', crew Charles Boniface and J Prodger and boats 'Pride and Envy' and 'Little Stranger'. They had sailed from Eastbourne at 1.30pm and were several miles off Beachy Head when at midnight the fury of the gale was at its height. With helms towards Eastbourne, a run was made for safety. Ben and Harry Erridge first thought of running 'Willing Boy' ashore at the 'Falling Sands' under Beachy Head, but it was too dangerous. 'Pride and Envy' got safely to Newhaven. 'Willing Boy' and 'Maud' were sighted by the lifeboat under command of the 2nd Cox'n 'Laddie' Simpson and a crew of five stood by while both boats beached at the Fishing Station. It was low tide and led by Tom Prodger, helpers pluckily brought the boats ashore at 5.00am. ('*No restoratives could be procured for the exhausted men till the customary hour of opening for licenced houses' 6.00am?*). The 'Little Stranger' having lost a dozen nets got ashore at 8.15am.

July 1904.

Suicide by drowning was the sad case of a female named Richardson, it was July and she was seen to run into the sea at the Fishing Station, witnessed by Thomas Hide, who was in his boat mending nets. With the assistance of Harry Lee, William Bollard Hide and an Allchorn, a boat was launched manned by Thomas Hide, Lee and bathing attendant Waymark who brought the body ashore and tried artificial respiration without success.

August 1904.

Later in the year came more peril and a tragedy but in August an article in the 'Anglers' News' reported '*At Beachy Head there has been splendid bass fishing. John Hide Snr. fisherman has caught 114 bass in a few outings. The bass range from 1lb. to 7lb. There is good fishing too at the Sovereign Rocks where boats get from 20 to 40 bream a day and a nice lot of rock whiting. Flat fish are also plentiful*'.

August also saw the rescuing of a visitor bathing near the Pier. He was being carried away by the strong tide when veteran swimmer Mr Thomas Gowland (Marine Parade) and Mr Coomber swam out and brought him safely ashore.

October 1904. The 'Pride and Envy' Tragedy.

'*After a brief spell of brilliant weather came a gale on 7th October in the English Channel off Folkestone when the Eastbourne Lugger 'Pride and Envy' was lost with her crew of 3. Owned by George 'Pincher' Hide of Anchor House Latimer Road, 'Pincher' was very concerned to hear of the loss of life and the substantial financial loss of the boat and her gear.*

The lost men were Charles Brown, Jesse Goldsmith and Samuel Barnard. The skipper Brown was about 45years a Lowestoft man who came to Eastbourne several years ago and married a daughter of Philip Huggett. She died in 1902 leaving four children Louie, Charles, Midget and Rosie. Louie attends a residential home. Midget lives with an aunt Annie Huggett, Beach Road and Rosie lives with her uncle James Huggett. Jesse Goldsmith was aged about 65years and formerly owned a boat 'Owl' which he was obliged to run aground at Birling Gap where she became a total loss. Samuel Barnard a young man lived at 6 Southwark Cottages leaves a widow (maiden name French) and three young children. The late Samuel was the son of an old inhabitant of the same name, who now drives a steam roller but was formerly a fisherman and one time master of one of the Luggers owned by Mr Popham in the 1880's. Young Charles Brown son of the late skipper of the 'Pride and Envy' was in Folkestone at the time of tragedy and had been to sea with his father'

One of the other Eastbourne boats present with the fleet at Folkestone was the 'Mizpah', having on board James, Phillip and William Huggett (relations of Charles Brown).

Mrs Huggett 196, Latimer Road received a telegraph from her husband William 'All safe'.

The Mayor opened a fund for the dependants of the drowned fishermen, upwards of £100 being raised. A special mention was made in the press of the following fishermen who acted as collectors. Harry Novis, Alfred Erridge, Fred Reed, Harry Allchorn, Fred Huggett, Tom Boniface, Charles Hide Jnr. Andrew Hurd and George Erridge. The Salvation Army also collected and a Concert was held at the Theatre Royal.

The benevolence of the Shipwrecked Fishermen and Mariner's Society came to the fore by giving monies to the bereaved families. It also granted £9.10s to George 'Pincher' Hide in respect of the loss of his boat and gear. Such small boats cannot obtain insurance his loss being much greater than the amount stated. On 27th October the body of Charles Brown was washed ashore at Hythe. Kent.

November 1904.

At 8.00pm in the evening of Monday 21st November, about ten of Eastbourne's fishing boats were off fishing when the weather turned for the worse. A westerly gale blew with rain and hail, as a result during the evening the boats, 'Willing Boy' crew Ben and Alfred Erridge, 'Gannet' Tom Boniface, 'Golden City' William Allchorn and the 'Servia' owner George 'Pincher' Hide, crew George Huggett and W Matthews were blown ashore at Wallsend (Pevensey Bay). Fortunately no damage was sustained by any boat.

Knowing that 5 or 6 boats were still at sea, Ben Erridge, Cox'n of the lifeboat made haste to the Fishing Station and the maroon was fired to assemble the crew of the lifeboat. At 10.30pm the lifeboat 'James Stevens No.6' was launched from the Fishing Station, the crew including the Cox'n were 2nd Cox'n William 'Laddie' Simpson, John Erridge, Archie Huggett, Tom Huggett, Ted Sayers, William Morley, William Sayers, Sam Hurd, George Erridge, William Bollard Hide, William Allchorn and Fred Reed.

Before the lifeboat could reach Pevensey Bay, the fishing boat 'Lady Eleanor' owned by George Huggett of Latimer Road, was washed ashore between Wallsend and the Sluice. The crew on board were Matt Ticehurst and William Erridge, brother of Coxswain Ben. When the 'Lady Eleanor' was close in shore a sudden squall struck her and blew away her foresail. Then her mizzen sail was blown away. The crew got the anchor out but it did not hold so the vessel was blown onto the beach where she quickly filled with water and broke up due to the heavy surf. So great was the damage she did not go to sea again. The loss to the owner George Huggett being £20. The nets and gear belonging to George 'Pincher' Hide may be repaired and are valued at £40. Assistance at the scene was given by the Coastguard who helped Huggett and Ticehurst ashore'

While the 'Lady Eleanor' was foundering, the lifeboat, which had been launched at high tide through heavy surf, made her way vigorously rowed by her crew towards Pevensey Bay. There were 4 fishing boats there and she stood by them as they successfully made their way back to Eastbourne and landed at the Fishing Station. The lifeboat continued to stand by as other fishing boats returned by a full moon. Among those who returned was the 'Star in the East', 'Mizpah', ' Maude' and 'Commodore'. Then with the last of the fleet landed the lifeboat came ashore about 1.00am.

December 1904. Another demand for a Harbour at Eastbourne.

The local Gazette contained the following report;

'With the present Eastbourne fishing fleet of 45 large and 30 smaller boats engaged, giving employment to 195 men with an estimated outlay including boats and gear amounting to £7,000 the Council should give consideration to have a Harbour at Eastbourne.

Bigger boats were needed to fish the deep waters in the Channel the present fleet not big enough to fish outside the 5-fathom limit. The fishing industry around the coasts was flourishing. Lowestoft as an example had 3 steam drifters in 1888 now a fleet of 175 existed.

Do not allow the Eastbourne fishing industry to decay for want of a Harbour. There was no response from the Council'. (Was it an 'image' thing? Empress of Watering Places).

January 1905.

The start of the year saw the death of fisherman Richard 'Dick' Hurd, of Poplar Road, Eastbourne. He was a son of Henry and Mary Ann Hurd. The funeral was largely attended and the pallbearers were; George Erridge, William Erridge, George Allchorn and cousin Ted Hide. Some mourners were the Widow, sons R Hurd, W Hurd and C Hurd, daughters Mrs W J Weeks, A Lee and R Green, Mr J and C Hurd brothers. The following cousins Mrs Fanny Bell, Benjamin Deacon Hide, Mrs H. Mockett, J. Mockett, Miss K. Mockett and aunt Mrs Ben Hide.

February 1905.

Langney Fort was washed away during a severe east wind.

March 1905.

Fisherman Jack Tuxford died.

September 1905.

The Erridge family were in trouble with the Council over the parking of their Bathing machines on the roadway (due to high tide) of the Royal Parade so as to cause an obstruction. Ordered to remove them forthwith.

October 1905. Another sad loss of an Eastbourne Fisherman.

Monday 2nd October at 5.00pm George Chester age 31, fisherman of Eastbourne, set sail alone in the small sailing boat 'Blue Bell' with the intention of trawling in the direction of Hastings. He proceeded to Wallsend (Pevensey Bay) where he was last seen by his brother Andrew, who was also fishing at 6.30 pm about a 1/4 mile from the shore. Andrew returned to Eastbourne on Tuesday morning and on finding his brother had not returned, became anxious for his safety. He sailed his boat 'Nona' along the coast towards Hastings and did not return until 4.00pm, but nothing was seen of his missing brother. It was feared that the boat had capsized in a squall about 7.00pm Monday evening. George Chester was a poor swimmer and had heavy boots and oilskins on. The missing man was single and lived at No.1, Gordon Terrace, Bexhill Road. He had trawled alone all the summer. Some days had passed and no sign of the missing fisherman had cast a gloom over the Fishing

Station. Flags on boats had been flying at half-mast, which was evidence that all hope for him had dispelled. Searches were made over the days without success until on the Friday when between 11-12 o'clock Harry Boniface and his son Henry were trawling in Pevensey Bay, when their net caught in a boat on the bottom. With considerable difficulty the bowsprit was taken out and a portion of the sail was recovered before she sank.

The bowsprit and sail were taken ashore and identified as belonging to the 'Blue Bell', the boat of George Chester. On Saturday morning a search party was formed consisting of the two Bonifaces, Andrew Chester, Archie Huggett, Jesse Huggett, John Prodger, 'Curly' Gibbs, William Allchorn, W Endie, William Reed and others. In four boats the fishermen set off for Wallsend at 9 o'clock. The Bay was dragged and the trawl net and coil of rope 'the warp' belonging to the 'Blue Bell' was found. At 1 o'clock the party returned without any further success. It had been thought the body would have been entangled in the nets but this was not the case. It was therefore possible that Chester had been knocked overboard before the boat went down. The 'Blue Bell' was about 16 feet long and 5 feet wide and had Lugger rigged sails.

George Chester had been in the habit of trawling alone for several summers, but when he went 'hooking' in the winter he always had assistance. In a fortnight's time he would not have gone out alone as he had made arrangements for a winter partner. His parents died when he was a boy and he had been lodging with his married brother at No.1, Bexhill Road. He was spoken of as being a very smart steady fellow, able to turn his hand to anything in the way of boat repair, sail making and the like. He had been a teetotaller and non-smoker all his life and regularly attended the Seaman's Institute, being quiet and well conducted. It was on the Monday that the body of George Chester was found face downwards in the rocks off the motor track at Bexhill. A walker made the discovery and told the Police. The inquest found a verdict of accidental drowning. George Chester and old hand Jack Reed were the only two Eastbourne men at that period that ventured to go trawling alone.

RESCUE OF THE CREW OF THE BARQUE "NEW BRUNSWICK"

EASTBOURNE, SUNDAY, 25TH NOVEMBER, 1883.
(After Campbell's "Hohenlinden")

On Eastbourne when the sun was high,
All cloudless the etheral sky,
And church bells rang out merrily
    For morning prayer that Sabbath day.

But Eastbourne showed another sight
When darkness swift displaced the light,
And tempest turning day to night
    Burst o'er the town so suddenly.

"A barque is wrecked off Beachy Head!"
This was the cry, No more was said
But, "Ho! out with the lifeboat there ahead,
    And to the rescue speedily".

Then yoked to horses twelve or more,
Across the Downs to Beachy's shore,
They dropped the lifeboat, mid the roar
    Of Heaven' dread artillery.

The cliff near Birling Gap, alas,
Had fallen and destroyed the pass,
A huge unsightly rugged mass
    Barring the way absolutely.

They bridged the gulf and launched the boat,
Midst ringing cheers from many a throat,
Of danger not a man took note
    On Beachy's shore that Sabbath day.

"Pray for us lads that we once more
May after duty reach the shore",
The Captain cried, as to his oar
    Each seaman bent right gallantly.

Midst furious blast and blinding spray
The Life Boat took the crew away,
Front off the shipwrecked barque that day,
    The barque from far Norwegia.

Now miles across the slippery down,
They will to reach our beautiful town,
Thus ends an action of renown,
    Worthy the days of chivalry.

Toll for the brave this eventide,
Ye Sabbath bells! With Heaven our guide,
We have the rescued by our side,
    And with them our bold mariners.

                                        A. F. S. T.

Poem. Rescue of the crew of the 'New Brunswick' lines written in honour of the bravery shown by Charles 'Bones' Hide and gallant crew of the Eastbourne lifeboat 'William and Mary'.

Chapter Eight

The Death of 'Bones' Hide

October 1905.

Trafalgar Day 21st October saw the death of Charles 'Bones' Hide. A fitting day to die for someone like 'Bones' a fine seaman and lifesaver to share Trafalgar Day with our great naval hero, Admiral Lord Horatio Nelson.

From 'Ruffian' to 'Life Saving Hero'.

Charles 'Bones' Hide was born 1849 at Climpson's Cottages, Lower Drove, Eastbourne, the 5th and youngest son of George 'Dot' and Mary Ann Hide. His brothers all fishermen were John, George Merrick, Samuel Beckett and Benjamin Charles. A sister Mary Ann married fisherman Henry Hurd. His nickname was acquired so the story goes, when born he could fit into a pint pot and as a youngster was all 'skin and bones'. As a young man he imbibed in the drinking of alcohol and became somewhat wild when under the influence and got into many a scrape and up before the local magistrates earning a reputation of engaging his fists rather than

Charles 'Bones' Hide age 35 years, Fisherman, Boatman and Lifeboat Coxswain (1849-1905).

his brain. One particular case of assault against Charles Light was reported with the following lines from H M S Pinafore:

'O, the British tar is a soaring soul
And free as a mountain bird
His energetic fist should be ready to resist
A dictatorial word
His eyes should flash and his chest protrude
And this should be his customary attitude'.

A headline over one case of assault in the local paper for 1872 described him as 'Ruffian'. Nevertheless his renown as a fearless and skilled seaman grew amongst the fishing and boating fraternity as he reached maturity. He saved many a person from drowning, having great strength and was an exceedingly fine swimmer. He was well known as the famous Coxswain of the Eastbourne lifeboat when she went to the rescue of the 'New Brunswick' in 1883.

In September 1874, 'Bones' along with 'The Peoples Friend' Tom Bennett saved the life of a male swimmer off the Wish Tower. At the time 'Bones' was working for his cousin John Head, bathing machine operator.

Another life saving exploit example was in August 1877 whilst working on the Pier a workman fell into the sea and was in imminent danger of drowning. 'Bones' being close by dived in and held the man up until a rope was thrown to him, he then held the rope between his teeth and by this method he and the drowning man were hauled to safety. As was the custom those days a collection was made on the spot among those that witnessed his gallant action and the good sum of 15s was handed to 'Bones'. A further result of this lifesaving exploit was, an onlooker, a London gentleman William Snooke wrote to the Royal Humane Society describing 'Bones's bravery and as a result 'Bones' was presented with the Royal Humane Society lifesaving medal in December 1877 by Mr F W Cavendish of Compton Place. At the presentation it was announced 14 lives had been saved from drowning by 'Bones' some while he had been engaged in fishing away from Eastbourne. The Eastbourne Chronicle in December published a poem by Joseph Lord praising 'Bones'. The first verse as follows;

> 'Bravely Charles Hide you well have done
> Blest is your Father with his son
> He fought in battles with the wave
> And held the hand which was to save
> And you have followed in his wake
> And are worthy of the name you take'.

'Bones' was home from sea for Christmas 1878 and was involved in the following incident in the 'Ocean Wave'.

Police Court 23rd December. 'Snowballing and Pot Throwing'.

'Charles Hide admitted assaulting George Field having thrown a pint pot at him, which hit him. Hide said as soon as he opened the door to the pub, a snowball hit him in the neck. And while he was sitting drinking his pint he was pelted with snowballs. Hide threatened to throw his pot at the first person he saw throwing at him. He had thrown the pot at a man named Dennis but had missed and accidentally hit Field. Field told the Court that after the assault Hide had expressed the reverse of regret. Hide was fined 6d and 10s costs'.

'Bones' was a member of the local Conservative Club and played in their cricket team. In one particular game against Heathfield CC July 1888, he played under captain Jesse Bollard Hide the Sussex and South Australia cricketer, his cousin, and scored 4 and 2 runs. No doubt contributing more to the after match festivities.

As the festive season approached 'Bones' attended in the month of December 1896, two contrasting social functions. The first being the Conservative Association dinner held at the Club Hotel. Dr. C. Hayman presided. Present were Admiral Field M.P, Sir Ellis Ashmead Bartlett. M.P and many local and county political dignitaries and of course 'Bones' Hide as member of the Central Ward branch. After a fine dinner

'Bones' in goal. The Saffrons, Eastbourne, January 1904.

and speeches the entertainment was provided by the Empire Music Hall artists, vocalists, acrobats and dancers.

A few days later was the Fishermen's Annual Supper held at the 'Ocean Wave'. 'Bones' Hide presided over a company of 40, who appeased the hunger of a days fishing with the substantial meat pudding supper, which the host and hostess Mr & Mrs Charles Post supplied. Masters of boats present, included, beside Chairman 'Bones' Hide, Messrs William Knight, John Erridge Snr. John Erridge Jnr. Charles Hurd, Jeffrey Allchorn, William Allchorn, George Hide Jnr. Charles Swain and others. George Hookham was in the vice-chair.

Characteristic and appropriate were the decorations of the room, flags, being set off with seasonable mottoes, chrysanthemums and other flowers. At the close of the supper, a harmonious evening followed, songs being rendered by Reuben Wood, Charles Hide, John Elms and George Hookham. Henry Sayers gave two solos on the mouth organ and a party of glee singers also helped to make things pleasant. During the evening Reuben Wood proposed that a slate club should be started and it was agreed to hold a meeting for that purpose. The health of Mr & Mrs Post and Chairman 'Bones' Hide was drunk, and, an hour's extension having been allowed, the party broke up after singing 'Rule Britannia' and 'God Save the Queen'. (From the above we learn that Joseph Mockett was no longer landlord of the 'Ocean Wave' Public House).

'Bones' in Goal.

On Saturday 22nd January 1904 a charity match between the Eastbourne lifeboat crew and the Sinbad Pantomime Company took place at the Saffrons football ground in aid of the Lifeboat Institute and Princess Alice Hospital.

'Bones' Hide was the stalwart goalkeeper for the lifeboat side and as the report goes, he reclined gracefully against one of the uprights. The other goalkeeper was a midget just 3 feet high. Everybody experienced good fun and it was said one lifeboat man sped down the field with the ball faster than he had ever sped on an errand of mercy, only to be given off side when he had the ball in the net. The incident of the match came in the second half when a penalty was awarded to the 'pantomimists'. The midget goalkeeper was called up to take the penalty. 'Bones' stopped smoking and balanced his pipe up in the rigging. The midget shot and 'Bones' scooped the ball up, a great save, only at the same time he was body tackled by a huge 'Mephistopheles'. The ball went out of 'Bones's' hands into the goal. Great cheers went up. 'Poor old Bones' was the cry. The Pantomimists ran out winners by 5 goals to 3.

The game was well supported, a large audience having watched. A cup was later awarded to the winning team and a remark was made that the lifeboat men were better at saving lives than scoring goals. The lifeboat crew football eleven was as follows: -

'Bones' Hide, Charles Ernest 'Chalky' Hide, Ben Erridge, William 'Laddie' Simpson, Tom Huggett, John 'Jack' Mockett, George J Erridge, William Huggett, Fred Huggett, Alfred Erridge, Andrew Hurd and Alf Hurd (linesman)

The death of Charles 'Bones' Hide.

The Eastbourne Gazette on 18th October 1905 carried the news that the veteran lifeboat man Charles 'Bones' Hide was lying seriously ill at his residence.

Then come Trafalgar Day, 21st October 1905. '*On the hundredth anniversary of the death of Lord Nelson, 'Bones' Hide dies. To share Nelson's Day what more could be asked. He passed away at his home 4, Eshton Terrace, Eshton Road, Eastbourne. Sussex'.*

The following are the reports at the time of 'Bone's' death, which was prominently reported;

'After an illness of about a month's duration, Mr Charles Hide, popularly known as 'Bones' passed away at a quarter to six on Saturday night at his residence at Eshton Terrace, Eshton Road and there is something singularly touching in the mournful coincidence that he, a brave and hardy lifeboat-man, should have died on Nelson's Day - the hundredth anniversary of the Battle of Trafalgar. In the deceased's front parlour were some pictures, which were amongst his cherished possessions. One of them represents Nelson on the deck of the 'Victory' at the time when the many coloured flags conveying the signal 'England expects every man to do his duty' were hoisted.

In the most populous districts of the town, and more especially in the neighbourhood of the Fishing Station, there was no figure more familiar than that of Mr Hide. The story goes that in his youth he was so extremely thin that he acquired the name of 'Bones', which clung to him to the end of his days. However this may be, there is no doubt that when he was in his prime he was a man who possessed almost Herculean strength. Although he was about the middle height, he was very deep chested; his neck and limbs also indicated the possession of great muscular power and endurance. Exposure to cold and rain gave his face a weather

beaten appearance. He had light hair and an exceptionally long moustache, which extended down on each side. The cast of his features showed that he was a man with a full share of resolution, and he spoke in a strong, not to say gruff, tone of voice. And he could on occasions use that vigorous language to which the British sailor is prone. ' Where are we going mates'? One of the lifeboat crew is said to have asked on the memorable day when the Eastbourne lifeboat was taken over the Downs to rescue a Norwegian crew who were tempest tossed. ' Where are we going?' growled 'Bones' Hide, 'We are going to B----y Birling Gap!'

Deceased was the youngest child of the late George and Mary Ann Hide, having four brothers and a sister; John Hide of Meads, George Merrick Hide of Anchor House, Latimer Road, Mary Ann Hurd (wife of Henry Hurd) of Latimer Road, Samuel Beckett Hide of Hydney Street and Benjamin Charles Hide of 154, Latimer Road. Deceased was also a relative of Jesse and Arthur Bollard Hide (Sussex County cricketers) and of Henry Bollard Hide.

The late 'Bones' Hide was sent to the Trinity Schools, and when he had to earn his livelihood he applied himself to seafaring pursuits, boating and fishing. Sailing yachts used for pleasure trips are now few in number, having failed to hold their own against the competition of steamers. Hide was one time skipper of Mockett's 'Skylark' and Bates 'Britannia'. The latter was the largest yacht, capable of carrying one hundred and forty passengers. A skilful and fearless seaman, Hide knew his business thoroughly. In the winter months he devoted himself to fishing and was a prominent figure at the meat pudding suppers. He was present, we believe at the gathering of fishermen, which was attended a few years ago by Admiral Field M.P. who gave a song (about a pack of cards) to the delight of his nautical listeners. For some time Hide was salesman at the Fish Market and he assisted his wife (who had a laundry business) by driving a cart, on which baskets of clothes intended for delivery to customers were placed. This vehicle was a curious looking one there seemed to be no regular seat for the driver, but Hide perched his bulky form upon it, and never lost his equilibrium.

It was through his connection with the Eastbourne lifeboat that Hide became widely known to the general public, when in November, 1883, a terrible storm sprang up and the news came that a vessel was in distress off Beachy Head, Coxswain 'Bones' and the crew took the lifeboat 'William and Mary' over the Downs and launched her at Birling Gap. A violent gale was blowing and it was raining and intensely cold. Hide's face was absolutely blue with cold but he was determined and the crew of the Scandinavian vessel were saved. The gallantry of the hardy lifeboat men had resulted in a memorable rescue. Hide and the crew were presented with a silver medal presented by the townsfolk. The pluck of Hide and his crew on that day will ever to be remembered as worthy of the brave seaman who had on his gravestone this stirring epitaph:

> Full many a precious life he saved
> With his undaunted crew
> He put his trust in Providence
> And cared not how it blew.

As recently as two years ago Hide was one of the crew of the Eastbourne lifeboat who having received a call went forth to rescue and had an immense experience

Captain Fred Collins, pleasure boatman of Brighton C.1900, a friend of 'Bones'.

when they had to come ashore at Hastings.

The death of his wife Esther, which occurred six months ago, was a severe blow. In his last illness, he suffered from jaundice and was attended by Dr.Heiser and devotedly nursed by his daughter Lottie. Happily his end was a peaceful one. After a period of sleep or unconsciousness he opened his eyes, a slight sound was emitted from his lips and he passed away without a struggle'.

A tribute from a daily paper said, 'He was known along the Sussex coast as 'Bones' and to use the words of one of his comrades 'a thorough old sea dog'. With his burly figure and flowing moustache, he was the personification of the hardy Vikings of old and many a kindly act of unostentatious charity, coupled with dashing heroism will carry his memory green for many a year. He performed many acts of life saving and received a Royal Humane Society medal for his bravery. He will be carried to his grave by his old colleagues of the lifeboat. On the announcement of his death, flags were hoisted at half-mast on all the boats at the Fishing Station and many and sincere were the regrets expressed at the loss of a popular and noble spirited man'.

The funeral of 'Bones' Hide took place at Ocklynge cemetery on Wednesday 25th October 1905. The following is as reported in the local newspaper;

'Funeral at Eastbourne. Lifeboat men present: -

The funeral of that hero in humble life, Charles 'Bones' Hide, formerly Coxswain of the Eastbourne lifeboat, took place on Wednesday, when the weather was fine and bright and the shimmering sea was calm and almost unruffled. And surely it was only fitting that the interment of one who had braved so many tempests should be conducted under peaceful and tranquil conditions.

Manifestations of sympathetic interest were not lacking. The flags at the Fishing Station were half-mast high, and there were other indications of sympathy for the bereaved relatives of a brave man whose life was probably shortened by his devotion to duty. The cortege, which started from the deceased's residence at Eshton - terrace, Eshton Road, consisted of a hearse and about thirteen carriages, including that of Eastbourne M P Mr Lindsay Hogg. By the desire of the family there were few floral offerings and the remains were enclosed in a handsome coffin.

The six lifeboat men, who walked by the side of the hearse and afterwards bore the coffin to the grave, were Thomas Swain, Edwin Matthews, William Bollard Hide, Ben Erridge, William Erridge and William Simpson. Of these Swain, Matthews, W.B. Hide and W Erridge were members of the old lifeboat crew of 1883. W Erridge is still a lifeboat man. Ben Erridge (Coxswain) and William Simpson are members of the present crew.

When the procession was formed it was headed by a number of lifeboat men and other seafarers. Among them were, John Mockett, Tom Huggett, William Huggett, Henry Boniface, George Erridge, John Erridge, Charles Ernest Hide, John Colstick, Albert Sayers, Reuben Reed, William Godden and others. Nearly all the seafaring men were most respectfully dressed in dark clothes with black peaked yachting caps, and their reverent demeanour did them credit.

First carriage: - (Children) Charles Hide Jnr. Ada Dartnell, Walter Hide and Miss Lottie Hide.

Second carriage: - (Children) Leonard Hide, Miss Tillie Hide, Edwin Hide, and John Hide of Meads. (Eldest brother)

Third carriage: - George M Hide, (brother) Mrs Samuel Hide (sister in law) Mrs Mary Ann Hurd (sister).

Fourth carriage: - Mr & Mrs Ben Hide (brother & sister in law), Mr Dartnell (son in law) Mrs Charles Hide (daughter in law).

The remaining carriages contained the following, the occupants being nephews and nieces except where otherwise stated: -

Fifth carriage: - Mrs Fanny Bell, John Hide Jnr. Mrs Mariah Simpson, and Albert Hide.

Sixth carriage: - Dennis Hide, Mrs Elizabeth Brewster, Miss Kate Hide, and Edward (Ted) Hide.

Seventh carriage: - Mrs Haynes, Sidney Hide, Richard Hide, and Mrs Sidney Hide.

Eighth carriage: - Ben Hide Jnr. George Hide Jnr. Sam Hurd, and Captain Collins of Brighton (friend).

Ninth carriage- H Barrow (brother in law), A Simmons, Mrs G Simmons, and G Rainsley.

Tenth carriage- Mr & Mrs J Barrow (brother & sister in law) and Mrs Carter.

Along the route and in the neighbourhood of the cemetery there were many sympathetic onlookers. The cortege having reached Ocklynge the coffin was taken from the hearse and borne, on the shoulders of the six chosen lifeboat men, into the cemetery chapel, where the Reverend. Dr. R.W.Pritchard conducted the first part of the service.

Deceased was a member of the Loyal Southern Lodge of Oddfellows (Manchester Unity) for thirty years and among the brethren present were P.P.G.M. Edward Ellis, P.P.G.M. Paul, P.G. James Andrews (Trustee of the Widow and Orphan Fund), P.G. Edwin Bloomfield, P.G. John Lower, P.G. George Hookham, P.G.W Brown and

P.G.J.H. Haine. At the graveside the Rev. Dr. Pritchard conducted the concluding portion of the Church of England burial service then the Oddfellows Burial Service was read by P.G. Bloomfield, and the brethren present threw sprigs of thyme into the grave'.

'Among those present was Mr Collins (the Skipper of the Brighton pleasure yacht 'Skylark' who was in nautical dress and wore a glazed boater hat), Mr James Morris, Mr Herbert Morris, Mr William Dennis, Mr A Infield (Hon. Secretary of the Eastbourne Lifeboat Committee), ex Councillor Thomas Bennett, Mr Jesse Bollard Hide (formerly Sussex County cricketer and a cousin of the deceased), Mr Sayers, Mr Fawcett (Royal Parade), Mr Henry Bollard Hide (cousin), Miss Graham and others including members of the 'Royal Ancient Order of Buffaloes' of which 'Bones' was a member'.

Among the floral tributes was a lovely artificial wreath in a glass case bearing the following inscription. 'From his brother fishermen and fishmongers, R.I.P''.

At the time of the funeral it was proposed that a subscription be raised for a memorial stone to be erected over the grave. Between £30 - £40 was required and this sum was raised among the townsfolk of Eastbourne. Dr Hilyard of 'Halewood' Carew Road acted as treasurer. Subscriptions could be left with the Hon. Secretary Charles Morgan 291, Seaside, Jack Mockett, fish salesman, Beach Road and Mr Clayden of the Seaman's Institute.

It was proposed that the marble memorial headstone to the late 'Bones' Hide bear a carving of an anchor and a suitable inscription. This was done and can be seen to this day in Ocklynge cemetery. So the life of Charles 'Bones' Hide ended. He is still remembered to this day by his and the descendants of Eastbourne's old fishing families.

Memorial to 'Bones', Ocklynge Cemetery, Eastbourne.

Chapter Nine

Spratting at Eastbourne and Through the Great War

1905. Watch Committee minutes.

October. Jack Sayers purchased the Net shop belonging to Sam Oliver and the agreement was transferred. Fishing Station. The committee agreed the following applications for transfers of capstans and Net shops No.21 Thomas Prodger (temporary), No.5 to Andrew Chester, Nos.8w and 11a to Mike Hardy, Nos.50 and 39w to Henry Sayers and George Hookham.

1906. Watch Committee minutes.

April. The Parade Inspector reported that Mike Hardy and Charles Boniface had not paid rents for their ground at the Fishing Station. Given till Easter to pay up.

1906.

John Hide (1837 -1918) eldest brother of 'Bones'

Old fisherman and boatman John Hide would regularly walk down from Meads

Eastbourne Fishing Station C.1906. Fishermen, left to right, Brothers John Hide, Samuel Beckett Hide, Benjamin Hide and extreme right Edward 'Ted' Hide, son of John.

Sprat punt boat 'Bill Bailey' coming ashore at Eastbourne Fishing Station. February 1906.

Eastbourne Fishing Station 1906. Holding fish is fisherman of Holywell, George Prodger age 84 years.

every day having retired as landlord of the 'Pilot Inn' to his Boat Stand and attend the Fishing Station where his son Edward 'Ted' carried on with fishing during the seasons. The family Net shop and capstans were on hand there and he helped with net mending and other tasks associated with the fishing trade. The 1906 photo taken at the Fishing Station shows John and others sported whiskers under their chins. This was a common thing among the fishermen of earlier days at sea when under sail and on open decks they were exposed to the elements. It was a protection against those elements and gave a degree of warmth and waterproofing under an oilskin. 1906 shows John Hide at the door of his Net shop at the Fishing Station, in the foreground fishermen George Prodger of Meads, aged 84 years. He like John Hide would have walked down from Meads.

1906 saw an article in the 'Daily Mirror' on Eastbourne sprat fishing. The original copy of the newspaper has survived but not in good condition.

Fisherman Fred 'Mucky' Erridge 1897-1990 knew 'Ted' Hide and recalled the following from memory. He described Ted's pleasure/fishing boat the 'Bill Bailey' as a 'Sprat punt boat' having a 'dipping lug foresail and 'standing lug mizzen'. The lug foresail was loose footed and she carried one crew, George Allchorn being his pal and regular crew. Tragically George was killed in action in 1915 serving with the Naval Brigade. Another crew for the 'Bill Bailey' was pal Tom Vine. Built in November 1903 by Tom Sisk, the 'Bill Bailey' was the biggest of three sister boats. The others being Alleyn 'Narny' Sayers' 'Runaway Girl' and 'Bogey' Allchorn's 'William and Dorothy' named after his two children.

As with all fishermen there are various 'spots' at sea where they drop their lines, pots and nets for their fish and shellfish by lining up particular landmarks from seaward. 'Ted' Hide was no exception as an old hand written sheet of paper of his shows where his 'spots' to fish off Eastbourne were.

Another tale told by 'Mucky' was, the time when 'Ted' Hide and George Allchorn were going long line fishing in the 'Bill Bailey', having prepared her and baited up the line, a long laborious task, they went for a drink, it was evening time. Having had plenty to drink in the Beach Hotel they eventually pushed off from the Fishing Station about midnight. On getting to the fishing grounds about 3 miles off they discovered they had left behind on the beach, the baited up lines. Old 'Mucky' did chuckle when recalling this.

A WONDERFUL CATCH of SPRATS at EASTBOURNE

LANDING THE NIGHT'S CATCH ON EASTBOURNE BEACH.

Large numbers of sprats are being landed at Eastbourne, but the prices fetched are ridiculously low, one boat being obliged to sell a night's catch of 20,000 for 18s.—about 10½d. per 1,000. The photograph shows the boat NN. 184 arriving at Eastbourne with 50,000 sprats on board.

Scene at the fishing village at Eastbourne. Shaking the sprats out of the net.

A good catch. There are 20,000 sprats in the catch now being shaken from the nets.

Sprat Catch at Eastbourne, February 1906, from an article in the Daily Mirror.

'Mucky' also related that William 'Bill' Fibbens was a sailmaker and during the summer months a boatman, having the top shop of Tom 'Tommy Ruin' Swain's Net shop for his sailmaking. Fibbens also ran a second hand shop in Seaside, occupied in later years by Meadows, an outfitters shop.

Fisherman Harry Mockett drowned at sea 14th-15th October and fisherman William 'Camboy' Sayers died December 1906.

January 1907. A Gallant Rescue.

'Humane Society Certificates were presented to fishermen George and Ben Erridge on 4th January 1907, at the Police Court for their gallant conduct in rescuing two men from drowning in November, 1906. 'The men had put off from the Fishing Station in a boat to go fishing, about 400 yds out the boat capsized, by struggling they both got into shallower water but by then one was unconscious. Seeing the incident both Erridges rushed into the sea up to their necks and took hold of the

Eastbourne Fishermen C.1900, seated Tommy Vine, standing Edward 'Ted' Hide.

unconscious man and the other and got them safely ashore. For ¹/₂ hour the Erridges' gave artificial respiration to the unconscious man who then recovered. Doctor Pollock examined both men and pronounced them fit to be taken home'

The prompt action by the Erridges' undoubtedly saved the man's life. Eyewitness reports fully corroborated their bravery.

'George 'Smuggler' Erridge of 57, Archery Road, aged 57, has been connected with seafaring all his life (principally fishing) and a member of the lifeboat crew about 30 yrs. About 1877 he went with others in the 'surf boat' and rescued two fishermen Mitchell and Adams, who, while fishing, capsized. He received £2. In September 1883 he was a member of

Eastbourne Fishermen C.1900. Left to right, George Allchorn, ? Sayers, Tommy Vine and 'Ted' Hide.

Fishing 'Spots' at sea off Eastbourne C.1900.

the lifeboat crew that went to the assistance of the barque 'Isabella' in distress off Bexhill, in severe storm conditions. Eight souls were rescued on this occasion. He was also a member of the lifeboat crew in that famous rescue of 1883, when they rescued the crew of the 'New Brunswick' off Beachy Head. For that bravery he received a silver medal. On several occasions he assisted in saving persons in difficulty whilst bathing in the vicinity of the Fishing Station.

Ben Erridge, of Olive House, Bexhill Road, aged 37, has been connected with seafaring all his life (principally fishing) a member of the lifeboat crew for 16 yrs, 6 yrs as Coxswain. He was a member of the lifeboat crew 15 yrs ago that went to the assistance of the barge, 'Eureka' in distress off the Pier and rescued 3 men and a woman. November 19th 1893 the 'Bantam' a Hastings Lugger was in distress off the Wish Tower, 4 crew were rescued. November 7th 1894 the steam yacht 'Ray', 7 crew rescued. About 18 yrs ago when fishing aboard the Eastbourne Lugger 'XL' owned by George 'Pincher' Hide at Plymouth he jumped overboard three times to rescue children that had fallen off the quay. Both deserving of the honour they not only deserved well of Eastbourne but of Great Britain'.

1907. Watch Committee minutes.

April. The Committee issued a warning to occupiers at the Fishing Station that worn out boats left on the beach contravened the Bye Laws and action would be taken if not removed.

May. A report was received that a tenant of a certain Net shop was sleeping in it. He was to desist.

April 1907.

At the Fishing Station in April, a lucky escape concerning the red light on the pole happened to Archie Huggett, fisherman, son of the late Jesse Huggett. It was Archie Huggett's job to light and hoist the red light to the top of the pole (to those at sea, a land mark and guiding light to the Fishing Station when dark) every evening. As Huggett was hoisting the light on a Saturday evening the chain broke and the heavy lamp almost fell on his head. Had it done so he would have almost certainly been killed. He avoided the lamp but in doing so struck his head against a wall, knocking himself out. Taken to his home in Beach Road he later recovered in time for his marriage at Christ Church 5 days later.

DINNER
TO
The Eastbourne Lifeboat Crew.

BEN ERRIDGE, First Coxswain.

DIPLOCK'S HOTEL,
Wednesday, December 19th, 1906.

Farncombe & Co., Ltd.

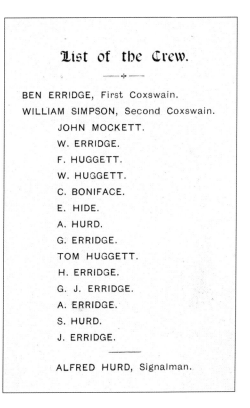

List of the Crew.

BEN ERRIDGE, First Coxswain.
WILLIAM SIMPSON, Second Coxswain.
JOHN MOCKETT.
W. ERRIDGE.
F. HUGGETT.
W. HUGGETT.
C. BONIFACE.
E. HIDE.
A. HURD.
G. ERRIDGE.
TOM HUGGETT.
H. ERRIDGE.
G. J. ERRIDGE.
A. ERRIDGE.
S. HURD.
J. ERRIDGE.

ALFRED HURD, Signalman.

January 1908.

The report of the 1907 herring and sprat catches were poor and price likewise, the catches not like the bonanza of sprats in 1906, and Archie Huggett came to the fore again at the Fishing Station. It was whilst he was attempting to launch his boat when due to a choppy sea, the boat filled with water and his sprat nets were washed along the beach and got covered with shingle. With the assistance of several fishermen they were recovered but not before they suffered considerable damage.

March 1908.

In March, Charles Boniface, fisherman and lifeboat man died at his home in Sidley Road, aged 45 years. A report at the time said he was skipper of the fishing boat 'Bonnie Kate' owned by George 'Pincher' Hide. Boniface was very popular among his fellow fishermen and boatmen. He was a hard working, steady, genial man and would be much missed. Over 50 fishermen attended his funeral, the coffin being borne by members of the lifeboat crew; Cox'n Ben Erridge 2nd Cox'n William 'Laddie' Simpson, John 'Jack' Mockett, Andrew Hurd, Tim Erridge, and William Erridge. Charles Boniface's wife had died in 1906.

1908. Watch Committee minutes.

March. The application by Viscount Curzon and Lt O A Bradford R N V R to purchase the Marine Club Boat House for use as a Drill Hall for the R.N.V.R. was approved.

August. Lease of the ground site was also approved.

November 1908	Borough Accountant's Report
Receipts from Watermen Licences	£ 5.4s.0d.
Receipts from Pleasure Boat Licences	£26.1s.0d.
Receipts from Capstan & Net shop Licences	£15.0s.0d.

Receipts were from October 1907 - September 1908.

It was also proposed to place a toll on fish from other Towns sold at Eastbourne Fish Market.

A Prawning competition at Birling Gap on 15th July 1908.

A great slaughter of these creatures succumbed to some 30 competitors. Mr E Ray won the silver medal for the championship of Sussex by catching 45 'brooders'. His total catch weighed 2lbs. Miss Peile won the ladies competition with a catch of 9 ounces. A very popular seaside pastime enjoyed among the rocks, by many local Eastbourne residents and visitors over the years. Methods of prawning amongst the rocks are 'Ginning' where a baited hooped net is laid in a rock pool then later retrieved by means of a hooked pole. (Plaice frames and 'jack abble' crabs are popular bait) 'Spooning' where the prawner using a pole with a hooped net at one end, runs it through and around the rock pools in search of prawns.('Brooders' are the big fat breeding prawns).

Fishermen's Light. August 5th 1908. Council Meeting.

Mr Archie Huggett is paid £29 per annum for cleaning, lighting and extinguishing this light and six lamps on the fishing station. He does his work very satisfactorily. The arrangement is to continue.

Prawning at Crowlink, 1907. Access gained via Coastguard Station cutting through chalk cliff to beach.

August 1908. Spanish Jack.

August 24th at the Police Court, a well-built Spaniard, John de Garcia, fisherman of Latimer Road was summoned for assaulting Charles Henry Prodger, also a fisherman of Beach Road. *'Garcia was aged about 30 years and of dark complexion. Prodger stated he was sitting on the beach beside a boat on a Sunday afternoon when Garcia came up to him and told him to take off his coat. Prodger refused so Garcia picked him up and knocked him to the ground and struck him in the face. Garcia accused Prodger of saying he was cunning. Prodger admitted saying this. Prodger then took off his coat and defended himself. Fred Huggett of Fairlight Road corroborated Prodger. Garcia said,*

Eastbourne Fisherman 'Spanish Jack' John de Garcia, 1912.

because he was a foreigner all were against him. William Huggett with whom Garcia lodged said he had had a dispute with Garcia, who then picked on Prodger. Garcia said he had to put up with a lot of abuse because he was a Spaniard. They called him the 'onion man' and the 'ice cream vendor'. He said he had been a chief engineer on Union Castle liners. Life was not worth living on Eastbourne beach and he had given up fishing. Garcia said he had money in the Bank'.

He was fined 20/-. The Bench commented that they were lenient because Garcia did not know the habits of this country'.

February 1909.

On February 23rd, George Merrick 'Pincher' Hide aged 68 years died at his home Anchor House, Latimer Road. He died early in the evening whilst reading a newspaper having for some time suffered from heart disease and had been attended by Doctor Sherwood. Reports in the local paper showed 'Pincher' to have been a prominent figure at the Fishing Station and one of the principal owners of fishing boats, special mention being made of his long service to the Sussex Sea Fisheries Committee.

Eastbourne Chronicle February 27th 1909.

'The seafaring section of Eastbourne, have lost a genial and popular friend in Mr George Merrick Hide who suddenly expired while reading at his residence Anchor House, Latimer Road. Mr Hide who was familiarly known as 'Pincher' leaves a widow and grown up family.

Mr Hide who was a member of the large family of that name which has been associated with the fishing and boating industry in Eastbourne for some generations, was the owner of the fleet of fishing boats sent each year to the herring grounds and the North Sea fisheries.

Occasionally he had success but mostly the expenses used up the proceeds of the catches.

He was a great champion of the fishermen's rights locally. Mr Hide on behalf of the fisher folk put in an appearance at the House of Lords against the building of the sea wall (Royal Parade) protesting that it would ruin their business. The whole case was fought out and the present Fishing Station was the result. He was a man

George 'Pincher' Hide (1840-1909).

of strong opinions and one it was not possible to 'talk over'. In appearance he was almost the counterpart of Dickens 'Pegotty'. A son of the late George Hide and brother of John, Samuel, Benjamin and the late 'Bones' Hide. He at one time had charge of the 'Anchor Tap' in the days of the late Mr Newman and of late years had bathing machines to the west of Grand Parade bandstand. He and the fishermen were always strong supporters of the late Mr John Haine of Cavendish Place. The funeral took place on Friday afternoon 26th February at Ocklynge cemetery. It was numerously attended. Preceding the hearse and walking two abreast were between thirty and forty of the local fishermen. There were about a dozen carriages carrying the family and chief mourners'.

A tribute to Pincher from Councillor J T Wenham published in the Eastbourne Gazette is as follows;

'I regard the death of Mr George Merrick Hide, as the passing of a type of manly race. To know him was to honour him; it was my privilege to gain his friendship as a boy, and once to gain the friendship of 'Pincher' Hide was to have a life long friend. His father 'Dot' Hide was a man of gigantic proportions, standing head and shoulders above his fellows, a weather beaten figure, brave as a lion, always ready like his sons, to risk his own life to rescue those in peril at sea. 'Pincher' was a worthy son of a worthy sire, and was looked up to by his class a leader, faithful friend and guide. His brother 'Bones' Hide who so recently passed away, has left a memory that will always be cherished, by those who honour the brave'.

J.T. Wenham.
Eastbourne. March 1st 1909.

September 1909.

A report stated 'Credit in connection with the recent saving of life at the bathing station is due to 1st class Boatman Henry Boniface, of 40 Sidley Road, who got the young man Berry out of the water'.

A brave act by Henry Boniface, no doubt not for the first time. Many a person had their lives saved from drowning by the diligent boatmen and fishermen on hand on the beach.

The Fish Market, a large oblong building with a cement floor at the Fishing Station had been operating now for a number of years and was the subject of a newspaper article in September.

'It was early morning and a single boat had landed its catch of about thousand mackerel and a few other fish, 'friers' dabs, codling, lemon soles, and plaice. John 'Jack' Mockett was the auctioneer. The sale being by 'dutch auction' there was a good crowd present including some women. Jack shouted, 'who'll give me fifteen shillings a hundred, fourteen and sixpence, fourteen shillings and so on down till *the mackerel were sold. Eastbourne beach is fairly well supplied with fishing boats and during the winter months a large quantity of fish is sent out of town'.*

A remark by the writer of this article to a fisherman at the Fish Market, that he supposed the boatmen on the seafront would soon be turning their attention to fishing evoked the reply, *'that whereas some of them were old fishermen, there were other boatmen who knew no more about fishing than the man in the moon'.*

On the subject of fish, 'Fishermen's Arithmetic' along the South Coast was something to wonder at. How many herring to the hundred? The obvious answer would be a hundred. But that is not so, at least not according to Brighton or Eastbourne fishermen. Down at Portsmouth, the fishermen sold a hundred herring to the exact hundred. But at Brighton you got 128 to the hundred and at Eastbourne you got 136 to the hundred. Herring it seems were sold by the 'worp', which is pronounced broadly as 'wurp'. A worp consisted of four herring at Brighton so there were thirty-two worps to the hundred of 128. Whilst at Eastbourne it was thirty-four worps to the hundred of 136.

Another distinction between Brighton and Eastbourne was that at Brighton the 128 was called a 'hundred', whereas at Eastbourne the 136 was styled 'the last tell'. Amongst Eastbourne fishermen the same regulation applied to mackerel, but at Brighton mackerel were sold at thirty-three worps to a hundred of 132. Still one more difference between the Sussex fishermen was that Eastbourne sprats were counted and sold by the hundred, whereas at Brighton they were sold by the bushel.

Still with fishing, the late Fred 'Mucky' Erridge gave the following information on the all-important net sizes used by local fishermen over the period he was alive (93 years).

Mackerel nets = 24 knots to the yard, the large Irish Mackerel nets = 28 knots to the yard, Herring nets = 32 knots to the yard and Sprat nets = 66 knots to the yard.

October 1909.

The 'White Slave' a motor boat belonging to Mr A.E. Dumbrill landlord of the Prince of Wales Public House caught fire off Beachy Head. Dumbrill who received burns to the face hands and arms was aboard with 3 passengers. He scuttled the 'White Slave' some 100 yards off Holywell. Later with the assistance of Mr Jessup engineer, fishermen Hide and Allchorn, the boat was salvaged at low tide and taken to the Fishing Station.

Christmas 1909.

The lifeboat crew were presented with monies collected for them. The crew were: - Coxswain Ben Erridge, 2nd Coxswain William Simpson £1.10s each. Crew: - John Mockett, George Erridge, Frederick Huggett, William Erridge, Thomas Huggett, George J Erridge, John Erridge Jnr. Andrew Hurd, Alfred Erridge, Henry Erridge, Charles Hurd, William Huggett, Sam Hurd, Charles Ernest Hide and signalman Hurd. £1.5s each,

July 1910.

Samuel Beckett Hide died July 4th 1910 aged 66 years.

October 1910.

Zero Tolerance Policing. Nothing to do with Fishing.

Annie Bumstead and Florence West, both children's' nurses of Saffrons Road, were summoned for obstructing the footpath in Grange Road. Both defendants had been warned by the Police to wheel their perambulators in single file, but they took no notice and continued to wheel them abreast on the pavement. They were asked if they understood and Bumstead replied, *'Yea, how stupid, when we are from the same family'*. It was near All Saints Church in Carlisle Road that a lady had to step off the pavement in order to pass the defendants. They denied this saying there was plenty of room on the pavement. The Bench did not record a conviction but ordered each defendant to pay 1/6d costs.

The fishing Lugger 'Bonnie Kate' owned by Albert Hide son of 'Pincher' called for the assistance of the lifeboat on Monday 31st October 1910. The report at the time states;

'A terrific gale force wind sprang up in the Channel about 11.15pm. All the Eastbourne fishing boats with the exception of the 'Bonnie Kate' were safely ashore. Watch was kept at the Fishing Station by Ben Erridge and the lifeboat crew who stayed until 2.30am in the morning on the lookout for the boat. Not getting any tidings of her it was thought she had made her way to Hastings and the lifeboat men went home'.

About 4.30am a message was received from the coastguard at Pevensey Bay by telephone, that a vessel was showing flares in the Bay and needed assistance. The bell was rung (a bell was affixed to the Coxswain's house in those days) and the crew quickly attended the lifeboat house. The 'James Stevens No.6' was got out in the darkness amid rain and gale force winds and hauled by willing hands over the beach and sands. (It was low water at the time). After launching she at once put her nose to the gale and after 55 minutes of strenuous pulling the lifeboat let out her drogue (sea anchor) and veered down on the 'Bonnie Kate' but not before being swamped twice with heavy seas. The distressed vessel was riding her anchors, having nearly all her canvas blown away by the storm and was in a perilous condition. The crew of three hands and skipper Jesse Huggett were down below in an exhausted condition having faced the gale all night. A stimulant (Rum?) from the lifeboat was put aboard for the crew to partake of. Cox'n Ben Erridge asked if the crew wished to be taken off, but as the weather seemed to be abating it was decided the lifeboat would stand by, which she did for three hours. When the storm had calmed the 'Bonnie Kate' made her way back to Eastbourne with the lifeboat in attendance arriving about 10.00am. The sea was still too rough to get her up so she rode at anchor for a further two hours before being hauled up.

The lifeboat crew had had a very trying time but their plucky compassionate action under perilous conditions called for the warmest praise'.

1910. Watch Committee minute.

December - The application by Henry Boniface to erect a Net shop using cement concrete was granted subject to supervision by the Borough Surveyor.

May 1911.

The lifeboat was called upon to give assistance because of a collision between two steamers off Eastbourne, the SS. Charlton and SS. Nyroca. The 'Nyroca' only slightly damaged proceeded to Southampton but the 'Charlton' ran ashore at

Langney Point. The lifeboat 'Olive' was launched off the beach at the Fishing Station and the east end fisherwomen showed great spirit by helping to pull and launch her. She stood by the stricken steamer until she was towed off and away by three Tugs to Dover. Tim Erridge was now Coxswain of the Eastbourne lifeboat, having taken over from his brother Ben (who had emigrated to Canada). The crew on this service were; Edwin Matthews, George Huggett, Charles Prodger, Andrew Hurd, Will Gibbs, Mike Hardy, Will Boniface, John 'Jack' Mockett, Reuben 'Cassy' Reed Snr. Luke Hide, Alfred 'Mucky' Erridge, George Erridge, William Huggett and Tom Huggett.

1911. Watch Committee minutes.

May. Fishing Station. Agreed that plot No.19 be transferred to Henry Boniface from Henry Fox. Mr Dumbrell's Net shop and capstan be transferred to Henry Sayers. Fish Salesman Charles Clarke granted plot No.16 Net shop. An application from William Erridge for a boathouse and to stand his Bathing machines on the Fishing Station was refused.

The Building committee stated that all plans for Net shops and capstans must be submitted to them.

September. Agreed that plot No.43 be occupied by Henry Sayers.

October. Fish Salesman Charles Clarke application for the transfer of Edward Allchorn's Net shop and capstan be granted.

August 1911.

A National Railway strike and no Fish trains arriving at Eastbourne. Two local fishmongers, Messrs Waters and Scotchmer chartered a supply of fish from Grimsby by boat. The steam trawler 'Rado' duly arrived and a total of 400 stone of fish were offloaded to the Fish Market. Strange when there were local fish caught, but perhaps, local boats could not meet the increased local demand. Indeed the importing of fish from Grimsby where there was usually a glut and cheaper prices competed with the local fishing industry.

1911 saw a total of 19 fishmongers trading through 26 shops, a big demand for fish. An example of how a fishmonger of Eastbourne made life hard for the local fishermen was the business of 'Scotchmer' No.6, Terminus Road, owned by a Mr G F Sleight who was also the owner of the world's largest fleet of 60 steam trawlers working out of Grimsby, with another 20 being built in 1914.

A visitor's post card, dated November 1911, told of the morning cry *'mackerel 1d each'* in the street.

March 1912.

A collision on 16th March occurred between the P&O liner 'Oceana' and barque 'Pisagua' off Beachy Head with some loss of life and the sinking of the 'Oceana'. Eastbourne's lifeboat 'James Stevens No.6' under Cox'n Tim Erridge attended and brought many survivors ashore. A total of 6 hours were spent over the rescue service. A fine effort by the Eastbourne lifeboat crew. £1million in gold and silver bullion was aboard the 'Oceana', which was later recovered by divers.

May 1912.

Eastbourne Lifeboat Crew, 'Oceana' rescue March 1912. Some crew members identified as back row extreme right, Joe 'Crickets' Prodger, next to him John 'Foot' Prodger, 4th from left Charles Ernest 'Chalky' Hide.
Front row 3rd from right Coxswain Tim Erridge and 2nd from right, 2nd Coxswain William 'Laddie' Simpson.

Amid mist and rain the barge 'Leslie West' went aground on a ledge of rocks at Beachy Head. The motor pleasure boat 'Britannia' skippered by Harry Sayers was soon alongside to give assistance until the lifeboat being towed by the motorboat 'Star of Peace' arrived on the scene. Coxswain Tim Erridge took control of the incident. The enterprising 'Britannia' returned to Grand Parade and took a full load of passengers to view the grounded barge. Later that day the barge was re-floated and made her way towards Dover.

November 1912. Aeronauts in danger.

An exciting adventure befell two gentlemen off Eastbourne. They had left London in a hot air Balloon in the morning intending to make a trip to Kent but due to the onset of fog and rain they finished up over the sea when darkness had fallen. The aeronauts did not at first realise the danger they were in but they had finished up two miles out to sea off Wallsend (Pevensey Bay). It was only when they were about 40 feet above the sea did they realise they were indeed at sea. As they descended into the water they cried out for help and by very good fortune the 'Bonnie Kate' fishing boat was in hearing distance with skipper J P Huggett and crew of P Huggett, John de Garcia and boy W Durrant aboard. Huggett ordered the boat's nets to be cut adrift and the crew pulled for the stricken balloon. The basket was almost level with the sea, how lucky. The aeronauts were taken aboard and some of the balloon's equipment. The envelope of the balloon was also taken aboard and all haste was made for Eastbourne. On being brought ashore the aeronauts, members of the Royal Aero Club, a Mr Nolan and Mr Arthur Towner lodged overnight in the Grand Hotel none the worse for their experience.

The fishermen later said that on hearing the cries through the fog thought it was from another fishing boat. Imagine their astonishment on finding the Balloon. But for their efforts the aeronauts would surely have perished. The nets they had cut loose were recovered by the fishing boat 'Stella' owned by John S Gowland and contained a thousand herring. They were compensated by the aeronaut gentlemen. (1923 fisherman Phillip 'Mug' Huggett said a sum of £30 was paid to the rescuers)

The above rescue regarding a manned Balloon was not the first to happen at sea off Eastbourne. The following incident happened October 1821.

'The sailing packet 'Thomas' was instrumental in saving the life of Mr Charles Green, the celebrated aeronaut, on the occasion of his ascent from the Gas Works, at Black Rock, Brighthelmston, with his Coronation balloon. The packet 'Thomas' had left some of her passengers and her Captain, Captain Clear, at Eastbourne, and was just off Beachy Head, in the charge of the Mate, Francis Cheeseman, who bore down upon the balloon, then unmanageable upon the water, and driving the vessel's bowsprit into the silk of the ariel machine soon liberated the gas and rescued Mr Green from his frail wicker-work basket car'.

(History of Brighthelmston. Erredge)

Fog, more dreaded than stormy weather in November 1912 continued as with the Balloon incident and Sayers Britannia II motor fishing boat towed the lifeboat to the assistance of a Spanish steamer 'Uribitrate' aground at Beachy Head.

With Cox'n Tim Erridge aboard his fishing boat 'Willing Boy' fishing for herring. 2nd Cox'n 'Laddie' Simpson was close by the lifeboat house when his son, a 12-year-old schoolboy, passed news of the incident to him. At the request of Simpson the maroon apparatus signal was fired (The Coxswain's bell had ceased to be used) and the crew assembled in haste and the lifeboat 'James Stevens No.6'under the command of 'Laddie' Simpson launched at 8.30pm.

The crew was made up of Joe Prodger, Sam Hurd, George Prodger, Alfred Erridge, Alf Hurd, George Allchorn, W Huggett, J Boniface, W Boniface, G Erridge Snr. George Erridge, Charles Ernest Hide, Fred Reed and William Allchorn. (A note in the local paper stated *'These names show that the 'old Bourne breed' is far from extinction'*). To assist the lifeboat and crew who were pulling away on the oars, Sayers boat 'Britannia II' owned by brothers Harry and Edward 'Ted' Sayers with a crew of Harry Sayers, George Hookham, John Godden and Percy Jessop took her in tow. On reaching the grounded steamer it was found the crew had been taken off by the Tug 'Alert'. Half an hour later the Newhaven lifeboat arrived on the scene, but it was the 'James Stevens No.6' that stood by until 4.00am. With the tide high and her crew back aboard, the steamer was pulled off with no damage and proceeded on her way. Another long standby service carried out by the Eastbourne lifeboat crew, what with Sayers 'Britannia II', a collective Eastbourne effort.

January 1913.

A prime example of the fishing community spirit came to the fore when Mike Hardy with a crew of two were spratting in his boat 'Doran' off Eastbourne when a gale sprang up and on coming ashore the boat was so damaged as to render it un-repairable.

Owing to the poor fishing season Hardy had no funds to make good his loss. (Fishermen could not get insurance for their boats) Immediately, a subscription was raised by his fellow fishermen and within two weeks enough money was raised for Hardy to afford a new boat to be built. Hardy's sincere thanks were published in the local paper.

October 1913.

Another charitable action by Eastbourne's fishermen and boatmen occurred when in October, as a result of the tragic mining disaster in Wales, Sayers Brothers organised a fishing excursion using their motorboats 'Britannia I' and 'Britannia II' and three punts 'Dreadnought', 'Uncle Alec' and 'Sunbeam'. Good fishing was had off Langney Point. The sum of £6 was raised and forwarded to the sufferers of the appalling mining disaster in Wales.

1913. Watch Committee minutes.

January. John Joseph Prodger's application for Net shop No.19 was granted.

August. William Allchorn's application to build a small lean to onto his Net shop was granted. It was reported that a non-resident Fish salesman was selling fish at the Fish market

A notice was to be put up at the Market banning the practice.

The Great War.

1914 and the laying of the foundation stone for the R.N.V.R. No.3 Company Sussex Division building was performed by the Mayoress Mrs Bolton. The building was to be 101 feet long and 41 feet wide and when completed would be ideal for the training of men. The building was completed by local builder Mark Hookham of Springfield Road. Fatefully, the local men of the R.N.V.R. a lot of them from fishermen/boatmen families were soon to go to war and many to lose their lives. The foundation stone is still visible on the remaining part of the wall retained when the building was demolished c.2000 to make way for a car park adjacent to the Fishermen's Club and opposite to Sovereign Court, Royal Parade.

1914. Watch Committee minutes.

June The newly formed Eastbourne Fishermen's and Boatmen's Protection Society requested to remove capstan No.9 by the Martello Tower at Langney Point to a position at Wallsend (Pevensey Bay). It would better service the boats coming ashore there and for permission to remove the hawser from its position at the Sluice to a point near capstan No.10 Martello Tower.

July 1914.

The 1st Battle Squadron of the Channel Fleet showed the flag at Eastbourne. The fleet comprised of battleships Marlborough, Colossus, Hercules, Neptune, St.

Vincent, Collingwood, Vanguard, Superb and light cruiser Bellona. What a sight they made. On their arrival it was reported that the children of All Saints Convalescent Home assembled on the veranda and gave three cheers. What a bonus for the boatmen, kept busy with trips to view the Fleet.

August 1914.

From 11 pm, on Tuesday 4th August 1914 a state of war existed between Great Britain and Germany and many Eastbourne fishermen, boatmen and members of the local Royal Naval Volunteer Reserve enlisted to serve their country.

Fishermen continued to fish under permit from the Admiralty. Pleasure boating also continued. What with the able bodied men going away it was left to the older generation to carry on. Reports showed thousands of visitors regularly coming to Eastbourne during those years. During hostilities fishing remained a hazardous occupation.

1915. Watch Committee minute.

January. Andrew Chester's application to place a windlass on plot No.6 at the Fishing Station was granted.

May 1915.

A great number of Sussex and Eastbourne men serving with the 2nd (Iron Regiment) and 1/5th (Cinque Ports) Battalions of the Royal Sussex Regiment were killed and wounded on Sunday 9th May at the Battle of Aubers Ridge, Richbourg, France.

Attacking 'over the top' at 5.40am *singing 'Sussex by the Sea' with the 2nd Battalion leading the Sussex men were decimated. In about an hour sustaining losses of, 2nd Battalion, 14 officers and 437 men dead, and hundreds wounded. The 1/5th Battalion, in close support of their pals in the 2nd Battalion, lost 11 officers and 191 men. Losses for the Royal Sussex that day were 25 officers and 628 men killed and hundreds wounded. One could say that 'the bloom of Sussex manhood died that day'. The small Sussex village of Wadhurst alone lost 21 of its men fighting with the 1/5th (Cinque Ports) Battalion. 'Heroes All'

*related by survivors of the attack.

The 2nd Battalion had been given the title of 'Iron Regiment' for their valour and steadfastness (we wont be druv) in battle by the German forces that had faced them since 1914.

The official total loss of British forces attacking in the Battle of Aubers Ridge was 458 officers and 11,161 men killed in one day. One of the highest losses sustained in a day of World War I. The whole assault had failed with no gain of territory. Such a great loss was kept from the British public at the time and never really brought to the fore as we had the losses at Gallipoli to bear.

That fateful day in May has the distinction of being perpetuated with the Battle honour 'Aubers' to the Royal Sussex Regiment and a service of commemoration was held on a regular basis until the final service at the Great Redoubt 1985. The Battle honours are laid up in St George's Chapel, Chichester Cathedral. *Forget not the men of 2nd and 1/5th Battalions*

Then, to repeat the slaughter, Sussex and Eastbourne men of the Southdown 'Lowthers Lambs' 11th, 12th, and 13th Battalions of the Royal Sussex Regiment on 30th June 1916, attacked over virtually the same ground at the Battle of Boars Head, Richbourg, with casualties of 17 officers and 349 men killed and hundreds wounded. Whilst not sustaining the losses of their comrades on 9th May 1915 it was nevertheless 'Another day that Sussex died'. It was the day that local man CSM Nelson Carter won the Victoria Cross for bravery under fire and later that day was killed in action.

July 1915.

Fisherman and boatman Dennis Breach of 71, Latimer Road, aged 76 years, died July 1915, leaving a widow. He was an uncle to Councillor Charles Breach of Matlock Road, Meads, and a life long pal of John Hide.

October 1915.

A postcard sent from Eastbourne to London 8th October. Message read *'Arrived safely, under neutral flag, No males thrown overboard. Eastbourne is full of wounded soldiers 3,000 here they say'*.

December 1915.

December 15th the Eastbourne Gazette published the following list of members of the Fishermen' and Boatmen's Protection Society serving in the Royal Navy:

William Allchorn Jnr	C J Burton	Luke Hardy	J Mockett
Jack Allchorn	Geo Erridge	Jas Hardy	H Novis
George Allchorn	G French	E Hardy	E Penney
H Boniface	J Godden	Sam Hurd	C Reed
W Boniface	W Godden	Fred Hurd	E Sayers
J Boniface	Luke Hide	A Matthews	W Simpson
C J Burton	Edward Hide	F Marchant	C Standing

The officers of the Society were: -
Chairman, Mr John S Gowland (Boat builder, Winchelsea Road).
Hon. Treasurer, Mr Henry Boniface.
Hon. Secretary, Mr J Godden.

1916. Watch Committee minutes.

The year of 1916 started with controversy. In January the committee meeting reported that boat builder and Councillor George Gausden applied for the tenancy of the late Dennis Breach's Net shop. Gausden said he was preparing plans for a new motor fishing boat. Objections to the application came from the Eastbourne Fishermen's and Boatmen's Protection Society representatives Ted and Henry Sayers who requested the tenancy not be given to him as he was not a fisherman and already had 3 Net shops. The committee did not grant the tenancy and made a stipulation that when a new tenant took over that Net shop he should pay Gausden £15 as he had already paid the widow of Breach the money to take over the Net shop. A champion of the fishermen, Gausden got no favours from them.

At this meeting it transpired that for some years persons other than fishermen and boatmen had been purchasing Net shops, this was against the regulations laid down when Mr Gilbert and the Duke of Devonshire gave the Fishing Station land.

Councillor Morgan told the meeting, *'For some time past when these Net shops have been for sale and they have been brought by other than fishermen. In fact gentlemen have them. This is preventing fishermen from buying them. I had the coxswain of the lifeboat come to see me. He has a capstan stand in front of a Net shop and when this Net shop was put up for sale it was put up to a figure that represented all the money he had. A gentleman standing by bought the shop over his head. The consequence is Coxswain Erridge has to carry all his gear* and fishing nets some 200 yards to the shop he did acquire. These gentlemen and others must be stopped from getting these shops'.*

BOARD OF AGRICULTURE AND FISHERIES.

PERMIT TO FISH.

The Board of Agriculture and Fisheries, by virtue of the Admiralty Orders for British Fishing Vessels and of every other power enabling them in this behalf, do hereby permit the Sea Fishing Boat *"Bill Bailey" N.N. 53,* *16.9 feet overall, owned by Edward Hide, 25, Longstone Road, Eastbourne* to fish during daylight hours only in the waters enclosed within a line drawn from Beachy Head to the Royal Sovereign Light Vessel, thence to Dungeness, thence to the North Folkestone Gate Light Vessel, and from thence to Folkestone Pier, subject to the Regulations printed on the back hereof.

This permit may be suspended or cancelled at any time by the Board of Agriculture and Fisheries, or by the Admiral Commanding at Dover, and shall not be deemed to authorise fishing in the area specified in contravention of any byelaw made by any Local Fisheries Committee or of any Orders made by the Naval Authorities in addition to those printed on this permit.

Any person fishing in contravention of the Admiralty Orders is liable on conviction to heavy penalties under the Defence of the Realm (Consolidation) Regulations, 1914.

SEALED by the Board of Agriculture and Fisheries this *26th* day of *July*, 1915.

Assistant Secretary.

Countersigned

Admiral Commanding, Dover.

P16   For Regulations see Over.]

(2928—2958) Wt.   —38 500 7/15 R.C.&S. 128

Fishing permit, July 1915.

This problem over the Net shops was brought about by the fishermen themselves. Being the original builders and occupier/owners the custom was to auction them off to the highest bidder (good money to be had). The Council unwittingly then granted the tenancy if there were no objections. With the formation of the Protection Society in 1914 it was realised this practice had to stop and on this occasion with the Gausden application things came to a head and indeed the Council did tighten up the tenancies. But it was down to the fishermen and Society to watch the situation. As a result of the above the Parade Inspector was ordered to draw up a current list of Net shop and capstan owners at the Fishing Station.

March 1916.

Eastbourne lifeboat and pleasure boats went to the rescue of the Senior Service when a flotilla of four naval motor patrol launches were in danger of going aground on the rocks at Holywell at 12.30pm March 1916 during very foggy weather. With no wind to assist in sailing the lifeboat she was towed to the scene by motor pleasure boats 'Royal Sovereign' owned by Jesse Huggett and 'Star of the East' owned by

Henry Matthews. All four naval launches were in very dangerous positions 'hove to' inside the Holywell ridge of rocks and the cliffs. Cox'n Tim Erridge made contact with captain of the flotilla and went on board the flagship and assisted the launches to clear the rocks and get to open sea and were last seen heading eastwards. A fine service by the lifeboat and pleasure boats during wartime.

Veteran fisherman and boatman Phillip Swain (a pal of Reuben 'Old Screw' Wood) died March 1916 at the home of his eldest daughter, 30 Avondale Road. Phillip was 94 years of age, popular, and well known amongst the fishing community. A tale he told, when 10 years old he along with his parents walked from Hastings to Eastbourne, there being no railway service at that time. Phillip a widower left a son and four daughters.

July 1916.

About 10.30pm the maroons went off at the lifeboat house, which brought an immediate response from her crew and helpers who lived down at the east end of town. The 'James Stevens No.6' Tim Erridge in command was launched with some difficulty and two fishing motor boats 'Royal Sovereign' owner Jesse Huggett and 'Star of Peace' owner Henry Boniface stood by ready to tow the lifeboat when she was clear of the shore. The call was to a collision between two vessels south of Beachy Head. As the lifeboat was off Beachy Head two recall rockets were sent up from the lifeboat house. The incident was not serious and both vessels involved were proceeding to the west. The shore helpers dug away at the shingle and stout wooden trows were placed ready for the beaching of the lifeboat. Ashore she came and a smooth return to the lifeboat house was made.

August 1916. Tower Street's 'Roll of Honour'

Affixed to a wall in Tower Street, Seaside was a named roll of 37 men, from nearly every house in the street representing men who were serving or who had died in the service of the Country, no doubt some of them fishermen. The roll was neatly framed and flanked by scriptural pictures with a prayer attached for the safety of the men. On each side was a vase of fresh cut flowers, the vases being regularly replenished by friends and family of the lost and serving men.

December 1916.

War service exemption tribunals were regularly held at the Town Hall for men who wanted exemption from war service in His Majesty's Armed Forces. One particular case was of Frederick Gell 28 years, fisherman, who had applied for exemption in December 1916. Adjourned for a week, Gell was told that under a new order the only fishermen exempted were those who had been rejected for the Royal Navy.

1917. Watch Committee minute.

July. Fishing Station. Net shop and capstan rents due from Ben Hide to be deferred until September.

July 1917.

Eastbourne National Service Sea Fishing Society was established at the Fishing Station by a group of well-intentioned local people, with a Mr Riddles as Hon. secretary, other members being Mr Frederick Cooke and Mr J. Saunders amongst them, with fisherman Sayers as attendant. The premises of the Society were adjacent to the Bowling Green at the Redoubt area. Three boats had been purchased along with fishing gear and bait ready for use.

The members must do the rowing themselves and it was hoped to purchase a motorboat in the near future. There was an absence of mackerel and a lateness of the fishing season in general. The Society stated the bulk of local fishermen were away at sea serving their country, hence this Society and it would provide fish for the local community.

December 1917.

A Fishing Station Fatality - William Frank Langley, a temporary postman of 62b, Sidley Road was killed and two others injured at 2.00am in the morning of Saturday 4th December when a wooden spoke of a capstan, which they were operating to haul a fishing boat up the beach broke. Fisherman Arthur Grooms of 17 Rye Street a witness explained that when the spoke broke the one in front swung backwards with great force striking the deceased on the head. Thomas Boniface of 42, Sidley Road father of the owner of the capstan, Henry Boniface, said the spoke in question was being used as a substitute. Had the men waited a different spoke would have been used. Langley died some two hours after the accident. At the inquest the jury brought in a verdict of 'Accidental death'

(Members of the public used to and still do 'give a hand' to haul and assist fishing boats ashore, shake out the nets and receive some of the catch). At the inquest it was stated of the difficulty and danger of boats coming ashore in darkness as the Fishermen's light could not be lit due to the War situation.

Leonard Beckett Hide, fisherman, lifeboat man and son of 'Bones' Hide lost his life in a similar accident to the above. It was May 1921, at Hastings beach when a capstan he was operating with others, broke and the forward spoke struck him on the head killing him instantly. Hundreds attended the funeral at Ocklynge cemetery. Eastbourne and Hastings lifeboat crews were there. Mark Hookham and Mr Cowper Smith represented the RNLI and Mr J R Siezmur Chairman of the Fishermen's Society attended. Messrs Tim Erridge (Coxswain) Charles Ernest Hide, George Erridge, and Sam Hurd represented the 1919 resigned lifeboat crew.

The 'twitten' showing cottage No. 37 home of Navarino Hide, and 'Ye Olde Bakery'. Molly Downing's 'Sweet shop' occupied the extreme right of picture.

Site of Molly Downing's 'Sweet Shop'. (See pages 257-258).

Chapter Ten

The Lifeboat Crew Resign, Ghostly Tales and a Home on the Beach

1918.

November 11th 1918 saw the end of hostilities and surviving members of Eastbourne's fishing and boating fraternity returned from military service. The war being over, the seafront became a peacetime environment again although it had remained busy during the war years. Fishing returned somewhat back to its pre war level with the return of the men. Sadly there were some well-known characters among the fishing fraternity never to be seen again. The war had taken its toll. Pre-war members of the lifeboat took up their duties again, sadly though William Boniface had lost his life in the service of his country.

February 1919.

A practice launch of 'James Stevens No.6' with several members of the regular crew that had been on minesweeping and other war patrol duties took up their accustomed places in the boat. Those that had just returned included 2nd Cox'n William Simpson (war service for 4 years), Bowman Jack Mockett, George Erridge, Charles Ernest Hide, George Prodger, Sam Hurd and Fred Huggett. Four others yet to be demobilised were William Huggett, Andrew Chester, Phillip Huggett and Michael Hardy.

Much praise is due to those gallant older fishermen that manned the lifeboat through the war years. Extremely dangerous at times. The lifeboat Hon. Secretary Mr Infield related occasions of their endurance. '*In all weathers by day and during the dark inky blackness of night they were called out time and again to risk their lives for others not knowing if they would see land again, the enemy submarine at times still in the vicinity of a torpedoed vessel.*

One night particularly our boat the 'James Stevens No.6' with her crew was beating about in terrible weather waiting for daybreak in order to ascertain their whereabouts. Her crew were literally coated in ice, and surrounded with wreckage, narrowly escaping coming in contact with a floating mine, and all the gruesome sights of casualties that accompany the sinking by torpedo or mine, of a vessel off Beachy Head'.

April 1919.

Bearing in mind what the Hon. secretary had said above, it does appear that things were not good over his and the committee's relationship with Coxswain Tim Erridge, and indeed the whole crew. In March 1919 Erridge tendered his resignation to take effect from 24th June. The local Gazette carried on April 2nd an advertisement for the position.

The problem arose through a call by the Coastguard for the Eastbourne lifeboat to be launched. The following is the report from the Gazette April 16th 1919.

Lifeboat men Resign En-Masse.

'The resignation of the first and second Coxswains and the members of the crew of the lifeboat have been handed in. The two Coxswains apparently have a grievance. On Sunday March 9th a call was made for the lifeboat to proceed to Birling Gap. Through an error on the part of a coastguard officer at Newhaven it was found that the boat was not required. The Eastbourne committee paid the members of the crew monies they were due, but refused payment to both Coxswains. The crew who considered this action grossly unfair, showed their indignation by resigning en-masse.

Application was made through the local secretary Mr Infield to the committee for the money and after much hesitation and consideration the committee decided to grant the application. The two Coxswains Tim Erridge and William Simpson in the meantime decided that on account of the 'unreasonable attitude' adopted by the committee, they refused to accept the money. It is understood, however, that should the offer of the committee be repeated, the Coxswains will be prepared to resume duty. At present there seems little prospect of a prompt settlement, and the affair has assumed a peculiar aspect by reason of the fact that the committee have advertised for a new Coxswain.

Since the inauguration of the lifeboat service in Eastbourne there has been peace and harmony (hardly, remember the 1883 famous rescue?) The only trouble has been with regard to allowances.

Ten years back when men in other parts of the country were receiving 25s, per annum for carriage practice money, the Eastbourne men received only 20s. This grievance was later corrected. The men are presently working on the following scale:

Winter practice, 7s 6d, summer practice, 5s, active service winter sunrise to sunset -15s per day, active service winter sunset to sunrise - 30s per day, active service summer sunrise to sunset 10s per day, active service summer sunset to sunrise - 20s.

The long service records of the present crew and Coxswains are, Alfred 'Tuppy' Sayers and William Erridge head the list each having 40 years service. Tim Erridge, 25 years (8 years as 1st Coxswain) T Huggett, 24 years. Jack Mockett, 24 years. Fred Huggett, 22 years, William 'Laddie' Simpson, 20 years (16 years as 2nd Coxswain) W Huggett, Alfred Hurd, Jack ' Foot' Prodger, Andrew Chester, 20 years each. George 'Quack' Erridge, 19 years. Charles Ernest 'Chalky' Hide, 18 years. Sam Hurd, 10 years. Mike Hardy, 5 years and George Prodger, 3 years'.

These were early days after the war and it may be that there was friction between the wartime crew and the returning crew? Contrary to what has been said about harmony, there had been over the past years and up to the present years professional keenness among the lifeboat men as all were skilful seamen well versed in the ways of the sea, and having their own opinions on who was a good Coxswain they could trust and put their faith in at sea. Indeed over the years it has been the case when the committee have selected a new Coxswain for the lifeboat, some members of the serving crews resigned.

1919. Watch Committee minutes.

April. George Erridge was granted tenancy of Net shop No.22a. Henry Fox accepted £100 for the purchase of his Net shop. Edward Hide's application for capstans Nos.11 &12. Net shop 33 and capstan 27 was granted.

Auction at the Fishing Station. Net shop No.22 to George Erridge for £20, No.18 to Fred Reed for £60, No.17 to E Penfold for £30.

George Huggett's application for plot No.27 now let to Mrs Elizabeth Hide was considered and resolved that Mrs Hide be given notice to quit and No.27 be let to George Erridge. The application by George Erridge for No.22 to be withdrawn. (Mrs Hide's son Thomas, who worked the business with her pleasure boats and bathing machines, had been killed in action in 1915 at Gallipoli, leaving her with no support).

May 1919.

Henry Boniface took over as 1st Coxswain and Mike Hardy 2nd Coxswain of the Eastbourne lifeboat. So a new era began with new crewmembers also being appointed.

Boatman Harry Tyrell of St Aubyn's Road was on hand at the Wish Tower to give assistance to 3 survivors from the Greek ship 'Epiros' as they came ashore in the ships boat.

The 'Epiros' having sunk in collision with the patrol trawler H M S Frost Axe. Strengthened by brandy administered by Harry Tyrell the survivors were given breakfast at the Grand Hotel. Sadly 9 sailors lost their lives in the incident.

1920.

During 1920 the Eastbourne & Fishermen's & Boatmen's Protection Society put in a request to the Council for a Quoits pitch for their use. Major McLean of 9, Royal Parade spoke up for the fishermen, proposing two sites for them by the Fishing Station. A site was found for them at Fishermen's Green. Quoits was very popular at this period of time. Leagues were formed and competition keen.

1920. Watch Committee minutes.

April. George Gausden requested to sell one of his Net shops to William Allchorn. Albert French had also applied to purchase it. It was resolved that the Net shop and capstan in front be let to William Allchorn. It was also resolved that William Erridge be allowed to purchase Net shop No.22 (not wanted by George Erridge) by instalments of £5 down and £1 per month balance.

September. Tom Sisk applied to build a shed for Boat building on land leased from the Gilbert Estate, east of the Sea Scouts Shed.

August 1920.

Fisherman Robert Bennett's wife Edith died at her home 17 Desmond Road August 1920. There were 15 children of the marriage of which 7 had survived.

September 1920.

The 26th September saw the lifeboat 'James Stevens No.6' launched to the rescue of the wrecked motor yacht 'Dyak' aground on rocks at Beachy Head;

'It was 5.00pm when the maroons went up and the crew launched under new Coxswain Harry Boniface. Being low tide difficulty was suffered in the launch and there being little wind the sail was useless and the crew had to row to the Head, being cheered by the crowds watching from the seafront. A Doctor Williams and his wife, both exhausted by their ordeal were taken aboard the lifeboat and return ashore at 7.45 pm to the Lifeboat House in front of a big crowd. The rescued couple were taken into the care of the Shipwrecked Mariners Society agent Mr Arthur Davies and lodged at the York Hotel. Before leaving the lifeboat, however, Dr Williams had called for three cheers for the gallant crew who had saved them from a perilous position and the cheers were given lustily from hundreds of throats. The motor yacht 'Dyak' was salvaged by Charles Clarke's motor fishing boat 'Mallard' skippered by Fred Huggett towing the yacht to the Fishing Station where she was beached'.

October 1920.

The 16ft fishing boat 'Sarah Ann Liza' on 6th October sank off Beachy Head, when manned by owner V. Graham and crew W Terry. They had the main sail up and were lying off between the two lighthouses when a sudden squall carried both sail and mast away and split the boats hull and she sank immediately. Terry being a poor swimmer was helped ashore by Graham. No mean feat considering the distance. The Mayor, Mr Duke headed a subscription to replace the boat at a cost of £50.

November 1920.

Foul weather brought about the launching of the 'James Stevens No.6' again on Monday,

15th November. On Sunday 14th a converted barge the 'Creterampart' 200 tons of London, made heavy weather down channel and eventually anchored off Holywell. The Eastbourne lifeboat crew stood by at the lifeboat house all night, then at 7.00am the barge grounded on Holywell Ledge and signalled for assistance. In the first instance the Coastguard Life Saving Apparatus Volunteers attended and the lifeline rocket apparatus was got out and two unsuccessful efforts were made to get a line aboard. The first hit the rocks and the second fell short of the barge by about 40 yards with 600 yards of line out. The lifeboat was then launched into heavy seas. To get to the stricken barge meant pulling into a severe gale, a formidable task what with having been awake all night. Making little headway the 'James Stevens No.6' still battled on but the Coastguard seeing their plight telephoned Newhaven and their lifeboat launched. Being a motor lifeboat and going with a following wind she made the grounded barge quite quickly. At this time the Eastbourne lifeboat had been battling for 4 hours and was still well off the scene. A Tug was requested to attend the barge while Newhaven lifeboat towed Eastbourne lifeboat to the grounded barge where she then 'stood by'. Newhaven lifeboat then returned home and the Tug 'Alert' towed the barge into Newhaven Harbour. The 'James Stevens No.6' and her crew got back to the lifeboat house about 7.00pm some 12 hours at sea in their gallant endeavours. The experiences that day proved that a motor lifeboat was a necessity for the Eastbourne Station.

Comradeship

Fisherman George 'Quack' Erridge of 13, Tower Street had an accident at the

Fishing Station whilst working on the roof of a Net shop. He slipped and broke his wrist doing a kindness for the owner, an old infirm fisherman friend.

December 1920.

The local Gazette reported the death of old fisherman George Paul.

He was born February 1837 and educated at St Mary's School Old Town, to which he had to walk to through, mainly, cornfields to attend from his home in Mann's Row, (now St.Aubyns Road) by the original Fishing Station. He did in fact become a teacher at St. Mary's for some years but later he took up the family calling of fisherman, being away on Luggers for up to 3 months and often related tales of the expeditions. He was a brother of fisherman and boatman Paul Paul.

May 1921.

A collision involving a large liner 'Benella' occurred close by the Royal Sovereign lightship at 1.00am during conditions of thick fog. 'The Eastbourne lifeboat crew were summoned to launch by firing two maroons and the 'James Stevens No.6' was launched at the Fishing Station within about 10 minutes. Among those that helped push her out were two young ladies named Mockett of Beach Road. They went up to their knees in the water.

Under Cox'n Henry Boniface the lifeboat searched for many hours, *'At times you couldn't see the other end of the boat the fog was a thick as soup,'* said Boniface. The lifeboat crew used up the emergency rations and of course the rum issue. Meanwhile the 'Benella' had been beached in Pevensey Bay and 1,300 passengers taken off. When the fog cleared Boniface made contact with the beached ship but there was no need for assistance so the lifeboat returned to Station. The 'Benella' was later floated off the beach and taken for repairs'.

1921. Watch Committee minutes.

January. Alfred W Erridge made application for plot No.23 at the Fishing Station, to erect a Net shop, also for capstan No.20. This was agreed and the Net shop still stands today alongside the popular Fish sales Net shop. A revolutionary Net shop of timber and concrete built by Alfred and his son Fred 'Mucky' Erridge.

April. An application received from George Gausden to sell Net shop No.10 to Henry Erridge was granted. It was also agreed that the Corporation would purchase it for £30 on behalf of Erridge and he would repay the sum in instalments of £10 with interest.

It was also reported that George Huggett had agreed to purchase Gausden's Net shop No.31. This was approved and the tenancy of this plot be transferred to Huggett on completion of the purchase.

June. The Fish Market. It was proposed to make a toll payable on fish and shellfish brought into Eastbourne other than by sea. This was an attempt to stop the wholesale import by rail, which could undercut the local fisherman who had a problem getting a living price for his catch. Tolls would have to be paid to the authorised agent at the Market who was Henry Boniface. A full list of tolls was drawn up and presented to the Watch Committee.

The toll issue was discussed over the following months till eventually in December that year a decision was taken not to impose tolls. The reason is not disclosed in the minutes.

December 1921.

The foundering of a small coasting steamer 'Flevo IV' some 9 miles off Beachy Head at 2.00am. The crew of 7 took to the ship's lifeboat and were later picked up by an Eastbourne motor fishing boat crewed by Arthur and Henry Matthews and Fred Reed and landed at Eastbourne about 11.00am. The sailors were taken to the Angles Hotel and their wants attended to by the Shipwrecked Mariners' Society.

The Black Ghost.

Strange scenes near the Fishing Huts. It was in December 1921, Jack ' Foot' Prodger told the hair-raising story of the 'Black ghost'.

'It happened in early December the time about quarter to six in half light of a December morning and the scene was the waste ground which skirts the right hand side of the Royal Parade in the neighbourhood of the Huts (Net shops).

Prodger said, 'He had, had no beer, no beer at all'. He was making his way down to the beach ready to take out his boat for a fishing trip. His son, Jack Jnr. who did not see the apparition, walked a short distance behind him, and both were weighed down with heavy hook lines they were carrying. Jack 'Foot' Prodger was thinking of nothing, just being in his usual placid state of mind, and suddenly it came out of the ground. Upon the murkiness of the early morning, a black figure was silhouetted and it walked steadily in front of the bewildered Prodger keeping always the same distance. It fairly turned his inside over. As to being a man or woman he did not know but it was bigger than him and wore a sort of big black overcoat right down to the ground. The figure appeared to have no feet it just glided along and it wore a big round hat. Three times Prodger stopped and the ghost stopped too. Prodger rubbed his eyes but the thing remained with him from when he had emerged from one of the roads near the Fishermen's Institute until he had crossed the waste ground that separates the Royal Parade from the Huts. Then said Prodger, 'It went down into the ground the same as it came up'. The place where it disappeared was close to the Huts. Prodger refrained from alarming his son 'For fear' that he would frighten him. Jack 'Foot' Prodger was aggrieved, regarding the haunting as a personal insult. He feels the ghost had no right to worry him this way. He would have gone for the thing if he hadn't been weighed down by the hook lines'.

Jack 'Foot' Prodger had no doubt his ghost was the ghost of a man who had committed suicide by hanging in a house in Beach Road, about two or three years ago. It is natural that he should come back especially about Christmas time.

The White Ghost.

This tale is different but in the same locality and in this case the ghost, was a luminous white and not so alarmingly close. It was seen by Mrs Goldsmith, caretaker at the Fishermen's Institute and she never confessed about it until Prodger's tale was told her.

'It was she said on a Sunday night whilst walking along the Royal Parade with the Net huts upon her left and the wide stretch of waste ground between them and her. Mrs Goldsmith was walking with her sister, when she looked across towards the

Huts when this thing appeared; it was like a white cloud. She had hardly time to feel frightened when 'pouf' it was gone, vanished into the Huts. The whole experience was but of a second's duration. Her sister saw nothing not having looked that way. The moon was shining brilliantly but the apparition had nothing to do with the moon in so far as that obliging luminary showed it up. Theories, were various, one fisherman said it was the ghost of Lord Kitchener. The White ghost was that of Irene Munro (murdered down at the Crumbles) because she walks on the Crumbles every night'.

The Ghost of Molly Downing.

The above tales bring to mind a previous apparition appearance concerning James 'Navarino' Hide and Mary Downing.

'Molly' as she was known married Joseph Downing, not much information on him but he was known to have been a publican in Eastbourne. The marriage was childless and when Joseph died in 1850 'Molly' went to live in the twitten in a little building at the sea end adjacent to 'Navarino' at 37 Marine Parade. She opened a sweetshop there and ran it until her death in 1863. She had become well known for a Court action in 1862 over a loan of £140 to James Hide Jnr. the son of 'Navarino' to purchase Bathing machines and his attempt to defraud her. She won the day.

It was in January 1864 that 'Molly' featured in a lecture by Robert Cooper a local brewer and spiritualist. The lecture took place at Diplock's Assembly Rooms, Pevensey Road, before a big audience.

'In confirmation of the appearance of spirits (ghosts) he gave the case of a well known character in Eastbourne, Molly Downing, an aged woman, who lived almost miserly, and who died a month or two since, at her residence in Sea-side. It was not his intention to bring the spirit of Molly to the platform that evening. (Laughter)' Mr Cooper went on to say, *' Molly kept a small shop, her stock in trade being consisting mainly of bull's eyes and other sweets. Being miserly she saved a great deal of money. After her death the property was occupied by a Mr Cook, who about 1 o'clock in the morning saw her apparition standing by his bedside. At about ½ past five the same morning Mr James 'Navarino' Hide and his two sons, all fishermen saw the same apparition some 15 yards from them on the beach. On being questioned Hide said he saw Molly as distinctly as ever he saw her in life. He halloed her and on approaching a kind of fire, or halo of light came around the figure and it then vanished. Cook although he had never seen Molly described the apparition so minutely to Mr Hide that both were satisfied it was Molly. (Derisive laughter and remarks came from the audience)*

Mr Cooper continued saying, ' At a recent spiritual séance Mary Downing's spirit came, and on being questioned as to what troubled her mind, she replied in the usual way, ' brandy'. (More derisive laughter)'

So there we are. Ghosts or not? As early as 1864 some did believe.

An interesting report appeared in the September 1st 1869 issue of the Eastbourne Gazette. The tale is about a rather evil spiteful unnamed woman;

Entitled *'A Stabbing'- 'The 'old blind man' daily seen on the esplanade with his shell work for sale, was stabbed on the side of the head by his wife, on Monday*

evening last after a quarrel. The old fellow bled profusely and is in a precarious condition. Our reporter attended the Police Court yesterday (Tuesday) morning when she was brought up. It is stated that the woman caused her husbands blindness some years ago by throwing vitriol in his eyes, and that she underwent penal servitude for the offence. About 12 months ago she was in custody on a charge of threatening his life, and was bound over to keep the peace, but failing to find sureties, underwent imprisonment. Formerly the couple occupied a little house or hovel near Sea Beach House, in which the famous Molly Downing died and her spirit (?) afterwards visited, but the couple afterwards removed to one of the little streets near the Rose and Crown, leading out of Langney road eastwards, and in this last named dwelling the serious offence of stabbing was perpetrated'.

So there we have it. A ghost sadly learnt of from a rather gruesome case. Perhaps 'Molly' visited that evil woman? It would have been a good thing if she had 'visited' James Hide Jnr. he was a very nasty wife beater and thief, imprisoned and finally dying in the Workhouse.

Ghost stories have abounded over the years around the Marine Parade area, especially in the properties in the twitten where the old bakery house was, particularly the cafe/restaurant 'Ye Olde Bakery'. Evidently in 1985 the Vicar of Christ Church visited the old bakery and blessed it in the hope that whatever was there would go away. The local papers in 1988-89 and 1994 covered the happenings. Some said it was a young man seen, others a figure of a woman standing at the bottom of the bed (this from a resident of the old bakery a Mr Nicholls) and stories of movement, lights going off and on and machinery being switched off. 'Ye Olde Bakery' was at the opposite end of the twitten to where Molly Downing lived. Her sweetshop cottage had been demolished around the 1980's. Perhaps it was then that she moved to 'Ye Olde Bakery'?

1922. Watch Committee minutes.

March. Charlie Clark offered his two Net shops to the Corporation. Estimated value £130 and £30. The Committee declined to buy them.

April. Re. Sale of Charlie Clark's Net shops. Full Council said 'No'. Asking price too much, only worth £75.

May. George Prodger to purchase No.31 Net shop from George Huggett by instalments. Committee had no objections. Prodger to arrange method of payment with Huggett.

It was decided by the Committee to hold a general discussion with the fishermen about Net shops and capstans. No further information forthcoming.

August. Application by Charles Prodger to rent capstan No.18 held by Charlie Clark and purchase of Net shop No.16 from him was agreed.

January 1923.

The motor fishing boat 'Lady Dora' with crew Jim and Joe Boniface and Bert Pelling aboard was overdue by 6 hours on 17th January. Great anxiety was felt by their fellow fishermen and the lifeboat under Cox'n Henry Boniface, brother of the two Bonifaces was launched at 8.00pm and returned to cheers at 9.30pm with the fishing boat in tow. It transpired her engine had broken down and she was making her slow way back under a small sail. The lifeboat had got in touch with the 'Lady Dora' by flare, some 5 miles out. The motor lifeboat 'Priscilla Macbean' was crewed with Mike Hardy 2nd Cox'n, Frank Whitmore, engineer, Jim Hardy, George Boniface, Fred Allchorn, Harry Hendy, Fred Reed, Ernest Sayers and Charlie Prodger. So Eastbourne's first motor lifeboat had performed her first service, no more pulling the oars.

1923. Watch Committee minutes.

March. Fishing Station. Andrew Chester's request to take over capstan No.7 previously held by the late J Reed was agreed.

April. The Gilbert estate sold the ex-Lifeboat house in Marine Parade to Mr G Stevenson. (Later becoming an electricity sub station. Still there to this day although much altered).

June. Fishing Station. Eastbourne Fishermen's and Boatmen's Protection Society (E.F.B.P.S). made a complaint that the Council bathing station encroached upon their ground and rights. The Council agreed with the Society. The Society then told the Council that they had no further objections but it must be clearly understood that it was on part of the Fishing Station.

August. An application by Fred Hurd for the transfer of Net shop No.34 to him and recently held by the late Benjamin Hide (cousin) was granted.

November. Andrew Chester's request for Net shop No.11 was granted.

December. Fishing Station. It was reported to the Committee that Henry Boniface had illegally let his Net shop to Roland Pragnell for boatbuilding and boat repairs. This became a long running affair with the Council. The Council taking Boniface and Pragnell to Court. (A report of the Court case appears further on in this book).

April 1923.

Answering the signal of two maroons at 12 noon to launch the lifeboat, Coxswain Henry Boniface was at that moment playing the cornet in the band of the Salvation Army at the Citadel, Langney Road. It was Easter Sunday 1st April 1923 and Salvationist Henry immediately jumped on his bicycle and pedalled furiously along Seaside only for the chain to break, quickly borrowing another bicycle he arrived at the boathouse in good time still wearing his Salvation Army uniform. He resorted to borrowing once more and borrowed a coat and hat from a bystander.

A large crowd had gathered and a cheer went up as the 'Priscilla Macbean' motor lifeboat, with a crew made up of George and Jim Boniface, Charlie and William Prodger, Michael and Harry Hardy and Fred Reed was launched into a dead calm sea and soon lost to sight motoring at full speed towards the Royal Sovereign lightship. The report was that two steamers had collided some 3 miles south east of the lightship.

The Hastings and Newhaven lifeboats were also in attendance. The Eastbourne boat spotted some wreckage but all in all it was a fruitless operation for all the lifeboats. A French cargo boat 'Surville' and American vessel SS 'Editor' 8,000 tons had collided but that was all they knew and no trace was found of either. In fact they both made Port under their own steam. Eastbourne and the other lifeboats returned to their stations after some 5 hours of searching.

May 1923. Fishermen's troubles at sea.

The E.F.B.P. Society sent a letter of protest to the Admiralty complaining strongly of the dangerous actions of HMS Kellet a survey ship whilst she was off Eastbourne recently.

The sailing boat 'Scout' owned by Fred 'Tinker' Novis and skippered by Patrick Erridge was nearly run down by the 'Kellett' whilst fishing over a shoal of rocks known as the 'Horse'. The 'Kellett' steamed so close to the 'Scout' she nearly capsized her. The 'Kellett' made a communication to the 'Scout' telling her to get off that position and return to Eastbourne or she could well be run down next time. The 'Scout' did then return to shore under duress.

A meeting was held in the Fishermen's Institute about the incident, Mark Hookham presiding. Secretary Arthur Sayers convened the meeting and Patrick Erridge related the facts of the incident. It was an ongoing problem with the HMS Kellett, she knew where the local fishing grounds were but continued be a source of danger to the fishermen. Extensive damage had previously been done to lobster pots and nets and indeed that present week 8 nets had been torn away. The laying of buoys under water by the 'Kellett' was a grave source of danger to fishing craft. Sayers said that the 'Kellet' had been operating in these waters for the past two summers and her Commander must be aware of the locality of fishing nets and pots. As well as the letter of protest to the Admiralty letters were also sent to M.P. Rupert Gwynne the vice-president of the Society and the Sussex Sea Fisheries. The resolution of protest was moved by Mr E Cruxford, seconded by Henry Boniface and carried unanimously. So was it a bloody-minded Royal Navy man or had the local fishermen obstructed his survey work? Evidently it was resolved amicably and after this no problems were reported

July 1923.

It came to notice in July that year of the strange lifestyle of fisherman and boatman Phillip 'Old Mug' Huggett and his wife Louisa; the national newspapers related the event. Huggett and his wife had for some considerable time been living and sleeping rough on the beach at the Fishing Station. In Fred 'Mucky' Erridge's time they lived by the Fish Market among the fish boxes. Phillip Huggett was aged 76 yrs and his wife a similar age. The story goes he had been born in the Eastbourne Workhouse. His father lived to the age of 94 yrs himself being a fisherman and boatman. Phillip's wife was the daughter of a Paris tailor cutter and her early days were lived in Paris. During this time she was an intimate associate of the daughter of the then French President and is said to have taught her English. She had several brothers and sisters holding positions of responsibility in Paris.

For many years the couple had rented a house in Beach Road, but on the house being sold, they were evicted and compelled to seek shelter on the beach. According to Fred 'Mucky' Erridge they were an eccentric couple. Several times Fred had seen Mrs Huggett washing the stairs down with buckets of water and a brush, the indoor stairs, mind you. She dressed oddly always a large overcoat on in the heat of summer and big boots worn without stockings.

Phillip Huggett stated that during his lifetime he had saved some 39 persons from drowning and received no recognition. Another occasion he along with others shared the sum of £30 awarded for salving an air Balloon and its crew that had dropped into the sea off Eastbourne. There is truth in this story, occurring back in 1912 but it's debatable that Philip was involved; two were Huggetts, Jesse and Jack according to the local report. Fred Erridge stated this to be the case. Bob Hunt fisherman and boatman related in 1965 that he knew the Huggetts well. 'Uncle Phillip' was a kind old gentleman with a white beard, and an expert sharp eyed 'Fretter'. He was a legend at finding coins etc among the shingle, a character indeed on the Eastbourne beach. (Fretting a local term for beachcombing now superceded by the metal detector)

Phillip 'Old Mug' Huggett, August 1923.

Louisa Huggett was charged with assaulting a Miss Lelliott at the Fishing Station in June 1925 by hitting her with a stick. Huggett said the girl kept making her dog bark and refused to stop teasing it. It annoyed Huggett who denied hitting the girl. The magistrate dismissed the case with a caution and ordered Huggett to pay costs. Huggett refused to pay the costs saying she wanted justice. Told in default she would serve 5 days imprisonment.

Huggett was gently led away out of the Court.

The Huggetts were still living on the beach in 1929. A case of theft against Louisa was reported in June that year when she appeared at the Magistrates Court on a charge of stealing from the Net shop of Harry Boniface, a quantity of net cotton and four 'snoozers' valued at 25 shillings. Although believing in the Bible, Louisa declined to take the oath, but affirmed, stating it was a mockery to take the oath. She denied the charge but was found guilty and fined 10s. The court was told she lived on the beach with her husband. Louisa told the court the price asked for rooms stopped her renting and she would not encourage profiteering. Living on through the 1930's Louisa is remembered to this day by Thelma and Pam Langford (of Erridge family stock) as 'Old Mother Prop' who used to hang her washing on a cloth line tied between the Net shops held up with a 'prop'. To others she was 'Old Mother Mug' (snoozers were spun cotton line varying between lengths of 12 inches - 2ft 6inches. Attached from line to fishing hook)

Another (famous) beach lady was 'Esther' Moggridge a weather beaten eccentric, (aged 60-70 yrs?) who lived on the beach against a groyne west of the Pier during the 1960's. Her abode was a ramshackle construction of driftwood and tarpaulin. A very spartan living, she survived on the beach for a number of years. The Council got her removed from the beach in 1964 after taking County Court proceedings but she returned and in 1968 removal proceedings were again taken against her. Afterwards, for a time she did live in a make shift (camp) behind the Co-Op Corner Store.

July 1923 saw the building of Tennis courts on Fishermen's Green. Royal Parade.

1924. Watch Committee minutes.

June. William Allchorn applied for the transfer of Net shop No.36 he had purchased from Lucas Hide the executor of the late Mrs Elizabeth Hide (George 'Pincher' Hide's widow) Granted. (No. 36 was known as the Big Shed/Luke's shed)

July. An application for transfer of Net shop No.28 and capstan opposite purchased from the executors of the late Mrs E Hide was deferred, capstan not granted.

September. Fred Reed was found to be in arrears of rent for his Net shop No.18, acquired for £60 in 1919. According to the Parade Inspector it was a genuine case of hardship. Ordered to pay arrears at 10/- per month.

December. Fred Hurd took over Net shop No.35 previously held by widow Mrs Ben Hide who has no further use for it.

1925. Watch Committee minutes.

January. Fishing Station. Application by Jack Allchorn for transfers of capstan No.30, capstan No.29 and plot No.37 to William Allchorn Jnr. all previously occupied by Lucas Hide was agreed.

July. 'Narny' Sayers requested the transfer of Net shop No.33 having purchased it from Edward 'Ted' Hide. Agreed.

A complaint (no details) had been received concerning the Fish Market run by Henry Boniface and Charlie Clark, fish sales man, both men to be interviewed.

Request for transfer of Net shop No.16 from Charles Prodger to John Joseph Prodger was granted.

October. Fred Hurd applied for permission to build a concrete Net shop between Net shops Nos.31-33. He was given permission as long as plans approved by the Building Committee. (Similar to that built by the Erridges?)

November. Tom Prodger took over capstan No.26 at Fishing Station from George Gausden.

December 1925.

Problems arose over the launching of the lifeboat. In early December whilst four Eastbourne fishing boats were fishing south of the lightship the weather turned nasty with a gale of wind dead off the land, two boats arrived back safely but two became well overdue. Evidently the assistant lifeboat secretary declined to let Coxswain Mike Hardy launch. One boat 'Britannia' successfully sailed back. A motorboat towed the other 'Silver Spray' in some hours later when the wind dropped.

The story goes that the Cox'n and fishermen were threatening to take the lifeboat and launch her. Due back at 12.00pm it was well past that time and the fishermen became worried for the safety of the men and boats. No distress signals had been received by the Coastguard. The assistant secretary Mr Richards contacted the Coastguard at Beachy Head and they advised him the wind would drop. But it was argued, *'better to launch, when there is a danger or a doubt, better to launch and find out'* Tim Erridge an ex Cox'n commented that there seemed to be a reluctance to launch these days. The Cox'n should be given the responsibility to launch. His experience should be paramount.

Further criticism arose because some days after the non launch of the lifeboat, a Brighton boat 'Helping Hand' SM 217 with 5 crew was night fishing for herring off Beachy Head when the wind increased to gale force and the seas grew heavy and whilst hauling in the nets they became entangled with the propeller. She was immobile so sails were set and she attempted to make Eastbourne. Come morning 2 miles off, her sails were carried away. She put down her anchor and signalled her distress by flying two baskets from her mizenmast. She hove at anchor for some 4 hours but nobody saw her signal (there was much criticism over this) so the crew rigged a jury sail and did get ashore by 6.00pm, it taking 2 hours. The skipper commented he had never experienced the like before and thought they would never make the beach.

When a boat is overdue and the fishermen on shore know it is, it is only right they want to see the lifeboat launched, better safe than a tragedy. In those years the boats were open to the elements, (no cosy cabins) and not all had motors, though even these broke down.

Sayers Bros. 'Eastbourne Queen' c1950, built by Pragnell's boat builders of Eastbourne.

Chapter Eleven

The 'Linnet Incident', Pragnell Boat Builders, Life-saving Apparatus Volunteers.

December 1925.

A near tragedy at sea occurred some days later after the above incident, it was about 2.00am on Friday 4th December when the Eastbourne fishing boat 'Linnet' RX 75 owner Henry Boniface, (ex Coxswain of the lifeboat, and an old, well known licensed boat owner) had been drifting for herring. She had a fair catch of some 4,000 fish aboard and was returning home when the 'Linnet' was run into and sunk at a point about 2 miles south west of the Lightship. There was considerable fog at the time. The incident began when noticing a vessel burning flares requesting help the skipper of the 'Linnet' turned her to go to the boat's assistance, when the mishap occurred. The 'Linnet' was cut in two and sank almost immediately. Boniface and two of the crew George Stockwell and Tom Towner grasped the offending ship's rail, but the other two 20 year John 'Jack' Hurd and 65 year William Erridge were thrown into the sea where they remained clinging to an oar until the vessel returned and took them aboard. They were very lucky to have been found considering the fog. Later all the crew were transferred to a Folkestone fishing boat 'Alfred' FE 164, taken to Folkestone and landed at 3.30pm. William Erridge was taken to hospital with a dislocated shoulder, the other survivors returned to Eastbourne. It was back to work next day, as survivor 'Jack' Hurd said, *'If you stopped working, you stopped eating'*

The vessel that ran down the 'Linnet' was the Spanish steamer 'Gordejula'. Later at the official enquiry into the incident the Spanish vessel was found to have been travelling at an excessive speed for the conditions prevailing at the time. The 'Linnet's' Henry Boniface and crew were awarded £1,200 in compensation. What a lucky escape for all.

A surviving crew member of the above boat 'Linnet'. John Wood Hurd a well-known character died at the age of 92 years, October 1996. 'Jack' as he was known was born 1904 into an old Eastbourne fishing and pleasure boating family and at the age of ten was sent to Plymouth to serve on a training ship returning home after six years. After working in the local fishing and boating business and having survived the life threatening experience in 1925, Jack joined the Royal Navy at the outbreak of war in 1939. He survived the war and returned to Eastbourne where he again took up the calling of fisherman and boatman. He had another lucky experience when the lifeboat went to his aid whilst encountering severe weather aboard his fishing boat off Eastbourne. Jack served in the lifeboat until 1968 and finally stopped fishing aged 70 years. During the years he was also employed on sea defences along Eastbourne beach. His knowledge of the tides and nautical ways stood him in good stead with this employment. Passing away in the local Royal Alfred Seafarers home he had a send off from the town's Lifeboat crew forming a guard of honour. A fitting tribute to Jack. For prosperity there is an audiotape of Jack singing the following lifeboat song. 'Pull for the Shore'

'Pull for the shore, sailors,
Pull for the shore,
Heed not the rolling waves but bend to your oars,
You're safe in the lifeboat, sailors,
Cling to life no more,
Leave that poor old stranded wreck,
And pull for the shore'.

What turned out to be a busy time for the lifeboat during the winter of 1925/6 continued with a call out in tremendous seas and a gale force southwester. On December 30th the lifeboat was launched to assist the SS 'Comtesse de Flandre' when she was blown aground west of Beachy Head under the Seven Sister cliffs. A Tug from Newhaven attended and attempted to pull her off but the cable parted. The Coastguard attended and with the rocket apparatus put a line aboard and 27 crew were transferred to the beach, thence by rope ladder up the cliff to safety. The 'Comtesse de Flandres' later floated off on a high tide and was taken into Newhaven for repair. After standing by in foul conditions for some hours at the initial grounding the Eastbourne lifeboat returned to station as conditions improved. But during those severe sea conditions crew member Harry Hendy had been injured and suffered from exposure. Sadly he died some time later from it is said, the severe experience he suffered.

John 'Jack' Wood Hurd (1904-1996).

January 1926. Steadfast women of Eastbourne.

Just before midnight January 1st 1926 and the lifeboat maroons went off. The SS 'Atlanteen' had lost her propeller in heavy seas and required assistance. Her position she reported as 8-12 miles south of Beachy Head. Tremendous breakers were rolling in on the half tide, down the ramp went the 'Priscilla Macbean' but she was thrown back by great waves onto a groyne but no damage was sustained nor injury. It seemed she would never get away. But with the unfailing bravery and steadfastness of the launchers, among them several local women, and with their endeavours being waist deep in the water they got her away to the cheers of Cox'n Hardy and his crew. What a gallant effort by the women of Eastbourne. As they wrung the water from their clothes and shook the pebbles out of their shoes the watching crowd cheered. All night the lifeboat searched for the distressed steamer but she had given the wrong position and was never found by the lifeboat, which returned to her station at 6.15am. A long fruitless night. The SS 'Atlanteen' was later found by another ship and towed into Dover Harbour'.

1926. Watch Committee minutes.

June. Fishing Station. C M Wood's Net shop No.45 was transferred to Sayers Bros.

July. A petition was signed by 60 fishermen in support of Pragnell boatbuilding firm using Net shop No.15 belonging to Henry Boniface for their business. (The Committee and full Council did not agree and took Pragnell and Boniface to court). This problem harked back to 1923.

The Committee agreed the transfer of Net shop No.17 from Tom Boniface to Henry M Boniface.

July 1926. Roland Pragnell. Eastbourne Boat builder.

7th July Eastbourne Corporation sued Henry Boniface and Roland Pragnell for one shilling each damages for breach of a covenant in respect of Net shop No.15 at the Fishing Station, or alternatively Pragnell for one shilling for trespass and also sought to prevent Pragnell carrying on business at Net shop No.15 in the trade of boat builder and repairer.

To give one an idea of how the above came about one must start back in 1879-85 when the fishermen of Eastbourne were forced off their ancient fishing site.

The part of foreshore east of the Redoubt was granted to the Corporation by the landowners, Mr Gilbert and the Duke of Devonshire for the sole use of the fishermen and boatmen in perpetuity as long they continued in their occupations. Certain areas of the beach were set aside for Net shops and capstans, other areas for net drying and mending. At that time several Net shops had been built and one building was occupied by the principal boat builder of the time George Gausden. Sites were let by the Corporation at a nominal 2/6d annually. Gausden later took over a site for Boat and Yacht building just across from the Fishing Station at the top of Beach Road. (Now the site of Sovereign Court)

About 1900 Thomas Sisk, boat builder went into partnership with Gausden eventually taking control of the business when Gausden retired. Roland Pragnell was apprenticed to Sisk and in 1923 took over the business in Beach Road from Sisk. What happened then was, in June that same year a fire destroyed the boat-building yard in Beach Road. This is where fisherman Henry Boniface comes in. He had in 1912 taken over Net shop No.15 and he let Pragnell take it over for boat building and repairing of fishing and pleasure boats. In September 1924 Pragnell advised the Corporation he had taken over No.15 from Boniface and asked for the tenancy to be transferred to himself. The Corporation refused Pragnell the tenancy and told him to quit, refusing to accept any rent, Pragnell stayed put.

So it all ended up in Court where in mitigation Pragnell told the Judge he was also engaged in fishing being the part owner with George Erridge of the boat 'Ben Macree' and his work at Shop No.15 was 2/3rds for pleasure boats. He said the Corporation had refused to accept his rent. The Corporation for their part maintained that Pragnell's business contravened the covenant covering the use of the Fishing Station. It was to be used solely for fishing and boating. For Pragnell it was put that George Gausden had used the Fishing Station for boat building in earlier days and at that time 1926, there was indeed a Tea chalet operating on the Fishing Station site and also the Angling Club had their premises there.

Fisherman Henry Matthews of 12, Wannock Road gave evidence that he had known Net shop No.15 for 40 years detailing its history saying, *'I don't come here to lie. You know I have a good character'*. He continued by saying Pragnell's Shop was a good thing for the fishermen. Concluding his evidence he turned to the Judge and said, *'God bless you sir, may you live long. Listen to me. Be good'*. His Honour smiled at the remarks and Matthews was with difficulty silenced. Fisherman Henry Erridge of 51, Sidley Road gave evidence in support as to the usefulness of Shop 15 which stood just to the west of the 1903 Lifeboat Station.

His Honour Judge Cann on 20th July gave judgement for Pragnell and Boniface saying there was evidence that Shop No.15 had been used for boat building and repairs going back to 1885 and in his opinion it was beneficial for the fishermen to have their boats repaired on site and there was no breach of the covenant by the defendants and no trespass by Pragnell. He ordered the Corporation to pay the whole of the costs.

Pragnell Boatbuilders at Net Shop No.15 Eastbourne Fishing Station, October 1930.

So the above was settled but over the years some of the Net shops at the Fishing Station had been used for other than solely by and for fishing. At times persons did obtain Net shops for their own personal yachts and boats solely for their pleasure and not commercial fishing

Roland Pragnell had two sons, Reg and Bill, both following in the business. During the 1939-45 war Pragnell's war effort was to build whalers for the Admiralty.

Just after the war Pragnell's business moved to Westham where under Reg along with son Rowland, into the family business at a young age, and George Stevens, using skills that had come through from a line of local boat builders starting c.1750's with Simpson, Gausden and Sisk, they built their boats in a large barn beside the pond in Peelings Lane. Fortunately there is shown for the record the construction of two fine pleasure boats 'Southern Queen' and 'Eastbourne Queen' for Sayers Brothers, built c.1947-49 at Westham. Acquired by Allchorn Bros in 1965 the 'Southern Queen' is still operating as a pleasure boat out of Sovereign Harbour and off the beach at Eastbourne by the firm Eastbourne Marine.

Reginald 'Reg' Pragnell. Eastbourne born and bred was educated at St Andrews Norway and St Phillips schools leaving at the age of 14 years to join his father in the family business serving a seven year boat building apprenticeship. Come the 2nd World War he served as a chief shipwright aboard cruisers and assault craft in the South Atlantic and Far East. Torpedoed off the coast of Africa he survived the war and returned to boat building. Then with the introduction of fibreglass built boats c.1950, Reg left boatbuilding and went into the house building and decorating industry. 1966 saw him take over as landlord of the former coach house inn Royal Oak and Castle, Pevensey, which he ran successfully for many years. Whilst a Publican he still found time to keep his hand in with boat building by constructing in his spare time small fishing boats in a yard at the back of the Minthouse, which is opposite the Pub.

Southern Queen under construction. Left to right, George Stevens, Barrie ?, Rowland Pragnell and Reg Pragnell.

1926. Watch Committee minute.

August. Discussing the above court case of Pragnell the Committee resolved that in future, plans must be submitted of all Net shop usages and proposed buildings erected at the Fishing Station.

'Southern Queen' painted and ready for engine fitting.

1927.

At the end of July a near tragedy at sea was averted by Mr Flude of 32, Carlton Road in his yacht 'Saucy Jean' when he went to the rescue of three boys from their capsized sailing boat off the Pier

Barn at Westham where Pleasure boats 'Southern Queen and 'Eastbourne Queen' were built by Pragnell's for Sayers Bros. 1947-48.

Reg Pragnell with 'Southern Queen'

head. The capsized boat was later recovered by fisherman Jesse Huggett.

1927. Watch Committee minute.

September. It was agreed to the transfer of Net shop No.21 to Edward 'Ted' Clark from his late father Charlie.

October 1927.

A challenge whaler race was fought out between local fishermen and the members of the R.N.V.R. The winning fishermen's crew were Tim Erridge, cox, P. Huggett, stroke, Alfred Erridge, Jack Huggett, Andrew Chester and Harry Boniface

That same month, lifeboat 'L.P. & S Helen' came on Station at Eastbourne. Becoming known to her crew as 'Plain Kate'

November 1927.

The death occurred on November 8th of William Henry Erridge 57, Channel View Road age 73, fisherman and boatman. Nicknamed 'Alligator' he was in the crew of the lifeboat at the famous 1883 Birling Gap rescue. At 12.20pm Erridge was at the Fishing Station assisting Jesse Huggett pull up his boat when he collapsed and died there on the beach. A fitting way to go on his beloved beach where he had spent all his working life.

December 1927.

There was a glut of herring in the Channel, so much so that one fisherman suffered a loss whilst fishing at night over the 'Hoss' (Horse) rocks about 3½ miles south east of Eastbourne. Jim Boniface was skipper of motor fishing boat 'Prince Albert' when she lost almost all her nets, carried away by a heavy shoal of herring, the loaded nets caught on the rocks, breaking away from the boat as soon as they attempted to haul in. Out of 55 only 8 nets were left and those mostly damaged. The lamp, set about 2 feet above the water was extinguished and broken. The loss was a severe one. Owner of the boat Mr French said the nets would cost over £100 to replace. 'Prince Albert's' crew were Jim Boniface, George Prodger, Alan Watkins and Joe Boniface. A similar accident occurred the following day to Jesse Huggett and the 'Royal Sovereign' fishing boat.

1928. Watch Committee minutes.

January. Fishermen H Boniface and J French made application to purchase the old Rocket House at the Fishing Station.

Frank Hastings of 11, Channel View Road applied for transfer of Net shop No.1 and capstan No.1 from Tim Erridge, said solely for fishing purposes. Granted.

March. Other applications for the tenancy of the Rocket House were made by Tom Sisk, Fred 'Tinker' Novis, Henry Boniface and J French. Not yet for rent according to owners, the Board of Trade.

April. The Board of Trade relinquish the Rocket House to the Town Council and it is let to boat builder Tom Sisk for 5/- per week.

A complaint was made to the Committee by the E.F.B.P. Society that Net shop No.1 was not occupied by a bona fide fisherman (Frank Hastings).

It was noted that Pragnell boat builder has premises at 16, Myrtle Road.

May. Pragnell granted Boat Stand No.69 at Royal Parade.

July. The case of Frank Hastings and Net shop No.1 and the complaint by the E.F.B.P. Society came before the Committee again. The Committee agreed with the complaint and resolve that the existing agreement should continue but a proposed alteration be refused. (Final outcome not known)

August. Pragnell granted a Motor boat drivers licence.

September. Fisherman Fred Reed in a letter offered to sell his Net shop No.18 to the Council. The Town Clerk advised he must sell or transfer to a fisherman, subject to approval.

A letter from the E.F.B.P. Society stated they had no objections to the transfer of Net shop No.40 to Fred Novis purchased from Arthur Sayers, Net shop No.12 to Jesse Huggett purchased from Samuel Hurd and Net shop No.49 to T G Swain Jnr. from his father Tom Swain. All the above were granted.

December. Fish Market. The Committee stated that locally caught fish to be sold before imported fish from other towns and that arriving by train. A regulation was duly made.

May 1928.

The death of fisherman and boatman Thomas Swain aged 72 years. He contracted blood poisoning through a cut to his arm whilst tarring his Net shop. Known affectionately as 'Tommy Ruin' he was a member of the famous 1883 lifeboat crew.

The summer of 1928 proved to be a most satisfactory season for most boatmen, due to the record spell of fine weather. Come October the fishermen were looking forward to and preparing for the approaching herring season due at the end of October through to Christmas thereafter which they would be occupied with 'long lining' for mainly dogfish and cod.

The herring season normally commenced at Grimsby 6 weeks before the herring arrived off Eastbourne placing the Eastbourne fishermen at a disadvantage. Grimsby herring were sent to Eastbourne and sold by the fishmongers as, 'local herring'. Thus when the herring did arrive local folk were a bit tired of 'local herring'. But thanks to the fish markets of Brighton and Hastings they took all that Eastbourne could catch. The lobster season had been good and with the approach of the herring this always signalled a great event among fishermen and long nights of activity. The fishermen of Eastbourne enjoyed a satisfactory season that year owing to the fine weather that blessed Eastbourne.

March 1929.

The Town Council refused to grant the application of Mr H Boniface to remove from the foreshore at Holywell and in front of the Fishing Station 200 tons of flints per month during the present year. The operation was to supply this material to the potteries and would create continuous local employment for six men.

Adrift in the Channel a large fairway buoy was sighted by the skipper of fishing boat 'Britannia II' and towed ashore at the Fishing Station.

June 1930. Collision at sea tragedy.

Midnight, June 1st and a collision between two steamers, the Swedish 'Inoger' and the Italian 'Literno' in the Channel saw the tragic drowning of 15 seamen of the Swedish vessel. There were three survivors, two picked up by the Italian ship, the other by the Eastbourne lifeboat 'Jane Holland' making her 1st gainful service. She spent many hours at sea searching and thereby hangs a tale.

It transpired that at 1.37am the Newhaven lifeboat was called out via the wireless. Eastbourne had no wireless and were contacted by telephone and told by Newhaven lifeboat station that the position of the collision was 7 miles south west of Beachy Head making it in Newhaven lifeboat's area and the steamer SS Literno was attending. When this was the case only one lifeboat was required to go and it was supposedly on the Newhaven patch. Newhaven station and lifeboat at 1.55am were given the true position as 2¹/₂ miles south of the Royal Sovereign lightship this being the Eastbourne lifeboat's area. Both Newhaven lifeboat and station failed to advise Eastbourne of the new position and it wasn't until some 1¹/₂ hours later that Eastbourne was given the true position and she launched. Meanwhile Newhaven lifeboat had picked up one body and landed it at Eastbourne pier head. Knowing their patch well the Eastbourne lifeboat under Coxswain Mike Hardy soon found a survivor clinging to an upturned boat. They searched the area for several hours without further success.

Much criticism of the lateness of the launch of the Eastbourne lifeboat was published in the local paper, more lives could have been saved but it was not Eastbourne's fault. Actually it was fortunate Eastbourne did not launch on the first occasion as she had no wireless and could not have been contacted. But there can be no excuse of not being told by Newhaven of the true position, which was on Eastbourne's patch. Indeed they knew their area well and could well have saved more lives if advised earlier of the true position of the collision. There was much public criticism of Newhaven lifeboat in the Eastbourne papers.

Fairway buoy recovered, adrift in the Channel by Sayers 'Britannia II', January 1930.

Being interviewed after the event, Eastbourne lifeboat man William Allchorn said, *'I have read the letters of criticism in the Gazette and it opens an old wound. (1883 Birling Gap rescue and salvage claim) but this time I think the facts are different. You see the Italian boat SS Literno, gave her position wrongly in the first S.O.S. she said she was south west of Beachy Head and so it was Newhaven lifeboat's job to go. Actually she was south east of the Lightship right opposite Eastbourne and the moment we got the proper message away we went. As it happened we came up on one side and the Newhaven boat had come up on the other. We spoke to the Newhaven men and they said the Italian ship had 2 survivors aboard, they reckoned 15 men had drowned.*

We decided that if anything was floating we should find it in the tideway. We went steaming down the tideway and Newhaven went southeast. At last we saw an object on the water thought at first to be a buoy but as we got nearer we saw it was a man kneeling on the bottom of an upturned boat. I felt desperately sorry for him as he sat in our boat unable to speak a word of English, but we did our best to cheer him up'.

Mr Alexander Robertson. Hon. secretary of the Eastbourne branch of the R.N.L. Institute said, *'If Newhaven had passed on that second message to us instead of holding it up for 1½ hours I believe we might have taken 2 more men from the sea and saved them'.*

Just why did Newhaven hang onto the new position and not tell Eastbourne? They knew the new position was on Eastbourne's patch. Eastbourne lifeboat men were very familiar with their patch and this is borne out by the fact that they soon picked up a poor soul, and who knows an earlier call could have saved others?

July 1930. Eastbourne fishermen to the rescue.

On Thursday, 3rd July, ½ mile off Beachy Head, W Matthews and 'Cassy' Reed were tending their lobster pots when a heavy sea arose.

Luckily they spotted a motorboat just as it capsized spilling 3 men into the sea about ¹/₂ mile from them. They immediately went to their aid saving all three and taking them ashore, the men visitors, were unhurt other than suffering from exposure to the sea. This type of rescue was not uncommon as those years saw plenty of visitors in boats off Eastbourne. Also the fishing fraternity numbers were many.

A whaler boat race was contested between the boatmen of Eastbourne and sailors of the visiting Royal Navy ship HMS Barham during July 1930. Watched by large crowds the boatmen proved too good for the sailors, a victory for Eastbourne. Sadly HMS Barham was torpedoed and sunk in the Mediterranean, November 1941 with great loss of life.

John 'Kruger' Prodger on right. John 'Foot' Prodger 2nd left C.1900.

October 1930.

October saw the death of a fisherman and member of the famous 1883 lifeboat rescue off Birling Gap. 78 year old, John 'Kruger' Prodger of Sidley Road from the old Eastbourne family was buried in Ocklynge cemetery on 27th. His coffin was borne by fishermen and lifeboat men namely: Jesse Huggett, Mike Hardy, Harry Boniface, F Morris, Jim Hardy and Alec Huggett. The Vicar of Christ Church, Rev. Fenning conducted the burial service. Flags at the Fishing Station flew at half-mast in memory of one of the 'Grand Old Men' of the lifeboat.

November 1930.

Just a month later 60 year old Charles Ernest 'Chalky' Hide, eldest son of the late Samuel Beckett and Sarah Hide and nephew of 'Bones' Hide died at his home in Sidley Road. A former Naval seaman, fisherman, boatman and lifeboat man he was well known and popular. 'Chalky' served the lifeboat from 1900 to 1920. He left a widow Kate. There were no issue. November also saw Reuben 'Cassy' Reed, 80 years become the third lifeboatman to pass away in two months, joining 'Kruger'

Prodger and 'Chalky' Hide. 'Cassy' a member of the 1883 crew was born and bred in Eastbourne and after serving for a period in the American Navy returned to his native town and occupation of fisherman and pleasure boatman.

Heavy weather in the English Channel saw a dramatic rescue off the Fishing Station at 2.30pm on Friday, 21st November. Eastbourne's herring fleet had returned safely ashore except fishing boat 'NN32 Ocean Spray' owned by Henry Boniface and crewed on this occasion by skipper George Prodger, Victor 'Navvy' Crick and H. Ekins.

The 'Ocean Spray' was about 400 yards off shore when her engine failed, she drifted eastwards shipped a heavy sea and was in danger of being driven onto a groyne. The anchor was put down and fortunately held although heavy seas were being shipped.

The lifeboat attempted to launch but was unsuccessful due to the low tide causing her to slew round 'broadside on' making it impossible to launch. The 'lizard' a guide rope had broken at a critical moment. A message to the Coastguard Station brought the Life Saving Apparatus Volunteers to the beach in minutes. The Rocket apparatus was set up and the very first shot landed clean across the bows of the 'Ocean Spray'. Within minutes she and her crew were hauled ashore landing opposite to the Gilbert (Princes Park) recreation ground. The bows of the vessel were splintered and broken but the crew safe. Victor 'Navvy' Crick said, *'The narrowest escape I've ever had. Although the anchor held it wouldn't have been long before the Ocean Spray was swamped'.*

It was a fine effort by L.S.A Volunteers, Coastguard Commander Ashcroft and Chief Officer Moat. The volunteers who answered the maroon were: A Wood, T Wood, F R Pragnell, W Pragnell, Fred Erridge, Jack Hardy and Ben Erridge.

The Life Saving Apparatus Volunteers can be said to have started back in 1809 when the Preventative Water Guard were formed to continue the fight against smuggling and that year took on the roll of lifesaving from ships wrecked upon our shores. At sea with boats and from the shore with a new invention the Manby Mortar Rocket invented by Captain G B Manby a boyhood friend of Nelson. The object was to propel a line to ships foundering on the shore and life being in danger. 1831 saw the Coast Guard take over from the Water Guard and by c.1840 Dennett's Rocket apparatus had replaced the Manby Mortar. In later years L.S.A volunteers were recruited locally and came under the control of Chief Officer of Coast Guard, receiving regular training with the firing of the apparatus and retrieving of persons from wrecks, reaping the benefits shown in the following statistic, 53 years from 1856 to 1909 17,446 lives were saved by Rocket apparatus from the shore. 1966 saw the local L.S.A volunteers absorbed into the Coast Guard Auxiliary Services and employed now to go over Beachy Head to save life and recover bodies, Beachy Head being a common spot to commit suicide. Usually victims total double figures annually.

Eastbourne had their L.S.A volunteers from the early days made up generally of the fishing and pleasure boating community. An example of those that served for the period 1919-1940 all living within 800 yards of the Rocket House at the Fishing Station is shown below: -

Dennett's Rocket Apparatus C.1840.

Life Saving Apparatus Volunteers. Drill exercise December 1932. (Rocket Apparatus equipment was stored in the Rocket House at the Fishing Station).

Name	Date of Birth	Enrolment Date
John Towner	15 01 1870	1919
Alfred Smith	09 06 1867	1919
Jack Hardy	18 05 1900	1924
William Erridge	01 10 1860	1919
Alfred Erridge	26 10 1897	1919
Frederick Reed	29 01 1882	1919
George Watkins	11 05 1882	1919
William Hindle	01 06 1873	1923
Albert Wood	03 03 1902	1921
Thomas Wood	20 11 1895	1921
William H Wood	29 06 1891	1921
Henry M Boniface	21 08 1901	1923
George Erridge	12 06 1878	1923
Thomas Knight	22 06 1884	1919
Arthur Knight	06 04 1894	1919
Frederick Jessup	29 11 1883	1919
Thomas Erridge	29 09 1901	1919
Thomas Prodger	01 06 1875	1924
George Pollard	22 03 1876	1924
Benjamin Goldsmith	23 08 1883	1924
Charles Stevenson	30 06 1885	1926
Francis Pragnell	13 01 1904	1926
William Kent	28 03 1901	1927
Edwin Fillery	28 03 1881	1927
Edwin Noble	03 11 1884	1928
Reginald Pragnell	06 11 1908	1928
Alec Huggett	30 08 1903	1928
Benjamin Erridge	Not recorded	1928
Roland Pragnell	03 12 1879	1932
John Davie	21 08 1904	1931
George Williams	28 03 1905	1932
George H Erridge	19 12 1904	1929

Charles F Reed	16 03 1892	1930
Henry C Erridge	06 10 1902	1937
William Pragnell	02 03 1912	1930
George Wood	20 12 1916	1924
John Hurd	29 07 1904	1938
Frederick Beck	30 03 1899	1936
Ernest Pakes	06 03 1891	1937

December 1930.

After the above escape, 'Ocean Spray' was again involved in a drama at sea. Her adventures in the Channel show that good and bad luck often run together.

'The middle of December saw the 'Ocean Spray' under her same crew leave the Fishing Station on a foggy afternoon for fishing grounds some 20 miles the far side of the Royal Sovereign Lightship. With the big ocean going vessels going sluggishly by in the fog, sirens blasting, the 'Ocean Spray' slipped across their paths and safely made the fishing grounds.

They had lines down and the fishing was good, then bad luck. The engine would only work in reverse gear. Not to be beaten the crew sailed and rowed her, and on taking up the lines found good catches. Good luck saw a bumper catch. Now they faced miles back to land but the fog was now very dense, so skipper George Prodger made for the Lightship and with skill and uncanny navigation, sailing and rowing the 'Ocean Spray' was brought within a few feet of the Lightship. A great feat of seamanship and luck combined. The Lightship crew lowered tools and materials for repairs and hot refreshments. After some time forward gear was engaged and after many thanks to the Lightship crew, the 'Ocean Spray' made for shore through the heavy fog and area of danger from the big ships and in due time heard the sea breaking on the foreshore. Forward hand 'Navvy' Crick, was landed and found their position was close to home and in a few minutes they were welcomed by waiting comrades.

Good luck being supreme because they had got home with a fine catch of fish for the morning market. But with the morning came bad luck. The price of fish had slumped and hardly paid their expenses, the crew's earnings therefore were poor. Such is the good and bad luck of these gamblers of the sea. One is struck with admiration for such men as these, as they re-bait their lines, with a song and a smile and drink their tea in the Fishermen's Institute to the jest of their mates. Let it be understood that the engine of the 'Ocean Spray' had expert attention and her skipper and crew are the most practical and steady men that can be found at the Fishing Station'.

1931. Watch Committee minutes.

January. William Prodger applied for the transfer of Net shop No.22 and capstans Nos.24 & 34 recently owned by his late father John Prodger. Granted.

February. Jesse Huggett laid claim to a piece of land at the Fishing Station required by the Lifeboat Institute for a turntable. The Corporation refuted his claim. (Outcome not known)

May. Fred Novis of 31, Seaford Road applied for the transfer of Net shop No.31 from George Prodger. (Retiring?) Granted.

June. Under the strict eye of E.F.B.P. Society on the Fishing Station it was noted that Ted Clark was using his Net shop as a store for chairs. By July the chairs had been removed.

Tom Sisk was released from his tenancy of the Rocket House.

February 1932. Fishing on hard times.

The winter of 1931-32 proved to be the worst for the fishing fraternity for many years; catches of fish were so small that they did not pay expenses. February saw freezing weather with northeast winds sweeping the country and while people were shivering at home the fishermen had gone out plying their trade with deplorable results.

An Eastbourne fisherman spoke of: *'The sprat season has been a failure. For the first 2 months I never made a penny and my average for the season is about 3 shillings a week'.*

Countrywide there was a depression in fishing - prices low as well as catches. Brighton fish market saw fish as cheap as it had ever been. Two fishermen who set out at 5.00am and went trawling to Newhaven and back showed after 12 hours at sea, a loss of 3-4 shillings caused by petrol expenses. Whilst they grumbled about their position the fishermen set a fine example to others by continuing to fish just to keep going.

A fisherman at the time said, *'We hear a lot about the poor unemployed, but what about the fishermen who are not making any money but keep on working? There are some persons who call themselves fishermen and boatmen but they are not really, they go to the Public Assistance for relief and get us a bad name'.*

Indeed the boatmen at that time of the year were busy preparing their pleasure boats for the summer. With the pleasure yachts undergoing their Board of Trade inspection it was a hive of activity seeing the rowboats undergoing scraping and varnishing bringing them up to the high standard as only Eastbourne boatmen knew how. Come the start of the season and they were a sight to behold, sadly now all gone.

Summer 1932.

Pleasure boating was still continued by some of Eastbourne's longshoremen families. Allchorn, Prodger, Boniface, Hardy, Novis, Sayers, Hide, Hurd among others. Of those that mainly fished Erridge, Chester, Huggett and Wood were prominent. At the Fishing Station the general rule was, Pleasure boating shops to be at the west side and fishing only to the east up to Tanhouse groyne. The fishermen enjoyed a good summer; 18 boats and some 120 men were employed in the industry. The mackerel going down Channel proved plentiful but one fisherman had the misfortune to lose 3 mackerel nets when a 2 cwt thresher shark some 9 feet long got 'caught' off Beachy Head.

Rowing Champions of Eastbourne 1932. Beating Eastbourne Rowing Club.
Left to right, John 'Jack' Prodger, George Erridge, Andrew Chester, Jesse Huggett, George Huggett, John 'Foot' Prodger.

Local rowing champions for 1932 were Eastbourne's fishermen and boatmen who beat the local Rowing Club..

Frank Nickson a teacher at Willowfield School and later Headmaster of Hampden Park Secondary School from 1940, made a return Channel crossing via Dover to Calais in a 15ft open motor boat with a 'Petters' designed air cooled engine. The boat was built by R. Pragnell & Sons in their Boat shed at the Fishing Station. The boat made 6 knots an hour. Nickson motored in the boat from Eastbourne to Dover. Made the crossing and back then returned to Eastbourne. The weather was stormy all the way back from Dover and Roland Pragnell remarked *'No fisherman would have been out in that weather'* Quite a feat by Frank Nickson in August 1932.

August 1932, on left Boatbuilder Roland Pragnell, on right Frank Nickson.

September 1932.

One of Eastbourne's evergreen retired longshoremen celebrated his 84th birthday in September. Henry 'Old Dusty' Matthews it was said, was like an old soldier - they never die and seldom fade away. A board announcing his birthday was displayed on a Boating pitch on the promenade. A fisherman and boatman all his life 'Dusty' had retired and sold his pleasure boat a year before. 'Dusty' resided beside another veteran of the sea, Albert 'Tuppy' Sayers in his 72nd year. They sailed together on many a fishing expedition. 'Tuppy' still operated his rowboats on the beach. 'Tuppy' also had the distinction of being a member of the famous 1883 Birling Gap lifeboat rescue. Both 'Old Dusty' and 'Tuppy' were good adverts for the Eastbourne sea air.

October 1932.

A general upturn in the fishermen's fortunes came the second week of October with the start of the herring season. With hopes of a fine 'harvest' Sunday night of the 16th, some 60 stone was brought ashore being the 'Longshore' smaller herring, as the bigger ones come by in November. Those first herring got 3/- a stone at the Fish market whereas in November the price would be 1/- per hundred (approximately a stone). There were some 16 to 18 boats employed locally with about 120 men. The 'Punt' type Eastbourne boats usually crewed by three men, were used for spratting, herring and trawling for other types of local fish, plus lobstering, crabbing etc. For the herring, boats would take about 50 nets, each 40 yards long, the boats being capable of taking 2 to 3 'lasts' of herring. That October night fishing proved to take the best catches. The arrival home of the boats and the shaking out of the nets was a long job, as much as 2 to 3 hours when a 'last' or two had been caught. The catch would be sold at the early morning Market with much of the herring going to Brighton market.

Herring not sold as 'fresh' were turned into kippers and bloaters - a process carried out in those days by the fishermen and fishmongers themselves. With 'Dees' (smoke sheds) in operation a strong 'scent' pervaded the Fishing Station area.

November 1932.

Come November the sprats came round and nets of a small mesh would have been prepared in October. Like the cotton herring nets, they were 'tanned' with 'cutch' boiled up usually in a bath and then 'dipped' and taken to the drying grounds (now car park for Treasure Island playground). The nets were fitted with corks along the top with a piece of 'scanting' (an old rolled net) fixed at the bottom to weight it down. Buoys were attached and the nets could be lowered to half a fathom, or one to two fathoms depth according to the level the fish were swimming. Fishing with 'long lines' (now no longer done) proved very profitable when going for cod, whiting, dogfish (bull and robin huss, interestingly fish that can open and close their eyes), skate and other like fish. A single line could be 2 miles long, containing 1,800 hooks baited with herring. Preparation was a long and arduous task especially in the winter months. Hauling in the lines was also hard work but all part of the fishermen's lot.

From the year 1884 a custom brick built single chimney Tanhouse which contained a coal burning boiler was erected at the east end of the Fishing Station for the use

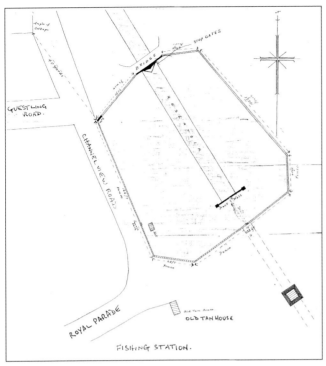

Site of the Tanhouse C.1884.

of the fishermen, hence the boundary groyne having the name to this day 'Tanhouse groyne' This groyne can be identified if a line is approximately taken from Channel View Road. The late Fred 'Mucky' Erridge related that, 'cutch' was produced from the bark of a tree and came in compressed 7lb slabs contained in 1cwt bags, to be boiled up with water. The Tanhouse fell into disuse and a bath on the beach amongst the Net shops was used for preserving the nets until the introduction of synthetic net.

The Fish Market.

A report on the workings of the above made interesting reading in November 1932.

'6.00am and the market was very well stocked with catches of herring, sprats and many other fish all neatly spread out for sale. Boats were still arriving on the beach with their night's catch, some huss and herring were taken straight to Newhaven and Brighton markets. The regular 5.30am Grimsby fish train also brought fish to Eastbourne'.

A lot of fish was needed by Eastbourne and some fishmongers bought straight from Grimsby. This on occasions tended to keep the price of local fish down. Grimsby fish was often sold as 'local'. Sharp practice was used when North Sea herring was sold as 'local' before the herring had even reached the English Channel. This sort of practice helped gradually to bring about a severe decline in Eastbourne fishing. Grimsby mostly undercut local prices and even when local was cheaper, local fishmongers and hotels still purchased from the Grimsby source making life hard for the Eastbourne fishermen.

To return to the Market, the report continued; *'It was a cold and windy place (situated roughly where the Eastbourne Rowing Club stands today). There were 50 -60 persons present selling, buying and moving fish, while some 20 vehicles stood by outside the Market with Hawkers barrows, carts and cycles. Fishmongers and women were among the regular fish buyers. The method of sale was by 'Dutch Auction'. Shortly after 7.00am the auctioneers were Edward 'Ted' and James Clark. 'Ted' Clark wore a herringbone tweed overcoat, muffler and cloth cap. He did the selling, 'Gather round,' he cried, 'A dollar (5/-), 4/6d, 4/2d, 4/-, thank you. (Sold). Two dozen 'dogs' 5'9d 5/6d, thank you. A conger eel and bull huss went for 1/9d. With a cry, 'Toes, Toes', heavy boxes of fish were hauled around. Sales made, pails*

and boxes filled and carted away. Herring shovelled up and weighed by the stone, sold and poured from the scale into a barrel and trundled off. It was an exceedingly busy scene. There were turbot and plaice and the Grimsby consignment contained some fine haddock and kippers and inspired the auctioneers comment, 'I say, I've got an oil painting here. I've got a bit of food here. The King couldn't eat better'. So it went on, a busy thriving scene. When all was done, washing and scrubbing down took place and the market was as the saying goes, 'all shipshape and Bristol fashion' ready for an early start the next day. The fish offal being taken to the Destructor works for disposal".

In 1954 complaints were received that strong language could be heard emitting from the Fish Market in the early hours upsetting the visitors in the front bedrooms of the guest houses along Royal Parade. The Chief Constable ordered the Constable of beat No.9 that covered the Fish Market to pay particular attention. Not an easy task as the very nature of business required loud language, but with the attendance of a Constable the strong language did ease.

December 1932.

Just before Christmas 1932, the brig rigged barge 'Alan Dean' foundered in heavy seas off Langney Point during the early morning and no one on shore witnessed the loss. The crew of three took to the ship's dinghy and at first light got ashore at the Fishing Station where they were met by Coastguard watchmen volunteers, Jim Hardy and George 'John' Erridge. The survivors were assisted ashore cold and exhausted and taken to the Fishermen's Institute where they received first aid, food and comfort. The 'Alan Dean' laden with oilcake and grain foundered at 4.00am and it took the crew 3½ hours to get ashore. The wreck was later blown up.

January 1933. Fishermen's Protest.

A problem that had been with the Eastbourne fishermen for some years was

Survivors of the foundered barge 'Alan Dean' December 1932 receive hospitality at the Fishermen's Club. Some club members identified possibly as standing from left; extreme left George 'John' Erridge, 4th left Jack Elms, 7th left John 'Sausage' Grooms and 8th left Ernest 'Chinaman' Sayers.

discussed down at the Fishing Station, on ways and means of improving the local trade. One suggestion was for local hoteliers to buy local fish and obtain it at a lower price. Fish from Grimsby and Lowestoft was still being bought. Local fish was fresher but there was no support from the local hotels. Even foreign caught fish was being sold as 'English'. The fishermen were obviously indignant. The foundation of a co-operative was discussed.

'There is no doubt that the foreign fish is killing our trade,' said Jesse Huggett, a prominent Eastbourne fisherman. *'People see it marked English', and thinking that it is English, they buy it. If a man was to hang up in his meat shop foreign meat labelled English he would get into trouble, but not as regards fish. There ought to be something done about it. A fisherman has no means of protection as other trades do. I know fishermen who have spent large sums of money in net, tackle and engine works and do not get enough money for their fish'.*

So the problem of foreign, Grimsby and Lowestoft fish made life hard, their large catches and industry, could, even with transport costs undercut the local fisherman. Eastbourne caught fish was regularly taken to Hastings and Brighton in order to get a fair price.

August 1933.

Conservation of fish was to the fore. A notice was posted at the Fishing Station re size of fish to be caught, net mesh sizes to be increased, but nets in stock before May 1st 1933 were eligible until they wore out. The Eastbourne fishermen's sales of fish were further effected, as in earlier days of good catches any number of small fish were thrown back but in the hard days of the 1930's they would be taken and fetch 18d a bushel at market. *'It is going to hit our chaps,'* said Ned Sayers. *'It is a good move. Bringing in small fish must effect the breeding. I think the fairest way would be to stop trawling for a fortnight or even a month at the time best suited to each town, for it would give time for fish to grow. It would be hard on Longshoremen but it would be best if trawling was stopped say within a mile all along the coast for a definite time each year'.*

Tributes were paid at the funeral of an old Eastbourne fisherman and boatman. 78-year-old William

The property with the arched door and sign on the wall was the family home of Edward Allchorn (died 1887) founder of the Allchorn Pleasure boat business and father of William. Originally the property opened out onto the shingle beach of the 'Stade' Fishing Station being No.39 Marine Parade. In 1886 William Allchorn was the householder. Later the property was incorporated into what is now Sea Beach House Hotel. Marine Parade.

C 1914. The family of William Allchorn, Fisherman and Pleasure Boatman at 15, Eshton Road. From left to right, standing at back, George, Florence, Harry, Fred, Annie and William Jnr. Seated centre row, Ethel, Father William and Mother Harriet (nee Prodger), Jack and Edith. Seated front row, Tom, Beatrice and Albert 'Sam'.

Fishermen William Jnr. and Tom Allchorn paying respects on the death of King George V. January 1936.

Allchorn's funeral was on 28th August, the service being at Christ Church followed by interment at Ocklynge cemetery. With over 60 years in the fishing and pleasure boat business a founder member of the Eastbourne Fishermen's and Boatmen's Protection Society, whose members lined the path to the Church. William for some 54 years was a member of the Shipwrecked Fishermen and Mariner's Society. With his cousin Ted Allchorn he won a regatta double scull race. The prize was two skiffs (row boats) named 'Grouse' and 'Partridge' and both still in use at the time of his death. William Allchorn was one of those Eastbourne fishermen who sailed in the Lugger fleets up north and down to Ireland - truly a 'son of the sea'. At the time of his death the family firm operated 4 motorboats, a speedboat and 20 rowboats.

Chief mourners were, the widow Harriet, Mrs Bailey sister, Harry, Fred, Will, Jack, Tom, and Albert, sons, Edie, Flo, Annie and Beat, daughters.

Other mourners, G Prodger, Mike Hardy, Jack Huggett, Tom Huggett, Fred Hurd, Jack Tuxford, E.W. Allchorn, Albert Sayers, Joe Allchorn, David Allchorn, Alfred Allchorn and Arthur Allchorn (Nephews)., William Erridge, J Bowler, T Prodger, G T Erridge Snr. G H Erridge, T Pollard, J Bell, C Foy, M Andrews, Jim Hardy, Alec Huggett, R Hardy, H Boniface Snr. E Gearing, F Novis, T Boniface, Jack Hurd, J Prodger Snr. J Prodger Jnr. Ted Sayers, Alleyn Sayers, William Hide and C Wood. Nurse Beck.

1933. Watch Committee minutes.

November. Net shop No.10 was transferred from the late Albert French to his son F E French and capstan stand to widow Caroline French. An application for the transfer to Allchorn Bros of Net shops Nos.36 & 37 and capstans Nos.37 & 38 previously rented by William Allchorn their late father, was granted.

January 1934.

1934 opened with the grounding off Langney Point of the vessel 'Plymouth Trader' 150 tons en-route from Gillingham to Truro. She went aground at 5.00am January 11th and successfully floated off on the next high tide. The 'Plymouth Trader' had the distinction of being one of the 'Lighters' used in the storming of the beaches at Gallipoli in 1915.

The winter months (October 1933 - January 1934) had proved poor for fishing and hardship was felt in many a fishing family home. January saw poor catches, for example, a boat with a crew of 4 caught only 2 stone of sprats in 4 hours, in total 1,000 sprats. Normal fishing times would have seen a catch of 60,000. The 2 stone caught, sold for 2/6d per stone, not worth catching. It was the cold spell in the previous December that sent the sprats down west according to the fishermen of Poole who enjoyed bumper catches while Eastbourne was sparse. With the shortage of sprat and herring there was no bait for long lining. Those Eastbourne fishermen who had been thrifty dipped into their savings, for others there was no buying of new tackle etc.

The month of January 1934 also saw a lucky escape for fisherman Nelson Sayers when he fell overboard from the boat 'Commodore' into an icy sea off Beachy Head whilst hauling the nets. He was quickly pulled back aboard by his crewmates. The 'Commodore' was fishing out of Newhaven at the time.

A Fishing Ordeal in Fog.

Rescued by lifeboat after 16 hours at sea - Eastbourne fishermen, skipper Alec Huggett, Fred Novis and Alan Brown left the Fishing Station in the boat 'Millicent' at 5.00am on Monday 19th to fish south of the Royal Sovereign Lightship. They had not returned by late afternoon. Jack Prodger in his boat 'Oceans Gift' had been out searching unsuccessfully for some four hours and on his return at 6.00pm the lifeboat 'Jane Holland' under Cox'n Mike Hardy was launched. At 9.00pm two lights were seen at sea approaching the Fishing Station, then a flare lit up the bow of the 'Jane Holland' and the waiting crowd cheered as she came into view towing the 'Millicent'.

Alec Huggett later described the ordeal that had been experienced;

'It was very foggy as we went out but cleared as we shot our lines. When we went astern the engine cut out. We left the lines and rowed for the Lightship where we tied up and went aboard. About 4.00pm the fog lifted so we went and made an attempt to get our lines in. A Steamer had cut one of our 'down's (line) off so that made our work of hauling the line doubly hard. It was dark and foggy when we finished, and we had to cross the shipping traffic lane to get back to the Lightship. There were two boats, one to starboard and one to port - one nearly run us down, but we lit two flares and good flares they were. As we approached the Lightship we came up against a strong flood tide and as we were making no headway rowing, the Lightship let go a 5-gallon drum with 120 fathoms of rope and we tied onto that until we did eventually pull to the Lightship. Our most anxious moment was when a Steamer was nearly on us. The Lightship crew treated us well and

Lifeboat crew of the 'Jane Holland' receiving Maroon-firing demonstration, October 1934.

Survivors of the fishing boat 'Millicent'. Left Alan Brown, Right Fred 'Tinker' Novis. November 1934.

arrangements were made to spend the night on board. However shortly after, the lifeboat arrived and towed the 'Millicent' and us back to Eastbourne'.

1934. Watch Committee minutes.

March. An application by A W Erridge to occupy capstan No.20 at the Fishing Station was granted.

September. A request by R Pragnell boat builder to strengthen Net shop No.15 was refused. The Council did not agree to it being used for fishing business.

November. The Committee ordered Pragnell to remove a motorcar kept in Net shop No.18 and proceedings were going to be taken in relation Net shop No.15. Pragnell removed the motorcar and dropped request to strengthen Net shop No.15.

1935. Watch Committee minutes.

March. Proceedings against Pragnell dropped by the Council as it was discovered that he was registered with the Board of Trade as part owner of fishing boat 'Ben Macree'.

July 1935.

Fisherman Tim Erridge caught a 'Tunny Fish' 3 miles off Eastbourne in his mackerel nets. A small one, but very unusual to be caught off Eastbourne.

A local report states that some 20 fishing boats were operating at the Fishing Station - a good summer for the fishermen, with catches being sent to Brighton and London.

August 1935.

The age old enemy and adversary the French were arrested with their fishing boat, poaching fish a mile off Langney Point. They were long lining. Apprehended by the Coast guard the French skipper was taken to Lewes Court. Pleading guilty as charged and fined. An age-old problem.

October 1935.

The herring season began with quite good catches brought by a strong inland breeze, landing as many as 2-3,000, but talk among the fishermen was the wish that there would not be a glut as had happened at Yarmouth and Lowestoft. A glut would mean low prices and a 3-day working week.

1936. Watch Committee minutes.

March. H Dyer of 102, Seaside made application for transfer of Net shop No.44 and capstan No.36. Enquiries showed Dyer was not a registered owner of a fishing boat and that the Net shop and capstan have been in the name of William Bollard Hide since 1921. Dyer claimed ownership of the Net shop since 1913. Further enquiries to be made.

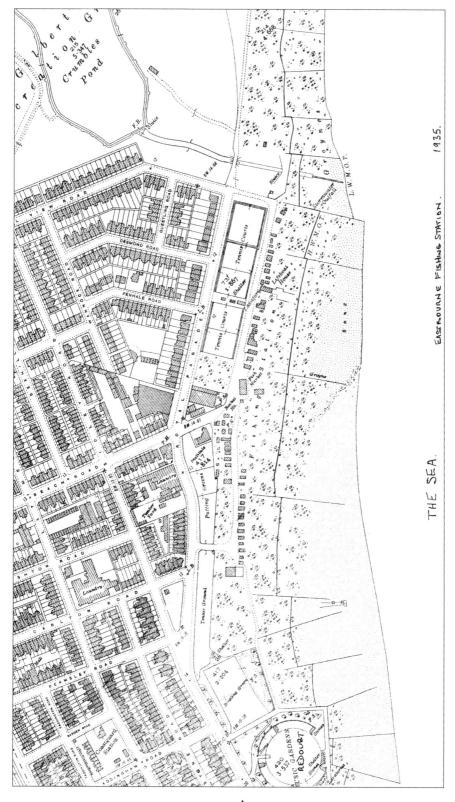

Plan of fishing station 1935 reproduced from an Ordnance Survey map 1935.

April. Enquiries showed that Dyer was not a fisherman of the Borough. Committee had no power to grant a licence of transfer in this case. E.F.B.P. Society also objected to a transfer being issued. Dyer was refused a transfer.

May. Dyer appealed saying he has the permission of the Gilbert Estate. The Council refused again stating he must also get permission of the Chatsworth Estate.

November. Plans submitted by Jesse Huggett to carry out alterations to Net shop No.12 were granted.

December. Application was made by William Allchorn for the transfer of Net shop No.38 and capstan No.31 previously held by the late Lucas Hide. Granted.

March 1936.

Fisherman Victor 'Navvy' Crick was fined for having no licence for his dog. He told the Court he had not been fishing since November 1935.

August 1936.

August saw the death of 79-year-old Mark Hookham well known builder established in 1883. A friend to all amongst the fishing and lifeboat fraternity. A strong swimmer he was south coast champion for the years 1879-1884. A stalwart of Eastbourne Swimming club for many years and involved with the local Lifeboat Institution by whom he was presented with a gold medal for his services. He was associated with the Sussex Mummers in the Christmas plays that they produced in the streets of Eastbourne prior to Christmas day. A regular on Jack Huggett's boat for the Christmas trips to the Lightship, he earned from Trinity House the right to board the Royal Sovereign Lightship at any time.

September 1936.

The Eastbourne Fishermen's and Boatmen's Protection Society held the very first Boatmen's Ran Dan race in September. A total of 12 boats entered crewed by members of the Society. Ran Dan rowboats had a staggered crew of 3 plus a Cox. Local nicknames and pseudonyms were adopted by the crews. In aid of Charities the races went on up to the 2nd World War.

November 1936. A liking for fish.

November saw the theft of a box of herring by John Smith and Henry Moon, the property of George Boniface of Channel View Road.

The same month fishermen Tom Prodger and Jack Bassett trawled up an old 300-year cannon in Pevensey Bay. It weighed 3-4 cwt, was 3 feet long. The muzzle contained a wooden plug. It was put on view at Sam Bustons shop in Seaside.

1937. Watch Committee minutes.

January. The tenant of the Rocket House is Arthur E Sayers.

May. Mr Ted Clark applied for the transfer of vacant capstan No.16. Granted.

March 1937.

22nd March and the opening of the Lifeboat Museum took place. The first curator was James 'Jimmy' Levoir an old sea salt born 1861, joined the Royal Navy 1877

CENTURIES-OLD GUN.—While trawling off Pevensey Bay Mr Tom Prodger and Mr Jack Basset " caught " a ship's gun several hundreds of years old. Mr Prodger is seen on the right of the picture which shows the gun encrusted with rock.

November 1936.

and on end of service joined the Coastguard thence on retirement he ran the Museum until his death in 1940.

Fisherman and Boatman Edward 'Ted' Walter Sayers died in the year 1937, aged 69 yrs of 39 Latimer Road. A well-loved character on Eastbourne's foreshore, he along with his brother Harry in 1901 began the well-known Boating firm Sayers Bros. Ted was actively connected with the old regattas and arranged 27 of them yearly without postponement. He left a widow, 5 sons and 3 daughters. Among those present including the Sayers family at the funeral were: William Allchorn, George Erridge Snr. and Jnr. John Colstick, E Godden, William Henry Bollard Hide, Fred Novis, Messrs Groom, Hurd, Chester, Ekins, Prodger and Jack Elms. The coffin was borne by Tom Allchorn, Harry Erridge, Jack Huggett, Jim Hardy, Jack Hardy and Albert Wood. Many more fishermen and boatmen lined the route from the Church. Another of Eastbourne's seafaring community gone.

1937.

The year of the coronation of George VI saw the Eastbourne fishermen and boatmen hold a special regatta. One of the competitions being a Coronation Ran Dan race. It was in a heavy sea that saw an exciting and close race with 9 entries. Result 1. A Addington, J Chester, F Erridge and G Erridge (cox). 2. G Prodger, G Erridge Jnr. E Clarke and C Prodger (cox). 3. E Huggett, R Steers, C Hurd and A Smith (cox).

Other results of races were Double sculls 1. Jack Huggett and George Smith. 2. C Wood and C Pack. 3.G Pollard and C Rayner.

An extra Ran Dan race with 6 entries was won by William Allchorn's crew. 1. T Allchorn, N Hurd, S Boniface and W Allchorn (cox). 2. J Chester, G Grooms, J

Grooms and W Grooms (cox). 3. M Hardy Jnr. G Sayers, H Hardy and Mike Hardy (cox).

1938. Watch Committee minutes.

June. Capstan No.35 vacant for a number of years was granted to W Erridge.

September. Application for capstans Nos.18 & 19 was made by Ernest Sayers. Henry Morgan Boniface who was leaving the town recently held them. (To take position as a Fisheries Officer)

December. Net shop No.42 and capstans Nos.24 & 34 owned by the late William Prodger were transferred to William Prodger.

December. Jesse Huggett was brought before the Committee due to a complaint from the Parade Inspector that he had sub-let Net shop No.12a to A Carter. This was against the regulations. Huggett was told to enter into a proper agreement. No action taken against Carter.

1939. Watch Committee minutes.

February. Jesse Huggett refused to agree to the above instruction. The Council resolved that unless Carter quit the Net shop Huggett be given notice to quit.

Further action was also taken regarding Net shop No.44. (See March 1936) occupied by H Dyer not a fisherman and not a tenant in respect of the Corporation he was given 14 days to quit. If not complied with Borough surveyor would remove the Net shop.

Net shop No.10 was transferred to Andrew Chester. An application was made by James Boniface for transfer of Net shop No.20. Arthur E Sayers tenant of the Rocket Apparatus House requested he sub-let it to Frank Smith, agreed, Smith granted tenancy.

March. Referring to H Dyer and Net shop No.44 the E.F.B.P. Society wrote a letter to the Committee stating that Dyer had never been a bona fide fisherman and had occupied the Net shop for many years without the knowledge or permission of the Corporation. The letter emphasised that use of land at the Fishing Station was restricted to men gaining a living from fishing. Dyer's notice to quit was delayed while further enquiries made.

Application was received to transfer Net shop No.38 from Arthur Sayers to Edwin H Sayers. Agreed.

May. The Council, Town Clerk and Chief Constable adhere to previous decision over Net shops regarding Huggett and Dyer.

October. An application by F Wyatt for the tenancy of the Rocket House was refused.

Chapter Twelve

Dunkirk, St. Valery and the Post War Years
Lifeboat Hero Tom Allchorn - The Rebuilding of the Fishing Station
Chesters - Last of the Fishing Families

1939. War begins.

As in the 1914-18 War many Eastbourne fishermen, boatmen and members of their families rushed to join the colours. But the horrors of war came quickly and sadness descended on the fishing community in October 1939, with the disastrous sinking of the battleship HMS Royal Oak at Scapa Flow.

Eastbourne men among the 900 lost were: -

AB. William Reed age 29, AB. William Carter age 22, Stoker George Pollard age 19, AB. Edward Coleman age 39, AB. Percy Colbran age 39, Boy Seaman George Standen age 16. AB. Charles Tester age 26.

Naval Chaplain lost was the Rev. James Cree whose mother lived at Lathom House, Howard Sq.

Known survivors were Boy Seaman Arthur Aldridge age 17 and AB. Albert Gearing age 38.

The Union flag flew at half-mast at the Fishermen's Institute in silent tribute to those of the fishing community and Eastbourners who lost their lives.

Another Eastbourne fisherman and boatman to pay the final sacrifice was Jesse Chester who went down with his ship the destroyer HMS Afridi when she was sunk in May 1940. Jesse a member of an old Eastbourne fishing family had previously had a lucky escape when in November 1939 the German ship 'Deutschland' sank the armed merchantman 'Rawalpindi'. Jesse was a member of that ship's company but shortly before the above action he had transferred to a captured Nazi merchantman as prize crew and was aboard her when the 'Rawalpindi' went down.

So England and the fishing community of Eastbourne were for the second time in 21 years placed in a state of war. Rationing came in very early and fisherman John Bassett was rationed to 18 gallons of petrol a month. *'Not enough,'* he said.

At a later Fisheries meeting it was put that, *'fishermen risks their lives to supplement the food supply yet motorists were getting petrol to use for leisure'.*

German submarines were active in the English Channel and off Eastbourne from 1939 and through most of the war years. As early as November 1939, from where the following 'tea' story comes the steamship 'Strydtvoorchristus' was torpedoed and sunk off Eastbourne. Dozens of chests of tea were washed ashore between the Pier and Pevensey Bay. The authorities issued this statement *'Tea once contaminated*

by sea water becomes poisonous' and a request was made for all tea salvaged from the shore to be taken to the destructor works to be burnt. As one can imagine what with rationing some of the tea found its way into homes, particularly of those folk that resided by the sea. One good lady on being told of the above warning produced a tin of the dried out tea and said with a smile, *'Yes, my son told me the Customs men told him the tea would kill in an hour after drinking. I had already enjoyed a cup ten hours before'.*

1940. Watch Committee minute.

January. Notice to quit Net shop No.12a was sent to Jesse Huggett terminating tenancy as Carter was still occupying the Net shop. Proceedings to be continued (the outcome of the Council's action against Dyer and Huggett is not known).

January 1940.

Among the Naval volunteers for service in Minesweepers were men of the fishing community some who had also served in the 1914-18 War.

Featured in the local paper at the time in answer to the Country's call were: -

George & Albert Wood, Arthur Clarence Hide, Charles Bishop, Patrick & James Jones, Fred Richardson, Jack Tuxford.

That same month 120 children of members of the Fishermen's Club enjoyed a party at the club premises. Fred Hurd was Father Christmas and great fun was had. Arrangements were in the hands of the following, Mr E Sayers (chairman), Mr E H Sayers (treasurer) and Mr C Young (secretary) assisted by the ladies section.

Fishermen join minesweepers.

On Saturday, 27th January the landlord of the 'Gildredge Hotel' Mr J Chilvers, honoured the lifeboat crew with dinner. There was no head table just a big square one. Served was a good old English dinner of boiled beef, Christmas pudding, cheese and biscuits and beer by the jug full. Among those present was Mr A Robertson. Hon Secretary of the local RNLI, Cox'n Mike Hardy, 2nd Cox'n Jack Huggett, Bowman Will Prodger, Tom Allchorn, Ernie Sayers, Fred Allchorn, Ed Matthews, George Boniface, Harry Thomas, Alec Huggett, Fred Novis, Mr E Verrall and Fred Clark. After the loyal toast, a toast was drunk to the absence of comrade Jack Tuxford who had gone minesweeping. Dinner over, there was humour and singing from Fred Clark, Jack & Alec Huggett. Cox'n Mike Hardy himself set them all going by singing: -

> *'We'll rant and we'll roar*
> *like true British Sailors,*
> *We'll rant and we'll roar*
> *across the blue sea,*
> *Until we strike soundings*
> *in the Channel of Old England.*
> *From Ushant to Scilly is thirty five leagues'.*

Perhaps the following once well-known local lifeboat ditty was sung? (Best sung with a liberal amount of beer flowing through the veins).

> *'Launch the lifeboat for my heart is brave and true,*
> *When dangers nigh, we'll all stand by,*
> *The Cox'n and the lifeboat crew,*
> *Heave Ho, Heave Ho,*
> *Launch the lifeboat for my heart is brave and true,*
> *When dangers nigh, we'll all stand by,*
> *The Cox'n and the lifeboat crew.*

March 1940.

The above crew were called upon to give one of their finest services in the 'Jane Holland' under Cox'n Hardy. The steamer 'Barnhill' was bombed a few miles off Beachy Head and set on fire. The lifeboat was launched just before midnight and reached the burning ship about 1.30am. 18 crew had already been taken off. The 'Jane Holland' took off a further 10 crew not without some danger from explosions and fire. Thinking this was all those on board, they were landed at Eastbourne but later at 5.00am it was reported that there was one injured man still aboard the burning vessel. The lifeboat launched again with a doctor aboard. Coming again to the stricken ship the seas were heavy and explosions and fires were still occurring. Bravely lifeboatmen Alec Huggett and Tom Allchorn volunteered to go aboard and search for the injured man. They were put aboard the 'Barnhill' by a Tug just as dawn was breaking. Making their way forward aboard the burning vessel and gaining some protection from the fire hose sprayed by the Tug, they came across the injured man who was the Ship's master, badly injured and semi conscious. Rendering first aid Huggett and Allchorn waited while Cox'n Hardy with skill and courage brought the lifeboat alongside the 'Barnhill'. With instructions from the Doctor the injured Master was lowered into the lifeboat and taken ashore. Altogether a worthy rescue in the tradition of the lifeboat service. The Master did

Alec Huggett Lifeboat man, Fisherman and Pleasure Boatman.

Thomas Allchorn Lifeboat man, Fisherman and Pleasure Boatman.

recover from his wounds. For their bravery, Alec Huggett and Tom Allchorn received the Lifeboat Institute's bronze medal; Coxswain Mike Hardy received a framed letter of appreciation and the crew awarded a total of £123

The steamship 'Barnhill' eventually went aground east of Langney Point and by April she had started to break up and some of her cargo in the form of label less tins of food flooded ashore. Warned not to salvage the tins the people of Eastbourne came in their hundreds and plundered the tins - a supplement for wartime rationing.

1940 also saw the banning of people from large areas of the Sussex foreshore and by June 1941, the only place sea bathing was allowed along the Eastbourne seafront was between the groynes opposite Lascelles Terrace and Howard Square - 100 yards in length, times daily 7 til 9.00am. Eventually the whole of the Eastbourne foreshore and parades were militarised and no sea bathing was allowed until near to the end of the war when bathing was allowed at the Holywell end of the seafront. Pleasure boating ceased for the duration of the war.

It should not go by without further mentioning Lifeboat Coxswain Mike 'Jersey Mike' Hardy of 75, Sidley Road, who became a long serving lifeboat man. An Eastbourne fisherman and pleasure boatman, it was in 1914 that Mike first served aboard the lifeboat then when war came later in that year he served in the Royal Navy aboard a minesweeper. In 1924 he became Cox'n serving until 1950 retiring at the age of 65 years. (5 years over the official retiring age).

He recalled *'When I started it was a pulling and sailing boat. Comparing the lifeboats now with those early craft is like comparing a wheelbarrow with a Rolls Royce'*.

Serving on 5 lifeboats he had been on 40 rescues in which more than 100 lives were saved. His proud boast was while Cox'n he *'never missed the boat'*.

After the episode with the 'Barnhill' Alec Francis Huggett fisherman and lifeboat man volunteered into the Royal Air Force and received an Officer's commission. The son of Mr and Mrs Jesse Huggett of Bay Cottage, Desmond Road, Alec served with distinction in Air Sea Rescue, with his knowledge of the sea being an asset to the service. For one action during a severe gale he received a mention in despatches for his skilful part in rescuing 5 men from a sinking vessel

April 1940.

William Henry 'Kilcraft' Erridge of 36, Eshton Road died 10th April 1940 aged 85 years leaving a widow of 79 years. A member of the lifeboat crew for some 40 years. He was a member of the famous

Michael 'Mike' Hardy, Lifeboat Coxswain, Fisherman and Pleasure Boatman.

'New Brunswick' rescue in 1883. He also survived being shipwrecked when he was skipper of the fishing vessel 'Linnet', being run down in the Channel by a steamship. His funeral was attended by the current crew of the lifeboat and his widow, Mrs Grey (daughter) Mr T Eade (Nephew) Mr Ben Erridge, Fred Erridge and Frank Erridge (nephews) Mr O Lansdell (nephew) and many others.

May 1940. Dunkirk.

The fishermen and boatmen of Eastbourne received an order from the Admiralty to proceed immediately with their fishing and pleasure boats to Dover on 30th May 1940 and there await orders for the evacuation of British forces from Dunkirk, France. It was 9.00pm when Eastbourne's little squadron set sail. Sayers Bros. sent the boats 'Britannia', 'Eastbourne Queen', and 'Grace Darling'. William Allchorn & Sons sent 'Enchantress' and 'Eastbourne Belle'. Henry Boniface sent 'Coronation' and fishing boat 'Commodore'. All manned by their Eastbourne crews they arrived at Dover at 6.00am, fully prepared to sail across the English Channel to take part in the evacuation and do their 'bit'.

The saga is continued by Ernest 'Glaxo' Sayers who on his return to Eastbourne said; *'We fully expected and wanted to take our boats across, but the Navy would have none of it. They commandeered our boats and that was that. They'll not get better boats, Tom Sisk and Roland Pragnell built them well'*.

It was to be the last voyages of 'Eastbourne Queen', 'Commodore' and 'Enchantress' - all being lost off Dunkirk. The Eastbourne lifeboat 'Jane Holland' was also commandeered and served at Dunkirk. She was badly damaged and initially abandoned there but was eventually towed back to Dover. Repaired, she went back into service at Eastbourne until 1949.

June 1940.

A week later Eastbourne fishermen and boatmen again answered their country's call. They sailed in an armada from Newhaven to take part in 'Operation Cycle' - the gallant action at St. Valery-en-Caux, Brittany, where an attempt was made to evacuate British and French troops. This time the intrepid Eastbourne men crewed their own open deck vessels across; other boats were manned by Naval ratings. Under the command of the Navy two days were spent with constant harassment from shelling and bombing attacks from enemy aircraft off St. Valery. They did indeed rescue some British and French soldiers successfully returning to Newhaven.

Eastbourne boats taking part in that gallant operations were: -

'Mizpah' 'Amaris' 'Golden City' 'Britannia III' 'Olive Joyce' 'Lady Doris' 'My Lassie' 'Hibernia' 'Albion' 'Ocean's Gift' 'Nona' 'Three Brothers' 'Hawfinch' 'Silver Spray' 'Ocean Spray' and 'Star of the East'.

Eastbourne men also crewed the Brighton boat 'Fair Irene'.

Those brave local men who took part in the operations were: -

Henry Erridge, Henry Boniface, Victor Crick, Albert Addington, George Henry Erridge, George John Erridge, Jack Allchorn, Edwin 'Ned' Sayers, Albert 'Sam' Allchorn, Ernest 'Glaxo' Sayers, William Sayers, Frederick Allchorn, Nelson Prodger, Nelson Sayers and Bevan Thornton.

On Wednesday afternoon 2nd July 1947, due recognition by the Council and people of Eastbourne was seen when these men were honoured with certificates of merit and the boats each received a bronze plaque bearing the legend 'St Valery 1940'. The presentation took place on the foreshore between the Pier and Bandstand - very apt. Some of

COUNTY BOROUGH OF EASTBOURNE

This is to Certify . . . .

that *George Erridge. Jnr.* of *473, Seaside, Eastbourne.* was a member of the crew of the M.V. *Amaris.* engaged in the evacuation of British Troops from St. Valery-en-Caux in June, 1940 (Operation "Cycle").

Mayor of Eastbourne

Certificate of Merit presented to George Erridge Jnr.

[Henry Charles] Erridge (decd.) | V. W. P. J. Crick | Alfred Frank Addington | George Henry Erridge | Henry Boniface | George John Erridge (decd.)

Jack Allchorn | Edwin Harold Sayers ("Ned") | Albert Edward Allchorn ("Sam") | Ernest Harold Sayers ("Glaxo") | William Walter Sayers

Heroes of St. Valery, 1940.

Frederick Allchorn | Nelson Prodger | Nelson Sayers | Bevan Thornton

these plaques can been seen to this day displayed in the Fishermen's Club, Royal Parade. Sadly both Henry and George John Erridge were unable to receive their due reward - both died before the end of the war.

Sea front out of bounds.

A curfew order was issued in July 1940 making the sea front out of bounds to the public between half an hour before sunset and half and hour before sunrise. These were the black out times. Beachy Head came within the above restrictions, no one being allowed on the seaward side of Dukes Drive and Warren Hill Road. People living on the parades had to obtain permits for the purpose of reaching their homes during the curfew hours. In December 1940 representations were made to the authorities by local fishermen in the hope that the ban on fishing be lifted soon, so that they could make a contribution to the town's food supplies and earn much needed money from their equipment lying idle.

June 1942.

Some Eastbourne fishermen were in the front line when in June 1942 they were attacked in their boat off Eastbourne. Three times an enemy aeroplane strafed the fishing boat containing the crew of Jack Huggett, Fred 'Tinker' Novis and Mickey Andrews. Huggett had shrapnel wounds to the shoulder, Novis was wounded in the shoulder and legs while Andrews had severe injuries to the stomach and leg, sadly losing a leg. What an experience for them, completely unarmed and at the mercy of the enemy. They were lucky to have survived with their lives.

Later in February 1944 fishermen from Pevensey Bay saved six American airmen from their ditched aircraft. The R.N.L.I. gave the fishermen a monetary award and they in turn gifted it back to the Institute. A fine gesture - it was reward enough for them to have saved the lives of their wartime allies.

1942. Watch Committee minute.

December. An application was received from Edwin H Sayers of 28, Latimer Road for transfer to him of Net shop No.53 presently held by Albert 'Tuppy' Sayers giving up due to advanced age. Edwin Sayers is a bona fide fisherman and owner of a large amount of fishing gear, as well as owner of a number of small pleasure boats. Granted.

John 'Jack' Prodger from the Eastbourne fishing family fished off Eastbourne during the 2nd World War being authorised to fish by Sussex Police under certain restriction as follows: He had access to the Fishing Station part of the beach from a point 130 yards from the west side of the Lifeboat house to No.3 Net shop. Times restricted to fish, sunrise until sunset and when weather conditions are such that there is visibility of not less than one mile and to be at his own risk. Jack kept a daily diary of catches, weather conditions and general happenings throughout the War years.

Father and son fishermen aboard 'Oceans Gift' C.1930, right John 'Foot' Prodger, left son John 'Jack' Prodger.

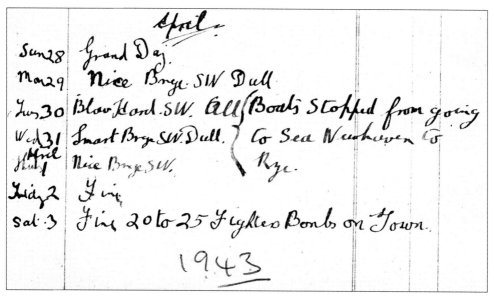

John 'Jack' Prodger's diary for April 1943. Eastbourne bombed.

1945. Watch Committee minutes.

March. Mrs Landsdell on behalf of her brother Frank Erridge made application for transfer to him of Net shop No.18.

December. An application from George H Erridge for transfer to him of Net shops Nos.22 & 22a and capstan No.13 from his late father George J Erridge was granted. An application from A W Erridge for transfer to him of Net shop No.19 and capstan No.18 tenanted by John J Prodger Jnr. granted. A W Erridge wished to relinquish tenancy of capstan No.20. This was granted.

The Committee discussed the tenancy of Net shop No.49 originally granted to Thomas Swain in 1928. As he does not now follow the occupation of fisherman the tenancy has to be determined.

January 1945.

In January, it was suggested in the local paper that the promenade be extended along past the Fishing Station removing or otherwise interfering with it. A letter of protest came back with the remark to leave well alone as the fishermen had a legal right to that area of beach.

May 1945.

May saw the first peacetime service of the Eastbourne lifeboat when she was called out to attend a capsized sailing boat. Later in October servicemen stationed in Eastbourne without the constraint of war caused problems on the beach damaging the rowboats of Fred Novis, George Grooms and Ned Sayers - drink being the underlying cause after the Pubs had closed.

August 1945.

With the end of the war in Europe and now Japan, Eastbourne fishermen held a meeting and decided to seek legal aid in their battle with the Government for compensation for losses due to the war. Eastbourne Fishermen's and Boatmen's Protection Society Hon. secretary A W Coppard said;

'Eastbourne fishermen have lost heavily over the war years. Boats damaged, property mined and wired off that it rotted away. Permits were needed to obtain material and were not forthcoming from the authorities. There was need to rebuild and earn a living'.

September 1945.

A subscription fund for the fishermen was raised through the local papers There was a dire need by them to replace lost equipment some which had been burnt by the over exuberant Victory celebration crowd who used it to fuel a bonfire held on the beach.

A cheque for £5 from the Misses Thornton started the fund.

Post War Years.

1946. Watch Committee minutes.

January. H Sayers of 76, Latimer Road applied on behalf of Messrs Sayers Bros for capstan No.35 at the Fishing Station. Granted.

May. A notice to quit Net shops Nos.29 & 30 had been served on the widow of Thomas Sisk but she had subsequently died. It was said that due to the dilapidated condition of the Net shops, they should be pulled down. Matter referred to Town Clerk.

May. Tenancy of Net shop No.49 and capstan No.43 was transferred from Thomas G Swain to Andrew Basil Chester.

November. Net shop No.16a and capstan No.14 tenanted by Frank Erridge of 51 Sidley Road and who has been called up to H M Service. Having sold his fishing boat and gear, wants to give up his tenancy. Mike F Hardy 75, Sidley Road bona fide fisherman, boatman and lifeboat Coxswain was granted tenancy.

February 1946.

The retirement of an old Eastbourne fisherman, boatman and lifeboat man Ernest 'Chinaman' Sayers, a member of the old Eastbourne seafaring family.

In the year of 1946, at the age of 86 years, Eastbourne's oldest fisherman, boatman and lifeboat man, Albert 'Tuppy' Sayers passed away. Related to Ernest, 'Tuppy' was born in the year 1860 in Eastbourne. A crewmember of the famous lifeboat rescue of 1883, another link with the old sailing days had gone.

June 1946.

Another link with the days of sail went in June that year with the death of fisherman and boatman Henry William Novis aged 82 years, the father of well-known and popular fisherman and boatman Fred 'Tinker' Novis. Henry along with other crew of the Eastbourne fishing Lugger 'Thistle' survived a severe storm at sea in the English Channel in 1893. The French fishing boat 'Avenir' skippered by the brave captain Papin rescued them.

After the war fishing took a downward trend. Mackerel fishing declined as prices for this fish went so low that it made it not worth catching. There was no incentive to drift net or long line for dogfish. Trawling for flat fish, plaice, soles etc, brought greater rewards. What with fuel rationing, times were not good for fishermen. The Sussex Fisheries District Committee protested to the Ministry of Food that housewives were unable to buy mackerel. In those days prices of foods were controlled. Fine really but as with the farmers who were financially subsidised, the fishermen also needed to have a living income but this was not the case. Chief Fisheries Officer Henry Morgan Boniface stated the present 3/3d a stone for mackerel should be at least 4/- to 5/- per stone.

Another problem facing the Sussex fishermen was the poaching carried out by foreign (French and Belgian) vessels, particularly in Rye Bay. The Royal Navy carried out constant patrols in 1946. Rye Bay, inside the 3-mile limit at the end of the war was rich in fish, sole, plaice etc. For the first two years of the war it had not been fished and then after only sparsely. As a Rye fisherman in 1947 put it *'It has been torn to pieces, what with the Frenchies and others'*.

With the added problem of wrecks of aircraft, ships and flying bombs the replacement cost of gear and a control price on top - all this did not help the fishermen's lot.

1947. Watch Committee minutes.

January. Tenancy of capstan No.43 was granted to Andrew B Chester of 11, Addingham Road. Net shops Nos.29 & 40 to be demolished and sold for timber. No.30 was demolished back in September 1946. (Thomas Sisk Net shop)

December. Fisherman John 'Jack' Prodger of 35, Seaford Road applied for the transfer to him of Net shops Nos.7 & 16 and capstans Nos.4 & 5 due to the death of his father John 'Foot' Prodger.

March 1947.

At the age of 83 years, fisherman and boatman Alleyn Nelson 'Old Rig' Sayers died at his home 48, Latimer Road. He was at the time Eastbourne's oldest fisherman and boatman, a title previously held by Albert 'Tuppy' Sayers. The title then went to Joe Prodger who was 82 years old. All of them belonged to the age of sail and their fishing expeditions took them away from home for a month at a time especially when they made trips to the Irish coast. They were the days when pleasure sailing boats lined the Grand and Royal Parades. Joe Prodger the new title holder served with Alleyn Sayers and Alleyn used tell the tale of when he had to 'fish' Joe out of the water with a boat hook, Joe having fallen overboard. Alleyn Sayers owned many sailing vessels that included 'The Pet', 'Runaway Girl', 'Noreen' and 'The Scout'. On the beach with his bearded profile he was always a great attraction to holidaymakers who liked to photograph him.

A skilled boatman Alleyn was renowned for skippering the sailing boat 'Delphine' in races against Arthur Matthews in his boat 'Royal Albert' in the years 1887, 1888 and 1889. Alleyn won them all. The boats were Lugger rigged, 'Delphine' being a 20 footer and 'Royal Albert' 22 feet in length. The 'Royal Albert' was 36 years old having been built by William Simpson in 1852. Many of his friends were present at the funeral and formed a guard of honour at the entrance to Langney Chapel. His nephew Stanley George of HMS Marlborough gave the salute. Owing to illness his widow was unable to be present. Family mourners included sons, Ned, Nelson and Arthur, brothers Ernie and Harry, nephews Stan Sayers and Stanley George and cousins Bill and Jack Sayers. Also present were Henry M. Boniface, George Boniface (chairman Eastbourne Fishermen's and Boatmen's Protection Society), William Allchorn, Tom Prodger, Fred Hurd and others from the fishing community.

July 1947.

The question was raised with the Council over the fishermen's red lamp at the Fishing Station put out of action during the war for security reasons. It had been previously maintained by the Council and not yet restored. The fishermen thought it would be a great asset if it were put back and essential when fishing at night. The lamp and mast were later put in place powered by electricity and remained in place until the Fishing Station was cleared and rebuilt c.1970. The lamp was then placed on Allchorn's big boat shed, but with the opening of the Harbour/Marina and moving of boats down there the lamp ceased to function and has not operated since. Just a few boats still operate off the Fishing Station beach these days 2009.

November 1947.

A report on local fishing in November 1947 showed fishermen at Eastbourne being forced out of business due to the high price of gear, nets, equipment and the price control of fish out of all proportion to their heavy losses. Eastbourne had but one tenth of its pre-war fishing fleet. Since the end of the war it was estimated that over thirty fishermen have been forced out of business and turned to other employment. The hard fact was that there remained only a few Eastbourne families wholly engaged in fishing. Namely; Chester, Huggett, Prodger, Erridge, Boniface, Hurd and the Pleasure boating and fishing families of Allchorn, Sayers, Boniface, Hardy, Novis, Grooms and in the end only the Allchorns 'Pleasured'.

The years were long gone when the Eastbourne fishing fleet was away for weeks at a time, going as far as the Irish Channel and landing their catch in Ireland. The price of new gear was 400 per cent over pre-war prices. Gear losses were heavy particularly between Newhaven and Rye as the seabed was littered with the wreckage from the war. This made trawling a hazardous task especially with unexploded ordnance on the seabed. Trawl nets could be ruined in single trip or even lost altogether.

Where the whole family were engaged in fishing many skilled hands soon made a new trawl but this did not offset the cost of rope, twine, cork, etc. Only those families with some finance behind them could carry on. For some, better the option to change occupations, take an easier course - sell up and become a labourer at £5 per week. For those men whose families with a tradition of earning a living from the sea for centuries, it was hard indeed. So the fishing community families of Eastbourne were gradually disappearing. The individual man took up fishing and indeed always will, but this never then nor ever will compensate for the loss of the traditional fishing family that blessed Eastbourne's foreshore for hundreds of years.

1948. Watch Committee minutes.

Applications now being referred to the Entertainment and Pleasure Ground Committee.

June. The transfer of Net shop No.23a was granted to Reginald Boniface.

October. With reference to the above it was decided that R Boniface may sub-let part of the Net shop to H J Boniface who is a bona fide fisherman.

December. The tenancy of Net shop No.20 held by J Boniface was transferred to John Bassett, bona fide fisherman.

1948.

618 cwt of fish valued £1,916 and 1949 - 939cwt value £2,037 was caught by Eastbourne fishermen.

1949. E & P Ground Committee minutes.

January. Parade Inspector Humphrey reported to the Town Clerk from information received that a vast majority of tenants of Net shops at the Fishing Station do not in fact earn their living wholly or primarily from fishing. (Year 1948 minutes above show an emphasis on 'bona fide' fishermen).

An application from Jack Allchorn and Stan G Sayers to swap Net shops Nos.43 and 44. Not granted.

January. An application was made by Henry Boniface for transfer to him of Net shop No.14 and capstan No.11 from Henry 'Dusty' Matthews. Boniface had already purchased above from Matthews. Transfer subject to the approval of Entertainment & Pleasure Ground Committee. (E&PGC)

March. Net shop No.14 and capstan No.11 to be transferred to William Smith 53, Bexhill Road from Henry Boniface. Smith had purchased a boat to fish.

April. Net shop No.14 and capstan No.11 transfer was completed.

May. March transfer noted by E&PGC.

June. The firm of Smith and Gibbs boat builders and repairers applied for a site at the Fishing Station. They were offered the tenancy of a site for 10/- per week.

July. An application by Edwin Sayers for capstan No.28 at Fishing Station was granted. Sayers had two Net shops.

Among the fishermen in the post war years at the Fishing Station, and well towards to the turn of the century could be found names such as Ted 'Cherry' Bradford, John Bassett a Coxswain of the lifeboat, Jack Hastings, 'Goosy' Wood, William 'Booner' Wood, Ron Wood, Harold and Stan Fox, Dick Hegarty, Neville Dean, Denzil Phillips and his son Roy, Graham Cole a Coxswain of the lifeboat, Sam Mottram, Roy Andrews, Brian Skinner and of course Sayers, Boniface, Allchorn, Erridge, Prodger, Chester, Huggett, Howell, Hurd, Pragnell and others with a touch of the sea about them. Sad to say not to be found on the beach these days.

An article in the Sussex County Magazine 1950 by W. d'Ivry Oakeshott sums up well the decline of the Sussex fishing industry and an insight into earlier days.

'It is a story of a twofold struggle - man against nature and man against man. Throughout the centuries the fight has been going on and while, in the case of man, it has been possible to take some sort of counter action, nature has proved unpredictable. An example of the tricks that nature can play is contained in a recent

report to the local committee of the Sussex Sea Fisheries. 'Drift-net fishing for herrings,' states the Chief Fishery Officer, Henry Morgan Boniface (a member of the old Eastbourne fishing family) 'has again been very disappointing. This is the fifth successive season during which the fish has failed to arrive in the due season. Before the war, the herring arrived with great regularity during early November and were found to be in considerable concentration from two to three miles from the shore until spawning took place just before Christmas. For some unknown reason, the herring has been inclined to concentrate along the French side of the English Channel and only on very few occasions have our boats been successful in taking even very moderate catches'.

'What is the remedy? It is for the fishermen to go after the herring - subject, of course, to the rules governing territorial waters - as they have done for hundreds of years past'.

'The search for more rewarding fishing grounds has gone on since the middle of the 7th century when, as legend has it, St. Wilfrid taught the South Saxons (Sussex folk) how to use nets. By the time the Normans came, the industry was well established and the Brighton and Eastbourne areas were producing large catches of herring and mackerel. Much was for local consumption, some going inland for sale.

The habits of the fish and their unwillingness to stay in one place indefinitely took the growing Lugger fleets further and further a field. Thus, in the 1400's, the Rye, Hastings and Eastbourne men used to regularly sail to the East Anglian coasts in search of herring and this they continued to do into the late 1800's.

In spite of the problems of road communication, the industry did reasonably well and in the 1700 - 1800's there was a flourishing trade between the Channel coast and London. Indeed, special provision was made in an Act of Parliament, exempting from toll on a turnpike road horses and drivers taking fish to London and returning.

But the fishing trips into the fishing grounds of the North Sea were plagued from time to time with battles against French boats, which not only 'poached' in English waters, but fished with nets of an illegally small mesh. In addition the fishermen had to fight armed privateers so much so that during the reign of Elizabeth I the Channel fishermen petitioned for protection.

The 1700's and 1800's also saw fishermen supplementing their income with smuggling, this was a profitable sideline although catches of herring and mackerel were their income mainstay. The late 1700's saw the health resort of Eastbourne start to attract visitors and pleasure boating began to cater for their needs. Summer months saw fishing boats renovated and adapted to take them to sea for pleasure and rowboats for hire. It became quite a living.

In the 1870's there were estimated to be 2,000 fishermen and 208 boys in Sussex. In 1875 it is recorded that 1,094 tons of fish were taken by rail to London. The 1880's were a booming time for the big Lugger fleets that went on fishing expeditions but these had dropped away by 1900'.

(Eastbourne then contained a large percentage of Lugger rigged 3rd class boats with 2-3 crew of up to 3-ton un-decked sprat punts, usually being ideal for use in the *summer pleasure boating business. In 1905 the value catch of fish at Eastbourne was recorded as £2,256).*

Many factors had changed up to 1950; The varying price of fish, the increased cost of boats and gear, the virtual suspension of operations during both world wars and the increase of shipping traffic in the Channel making for greater pollution of the water and of course with the increasing population, the discharge of sewage. More important still perhaps is the fact that the internal combustion engine was adapted to boats gradually from 1900 and provided more opportunity to fish and overfish the grounds. With no problems of waiting for the tide and wind, putting to sea became somewhat easier.

In 1950 just 10 boats operated from the Fishing Station at Eastbourne.

1950. Entertainment & Pleasure Ground Committee minutes.

February. Messrs Smith and Gibbs finalised and took up a site.

March. A request by R A Hegarty for the transfer to him of Net shop No.23a and capstan No17 was granted. He was a full time bona fide fisherman.

June. It was discussed in Committee proposals to change/move/ update the Fishing Station. Plans were afoot for a new Fishing Station to replace the present run down one but the Town Clerk Frank Busby said the plans had not yet been approved and should be submitted as a Private Bill in Parliament.

Mr Frank Smith and Mr Fred Gibbs had made an application to build a boathouse for their business to be included in the plans. It was stated that 70% of their work included boatbuilding and repairs to fishing craft and 30% in respect of pleasure craft. The application was approved in principle to be included in the new plans.

But it was to be many years before the new Fishing Station was completed and it is not known whether Smith and Gibbs got their custom built boathouse?

One of Eastbourne's Lifeboat Heroes.

31st December 1950, Thomas 'Tom' Allchorn aged 49 years, fisherman, pleasure boatman and lifeboat man was elected by ballot to take over as Coxswain of the Eastbourne lifeboat 'Beryl Tollemache' succeeding the retiring Mike Hardy. A popular member of the crew with 20 years previous experience 'Tom' held the Lifeboat Institute's bronze medal for bravery in the 'Barnhill' rescue 1940.

After landing from a sprat fishing trip he went to the Lifeboat Station where he was elected Coxswain. Then after congratulations from the crew he went back to finish shaking out from his nets some 40,000 - 50,000 sprats.

Two of Tom's brothers were in the crew, Jack 2nd mechanic and Fred radio operator aged 60 and oldest member of the crew. A married

'Tom' Allchorn, Coxswain Eastbourne Lifeboat.

SS Germania aground at Beachy Head, May 1955.

man with two children, Tom was one of five brothers who operated the biggest pleasure boat 'William Allchorn' on the beach along with the 'Eastbourne Belle' and 'Enchantress' two of their other boats.

Tom's position in the lifeboat required full time attention and was a gruelling task often fraught with danger. Five years later in May 1955, Tom and his crew of the lifeboat 'Beryl Tollemache' were put to the supreme test when after a six hour battle in gale force winds and heavy seas they saved and brought ashore the crews of two fishing boats and a group of salvage men aboard the wrecked steamer 'Germania'

The drama unfolded due to the foundered 'Germania' being on the rocks with a broken back below the foot of Beachy Head some time previous to the incident. A salvage crew worked aboard and off loaded cargo into hired fishing vessels. Then came that day in May with the worsening of the weather things became very dangerous and the lifeboat was called out. After rescuing the crews of the fishing boats that were drifting helplessly before the storm and landing them at the Fishing Station, 'Beryl Tollemache' sustained a damaged starboard prop shaft but nevertheless when called upon to return to the 'Germania' she did so without question. The 'Germania' with a broken back was being battered by heavy seas putting the salvage crew aboard in great danger. The 'Beryl Tollemache' arrived just as the Birling Gap and Eastbourne rocket life-saving apparatus crews on the cliff top were preparing to take off men from the 'Germania' by breeches buoy. The Eastbourne crew had managed with great difficulty to get a line to the 'Germania', darkness was falling and with a gale force wind it was a fine effort by them. The transfer was fraught with danger but the 'Beryl Tollemache' saved the day as her lights showed those on the cliff top she was approaching. Handled with great skill she went alongside the stricken vessel and with the aid of the beam of the searchlight from the cliff top the salvage men were rescued.

Of the rescue Cox'n Tom Allchorn said, *'I never thought we would get them off. With the sea that was running it was a miracle how they managed to scramble down the rope ladder into the boat'*. The saved men were landed at 10.00pm.

This was the second service in ten days to the 'Germania'. When she first went aground on the rocks in heavy seas the 'Beryl Tollemache', Tom and his crew kept a 26 hour vigil alongside, eventually, under extreme worsening conditions, rescuing the crew.

In recognition of both services Tom was awarded by the Lifeboat Institute, a second service clasp to his medal (awarded 1940) and the Maud Smith award for the bravest act of life saving for the year 1955. The perilous magnitude of the situation and Tom's courageous seamanship and endeavour is borne out by the Institute's awards. The presentations were made by the Duchess of Kent.

Tom retired from lifeboat service in 1961 aged 60 and worked for some time with the family pleasure boat business. He died aged 70 years at his home 39, Ringwood Road. At his funeral the coffin was draped with the Lifeboat flag and lifeboat men led by Coxswain Derek Huggett formed a guard of honour. Family mourners were Mrs P Allchorn, widow, Mr and Mrs A Allchorn, son and daughter in law, Mr and Mrs M Hobbs, daughter and son in law, Mr and Mrs A Allchorn, brother and sister in law, Mrs L Bradford, sister, Mr P Povey, brother in law, Mrs F Allchorn, sister in law, Mr B Allchorn, nephew and Mrs Allchorn, Mr C Allchorn, nephew and Mrs Allchorn. Also present Mr and Mrs H V Hobbs, Mr and Mrs R Walter, Mr W Wood, Mr R Wheeler and Mr V Hunnisett.

1951.

The Sussex Sea Fisheries Committee made a complaint in 1951 about the unfair competition between Sussex and foreign Belgian and French fishermen. Their vessels were using small meshed nets and were denuding the Channel of immature fish to the eventual detriment of our fishermen. Another serious problem was the delineation of the 3-mile limit. The existing limits followed the coastline, the Belgian and French vessels being within their rights to fish several miles inside Rye Bay. It was suggested that the 3-mile limit be based on a line drawn from headline to headline. Would the Belgian and French agree? - Never. (Whatever mile limit was in operation it had never bothered them over the centuries and they had continually 'poached', having scoured their own inshore waters of any size fish. A typical 'dog in the manger' attitude)

With the coming of the European Community and Britain joining in 1973 the Belgian and French fleets ignored our 6-mile limit and fishing stocks suffered. Successive governments have 'shared' our fishing grounds with our 'European friends'. Quota systems were brought in but ignored by the French and by the winter of 1980-81 a great problem faced the local fishermen. 'All take and no give' not helped by some British fishermen who sold their boats and quotas to the foreigner. British traditional fishing grounds are still in crisis. The year 2000, Herring, Sprat, Cod and many other species banned from being caught or catches seriously restricted. Up to the present day (2009) the situation is still dire.

1954.

The symbol of the trade, of the thigh booted old salt mending his nets on the foreshore had long gone by the 1970's. Drifting and long lining had now gone, trawling being the greater part of fishing - a bad thing for the inshore grounds.

And so the sorry story continued with a report in the local press in 1954.

'Since the end of the war matters had become progressively worse and unless the Government subsidised the fishermen as they did the farmer, the fishermen of England may become a thing of the past. Mr Andrew Chester Snr. with 38 years fishing experience said that nets could be bought at 16s to 18s each before the war, now they were over £4 each. Each year a boat must be provided with about 12 new nets, and each boat uses 50 nets. High prices and poor seasons are the main cause of the dwindling of the industry locally. 'Longshore fishing will die right out unless the Government does something about the high prices fishermen have to pay for nets and other materials,' Mr Chester declared. The subsidy on fish is on the catch or no pay system. Fishermen get 10d per stone of fish caught and gutted, and 8d on fish caught but ungutted. If they catch nothing due to bad weather or lack of fish, they get nothing. The farmer, however, gets a subsidy on land sowed whether his harvest is a success or not, Mr Chester pointed out'.

An equally gloomy picture was painted in the annual report of the Sussex Sea Fisheries local committee, which stated as far as herring fishing was concerned, *'today, there is only a skeleton of the considerable fleet of inshore drifters. The price of gear made it impossible for small owners to equip for fishing'.*

But in 1954 all had not gone, there were still some Sussex longshore fishermen that kept a scrap or two of herring net, though hardly worthwhile. They combined herring fishing in its brief season with shellfish potting and trammelling. Sometimes they got herring in the trammels (nets of double mesh). Hauling a net out of the North Sea at 3 o'clock on an October morning with a steam winch is grim work. Manhandling a net in a twelve-foot boat in November, in the ever-vicious cold sea off Beachy Head isn't too clever as is said. With the cry of 'Up, up, up' as the net is hauled in and the silver fish with scales of mother of pearl come aboard.

1960. E & P Ground Committee minutes.

February. Mr Alan Pitcher terminated his tenancy agreement at the Fishing Station of Net shop No.2 and capstan No.1a.

The 5th Eastbourne St Mary's Scout Group requested the use of a Net shop for storing of boats etc. The Town Clerk pointed out the legal position to the Committee re. Net shops at the Fishing Station. (For use of bona fide fishermen and boatmen only).

But is was resolved by the Committee that an agreement with the Scouts for a Net shop would be granted, with one months notice at 5/- per annum.

The Town Clerk reported that Mr John Bassett tenant of Net shop No.20 was using a capstan for which there was no agreement in force. It was resolved that Mr Bassett be required to enter into an agreement in respect of the capstan sited in front of his Net shop at 2/6d per annum.

A discussion took place regarding the use of the beach near Princes Park for amateur and part time fishermen. There had been an agreement in 1951 with the Association of Boat owners for the use of groynes Nos.4 & 5 (East Sussex River Board groynes).

The Parade Inspector stated this section of the beach had not been used by the Association for 2-3 years. It was then resolved that the Town Clerk be authorised to give amateur and part time fishermen and the boat owners Association notice of terminating the agreement with regard to this section of the beach.

The local Chamber of Commerce suggested a concrete slipway be built.

March. Mr Alan Pitcher gave notice of terminating the agreement for Net shop No.44.

April. Eastbourne Sea Cadet Corps who used the R N V R premises as HQ for Training Ship H M S Marlborough requested a lease of 3 Sheds to the south west side of their HQ, for a period of 7 years. Granted at a fee of 1/- per annum.

May. Eastbourne Rowing Club requested to lease the Rocket House. Request was denied as it was used as a store by the Council.

With reference to the proposed slipway, the Town Clerk said that the fishermen and boatmen had not been consulted. A site suggested was adjacent to the Seaplane sheds site. (At that time still standing and used by the Tramway Company. Then later demolished and the Leisure swimming centre built on the site).

March 1961.

An application by B Grant of Pevensey Bay to place a boat at the Fishing Station for fishing was deferred.

June 1962. E & P Ground Committee minutes.

Fishing Station. The Town Clerk submitted an application from Mr A B Chester for tenancy of the capstan between his Net shop and the Lifeboat slipway. It was resolved that the Chairman be given power to act in dealing with this application, subject to the General Manager's enquiries that the application be bona fide. Agreement to be prepared by the Town Clerk. The Town Clerk read a letter from Mr J Venus for permission to place his fishing boat on the beach at the Fishing Station.

Both above requests were granted.

July. The Town Clerk referred to a report by the Parade Inspector following his enquiries at the Fishing Station over a long period. It appears the Fishing Station had fallen into part disuse and for wrong use as laid down in the original agreement. Time was coming to demolish and re-develop. The Town Clerk then reported on the legal position and the Committee then resolved that the Town Clerk terminate agreements in respect of Net shops Nos. 3, 4, 6, 8, 9, 11a and 12.

September. The Town Clerk referring to the decisions of the July meeting read letters received from Mr William H Wood asking that his eldest son be permitted to take over tenancy of Net shop No.4 and Mr Mike F Hardy also asking that his son be permitted the tenancy of Net shops occupied by himself. A decision was put back until October.

October. The Committee having inspected the Fishing Station resolved that consideration would be given to improve its appearance.

Mr Mike F Hardy's request reference Net shops Nos.8 & 11a not granted and proceedings to be taken to recover possession. (Reason not given) Mr William W Wood's request was granted subject to a new agreement with his son William Wood Jnr. and subject to repair or rebuilding Net shop No.4. The Town Clerk reminded the Committee that he had been authorised to terminate agreements for Net shops Nos.9 & 12 occupied by J Huggett. He stated that Mr Neville Dean who earned his living from fishing had made application for the tenancy of Net shops Nos.9 & 12. Granted as long he as puts the Shops into a reasonable state of repair.

November. Fishing Station. The Town Clerk submitted an interim report on the Fishing Station giving particulars of tenancies and conditions of every Net shop, capstan, winch and winch hut. The report disclosed the following:

a) It was evident that some Net shops were being used either by unauthorised persons or for unauthorised purposes and action should be taken at once to secure the Net shops, where vacated and removed.

b) In a few cases the tenants or trespassers had left or would shortly leave the Net shops and a supplementary estimate of £116 was required so that the premises could be demolished at once.

c) That clearance work on a large scale must be carried out. £832 should be included as a specific item of expenditure for next year. Authorization was requested from the Committee to terminate agreements in respect of Net shops Nos.14, 20, 21, 25 and 42 also capstan stands used with them.

(The Council was determined to clean up the Fishing Station site, which can only be blamed on the fishermen themselves. They knew the regulations, the Net shops were only for fishermen but it could be supposed with few taking up the occupation an income could be gained by illegally sub-letting and in some case selling with no notification to the Council. Although some fishermen did maintain their Nets shops to a high standard, others did not. No sign of the E.F.B.P. Society involvement yet, but they surely would be)

1963. E & P Ground Committee minutes.

April. The Town Clerk reported that within his department, research had been carried out into the history of the Fishing Station and he submitted a summary of information obtained. He referred to the legal complexities on which opinion of G H Newsom QC had been obtained. The Town Clerk explained the views given by the QC that it would appear possible to provide premises for bona fide fishermen and boatmen on half of the present Fishing Station area. If suitable accommodation and facilities were available, thereby allowing the remaining half (western section) to be used for other purposes. To achieve this objective it would be necessary to negotiate with the Trustees of the Gilbert Estate and Chatsworth Estate Settlement and the fishermen and boatmen whose licences were determined. The Committee resolved that the Town Clerk be authorised to negotiate with the above with a view to reducing the Fishing Station to approximately half, thereby releasing the remainder of the area for uses consistent with the development and improvement of the seafront.

September. Fishing Station. The Town Clerk reported on his discussions with the Gilbert and Chatsworth Trustees and they were happy to transfer the land in question to the Corporation for development as they saw fit. (The original agreement over the land at the Fishing Station was, when no longer required or not used by the fishermen the land would revert to original owners, the Gilbert and Chatsworth Estates).

The Borough Surveyor had submitted a plan indicating a way that the released land might be used. One idea was to construct a Children's centre on the area of the net drying grounds. He further reported that all bona fide fishermen and boatmen could be provided with reasonable accommodation on the section of the Fishing Station, east of Beach Road in the event of the re-development of the Fishing Station. It was resolved to go ahead and that the Eastbourne Fishermen's and Boatmen's Protection Society be thanked for its co-operation.

The E.F.B.P. Society having the freehold of their Club premises and some land, were in a strong negotiating position regarding the development and had agreed to compromise over the land under their control by moving their premises and ceding some land to the Council. They would demolish the old Institute (Fishermen's Club) and design a new one to be built with assistance from the Council.

They agreed to the demolition of the Net shops and in their place would be brick customs built Net shops to accommodate those few fishermen left. (The result can be viewed to this day).

A sub committee of Albert 'Sam' Allchorn, Dick Hegarty, Fred Erridge and Andrew B Chester was formed to liaison with the Council over the proposed plans and from then on it was hard work but it bore fruit when finally the new Club premises were completed by the end of February 1967 and officially opened by Club President Eric Owen on 9th March.

October. Parade Inspector W R Edwards tendered his resignation to take effect from December after 4¹/₂ years in the job.

November. The Town Clerk reported that the Children's Playground would hopefully be built by April 1964 and the Committee generally agreed to go ahead with the development of the Fishing Station area.

December. Mr Arthur Roland Ricketts was appointed Parade Inspector.

1964. E & P Ground Committee minutes.

January. A plan drawn up by the Borough Surveyor re. the Fishing Station development was submitted to the Committee with the proposed erection of 10 Net shop buildings for the fishermen and boatmen east of Beach Road and new sites earmarked for the Fishermen's Club, Angling Club, Sea Cadets and car parks. Estimated cost for the Net shops £24,000. Building a sea wall was proposed but not proceeded with. Details of the letting of Net shops was approved with the agreement of E.F.B.P. Society and adopted.

July. Further plans were submitted by the Borough architect showing the layout of the new Fishing Station and remaining Net shops to be demolished. Nos.1, 4, 16, 16a, 17, 18, 19, 20, 21, 35, 40, 41, 47 and 48. The Erridge concrete Net shop to be left on site (still there to this day next to the Fish sales shop)

November. The estimated cost to build the Net shops had risen to £29,000.

1965. E & P Ground Committee minutes.

January. It was decided to have corrugated asbestos roofs for the Net shops.

February. The Town Clerk reported to the Committee that a total of 9 new Net shops would be built on land originally granted by the late Mr Gilbert to the Corporation for use as Fishing Station. This land was subject to rights of reverter to the Trustees of the Gilbert Estate in the event of it ceasing to be used as a Fishing Station. Although it might be many years before the land in question ceased to be used as a Fishing Station the Trustees were willing to release their rights of reverter at this stage, subject to a requirement that the plans of buildings proposed to be erected should be submitted to the Trustees for their approval. It was resolved by the Committee that the Town Clerk complete a Deed of Release on the terms indicated.

It was also resolved that the remaining 9 fishermen and boatmen be granted 5 years leases on the new Net shops and assistance be given in moving into them.

The Fishermen's Club proposed new premises were submitted for approval.

March. E.F.B.P Society Club premises plans approved.

April. Permission was given to Allchorn Bros to place a 1000gallon diesel tank alongside their present premises at the Fishing Station. A proposal to build a new Sea Cadet HQ on the Tennis Courts, Royal Parade was not granted.

1966. E & P Ground Committee minutes.

January. Provision made in revenue estimate for years 1966-67 for renewal of Net shops.

1967. E & P Ground Committee minutes.

February. A proposal was made by the E.F.B.P. Society on behalf of member Mr J Venus to erect a winch stand 8ft x 5ft x 4ft high. This would be temporary pending building of Net shops on the northeast section of the Fishing Station.

March. Referring to the above, Mr Venus had been fishing regularly for 5 years and earned his living as a fisherman. A licence to erect a winch stand had been granted to Venus in 1962. This winch stand had been removed the same time as old Net shop No.13 had been demolished. Venus had a 30ft diesel driven fishing boat and was hoping to be granted a lease of a new Net shop when they were built.

April. The Town Clerk reported that capstan No.27 had belonged to the late Fred Novis and was now being used by Mr H Cherry. This capstan was due to be demolished and Cherry given 3 months notice to remove his boat and capstan. He was granted permission to beach his boat east of Princes Park. Annual fee 21/-.

November. The Borough Architect submitted a revised plan of the Fishing Station indicating sites of 6 new Net shops to be let to the fishermen and boatmen. He stated that since the original layout was prepared the demand for 10 had reduced to 6 Net shops.

1968. E & P Ground Committee minutes.

April. An application was made by Mr L W Gallard to erect a winch stand at the Fishing Station. He would be engaged fishing full time at the end of April. The E.F.B.P. Society supported his request. Gallard had enquired about renting one of the new Net shops to be erected. A winch stand licence was granted.

October. The Town Clerk read a letter from Ross Group Ltd, which stated that one of their subsidiary companies John Dryden & Co Ltd, had a licence to use the Fish Market on the Fishing Station under terms of an agreement.

1969. E & P Ground Committee minutes.

March. Fishing Station. New premises would be provided for Messrs Allchorn on the eastern section. A large Net shop was required; they would then be able to move their boats and equipment to the new site. At present Allchorns had boat sheds next

to the site of the proposed new Angling Club. (A big Net shop No.5 was built to accommodate the Allchorn pleasure boats 'William Allchorn' and Southern Queen' and is still there to this day).

April. The Pier speedboat operator M R Poolman was given permission to place a fuel tank at the Fishing Station. Fishermen Mr D E Eade and Mr V Hunnisett were given permission to install a winch at the Fishing Station. It was agreed that Mr J Venus would use the Allchorn winch until they moved to their new premises.

September. The Eastbourne Herald announced the following report on the Fishing Station. A total of £62,000 was to be spent over 3 years on redevelopment between the Fish Market and Tanhouse Groyne. 5 new Net shops and a new boathouse (Allchorn's) to be erected. The fishermen and boatmen were anxious, having

Albert 'Sam' Allchorn, Pleasure Boatman, Fisherman and Lifeboat man.

Pleasure Boatmen, sons of 'Sam' Brian on left with brother Colin 1986.

The Chester family. Left to right, Andrew Jesse, Roy William, Andrew Basil and Andrew William.

NN31 'Olive Joyce' coming ashore 1936. She served at the St.Valery, France evacuation, 1940.

agreed to a substantial reduction in the area available for their purposes, that there should not be any further loss. It was the net drying area under discussion that the Council wanted to take over and sought agreement with the Eastbourne Fishermen's and Boatmen's Protection Society Club Ltd. They wanted this area kept available for the use of bona fide fishermen and boatmen. This did not happen.

So by 1972 the new Net shops were built and a smaller Fishing Station was functioning. New Sea Cadet HQ, Angling Club premises were built followed by the Children's Playground plus an adjoining car park on what had been the fishermen's net drying area, consigned to history.

February 1975.

The death occurred in February of 77-year-old Albert 'Sam' Allchorn, fisherman, boatman and lifeboat man. Another of the Allchorn stock who had spent his life on Eastbourne beach and devoted himself to the Eastbourne Fishermen's and Boatmen's Protection Society and Club, a founder member he served as Trustee, President, Chairman, Hon Secretary, committee member guiding the Club through to see new premises built, carrying on a tradition that started with his forebears back to 1839 when the 'East-Bourne Fishermen's Compensation Fund Society' was formed. The last remaining son of William Allchorn, he joined the well-known Allchorn boating firm during the 1st world war. During the 2nd World War he was one of the local boatmen who helped to evacuate soldiers from St.Valery, France. A notable figure to be seen on the seafront giving trips to visitor and local persons aboard the Allchorn boats. *'Sam Allchorn was a great character known by everyone on the beach, up the front, or at the Fishing Station'.* 'Sam' left a widow Pansy and sons Brian and Colin both boatmen of Eastbourne.

Possibly the last Eastbourne fishing community family to fish were the Chester brothers Andrew Basil and Roy. Long established fishermen, the Chesters also ran a Fishmongers shop, Andrew Chester & Sons from 1956. This had started life as 'Bustons' c.1880 in Seaside, situated between the then White Hart pub and Gaiety Cinema. When in 1968 the brothers retired from fishing following the death of Andrew William Chester, they continued to trade from the shop until 1993.

The Chester family go back a long way in the fishing history of Eastbourne. As an example Ralph Ravenshear columnist with the Eastbourne Herald wrote a fine obituary to Andrew William Chester (1878-1968) when he passed away in June 1968 aged 90 years at his home in Penhale Road, just yards away from the Fishing Station.

'He built a reputation around his name during more than 60 years active work at sea that will live long in the memories of the local seafaring community. He left school at the age of 13 years in order to go to sea and earn his living. While in his teens he rowed the 8 miles out to the Royal Sovereign lightship on fishing trips. Sea fishing was his life and even in his leisure hours he was always at sea. He was a member of the Eastbourne lifeboat crew beginning in the 1890's.

A prominent figure in the town through the years. To many he became known as 'Doctor Andrew' because of the skill he attained in on the spot' operations' of taking hooks out of fishermen's hands. Marrying Lily Huggett from the well-known fishing

family. He continued fishing with his sons Andrew Jesse and Jesse Guy (sadly lost serving aboard HMS Afridi, sunk 1940) and two grandsons Andrew Basil and Roy William, until he was 75. But still had his fishmonger's shop in Seaside, and this with the fishing business will be carried on by his grandsons.

The funeral took place at the Salvation Army Citadel followed by interment at Ocklynge Cemetery'.

On shore with fishing boat 'Olive Joyce' Jesse Chester with skate. February 1936.

The local Lifeboat secretary Alderman Cecil Baker paid a moving tribute to Andrew Chester at the funeral service at the 'Citadel'

'After recalling Mr Chester's proud sea-faring record as a member of the 'William and Mary' lifeboat at the turn of the century and as a fisherman, Alderman Baker said

C.1930 The Chesters at their 'pots' - Eastbourne Fishing Station.

that he mourned for a man who had had a hard life. *'Fishing or life saving by a boat driven by oars or sails in calm or storm was a job for the finest seaman and certainly not one for the faint-hearted.*

Highly respected in the community he did much good and when duty or danger called, was never found wanting'.

Among the family mourners was Brigadier Olive Chester, his daughter who served as a missionary in China for 25 years. A 3ft long floral boat from his grandchildren was borne in front of the coffin.

Being blind in both eyes towards the last years of his life Andrew had a 'miracle' operation, which restored his sight, and his first request was to be taken to see his beloved English Channel.

So with the loss from the fishing trade of the Chesters, Eastbourne has, to any knowledge, none left of the original traditional fishing community families involved down on the foreshore or out of the Marina. But it can be said that those men that fish today out of the Marina and off the beach are carrying on a centuries old tradition of fishing out of Eastbourne.

Locally, the 1980's and probably before, saw an old method of fishing taken up, namely, trammel netting that consisted of 3 nets, 4-5feet high and 60 yards long. In all similar to drift net fishing but fixed and weighted to the seabed. The 3 nets placed one in front of the other with cork floats and having buoys to mark their position. The nets are dropped or 'shot' overboard, a good site being close to a wreck on the seabed.

Andrew William Chester 'netting' at the 'Cats Rest' Net shop. Previous owner of the 'Cats Rest' was 'Bonky' Jack Reed.

The sea as ever a dangerous place to work has sadly has taken the lives of our fishing fraternity over the centuries and another such tragic happening occurred in December 1997 when fisherman Peter Hamper was lost at sea whilst fishing alone off Eastbourne in his boat 'Karen Lynn' NN407. The lifeboat along with some 22 vessels, helicopters and aeroplanes made a thorough search of the sea without success. A sad affair - especially at Christmas time, Peter joining those who go to sea in ships, and lose their lives engaged in that special way of life.

1998 saw 43 boats registered for fishing at Eastbourne, the majority working out of the Marina indicating an upturn in the fortunes of fishing at Eastbourne.

The present day scene (2009) on the beach at the Fishing Station is one bare of activity - just some 3 boats lying on the shingle. A Net shop of note is the late Fred 'Mucky' Erridge's Net shop built 1921, alongside the busy fishmongers shop.

Frederick Erridge (1897-1990) born into an old Eastbourne seafaring family never lived less then some 200 yards from his beloved beach all his life. Nicknamed 'Mucky' a title given through the wit of

Andrew Jesse Chester aboard 'Olive Joyce' C.1930.

Eastbourne Fishing Station C.1950. The Chester family aboard their boat NN106 'Irene' built in Newhaven, cost £1,000, 10 metres long. Fitted with 2 Ailsa Craig diesel engines. To the left is Mike Hardy's boat 'Hibernia' used for fishing and pleasure boating. Just forward of the 'Irene' can be seen the bow of Chester's other boat NN31 'Olive Joyce'.

fishermen. Fred on all occasions was the cleanest and smartest turned out fisherman one could ever meet. Small of stature and wiry framed, at the age of 92 years, a sharp witted mind but with failing eye sight he could still be found daily in his Net shop 'messing about'. Since leaving the sea he became a prolific producer of hand made 'Prawn Stalker' pots for those that potted for prawns. Fred maintained the best bait being 'Jack Abbles' (small green crabs).

On his retirement from active fishing his two boats lay on the beach in front of his Net shop for many years. The first a big beach motorboat 18 feet long NN193 with an elliptical stern, named 'Dawn of Hope' built by Cantells of Newhaven c.1920 for crew of two. The second an ex Bathing Station boat 15 feet long NN129 with transom stern named 'Rose of Devon' built by Gausden and Sisk, Beach Road c.1900 used for prawning only. Both fittingly on Fred's death were burnt where they lay.

The like of 'Fred' never to be seen again on the beach at Eastbourne.

Fishermen, Andrew Basil Chester on the left with brother Roy, long lining off Eastbourne aboard their boat 'Irene' C.1950.

Chester's fishing boat NN106 'Irene' coming ashore. Now fitted with cabin.

Fred 'Mucky' Erridge (1897-1990) fisherman of Eastbourne in his Net shop 1989.

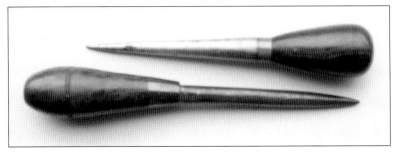

Fred's working tools. 'Marlin spikes'

Fred's Net shop built in 1921 with his boats NN129 and NN193 on beach.

Reg No	Name of Boat	Owner first name	Owner surname
NN8	KATHLEEN	BRIAN EDWARD	ALLCHORN
NN15	PISCES	PHILIP	HOLLWOOD
NN17	FOXY LADY	GLYNN DAVID	BURTON
NN25	SEARCHER	BRIAN GEORGE	SKINNER
NN36	JAN	CHRISTOPHER	SHARP
NN51	MAX 11	ROLAND D.	McGREEVY
NN60	J. D.	JOHN A.	DOBELL
NN67	BAMBINO	JOSE LUIS	NUNES
NN68	SECCUSS 11	BERNARD	GOODWIN
E81	TRACY LYNN	C. L.	BIRLEY
NN95	CHRISANN	PAUL MAURICE	SMITH
NN96	SEAJAY	SIMON MARK	PEASGOOD
NN105	RHIANNON	CHRISTOPHER	VESSEY
NN106	VERGOYER	JOSEPH	WATT
NN120	ROBERT CLARE	WILLIAM F.	CORNISH
NN145	GEORGE RANDSON	PETER	WARREN
DH148	ROYAL SOVEREIGN	P.	STOREY
NN174	LIFTOFF	GEORGE RONALD	BERRY
NN200	PIONEER	TONY	RICHEY
NN201	FREDERICK ROSE	MARK DARREN	WOODLEY
NN241	JEAN	BRIAN	WESTGATE
N/N	NEW BOAT (?)	MICHAEL	SMITH
NN279	ROMA IV	FRANK	SHAW
NN354	JOLLY ROGER	BERNARD	GOODWIN
RX370	E. J.	GRAHAM	COLE
RX374	MIDNIGHT SUN	GRAHAM	BARKER
RX381	AMY 11	LEE	BARTON
NN384	HARD GRAFT	NIGEL	HOLBROOKE
NN391	ALBION ROSE	GRAHAM	BARKER
NN405	SHARLISA	BRIAN ARTHUR	JOHNSON
NN407	KAREN LYNN	PETER DAVID	HAMPER
NN436	SEA CREST	GEORGE RONALD	BERRY
WH456	AMY G.	SEAN STUART	McCORMACK
SM462	JUBILEE	NEIL P.	MESSENGER
NN482	MARY ELIZABETH	MARTYN THOMAS	BURGESS
NN483	MOONRAKER	DAREN	BEAL
NN491	BOY ALBERT	FRANK	SHAW
NN498	REBECCA LOUISE	PAUL	SHADBOLT
NN500	WIN	WALTER GEORGE	POOLMAN
NN565	ARDEN LADY 11	MARCUS RONALD	HARVEY
NN700	TETRA	NEIL JAMES	PATTERSON
NN706	RO-AN	MARK RONALD	HARVEY
NN506	CHIC-O	RICHARD	IVES

Eastbourne Fishing Boats 1998

Eastbourne registered fishing boats and owners 1998.

Chapter Thirteen

Some Tales of the French & Belgians.
The Ramsgate and Newlyn Riots

It seems to some that the French have always been a thorn in the flesh of an Englishman especially those that live and lived on the southern coast of our shores. The fishing fraternity will tell of downright aggression at sea and of poaching in English waters.

French and indeed Belgian aggravation at sea goes back centuries, there being incidents going back to the 1600's not including of course the battles for command of the seas to protect our Island. From a fishing point of view Roy Clark's book 'The Longshoremen' tells of the French and Belgian trawl boats cutting, damaging and stealing English fishermen's nets. It was the English drift net boats they attacked using what was called a 'devil' - a device drawn in front of their trawl net.

In spite of an agreement between Governments in 1868, referring to drift and trawl fishing, which laid down that *'Trawl boats shall not commence fishing at a distance less than 3 miles from any boat fishing with drift nets and if trawl boats had already shot their nets, they must not come nearer than 3 miles to drift net fishing boats'.*

Nevertheless the French and Belgian boats being bigger and having crews outnumbering the English, held the whip hand and their deliberate cutting of the English nets was quite out of order. These offensive incidents continued off the East coast and English Channel for many years with regular losses of fish and nets by the English fishermen. To say bad blood existed was an understatement.

In 1677 protection was given by the Royal Navy to the English boats fishing off Rye against the French unlawfully fishing in English waters. Off Rye were rich fishing grounds called the 'Sowe'. A report from the 'Times' March 1841, tells of *'a Hastings Lugger being attacked by a French boat, in Rye Bay. It is regretted that French fishermen are determined not to comply with fair provision of the convention (12 mile fishing limit off the English coast) For some they have infringed on the agreement. Recently a French Lugger attempted to run down a Hastings boat and threw ballast boulders at the smaller boat, causing her crew to take refuge below. Due to repeated trespass, HMS Rapid was on hand to protect the English boats and was obliged to open fire on a French boat to make her sheer off. The 'Rapid' on occasions had detained French boats and their crews'.*

November 1861 and a report of a collision and fight at sea was published in the Illustrated London News between a Ramsgate fishing boat 'Prince Arthur' and a Boulogne boat No.431. It was 2.00am on the morning of 4th October, The 'Prince Arthur' was drift fishing normally under the correct way at sea, properly showing her lights when she was run into by the bigger French boat which showed no lights.

THE ILLUSTRATED LONDON NEWS

REGISTERED AT THE GENERAL POST-OFFICE FOR TRANSMISSION ABROAD.

No. 2483.— VOL. LXXXIX.   SATURDAY, NOVEMBER 20, 1886.   WITH TWO SUPPLEMENTS : **SIXPENCE.**
AND TINTED PICTURES | By Post, 6½p.

No1. French trawler, No2. A 'Devil', No3. English Herring drifter.

The French crew then commenced with ballast stones, to stone the Ramsgate crew, who had to take refuge and when the French crew made to board the Ramsgate boat the mate went below and armed with a fowling gun let off three shots of powder. But when the French did not retreat he fired a small shot charge. The French then withdrew but only after causing considerable damage to the 'Prince Arthur' and injuring her master and crew.

So it went on and in the year 1886, a 'Times' report for 1st October, related the tale of the seizure of two English oyster boats, being arrested by the French authorities and taken into Le Havre for allegedly having undersized oysters aboard. However the boats were soon released after a check showed, out of 48,000 oysters only 5% were undersize, well within the agreed limit. News of the arrest soon travelled through to the English fishing fleets and a further report in the 'Times' 6th October, stirred things up when 11 English boats were detained in Le Havre alleged to have illegally entered French waters. English boats were only allowed to do so through stress of weather conditions. The Foreign Office became involved in attempting to get their release.

So it was that the same day eleven French mackerel boats put into Ramsgate Harbour to revictual and sell their catches (This was another source of aggravation to the English fishermen. They were unable to sell their catches in French ports due to an impossible tax placed on them and other restrictions) 'not fair play' as they said. Inflamed by the injustice of it all, what with the net cutting and stealing of nets the following incident occurred.

Eastbourne fisherman in affray at Ramsgate.

Frederick French an Eastbourne fisherman serving aboard the Eastbourne Lugger 'Little Florence' owned by George Gausden and registered in Newhaven, fed up with the attitude and behaviour of the French, became involved with others in an attack on the French mackerel boats in Ramsgate Harbour on 7th October 1886. It appears Fred French took the lead and boarded a French boat that he alleged had English fishing nets aboard. He had an altercation with a French fisherman, violence ensued and Fred French finished up having an axe blow to his knee causing him some injury. The French boat attacked by other English fishermen had its lines, sails and halyards severed. A general riot followed between the English and French fishermen. In the end the French sought protection from the Harbour authorities and peace was restored, but not before the Frenchman who had assaulted Fred French was arrested, charged and placed in a cell.

The next day 8th October, the French government ordered the release of the English boats from Le Havre and requested the English government look after the well being of their fishermen.

The injury to Fred French was not serious and after treatment he returned to his boat 'Little Florence'. The incidents were widely reported in the National newspapers and on the Continent, all expressing regret over the ill feeling that existed between the French and English fishermen. During the next few days, tales came in of incidents regarding the French behaviour at sea. One in particular told of the Rye Lugger RX120 'Sweet Hope' being rammed and damaged by a Boulogne boat.

Ramsgate Riot 1886.

At Ramsgate Magistrates Court 13th October, French fisherman Louis Lemaire appeared charged with assaulting Frederick French. After hearing the evidence the case against Lemaire was dismissed and he was freed. (Orders from higher places?)

Ramsgate Riot 1886

The Court expressed regret over the bad feeling that existed between the English and the French.

Frederick French was 51 years old when the above took place, having been born in Eastbourne 1835. Married and from a fishing and boating family he at one time (1871) lived in Manns Row adjacent to the original Fishing Station.

The local paper in Eastbourne on 23rd October, reported the above incident followed by comments from a local fishmonger related below.

'They're always at it. When I first entered the fishing business we were fishing off Eastbourne with a drift net some 1¹/₂ miles long when a French boat came up, cut it and took it in. We chased them to Boulogne. They swore it was adrift and they had found it and demanded we pay salvage to get it back. The Boulogne authorities believed them and wouldn't listen to us so we had to pay £10 to get it back. This was all part of the problem at Ramsgate when Fred French was assaulted. I know Fred well, a rough chap he is too. It's a word and a blow with him. The French boats are larger than ours and carry a crew of 14 men while ours carry just 5. The English can do little when the French become aggressive and order the English boats away from the good fishing grounds with the threat of violence. There ought to be a sloop of war out there to watch'.

The Eastbourne Gazette November 1886 carried the following story about 'Devils'

'The presence of foreign spirits in the vicinity of Eastbourne has been proved to the satisfaction of the law. 'Evil Spirits' are those that are known as 'Devils'. In short they are sharp-clawed instruments used by French trawlers for the purpose of cutting fishing nets belonging to other vessels. Their bullying attitude must be stopped'.

August 1886 - French fishing boat captured ¹/₂ mile off Langney point.

'Seen at anchor the local Coastguard put off and when alongside the French boat, ordered the master to take up her anchor, there attached to it was a fishing line some ¹/₂ mile in length hooked, and attached was many fish. (A crafty way to fish whilst innocently appearing to be at anchor) The master was arrested and the boat taken to Newhaven where later the master pleaded guilty to breaking the fishing laws. Fined £8'.

The Belgians of Ostend have a go at the English fishermen.

The following is from a report at the time.

'1887 and the last week of August saw long standing antagonism between the Belgian and English end in riots at Ostend. The Belgians were jealous of the good cargoes of fish brought into Ostend by the English boats and of their superior catches on the fishing grounds. They had of late been deliberately damaging the English nets. The English boats could get a better price in Ostend than Billingsgate for their fish. The Ostend fishermen were poorly paid for their fish in comparison to the English who could sell their cargoes freely in Belgian ports. The Ostenders could make little profit in English ports due to the syndicate of middlemen. Hostility reached a crisis on 23rd August when several English boats came into Ostend just as the Belgians returned from their cod fishing. Fearing their fish would be worthless they attacked and spoilt the English fish as it was being landed. This led to a general

fray and the gendarmes were called to protect the English. Next day a new attempt was made to land the English fish, but the mob had so increased that serious rioting ensued. The Civic Guard were called out and tried to restore order by firing over the heads of the rioters, without avail. The Belgian fishermen bared their chests and demanded to be killed rather than endure the privations produced by English competition. The Civic Guard duly obliged, opening fire killing five of the rioters, wounding others. The military attended and assisted in restoring order. The English boats all left Ostend as soon as possible, the port being closed to the English for some time after.

Did the Ostenders have a legitimate complaint? The Ostend fishermen numbered 1,100 with 190 boats and the futility of their claim that English competition swamped their market is shown by the fact that for the previous year, three quarters of the wholesale of fish at Ostend came from Belgian boats'.

Over the years the problem with the French continued but never to the violent extent as in 1886. It wasn't only the French where problems arose over fishing. The English often fell out between themselves. One particular incident happened in 1896, known as the 'Newlyn Riots'. It was in mid May when the Yarmouth, Lowestoft, Eastbourne and Hastings mackerel fleets were down off Cornwall fishing, when on a Sunday they landed large catches at Newlyn. This upset the local Newlyn fishing community, as they were God fearing and never put to sea on the Sabbath. Physical attacks of violence were made on the non-Newlyn fishermen and damage was caused to their boats while in harbour and even when they put to sea to escape the Newlyn fishermen followed and attacked them at sea. This behaviour continued for some 3 days and in the end the military were called out with 3 gunboats and peace was restored.

Ostend Riot 1887.

At the quarterly meeting of the Sussex Sea Fisheries committee in August 1898, the problem of French fishermen, fishing within the then 3 mile limit was discussed and a proposal by Brighton fishermen for a 3 month closed season on their fishing grounds was considered.

That same month there was an incident off Beachy Head when a pleasure boat 'Dauntless' capsized and the occupants were rescued by a passing Norwegian barque.

On shore the incident was witnessed and the yacht 'Skylark' put off to get to the scene. However before the 'Skylark' got there a French fishing boat 'Emelie' from Boulogne had salvaged the 'Dauntless' by hauling her aboard their vessel. The crew of the 'Skylark' offered the French £5 salvage but this was refused. The French were then requested to put into Newhaven and get fair and full salvage compensation from H.M. Customs. This they refused to do and set sail for France, the 'Dauntless' never to be seen again.

1945 and the Sussex County Magazine carried a report of recent poaching by French boats in Rye Bay and later in 1948 it contained another report that the *'fishermen of England'* still run their daily and nightly risks, stating the case of the Hastings boat 'Pioneer' being rammed in broad daylight by the Boulogne steam trawler 'Vierge de Lourdes' and badly damaged in Rye Bay. Both the above evoke memories of the conflicts over the centuries.

But acts of humanity did on occasions occur at sea between the English and French.

To give a couple of examples there was in March 1875 an incident off Beachy Head when a French fishing boat 'Jeanne Louise' of Treport was run down by a passing Schooner. The crew of the Brighton Lugger 'Rosy' who saved 5 of the crew witnessed the incident but sadly another 3 drowned. The survivors were landed at Brighton and received the services of the Shipwrecked Mariners Society.

Another incident was closer to home when as previously recorded the brave Captain Papin and his crew of the Boulogne boat rescued the Eastbourne crew of the Lugger 'Thistle' in November 1893.

Eastbourne Pleasure Boatmen in the 1920's. left to right - Alleyn Sayers, Bill Prodger, Jack Mockett, Bob Hunt. In foreground - Monty Blower.

Chapter Fourteen

A Bit More about the Pleasure Boatmen of Eastbourne

The following information and photographs add to Eastbourne's seafront history of an era the like never to be seen again.

Boatman Edward 'Ted' Hide with Grandsons Edward John and Jimmy C.1935.

May 1872 saw the Eastbourne Steam Yacht Company formed by, and the idea of local business men Dr Hayman, Mr C Diplock, Mr J Horne, Mr F M Gimson, Mr C Jarrett, Mr J Vine, Mr C Tomkinson and Mr T S Gowland. Secretary Thomas S Gowland. It was for the purpose of working steam vessels to ply from the new Pier to Brighton, Hastings and pleasure trips out to sea and off Beachy Head. An added attraction for the town but a great challenge to the livelihood of Eastbourne's pleasure boatmen.

It was in June 1872 when the hired steamer 'Rapid' made a maiden trip from the Pier. Licensed to carry 240 persons of 100 tonnage, 100 feet long 16 feet wide with an 80 horsepower engines, her speed was 10 miles per hour. Leaving at 11am she had 120 passengers for this first trip, which was to Seaford thence to Hastings returning to Eastbourne at 3pm. Later in the evening she took a trip to Beachy Head. A successful day for the Company, it was anticipated to run trips daily through the summer season.

C.1935 Fisherman and Boatman Edward 'Ted' Sayers with Grandson Michael Longley who followed the family tradition of Pleasure Boatmen.

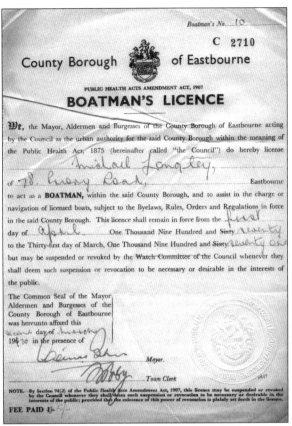

How long this Company operated is not known as no more information has come to notice. Surely not welcomed by the boatmen and indeed in later years the big paddle steamer Companies operating up to and beyond the 1st world war took away a lot of their business.

Application was made in 1874 to the Secretary of State to confirm certain Bye Laws made for the regulation of Pleasure boats plying for hire at Eastbourne. Duly confirmed they came into force in 1875 and a charge made to purchase a copy. Few Boatmen purchased them so in August 1876 the Local board decided to give free copies to the Boatmen and those that had paid for a copy could get their money back.

Boatman's licence issued to Michael Longley 1970.

Sayers Brothers boatmen C.1950 kneeling left to right, Unknown, Eddie Knight and Alan 'Tar' Pitcher. Standing left to right. Ernest 'Chinaman' Sayers, Unknown, Unknown, Unknown, William 'Booner' Wood, Stan Sayers, Ted Sayers, Alec Huggett and Ernest 'Glaxo' Sayers.

1877 and the Boatmen requested of the Local Board to be allowed to carry 16 feet length sails in their pleasure boats as they previously had before the Bye Laws were made. The Local Board agreed and it was included in a new published set of Bye Laws.

A few more nicknames.

'Booner' William Wood.
'Redpole' Alfred Hurd.
'Turpin' Richard Hurd
'Tar' 'Paint It' Alan Pitcher.
'Bert' Albert Boys.
'Sheeny' William Kent.
'Doctor' Andrew William Chester.

C.1959 Sayers Pleasure boat 'Britannia' with Boatmen left to right, Ernest 'Chinaman' Sayers, Alan 'Tar' Pitcher, Mike Longley and Ted Sayers.

Eastbourne Fishermen and Boatmen at their Arch. August 1883.
Visit of Prince and Princess of Wales.
Bottom picture shows extreme left: Louisa 'Cushy' Hide, daughter of 'Navarino' Hide.

Eastbourne Fishermen, Boatmen and Lifeboat men Unionists of 1886. Names of some of those in the photo approximately row by row from the left bottom; Jim 'Snob' Merritt, George 'Gruff' Hide, Will Erridge, Jack Erridge, Edwin Ticehurst, Joseph Mockett, Reuben 'Old Screw' Wood, Edwin 'Lord' Matthews, Jim Hide, Billy Stanbridge, Will Sayers, 'Keen eyed Dickey' Hide, Dennis Breach, John 'Trunky' Colstick, William 'Old Bollard' Hide, Dick Carter, Dorien Knight, 'Bones' Hide, Will Wood, Henry Novis, Charlie Hurd, Albert 'Tuppy' Sayers, Reuben Wood, - Morris, - Morris, Jack Dove, Joe Prodger, Fred Hurd and Harry Mockett. Some of the 1883 Lifeboat crew are wearing their medals.

CHAPTER ONE

Lifeboat man William 'Laddie' Simpson. Portrait by Charles Charles 1912.

Thomas 'Old Tom, the Peoples Friend' Bennett 1923.

1932 Fretting (beachcombing) on Eastbourne beach.

Eastbourne Fishermen and Boatmen C.1925.

Fishermen's and Boatmen's Arch. Visit of Prince of Wales, July 1931.

Eastbourne Fishermen and Boatmen C.1925.

Prodger's 'Oceans Gift' Sprat catch 1930.

Alleyn 'Narny' Sayers 'Runaway Girl' Sprat punt and catch C.1930.

'Bogey' Allchorn's 'William and Dorothy' Sprat punt C.1937.

Fishermen of Eastbourne C.1930. Left to right, Harry 'Uncle' Boniface, Henry 'Dusty' Matthews, Jack Mockett, Jack Elms, Alf Boniface, Tom 'Flummy' Prodger and George Prodger.

January 1934. Net preparation.

February 1935. A 'Siver' of sprats.

October 1932. A fine catch of tope. Baiting up long lines. Each line 2 miles in length and some 2,000 hooks. Trimming lamps for the night's work.

New Herring nets. Possibly left to right, 'Navvy Crick, Harry 'Early Doors' Allchorn and 'Tishy' Huggett.

Fishermen, father and son, George 'John' and George Erridge C.1930.

Fisherman George 'John' Erridge with his boat, September 1927.

Net shops and the Erridges 'shaking out' C.1930.

Huggett fishing family C.1930. Left to right, Father Jesse with sons Derick and Alyn on return from a fishing trip.

Fisherman and Boatman, John 'Foot' Prodger.

Fishermen of Eastbourne 1931. Possible names. Left to right, Unknown, John 'Jack' Prodger, William 'Young Flummy' Prodger, Unknown, Joe 'Crickets' Prodger and Tom 'Flummy' Prodger.

Tanning nets. Possibly Left to right, Will Prodger, Nelson Sayers and George 'Quack' Erridge, October 1930.

The Allchorn family tanning nets, October 1928.

June 1936. Left to right, Harry Erridge and Harry Boniface tanning.

On the net grounds Royal Parade. Tom and Albert Wood, October 1930.

C.1960 'Jack' Prodger (facing) and Tom Allchorn shown splicing anchor cable of Pleasure boat 'William Allchorn' outside 'Lukes' Net shop.

Net work. Left to right, Jesse and Alec Huggett, September 1932.

The 'Old Uns' shaking out C.1960. Left to right, Tom Allchorn, Will Prodger and Fred Allchorn.

Possibly the last clinker built fishing boat NN83 'New Moon' to be seen on Eastbourne Fishing Station, June 2000, built by Lower of Newhaven.

Some fishing boats of Eastbourne C.1970-80.

January 1965. An extra high tide.

Eastbourne Fishing Station before demolition and development C.1964.

Fishermen's 'light' pole coming down C.1969.

Fishing Station view east C.1969.

Fishing Station view west C.1969.

Knight. Thomas	30	Burfield Row.
Knight. William	40	Marine Parade. No.12.
Luxford. John	25	Anchor Tap Hotel.
Maynard. Robert	35	Puddle Dock.
Maynard. William	36	Puddle Dock.
Paul. Jonathan	30	Mans Row.
Paul. William	35	Hurst Cottages. No8.
Paul George	55	South Street.
Simpson. George	30	Prospect Row.
Simpson. John (Boat builder)	40	Ordnance Building, Seaside.
Simpson. Richard	75	Prospect Row.
Simpson. Jarreld	40	Prospect Row.
Simpson. William	35	Prospect Row.
Sutton. William	55	Mans Row.
Swain. Thomas	45	Ordnance Building, Seaside.
Swain. Thomas. Jnr.	25	Ordnance Building, Seaside.
Swain. James	20	Ordnance Building, Seaside.
Thomas. William	30	H ? Cottage.
Waymark. Abraham	35	Mans Row
Waymark. Isaac	45	Burfield Row.
Waymark. James	25	Burfield Row.
Waymark. John	60	South Street.
Waymark. Jonathan	45	South Street.
Weston. Thomas	35	Wish Cottage
Wood. Abraham	15	Wish Cottage
Wood. Edward	35	The Seaside.
Wood. John	50	Prospect Row.
Wood. Thomas	46	Meads.
Young. John	77	Meads Street.

1851. Census.

All Fishermen unless otherwise stated.

Name	Age	Status	Born	Address
Allchorn. Edward	67	Married	Eastbourne	15, York Buildings.
Allchorn. Samuel	55	Married	Eastbourne	Brewers Arms.(Beer Shop)
Breach. George	25	Single	Eastbourne	Meads.
Breach. Thomas (Pauper)	70	Single	Eastbourne	Holywell.
Carter. William	29	Married	Eastbourne	Head's Cottages.
Collins. Jacob (Fisherman Boy)	15	Single	Eastbourne	Meads.
Collins. Reuben	49	Married	Eastbourne	Meads.
Collins. Reuben	19	Single	Eastbourne	Meads.
Cox. George	48	Single	Eastbourne	8, Hursts's Cottages
Cummins. Henry	39	Single	Eastbourne	3, Hurst's Cottages.
Cummins. John	43	Married	Eastbourne	Ford's Cotts, Drove Way.
Erridge. George	25	Married	Eastbourne	3, York Buildings.
Hard. William	58	Married	Eastbourne	7, Hurst's Cottages.
Head. John	40	Married	Eastbourne	Post Office. Seaside.
Head. William	43	Married	Eastbourne	Ordnance Cotts, Seaside
Hide. George	37	Married	Eastbourne	3, Climpson's Cotts, Seaside
Hide. James	52	Married	Eastbourne	Sea Road, Cottages.
Hide. John	64	Widowed	Eastbourne	Post Office. Seaside.
Hide. Philip	19	Single	Eastbourne	Sea Road. Cottages.
Hide. William	34	Married	Eastbourne	Marine Cotts, Drove Way.
Hollobone. Alfred	21	Single	Lewes	South Street.
Huggett. Henry	38	Married	Eastbourne	Brown's Cottages.
Hurd. John	59	Widowed	Eastbourne	6, York Buildings.
Knight. Samuel	67	Widowed	Eastbourne	Sea Road. Cottages.
Knight. Thomas	39	Married	Eastbourne	9, York Buildings.
Knight. William	25	Single	Eastbourne	Seaside Road.
Maynard. William	50	Married	Eastbourne	Watts Lane.
Maynard. Robert	47	Married	Eastbourne	Watts Lane.
Mitchell. Thomas	63	Married	Eastbourne	4, Marine Parade.
Prodger. George	26	Married	Eastbourne	Meads.

Sayers. James	16	Single	Eastbourne	4, Hurst Cottages.
Sayers. William	28	Married	Hailsham	Sea Road, Seaside.
Sayers. William	54	Married	Eastbourne	4, Hurst Cottages.
Simpson. John (Boat builder)	53	Married	Eastbourne	1, Tower Road.
Simpson. John	16	Single	Eastbourne	1, Tower Road.
Simpson. Richard	86	Widowed	Eastbourne	Marine Cot. Drove Way.
Simpson. William (Fisherman/Sailmaker)	48	Single	Eastbourne	Marine Cot. Drove Way.
Sutton. William	65	Married	Eastbourne	4, York Buildings.
Waymark. George	32	Married	Eastbourne	Brown's Cottages.
Waymark. Isaac	55	Married	Eastbourne	Cottage on Beach.
Waymark. John	72	Married	Eastbourne	Seaside Road.
Weston. Thomas	48	Married	Stone, Kent	3, Wish Cottage.
Wickham. Walter (Fisherman/Beershop)	33	Married	Eastbourne	Fisherman's Arms.
Wood. Abraham	28	Married	Eastbourne	18, York Buildings.
Wood. Richard	30	Single	Hastings	Seaside Road.
Wood. Thomas	56	Married	Eastbourne	Meads.
Wood. William	52	Widowed	Eastbourne	2, Hurst's Cottages.
Wood. William Jnr.	15	Single	Eastbourne	2, Hurst's Cottages.

Wives of fishermen of Eastbourne at sea.

1851 Census.

Name	Husband of	Address
Allchorn.	Barbara	Ford's Cottages. Drove Way.
Allchorn.	Caroline	Marine Cottages. Drove Way
Allchorn.	Emma	Marine Cottages. Drove Way
Allchorn.	Harriett	Marine Cottages. Drove Way
Brown.	Sarah	48, Seaside Road.
Chandler.	Sarah	Brown's Cottages.
Cummins.	Anne	17, York Buildings.
Dyer.	Ann	Holywell.
Dyer.	Sarah	Ford's Cottages, Drove Way.

French.	Mary Ann	1, Bryar's Buildings.
French.	Sarah	1, Bryar's Buildings.
Gausden.	Hannah	Meads.
Godden.	Eliza	Meads.
Hide.	Jane	Sea Road.
Hurd.	Susan	Haine's Cottage.
Jackson.	Sarah	Climpson's Cottage, Barrack Ground
Mitchell.	Caroline	19, York Buildings.
Paul.	Harriet	Brown's Cottages.
Prodger.	Phyllis	Meads.
Swain.	Jane	Marine Cottages, Drove Way.
Swain.	Mary Ann	60, Seaside Road.
Verrell.	Lydia	3, Tower Road
Waymark.	Mary	Marine Cottages, Drove Way.
Waymark.	Susan	Climpson's Cottages.
Wood.	Mary	7, York Buildings.
Wood.	Sarah	8, York Buildings.

1861 Census.

Seaside Area.

Name	Age	Status	Born	Address
Allchorn. Edward	76	Married	Eastbourne	14, Mans Row.
Allchorn. Samuel	67	Married	Eastbourne	Olive House. Lower Drove.
Carter. Edward Foresters Arms.	24	Single	Eastbourne	1-2, Meadow Place.
Carter. Joseph	30	Married	Eastbourne	3, Reeds Cottages.
Carter. William	39	Widowed	Eastbourne	8, Tower Street.
Chandler. Thomas	38	Married	Chart? Sutton Kent	2, Kings Arms Row?
Cox. George	58	Single	Eastbourne	5. ? Cottages.
Cummins. Henry Seaside Rd.	48	Single	Eastbourne	Brewers Arms, (lodger)
Erridge. George	36	Married	Eastbourne	2, Mans Row.

Head. John	67	Married	Eastbourne	6, Mans Row.
Hide. George	47	Married	Eastbourne	4, Beach Cottages.
Hide. John	23	Single	Eastbourne	4, Beach Cottages.
Hide. George M	21	Single	Eastbourne	4, Beach Cottages.
Hide. Samuel. B	17	Single	Eastbourne	4, Beach Cottages.
Huggett. Henry	48	Married	Eastbourne	5, Mans Row.
Huggett. Joseph	38	Single	Eastbourne	1, Hanover Place.
Jackson. William	43	Married	Eastbourne	9, Alma Cottages.
Knight. Thomas	51	Married	Eastbourne	9, Mans Row.
Sayers. William	39	Married	Hailsham	12, Mans Row.
Simpson. John (Boat builder)	62	Married	Eastbourne	Cottage in Tower Road.
Swain. Thomas	68	Married	Eastbourne	3, Beach Cottages
Waymark. Charles	29	Single	Eastbourne	5, Beach Cottages
Waymark. John (Retired Fisherman)	82	Married	Eastbourne	1, Albion Cottages
Wood. Abraham	38	Married	Eastbourne	17, Mans Row.
Wood. Edward (Boatman)	47	Married	Eastbourne	3, Mans Row.
Wood. John	40	Married	Salcombe, Devon	3, Kings Arms Row

Wives of Eastbourne fishermen absent at sea.

1861 Census.

Seaside & Grand Parade Area.

Name	Husband of	Address
Allchorn	Caroline	14, Marine Cottages.
Brown.	Sarah	48, Sea Houses.
French.	Ann, Widow of Fisherman.	2, Marine Cottages.
Hide.	Jane	40, Sea Houses.
Hide.	Sarah	36, Marine Parade.
Mitchell.	Mary, Widow of Fisherman	4, Marine Parade.
Paul.	Mariah	34, Marine Parade.
Waymark.	Mary	6, Marine Cottages.

1861 Census.

Old Town Area.

Name	Age	Status	Born	Address
Paul. Jonathan	57	Widowed	Eastbourne	South Street.

1861 Census.

South Street-Meads Area.

Name	Age	Status	Born	Address
Boniface. James	20	Single	Eastbourne	Meads Street.
Collins. Jacob	26	Married	Eastbourne	Holywell.
Collins. Reuben	29	Married	Eastbourne	Holywell.
Godden. William	41	Married	Eastbourne	Meads Street.
Gosden. James	41	Married	Eastbourne	Meads.
Lane. Samuel	56	Widowed	Eastbourne	Holywell.
Luck. George	36	Married	Eastbourne	Wish Tower Cottage.
Prodger. George	35	Married	Eastbourne	Meads Street.
Wood. Jacob	37	Married	Eastbourne	Meads.
Wood. Thomas	66	Married	Eastbourne	Meads Street.

Wives of Eastbourne fishermen absent at sea.

1861 Census.

South Street- Meads Area.

Name	Husband of	Address
Huggett.	Elizabeth	Meads Street.
Huggett.	Martha	Meads.

1861 Census.

Meads Area.

Name	Age	Status	Born	Address
Collins. Reuben	59	Married	Eastbourne	Holywell.
Prodger. Thomas	29	Married	Eastbourne	Holywell.

Wife of an Eastbourne fisherman absent at sea.

1861 Census.

Meads Area.

Name	Husband of	Address
Dyer.	Ann	Holywell.

1871 Census.

Parish of St.Saviours.

Name	Age	Status	Born	Address
Collins. John	29	Married	Eastbourne	27, South Street.

1871 Census.

St.Johns Ward, Meads.

Name	Age	Status	Born	Address
Collins. Jacob	35	Married	Eastbourne	1, Coppards Cottages.
Collins. Reuben	39	Married	Eastbourne	Coppards Hut.
Dyer. Ann (Wife of Fisherman).	51	Married	Eastbourne	5, Harts Cottages.
Gausden. George (Boat builder)	24	Married	Eastbourne	Podovers Cottages.
Godden. William	51	Married	Eastbourne	5, Meads Street.
Godden. George	22	Single	Eastbourne	5, Meads Street.
Lane. George	34	Single	Eastbourne	2, Stevens Cottages.
Lane. Samuel	68	Widowed	Hailsham	8, Harts Cottages.
Markwick. Ellen (Wife of Fisherman)	28	Married	Eastbourne	4, Stevens Cottages.
Prodger. George	46	Married	Eastbourne	6, Ship Yard Cottages.
Prodger. George	21	Single	Eastbourne	6, Ship Yard Cottages.
Wood. Charles (Publican-Fisherman)	38	Married	Eastbourne	The Pilot Inn.
Wood. Jacob	47	Married	Eastbourne	9, Ship Yard Cottages.
Wood. Charles	18	Single	Eastbourne	9, Ship Yard Cottages.
Wood Thomas.	76	Married	Eastbourne	4, Ship Yard Cottages.
Wood. Charles	45	Single	Eastbourne	4, Ship Yard Cottages.

NB. In the census Harts Cottages are wrongly shown as Coppards Cottages & vice versa. In this list they are correct.

1871 Census.
Parish of Holy Trinity.

Name	Age	Status	Born	Address
Allchorn. Thomas (Boatman)	50	Married	Eastbourne	58, Seaside.
Allchorn. Edward	86	Widowed	Eastbourne	48, Seaside. (Lodger)
Brown. William (Fish Salesman)	49	Married	Eastbourne	48, Seaside.
Head. John (Fish Salesman)	61	Married	Eastbourne	37, Seaside.
Hide. James (Boatman)	72	Married	Eastbourne	Navareen Cottage.
Hide. Philip	39	Single	Eastbourne	Navareen Cottage.
Hide. Louisa (Bathing Machine Woman)	36	Single	Eastbourne	Navareen Cottage.
Hide. Richard	54	Widowed	Eastbourne	40, Seaside.
Hide. William B	53	Married	Eastbourne	36, Marine Parade.
Hide. Frederick B (Fisherman/Carpenter)	26	Single	Eastbourne	36, Marine Parade.
Hide. William. B	20	Single	Eastbourne	36, Marine Parade.
Huggett. Joseph	42	Married	Eastbourne	57, Pevensey Road.
Knight. Sarah (Bathing Machine Proprietor)	68	Widowed	Eastbourne	49, Seaside.
Knight. William (Fish Salesman)	45	Married	Eastbourne	35, Marine Parade.
Longhurst. Caroline (Fish Hawker)	42	Married	Battle	88, Pevensey Road.
Mitchell. Thomas	59	Married	Eastbourne	38, Langney Road.
Mitchell. William	53	Married	Eastbourne	30, Marine Parade
Parks. Jane (Wife of Fisherman)	42	Married	Middlesex	59, Pevensey Road.
Paul. Paul	45	Married	Eastbourne	28, Marine Parade.

1871 Census.
Parish of Christ Church.

Name	Age	Status	Born	Address
Allchorn. Edward	54	Married	Eastbourne	14, Marine Drove.
Allchorn. James	42	Married	Eastbourne	3, Cottages on Beach.

Allchorn. Mary (Widow of Fisherman)	70	Widow	Eastbourne	23, Marine Drove.
Allchorn. Mary (Wife of Fisherman)	27	Married	Eastbourne	3, Elealeh Place
Boniface. Charles	29	Married	Eastbourne	12, Warrior Square.
Boniface. James	30	Married	Eastbourne	11, Warrior Square.
Breach. Dennis	31	Married	Eastbourne	? Warrior Square.
Carter. William	49	Married	Eastbourne	4, Cross Street.
Carter. William	36	Married	Eastbourne	2, Dennis Cottages.
Chandler. Thomas	48	Married	Eastbourne	15, Tower Street.
Cox. George	70	Married	Eastbourne	2, Willow Walk. (Lodger)
Cummins. Henry	21	Married	Eastbourne	8, Brown's Cottages.
Cummins. John	38	Married	Eastbourne	3, Cambridge Terrace.
Cummins. Henry	59	Single	Eastbourne	57, Sea Houses. (Lodger)
Climpson. Obediah	37	Married	Willingdon	23, Tower Street.
Dunnett. Samuel	21	Single	Eastbourne	Brewers Arms. (Lodger)
Dyer. Sarah (Wife of Fisherman)	58	Married	Eastbourne	9, Alma Cottages.
Dyer.George F	28	Married	Eastbourne	9, Alma Cottages.
Ellis. Robert	31	Married	East Dean	1, Poplar Row.
Erridge. Charles	35	Married	Eastbourne	3, Cambridge Terrace.
Erridge. George	49	Married	Eastbourne	2, Manns Row.
Erridge. George	18	Single	Eastbourne	2, Manns Row.
Erridge. William	16	Single	Eastbourne	2, Manns Row.
Erridge. John	30	Married	Eastbourne	9, Manns Row.
French. Frederick	36	Married	Eastbourne	17, Manns Row.
French. James	28	Married	Eastbourne	15 Tower Street.
French. Sarah (Wife of Fisherman)	54	Married	Eastbourne	Cottage on the Beach.
Harris. John	31	Single	Warbleton.Sx	21, Willow Walk.
Hide. George	57	Married	Eastbourne	4, Cottages on Beach.
Hide. George M. (Fisherman/Fish Buyer)	31	Married	Eastbourne	4, Albion Cottages.
Hide. John	33	Married	Eastbourne	1, Elealeh Place.
Hide. Samuel. B	26	Married	Eastbourne	7, Cambridge Terrace.

Hide. Elizabeth (Widow of Fisherman)	46	Widow	Eastbourne	12, Marine Drove.
Huggett. Henry	47	Married	Eastbourne	5, Manns Row.
Huggett. James	35	Married	Eastbourne	1, Manns Row.
Huggett. James P	23	Married	Eastbourne	1, Leslie Street.
Huggett. Jesse	21	Married	Eastbourne	7, Brown's Cottages.
Huggett. Samuel	25	Married	Eastbourne	8, Tower Place.
Hurd Henry	43	Married	Eastbourne	5, Tower Place.
Hurd Henry	37	Married	Eastbourne	8, Cambridge Terrace.
Hurd. John	49	Married	Eastbourne	4, Marine Buildings.
Jackson. William (Seaman)	55	Married	Eastbourne	4, Cambridge Terrace.
Jackson. William	19	Single	Eastbourne	4, Cambridge Terrace.
Jones. Joseph	29	Married	Eastbourne	27, Marine Drove.
Knight. Thomas	38	Married	Eastbourne	13, Manns Row.
Manser. Mary Ann (Widow of Fisherman)	30	Widow	Eastbourne	44 Leslie Place.
Matthews. Arthur	27	Married	Westham.Sx	Seaside Road.
Matthews. Edwin	28	Married	Eastbourne	8, Tower Place.
M'Mullen.? Elizabeth (Wife of Fisherman)	33	Married	Eastbourne	4, Brown's Cottages.
Mitchell. Caesar	44	Married	Eastbourne	2, Cottages on Beach.
Mitchell. Charles	18	Married	Eastbourne	2, Cottages on Beach.
Mockett. Joseph	27	Married	Eastbourne	Ocean Wave, Tower Place.
Novis. Thomas	28	Married	Eastbourne	1, Strettons Cottages.
Sayers. Alleyn	32	Married	Eastbourne	15, Warrior Square.
Sayers. Henry	47	Married	Hailsham	7, Cambridge Terrace.
Sayers. Weller	50	Married	Hailsham	4, Manns Row.
Sayers. George	19	Single	Eastbourne	4, Manns Row.
Sayers. Albert (Fish Boy)	11	Single	Eastbourne	4, Manns Row.
Simpson. William C (Sailmaker)	68	Married	Eastbourne	15, Marine Drove.
Simpson. William	40	Married	Eastbourne	10, Warrior Square.
Swain. James	47	Married	Eastbourne	9, Warrior Square.
Swain. Philip	47	Married	Hastings	4, Tower Place.

Name	Age	Status	Born	Address
Tutt. Richard (Fishmonger)	30	Single	Eastbourne	3, Whites Cottages.
Tutt. Samuel (Fish Hawker)	28	Single	Eastbourne	3, Whites Cottages.
Tutt. Jesse (Fish Hawker)	26	Single	Eastbourne	3, Whites Cottages.
Tutt. John (Fish Hawker)	24	Single	Eastbourne	3, Whites Cottages.
Verrall. James (Boatman)	30	Married	Eastbourne	21, Manns Row.
Waymark. Rosetta (Wife of Fisherman)	52	Married	Eastbourne	3, Brown's Cottages
Waymark. Charles	17	Single	Eastbourne	3, Brown's Cottages
Waymark. Jane (Widow of Fisherman)	73	Widow	Eastbourne	2, Cambridge Terrace.
Waymark. John	54	Single	Eastbourne	2, Cambridge Terrace.
Wood. Abraham	49	Married	Eastbourne	8, Tower Place.
Wood. Edward (Boatman)	56	Married	Eastbourne	3, Manns Row.
Wood. Edward	40	Married	Eastbourne	10, Brown's Cottages.
Wood. George	48	Married	Hastings	11, Manns Row.
Wood. Richard	78	Widower	Eastbourne	2, Lucks Cottages.

1881 Census.

Parish of Christ Church.

Name	Age	Status	Born	Address
Allchorn. Edward	64	Married	Eastbourne	4, Addingham Road.
Allchorn. James	53	Widower	Eastbourne	1, Beach Cottages.
Allchorn. Richard	62	Married	Eastbourne	44, Duke Street.
Boniface. Charles	38	Married	Eastbourne	1, Tower Place.
Boniface. James	41	Married	Eastbourne	8, Tower Place.
Boniface. Thomas	28	Married	Eastbourne	13, Tower Street.
Carter. Joseph	50	Married	Eastbourne	2, Cambridge Terrace.
Carter. Richard	23	Married	Eastbourne	7, Carlton Road.
Chantler. Thomas	58	Married	Eastbourne	13, Tower Street
Colstick. John	28	Married	Eastbourne	5/6, Tower Place.
Erridge. Alfred	20	Single	Eastbourne	2, Mann's Row.
Erridge. George	53	Married	Eastbourne	2, Mann's Row.
Erridge. William	26	Single	Eastbourne	2, Mann's Row.

Erridge. Richard	27	Married	Eastbourne	2, Mann's Row.
Erridge. George	28	Married	Eastbourne	2, Mann's Row.
Erridge. William	31	Married	Eastbourne	3, Latimer Road.
Gausden. George (Boat builder)	34	Married	Eastbourne	80, Seaside
Goldsmith. John	36	Married	Warbleton.Sx	13,Leslie Street.
Hide. Charles (Fisherman/Captain of Sailing Yacht)	30	Married	Eastbourne	3, Warrior Square.
Hide. George	67	Married	Eastbourne	4, Beach Cottages.
Hide. Albert	18	Single	Eastbourne	4, Beach Cottages.
Hide. James	28	Married	Eastbourne	11, Tower Street.
Hide. James	57	Married	Eastbourne	Shed on Beach.
Hide. Richard	32	Married	Eastbourne	73, Seaside.
Hide. William	29	Married	Eastbourne	25, Marine Drove.
Hide. Samuel	36	Married	Eastbourne	5, Addingham Road.
Hide. Elizabeth (Bathing Machine Lady)	55	Married	Eastbourne	3, Burfield Cottages.
Huggett. James	53	Married	Eastbourne	32, Duke Street.
Huggett. Frederick	36	Married	Eastbourne	2, Willow Walk.
Huggett. Jesse	30	Married	Eastbourne	6, Holman Terrace.
Hurd. George	25	Single	Eastbourne	72, Seaside.
Hurd. Henry	47	Married	Eastbourne	9, Cambridge Terrace.
Hurd. John Wood	30	Married	Eastbourne	112, Seaside.
Hurd. Richard	27	Married	Eastbourne	6, Mann's Row.
Jackson. William	67	Married	Surrey	4, Cambridge Terrace.
Jackson. William	28	Married	Eastbourne	10, Alexandra Terrace.
Jones. Joseph	36	Married	Eastbourne	4, Marine Drove.
Knight. Charles	27	Married	Eastbourne	8, Mark? Terrace.
Knight. Thomas	71	Married	Eastbourne	14, Mann's Row.
Knight. William (Boatman)	32	Married	Eastbourne	2, Hanover Place.
Matthews. Edwin	39	Married	Eastbourne	6, Chapel Drove.
Mitchell. William	63	Married	Eastbourne	1, Burfield Cottages.
Mockett. John (Fisherman/Publican)	28	Married	Eastbourne	'3 Compasses' 95, Seaside.

Prodger. George	56	Married	Eastbourne	2, Artillery Cottages, Seaside
Prodger. John	29	Married	Eastbourne	2, Old? Cottages, Seaside.
Reed. Reuben	31	Married	Eastbourne	17, Tower Street.
Sawyer. James	26	Married	Hastings	10, Warrior Square.
Sayers. Alleyn	42	Married	Eastbourne	14, Warrior Square.
Sayers. Alleyn N	17	Single	Eastbourne	14, Warrior Square.
Sayers. George	29	Single	Eastbourne	9, Alexandra Terrace.
Sayers. William	60	Married	Eastbourne	4, Mann's Row
Simpson. William (Boat builder)	50	Married	Eastbourne	8, Tower Place.
Simpson. William. E	17	Single	Eastbourne	8, Tower Place.
Swain. Charles	27	Married	Eastbourne	18, Longstone Terrace.
Swain. Philip	59	Married	Eastbourne	18, Chapel Drove.
Thwaites. James (Boat builder)	38	Married	Hastings	4, Holman Terrace.
Tutt. Samuel	39	Married	Eastbourne	3, Lower Drove.
Waymark. James	64	Married	Eastbourne	1, Beach Cottages.
Waymark. William	34	Single	Eastbourne	53, Seaside.
Wood. Abraham	58	Married	Eastbourne	4, Chapel Drove.
Wood. Thomas	19	Single	Eastbourne	4, Chapel Drove.
Wood. Edward Seaside.	52	Married	Eastbourne	8, Brown's Cottages.
Wood. Edward (Boatman)	66	Married	Eastbourne	3, Mann's Row.
Wood. Jacob	57	Widower	Eastbourne	10, Warrior Square.
Wood. Thomas	27	Married	Eastbourne	10, Warrior Square.
Wood. Samuel	51	Widower	Eastbourne	12, Warrior Square.

Wife of Eastbourne fisherman absent at sea.

1881 Census.

Parish of Christ Church.

Name	Husband of	Address
Matthews.	Eliza	8, Mann's Row.

1881 Census.
Parish of Holy Trinity.

Name	Age	Status	Born	Address
Allchorn. William (Licensed Boatman)	51	Married	Eastbourne	39, Marine Parade.
Brown. William (Bathing Machine Owner)	59	Married	Eastbourne	29, Seaside.
Fibens. William (Sailmaker)	24	Married	Eastbourne	108, Pevensey Road.
Hide. George M (Manager/Fisherman)	41	Married	Eastbourne	Anchor Tap, 26, Marine Parade.
Hide. James (Licensed Boatman)	83	Married	Eastbourne	Marine Cottage, 40, Marine Parade.
Hide. Richard (Fishmonger)	61	Married	Eastbourne	15, Seaside.
Huggett. Joseph	52	Married	Eastbourne	57, Pevensey Road.
Lane. Samuel (Unemployed Fisherman)	77	Widower	Eastbourne	21, Pevensey Road.
Merritt. James	23	Married	Surrey	100, Pevensey Road.
Paul. Paul	55	Married	Eastbourne	28, Marine Parade.
Tutt. Jesse	33	Single	Eastbourne	29, Pevensey Road.

1881 Census.
Parish of St. Johns. Meads.

Name	Age	Status	Born	Address
Boniface. Henry	25	Single	Eastbourne	Holywell Cottages. Chalk Pit.
Collins. Mary (Widow of Fisherman Reuben Collins).	81	Widower	Eastbourne	Blacksmith Arms Cottages, Meads Road.
Collins. Reuben (Son of above)	50	Married	Eastbourne	Holywell Lodge.
Collins. Jacob	45	Married	Eastbourne	1, Coppards Cottages, Meads Street.
Gausden. Edward (Boat builder, son of George Gausden)	32	Single	Eastbourne	Cottage, Meads Street.

Gausden. James	61	Married	Eastbourne	2, New Cottages, East Dean Road.
Godden. William	62	Married	Eastbourne	Blacksmith Arms, Cottages, Meads Road.
Hide. John	43	Married	Eastbourne	Pilot Inn.
Markwick. Jasper	41	Married	Eastbourne	6, Harts Cottages.

1891 Census.

Name	Age	Status	Born	Address
Allchorn. Edwin (Boatman)	30	Single	Eastbourne	184, Seaside. (boarder)
Allchorn. Henry	40	Married	Eastbourne	162, Seaside.
Allchorn. James	74	Married	Eastbourne	23, Langney Road.
Allchorn. James	60	Widower	Eastbourne	5, Thorne Terrace, Latimer Road. (boarder)
Allchorn. Jeffrey	29	Married	Eastbourne	5, Thorne Terrace, Latimer Road. (boarder)
Allchorn. Samuel	48	Married	Eastbourne	149, Seaside.
Allchorn. William (Boatman)	61	Married	Eastbourne	39, Marine Parade.
Allchorn. William	31	Married	Eastbourne	6, Tower Street.
Boniface. Charles	49	Married	Eastbourne	4, Haywards Cottages.
Boniface. Henry	34	Married	Eastbourne	2, Marina Terrace, Beach Road.
Boniface. Tom	37	Married	Eastbourne	3, Marina Terrace, Beach Road.
Breach. Dennis (Boatman)	51	Married	Eastbourne	8, Warrior Square.
Brooks. James (Captain of Yacht)	40	Married	Hampshire	1, Gausden Mews, Gausdens Yard, Sidley Road. (boarder)
Collins. Jacob (Boatman)	55	Married	Eastbourne	1, Coppards Cottages, Meads Road.
Collins. Reuben (Boatman)	59	Married	Eastbourne	11, Wallis Cottages, Meads.
Cummins. Henry (Seaman)	27	Married	Eastbourne	Northall Villa, The Crumbles.
Erridge. Alfred	28	Married	Eastbourne	4, Archery Terrace, Archery Road. (visitor)

Erridge. George	69	Widower	Eastbourne	2, Gausdens Cottages, Sidley Road
Erridge. George	39	Married	Eastbourne	2, Springfield Terrace.
Erridge. William M	38	Married	Eastbourne	2, Springfield Terrace.
Erridge. John	50	Married	Eastbourne	5, Marina Terrace, Beach Road.
Erridge. William	30	Married	Eastbourne	9, Warrior Square.
French. Tom	15	Single	Eastbourne	12, Gausdens Cottages, Sidley Road.
French. William	31	Single	Eastbourne	2, Thorne Terrace, Latimer Road.
Godden. William	42	Widower	Eastbourne	3, Springfield Terrace.
Hide. John (Publican/Boatman)	58	Married	Eastbourne	The Pilot Inn
Hide. John (Boatman)	23	Single	Eastbourne	The Pilot Inn
Hide. George M (Boatman/Fisherman)	51	Single	Eastbourne	1, Tower Place, Latimer Road.
Hide. George M	20	Single	Eastbourne	1, Tower Place, Latimer Road.
Hide. Osman (Apprentice to Boat builder)	13	Single	Eastbourne	1, Tower Place, Latimer Road.
Hide. Samuel B	46	Married	Eastbourne	1, Hydney Street.
Hide. Charles.	41	Married	Eastbourne	2, Eshton Terrace.
Hide. Richard	43	Married	Eastbourne	2, Eleanor Terrace, Beach Road.
Hide. Richard (Boatman)	74	Married	Eastbourne	92, Pevensey Road.
Hide. Frederick B	45	Single	Eastbourne	18, Marine Parade.
Hide. William B Taddington Road.	39	Married	Eastbourne	3, Compton Terrace,
Hide. Albert	28	Single	Eastbourne	11 Warrior Square. (lodger)
Howell. Walter (Boatman)	31	Single	London	6, Portland Terrace.
Huggett. James P	24	Married	Eastbourne	4, Hope Cottages.
Huggett. James	43	Single	Eastbourne	447, Seaside.
Huggett. Frederick	17	Single	Eastbourne	447, Seaside.
Huggett. Phillip (Fishboy)	14	Single	Eastbourne	447, Seaside.
Huggett. Jesse	40	Married	Eastbourne	1, Marina Terrace, Beach Road.

Huggett. Jesse	18	Single	Eastbourne	1, Marina Terrace, Beach Road.
Huggett. James	36?	Married	Eastbourne	7, Tower Place, Latimer Road.
Huggett. Joseph	62	Married	Eastbourne	57, Pevensey Road.
Hobby. Edmund	66	Widower	Hampshire	45, Leslie Street. (lodger)
Hurd. John	69	Married	Eastbourne	156, Seaside.
Hurd. George	35	Single	Eastbourne	156, Seaside.
Hurd. Charles	26	Single	Eastbourne	156, Seaside.
Hurd. Fred	22	Single	Eastbourne	156, Seaside.
Hurd. John	40	Married	Eastbourne	184, Seaside.
Hurd. Henry	59	Married	Eastbourne	9, Eshton Road.
Hurd. Alfred	24	Single	Eastbourne	9, Eshton Road.
Knight. Albert (Boat builder)	33	?	Southwick	2, Sutton Terrace.
Knight. William (Boatman)	42	Married	Eastbourne	9, Beamsley Road.
Longhurst. Catherine (Fishwoman)	62	Widow	Eastbourne	4, Beach Road.
Matthews. Arthur (Publican/Boatman)	47	Married	Pevensey	Beach Hotel.
Matthews. Arthur (Boatman)	22	Single	Eastbourne	Beach Hotel.
Matthews. Edwin	22	Married	Eastbourne	6, Burfield Road.
Novis. Henry	25	Married	Eastbourne	6, Portland Terrace.
Maynard. George	72	Widower	Eastbourne	323, Seaside.
Mockett. Joseph (Publican/Boatman)	48	Married	Firle	Ocean Wave, Tower Place.
Mockett. Henry (Boatman)	25	Single	Eastbourne	Ocean Wave, Tower Place.
Mockett. John (Boatman)	19	Single	Eastbourne	Ocean Wave, Tower Place.
Oliver. Samuel	47	Married	Eastbourne	6, Latimer Road.
Parks. George	63	Widower	Hailsham	4, Eshton Road.
Parter. John	28	Married	Hastings	5, Bexhill Road.
Paul. Paul (Retired Fisherman)	65	Married	Eastbourne	28, Marine Parade.
Payne. George (Yacht/Boat builder) see Sisk	29	Married	Kingston	1, Sutton Terrace, Fairlight Road?
Penfold. Charles	32	Married	London	15, Eshton Road.

Prodger. John	39	Married	Eastbourne	3, Gausdens Cottages, Sidley Road.
Prodger. Thomas	17	Single	Eastbourne	3, Gausdens Cottages, Sidley Road.
Reed. Reuben	40	Married	Eastbourne	13, Gausdens Cottages.
Sayers. Albert (Boatman)	29	Married	Eastbourne	9, Beamsley Road.
Sayers. George (Boatman)	37	Single	Eastbourne	217, Seaside. (lodger)
Sayers. Thomas (Boatman)	55	Married	Hailsham	15, Tower Street.
Sayers. William (Boatman)	24	Single	Eastbourne	7, Tower Place (lodger)
Sisk. Thomas H (Yacht/Boat builder)	25	Single	Kent	1, Sutton Place, (lodger) Fairlight Road?
Swain. Thomas	34	Married	Eastbourne	182, Seaside.
Ticehurst. Edwin (Boatman)	28	Single	Eastbourne	38, Cavendish Place.
Ticehurst. Matthew (Boatman)	19	Single	Eastbourne	38, Cavendish Place.
Tutt. Richard (Fish Dealer)	52	Married	Eastbourne	1, Lower Drove.
Tutt. Samuel (Boatman)	49	Single	Eastbourne	3, Lower Drove.
Tutt. Henry (Boatman)	46	Single	Eastbourne	3, Lower Drove.
Tutt. Jesse (Boatman)	44	Single	Eastbourne	3, Lower Drove.
Tutt. John (Boatman)	40	Single	Eastbourne	3, Lower Drove.
Tutt. William	18	Single	Eastbourne	1, Eshton Road.
Tookey? John H (Captain of Fishing Lugger)	32	Married	Plymouth	2, Haywards Cottages.
Thwaites ? James D (Boat builder)	48	Married	Hastings	229, Seaside.
Verrall. James (Boat builders Carter see Brook)	55	Married	Eastbourne	1, Gausdens Mews, Gausdens Yard, Sidley Road.
Wood. Abraham	69	Married	Eastbourne	6, Sidley Road.
Wood. Charles	65	Single	Eastbourne	2, Blacksmiths Arms, Meads. (Lodger)
Wood. Charles (Boatman)	39	Married	Eastbourne	50, Susans Road.
Wood. Charles	38	Married	Eastbourne	3 Eshton Road.
Wood. Edward	67	Widower	Eastbourne	1, Old Lime Tree Cottages.
Wood. Samuel	61	Widower	Eastbourne	12, Warrior Square.

Wood. Robert (Boat builder)	37	Single	Eastbourne	12, Warrior Square.
Wood. Thomas	29	Married	Eastbourne	2 Sidley Road.
Wood. William	54	Married	Eastbourne	4, Holywell Cottages. Meads. (Lodger)

Bibliography

Beckett publications. *Eastbourne Gazette and Herald.*

Eastbourne Chronicle.

The Argus.

The Times.

Daily Graphic.

East Sussex Advertiser.

Sussex Weekly Advertiser.

Illustrated London News.

British Library. Colindale. London.

Eastbourne Central Library.

Eastbourne Local History Society.

Eastbourne Town Council Minutes.

East Sussex Records Office.

Towner Art Gallery.

Compton Place Accounts and Correspondence. Volume 117.

Memoirs of William Hickey by Peter Quennell.

Old Eastbourne by Rev.W.Budgen.

Eastbourne Memories by George Chambers.

Contraband County by Mark Bullen.

The Journal of a Deal Pilot by Will Stanton.

Sussex County Magazine 1927-1956 by Arthur Beckett.

Eastbourne Fishermen and Boatman by Tom Reed.

The Seas of Britain by Peter Dawlish.

Coastwise Craft by T.C.Lethbridge.

The Longshoremen by Roy Clarke.

The Maritime Economy of Eastern Sussex 1550-1700.
  No.11 and Urban Employment and Population in Sussex 1550-1660 Volume113
  by Colin E Brent.M.A.D. Phil.

Diaries 1754-1765 of Thomas Turner.

The Fisheries of the World by F.Whymper.

Brighton Fishing Museum.

House of Lords. Archives.

Ship and Boat Name Index

Surname Index